American Graphic Designer

A biographical essay
by Adrian Shaughnessy

1. Herb Lubalin and friends in the steam room. From left to right: Herb Lubalin, Seymour Chwast, Lou Dorfsman, Gene Federico, Bernie Zlotnick. Herb's towel has been photographically extended. The picture was taken at Grossinger's, the famous resort in the Catskills. Date: c. 1967. Photo courtesy of Bernie Zlotnick.

2. Herb Lubalin (left), with twin brother Irwin (right) and sister Charlotte (known as Bobby).
3. Herb Lubalin as a young man. All photographs kindly supplied by Peter Lubalin.

1

Family and Early Life

Herbert Frederick Lubalin rarely talked about his childhood in interviews. As we shall see throughout this investigation of his life and work, he wasn't much of a talker. His grunts were famous, and his staff and partners learned that a Lubalin cough was more than just a cough. He did his talking through his highly charged manipulation of lettering, which gave him license to convey meaning far beyond that of the mere words themselves.

In interviews, he tended to confine himself to professional matters, yet as far as we can tell, he appears to have had a happy, if unremarkable, childhood. He was born in New York City in 1918. From census records we know that in 1920 his family lived in the Bronx. At some point they moved to Edgemere, Long Island, where the young Lubalin spent his childhood catching fish — a recreational activity he was to continue for the rest of his life. Some published accounts give his father's name as Sol, with his occupation listed as 'musician'. Herb Lubalin's father was indeed a musician, but his name was not Sol; it was Joseph, and he had been born in Russia. Lubalin's mother's name was Rose, and she was of German origin, although the census states that she too was Russian.

The Lubalins were a musical family. Joseph was a professional musician, a trumpet player, and Rose was an amateur singer. They had three children: twin boys, Herb and Irwin, and a daughter called Charlotte (known as Bobby, fig.2). The family was Jewish, tight-knit and surrounded by relatives. Saturday nights were devoted to family music sessions. In a rare instance of autobiographical detail, Herb Lubalin told one interviewer that his father wanted him to be a doctor; his mother hoped he would become a lawyer.

Herb Lubalin's relationship with his twin brother was among the closest of his life, yet in temperament they were polar opposites. Irwin, who died aged 90 in 2008, was described in his *New York Times* obituary as 'a man of great humor, joie de vivre and vitality.' These were not words that could be used to describe Herb. His friend and fellow designer, Lou Dorfsman, called him 'a very quiet fellow' and his sister-in-law said he was 'deafeningly quiet'. Everyone who knew him remarked on his taciturn nature: it was only in the lecture theatre, at the height of his fame, that he became loquacious.

Irwin went into business and rose to senior executive level at Avnet, a giant distributor of electronic components and subsystems — the company was later to become a client of Herb's studio. Herb, by contrast, had a famously relaxed attitude to business. In later life, often to the dismay of his business partners, he would take on work that was far from profitable, but that fed his insatiable creative appetite. Yet the Lubalin philosophy of putting quality of work above profitability was to serve him well: not only did he have a prosperous studio (loss-making assignments were counterbalanced with more profitable ones), but also, thanks to the far-sighted alliances he formed with some of the key figures in American typography and typesetting, he was to benefit financially from the phototypesetting boom of the 1970s.

Although Herb and Irwin headed in quite different directions in their respective careers, it seems that Irwin was not without ability in the visual arts. In the current brand guidelines for Avnet, there is a footnote stating that Irwin Lubalin was the original designer of the Avnet logo 'sometime in the '80s'. No mention is made of his more famous twin brother.

The young Herb Lubalin's high school academic record was so poor that, unlike his twin, he failed to gain a place at the free City College of New York, the first free public institution of higher education in the United States. But he had a reputation for being artistic, and despite the disadvantage of congenital colour-blindness and, it is widely reported, an inability to draw figuratively, he gained notoriety at high school for his 'highly erotic nude drawings of Tarzan and Jane'. This suggests that he had at least some ability to make recognizable forms. It is also evidence of an impish sense of humour that is frequently commented on by those who knew him. The designer, writer and fellow Cooper Union graduate Marilyn Hoffner described the adult Lubalin as having a 'wicked streak'. Lou Dorfsman, in an essay that he wrote about Lubalin, tells the story of how the two were once playing a game based on creating

fictitious headlines to advertise famous products. To promote Preparation H, a product that claimed to cure haemorrhoids, Lubalin suggested: 'Use Preparation H and kiss your haemorrhoids goodbye.'

For poor people with artistic talent in early 20th-century New York, there was always the sanctuary of the Cooper Union. In 1935, Lubalin applied for entry and was accepted ('I was 64th out of 64 applicants,' he later claimed). For the next four years he was to find a congenial home that allowed him to grow in confidence and intellectual ability, and to discover his life's calling — graphic design.

Lubalin was helped in his mastery of the graphic arts, and typography in particular, by his ambidextrousness. Naturally ambidextrous people are rare — an estimated one in every hundred. Herb Lubalin's manual dexterity was a source of amazement: one former employee recalls seeing him simultaneously 'sketching letterforms with his left hand while signing checks with his right.'

In an interview in the Japanese magazine *Idea* (1969), Lubalin discussed his uncommon ability and how it jump-started his career: **'Calligraphy is handwriting, that must be done with the right hand because of the angle of the pen. Everybody in school thought that I was left-handed because I drew with my left hand and I always used my left hand. So when they gave us an assignment, the teachers said to me, "I know this puts you under a tremendous handicap because you are left-handed and you must do this with your right hand." I did not bother to tell him that I do all my writing with my right hand. Since calligraphy is really handwriting I found the job very easy. When I completed it I got the highest mark in the class, not because I was the best but because the teacher felt that I had overcome this great handicap and I'd done this job with my right hand. I guess this gave me some confidence because from that time on I did very well.'**

The Cooper Union was to give Lubalin more than self-confidence; it also gave him a wife. It was there that he met a student called Sylvia Kushner who was to become his first wife and the mother of his three sons. The marriage lasted until Sylvia's death in 1971. In a widely reported remark made in an interview, Lubalin described her as the most talented student ever to come out of the Cooper Union: **'Unfortunately, we had three children right away**

so she was never able to exploit her talent. She was a very fine fashion designer. And just recently as the kids have grown up, she's going back to designing and she gets involved every now and then in fashion design problems. And she's also a very fine painter. She wins all kinds of awards for painting.'

Lubalin made one other highly significant association at Cooper Union: he formed a lasting friendship with the designer and art director Louis Dorfsman (the latter also met his wife, Ann Hysa, while attending Cooper Union). The two men were to remain friends and colleagues until Lubalin's death in 1981.

2

The Cooper Union

The artists, designers and photographers who graduated from the Cooper Union for the Advancement of Science and Art in the years between the two World Wars were to shape graphic design and advertising in mid-20th-century New York in ways that are still felt today. One of the school's most famous graduates of that period, the photographer Carl Fischer, noted: 'for a while — for one brief, shining moment — Cooper Union was Camelot.'

The school was established in the East Village in New York in 1859 as one of the first academic institutions in the United States to offer a free education to working-class children and to women. The college was founded by Peter Cooper (p.10, fig.5), the son of a poor, working-class family, who, despite having less than a year of formal schooling, went on to make substantial contributions to the industrialization of America, including designing the first American-built steam locomotive (called the Tom Thumb) and becoming a founder member of the company responsible for the first transatlantic telegraph cable. Cooper acquired vast wealth through involvement in real estate, insurance, railroads and telegraphy, and was once a presidential candidate, standing for the Greenback Party, a political body with an anti-monopolist philosophy.

Cooper's lack of education bred in him the desire to give talented young people the privilege of a good, free education. He believed that the children of immigrants and the working class deserved access to learning, and spent the last 30 years of his life creating and nurturing a school for the 'boys and girls of this city, who had no better opportunity than I.'

Since its inception, the Cooper Union has occupied a prominent position in American public life. Various presidents, from Lincoln to Obama, have made speeches in the school's hall, and, thanks to Peter Cooper's philanthropic vision, it has educated countless artists, architects and engineers, many of them leaders in their fields.

Herb Lubalin was just the sort of candidate that Cooper had in mind when he founded his institution. For Lubalin, it was the start of a lifelong association with Cooper Union — first as a student and later as a teacher. In 1976, he was appointed Professor of Design, and such was the depth of his attachment to the institution that the designer Kevin Gatta — a graduate of New York's Pratt Institute — recalled being worried that he wouldn't get a job in the Lubalin studio simply because he wasn't 'a Cooper guy'. He needn't have worried; in 1979 he joined Lubalin's team as an intern.

In a privately published memoir, the photographer Carl Fischer wrote: **'The school was adjacent to the ram-shackle, screeching Third Avenue elevated line and cheek by jowl with the grungy Bowery and its inhabitants, some of who would sleep on the school steps. Around the corner was our annex, McSorley's Old Ale House, the misogynist pub that did not then admit women.'**

Lubalin flourished at the Cooper Union. It was the making of him, and the foundations laid by his education can be seen in his mature work. He told *Idea* magazine that the school did not particularly stress technique. 'They were more interested in thinking and creating ideas than design,' he said. It is a view corroborated by Fischer, who was so concerned about the lack of practical skills in the curriculum that he decided to complain to the head of the school, Professor Dowden: **'I asked why they were not given instruction in the practical tools needed for freelance assignments: how to scale photographs, how to order Photo-stats, how to make mechanical paste-ups for the printer? I had uncovered a flaw in their system. The compassionate Professor Dowden showed no compassion.**

We would learn those mundane skills after we finished school, he told me; Cooper was a place where we were to stretch our imaginations. It was a secular faith that left us with a zeal to excel and, conversely, with a sense of guilt if we did not.'

For Lubalin, there was no doubt about the merits of his training: 'When I got out, I had an advantage over other designers because, although I was technically very bad, I was able to think out problems and find creative solutions faster than most others.' This quote tells us a lot about Herb Lubalin. It defines his working methodology, which was made up from a concoction of speedy conceptual thinking, rapidly sketched ideas, and a remarkable ability to surround himself with people capable of delivering the craft and polish that became the hallmark of everything he did.

Lubalin graduated in 1939. Few would have guessed that the skinny, colour-blind, ambidextrous kid with lousy academic grades was about to set out on a journey that would result in him becoming one of the most influential graphic designers of the 20th century. Besides Lubalin and Dorfsman, the roll call of former Cooper Union students is stellar: Milton Glaser, Edward Sorel, Seymour Chwast, Tom Carnase, Carl Fischer, J. Abbott Miller, Ellen Lupton, Tom Kluepfel, Stephen Doyle, Emily Oberman, Mike Mills, Alexander Isley and Carin Goldberg.

Today, the art school is housed in a gleaming ocean liner of steel and glass called the New Academic Building (p.10, fig.6). It sits at 41 Cooper Square, close to the old redbrick Victorian building that Cooper built (p.10, fig.4). Designed by Thom Mayne of Morphosis architects, it was completed in 2009. The school has approximately 1,000 students studying, art, architecture and engineering, and gives every student a full-tuition scholarship (although, in the *New York Times* of October 31, 2011, it was reported that tuition fees might have to be charged in the future). It houses the Herb Lubalin Study Center, a resource established to hold the work of Lubalin and other significant designers.

In an interview I conducted with the art director Al Greenberg, best known as the founding art director of *GQ* magazine, and a Cooper Union alumnus, he told me: 'They should rename the place — the Lubalin Union.' He wasn't being flippant.

4
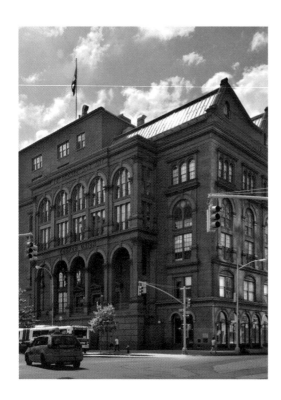

5

6

7

8

9

10

4. The Cooper Union Foundation Building at Cooper Square and Astor Place, New York City.

5. Peter Cooper, inventor and businessman, and founder of the Cooper Union in 1859. Lettering: Tom Carnase.

6. Cooper Union's new academic building, 41 Cooper Square, New York City. Completed in 2009.

7—9. Shots taken within the Herb Lubalin Study Center of Design and Typography in the Cooper Union.

Founded in 1985 by the Cooper Union and friends of the late Herb Lubalin, its mission is the preservation of design history through its core collection of the work of Herb Lubalin and its extensive library and archive of design ephemera. All materials are available for viewing by appointment (pp.432—35). All photographs (except fig.5) by Claudia Klat.

3

Beginnings of Professional Life

Herb Lubalin was born at the end of World War I and emerged, as a young man, into a world overshadowed by World War II. The war in Europe had a direct impact on his early career. Many in his chosen profession had been drafted into the army, which meant that the competition for jobs was greatly reduced. As a prospective parent, Lubalin was exempt from military service, but shortly after the birth of his first child, Lubalin was surprised to receive his call-up papers. His friend Lou Dorfsman — who served in the U.S. Army from 1943 to 1946 — published an account of this episode in Lubalin's life: **'All of Herb's friends and relatives got together and planned a pre-induction bash for the night before his date with the draft board. The big blowout was to take place somewhere in Greenwich Village. By that evening, Herb had developed a devil-may-care macho attitude about serving. The evening began with Martinis. Herb had his straight up, which was a joke since he could get bombed on a chocolate malted in those days. He knocked off the first Martini and ordered another. He was getting loquacious, which signaled that the Martinis were working. If you knew Lubalin, you'd know that he never talked — he was the quietest guy around, except with girls. (We once went to Los Angeles on a business trip and he said nary a word for six hours.) Around the third Martini, Herb was feeling sick. We escorted him to the men's room just in time. He faced the urinal and threw up. Suddenly he crumpled and fell, head first, into the urinal. His jaw broke in several places. We rushed him, by taxi, to the emergency room at New York Hospital. He had his face wired up every which way. Unable to speak at all, he was hospitalized for several weeks and fed through a straw. He lost a few pounds, which he could hardly afford. He couldn't talk to girls. He missed his induction into the Army or Navy. As good fortune had it, during Herb's recuperation, the draft board changed its guidelines for draftees and all fathers became exempt from service for the duration of the war. This was particularly notable since Herb was now down to 100 pounds.'**

Prior to his graduation in 1939, Lubalin had his first taste of public acclaim as a graphic designer. He entered the McCandlish outdoor poster competition, which was open to both students and professionals, and was awarded second prize. His entry was significant because it was the first recorded instance of his habit of graphically substituting the letter 'o' with a round object — in this case, the 'o' in the slogan 'It's Tops' was replaced with a Hires Root Beer cap. It was a graphic trope that Lubalin was to use repeatedly throughout his career (p.14, fig.19).

Lubalin's first job, in 1940, was lettering for exhibitions for the New York World's Fair. He worked alongside Dorfsman and earned $8 a week. In *Idea* magazine (No.77, 1966, p.13, figs.12—14), under the heading 'My Graphic Life History', Lubalin noted that between 1941 and 1943, he 'designed classified real estate and job opportunity ads for a small agency' and 'specialized in book and book jacket designs.' During this period, he worked for an agency called Deutsch & Shea Advertising, and in 1943 he became art director for *Men's Wear*, a magazine owned by Fairchild Publications, a company founded in Chicago in 1892. The following year, he took a post as art director at Reiss Advertising, an agency that specialized in electrical goods. This was followed shortly by his arrival at the highly regarded Sudler & Hennessey agency. Lubalin was to stay with S&H from 1945 until 1964. In 1955, he was appointed creative director and vice president of the agency, and that same year he became a director of the company's consumer advertising arm — Sudler, Hennessey & Lubalin. It was the first time that he had his 'name on the door', a practice that he was to follow for the rest of his life.

Although he was ultimately to leave advertising for design, Lubalin's skills as a designer, along with his individualistic approach to typography and layout, were refined by his time in advertising. It could be argued that he discovered his own personal creative philosophy while immersed in the great American advertising project of the 1950s and 1960s.

What is meant by this phrase? When we look at Lubalin's typography, we see undoubted flair and faultless execution, but we also see *ideas*. Unlike his predecessors in the

10, 11. Booklet covers for two of the schools within the Cooper Union. Designed by Herb Lubalin and Tony Di Spigna. Lubalin set a competition among his students to design an identity for the Cooper Union. Date: c. 1975.

12—14. Front cover and spreads from Japanese design magazine, *Idea* (No.77), 1966. The issue featured an extensive interview with Herb Lubalin, and indicates his growing international reputation in the 1960s.

Modernist school, who sought only to convey the message in purely neutral terms, Lubalin had the ad man's instinct to embellish and emphasize the message. He even had a name for it — Graphic Expressionism.

4

The Conceptual Typographer

Lubalin's creative philosophy of Graphic Expressionism was not an immaculate conception. In an interview in *Graphics Today* (July/Aug 1976), he cited Cassandre, Lester Beall, Will Burtin, McKnight Kauffer and Paul Rand as figures who had provided him with 'tremendous inspiration'. But he knew that to emulate genius you had to be more than a starry-eyed admirer; you had to work hard and learn your craft to its fullest extent. 'We worked like dogs,' he told *Graphics Today*. 'Guys like Lou Dorfsman, Gene Federico, George Lois (you could go on naming them) — we came up in the Depression and it was impossible to make a living. We knew that we had to be good and so we learned what students don't learn any more — the entire field. There's no area of design I don't feel confident in.'

Unlike Paul Rand or Lester Beall, Lubalin rejected Modernism on the grounds that it was unsuited to the exuberant mainstream American imagination. He told *Idea* magazine: 'The American people react to ideas. We are a concept-conscious society. At the same time we are not exactly recognized for our appreciation for the aesthetics of fine design.' Lubalin favoured a more eclectic, freewheeling style that allowed him to reference the vernacular modes and fashions of an older America. He was known in his youth to collect old type specimen catalogues, and when he came to edit the typography journal *U&lc*, he frequently published articles on typographic arcana. The design historian and writer Steven Heller told me about his first encounter with Lubalin: **'When I met Herb after so many years of adoration (to me he was graphic design), he relished my interest in satiric art, which I was writing about a lot, and assigned my first piece in U&lc. He had bought a run of**

19th-century Punch. He didn't know the history and wanted to learn more. That's where I came in. But more important, he wanted to publish these vintage pictures, covers and cartoons. He loved the Victorian aesthetic. This to me was also typical of his generation of designer — hoarders, collectors, interpreters.'

Ample evidence of Lubalin's interest in vernacular and pre-modern styles of design can be found in his work. The logo for his first studio — Herb Lubalin, Inc. — can be seen as a homage to the famous New York, New Haven and Hartford Railroad logo (the ornate lettering was done by John Pistilli, one of the first of Lubalin's trusted accomplices in the creation and refinement of letterforms; p.17, figs.20—21). In later life, Lubalin is said to have turned down the chance to 'redesign the Coca-Cola lettering' on the grounds that 'you don't tamper with a piece of American graphic design history'; and he is often identified with the trend for Art Deco and Art Nouveau revivalism that swept through U.S. visual culture in the late 1960s and early 1970s.

There is an additional element found in Lubalin's work that is worthy of discussion: squint your eyes at some of his asymmetric, interlocking, free-flowing typography and you could be looking at Talmudic scripts. This impression is reinforced by the blackness and heft of many of his individual letterforms and his use of small, sharp serifs, but it also comes from the illustrative nature of his typography — the sense that we are invited to grasp meaning beyond the words themselves.

Orthodox Jewish law forbids the creation of images that can be worshipped as idols, yet Hebrew letterforms are vivid graphic formulations suffused with symbolic meaning. The typographer Martin Mendelsberg wrote: 'Hebrew letters are not merely a convenience of language, but are considered in Jewish tradition to be essences that sustain the structure of the world. The shape, name and numeric value of each letter have lessons to teach us about our spiritual and religious lives.' Does this partly explain Lubalin's aptitude for resonant typographic constructions? Does it offer a clue to Herb Lubalin's mature practice of creating striking 'word pictures'? The Hungarian-born typographer Peter Gabor has noted the Talmudic heritage embedded in Lubalin's work: **'Herbert Lubalin's power rests in the conjunction of the two universes of text and image. Text becomes image and image reinforces the text. His is a deeply**

Jewish approach, by way of Talmudic tradition, in the way [Lubalin] incessantly seeks multiple meanings ...'

Lubalin was not religious — a fact confirmed by his son Peter: 'We were Jewish by ancestry,' he told me, 'but we had Christmas trees.' But growing up in a more traditional Jewish household, he would have been exposed to Talmudic script from an early age. In his mature work there are examples of his use of actual Hebrew letterforms, such as his ad for the Federation of Jewish Philanthropies of New York and his poster for VGC (p.14, figs.15—16). And his most revered and important client, the radical publisher Ralph Ginzburg, recalls that when Lubalin was submitting ideas for the masthead for *Avant Garde* magazine (a project that we will return to in greater detail), one of his rejected proposals involved producing the words 'Avant Garde' in Hebrew.

In a revealing essay that Lubalin wrote for *Print* magazine ('Herb Lubalin's Typography Issue', May/June 1979), he spelt out his philosophy of imbuing letterforms with 'multiple meaning': **'Graphic Expressionism is my euphemism for the use of typography, or letterforms, not just as a mechanical means for setting words on a page, but rather as another creative way of expressing an idea, telling a story, amplifying the meaning of a word or a phrase, to elicit an emotional response from the viewer. In other words, typography to be used as an alternative to photography and/or illustration, or to be synergistically combined to enhance the impact and memorability of a graphic statement.'**

Because of his singular and idiosyncratic development of Graphic Expressionism, Lubalin's place in graphic design history is secure. But what did he contribute to the evolution of the craft? Was he merely a skilful appropriator of styles and graphic idioms? Was he the father of conceptual graphic design? Was he the first postmodernist? Or was he a genuine American original to rank alongside Beall, Rand and Bass? In writing this biographical investigation, my aim is to answer these questions and to place Lubalin in the continuum of modern design history; but to do this it is necessary to look at the evolution of American graphic design and how it might have impinged on the young Lubalin.

5

American Graphic Design Pre-Lubalin

The years after World War II were a boom time for graphic design in the United States. An authentic American voice had been forged out of a combination of indigenous styles, European Modernism and various avant-garde art movements, such as Surrealism, Dada and Futurism. This fusion was expressed most potently by the American-born designer Lester Beall in the posters he designed to promote President Roosevelt's attempts to help the poor of the 1930s Depression: they were a maverick fusing of the American vernacular with radical developments in typography from Europe. Beall noted that 'American political posters, the recruiting posters of the Civil War and *Die Neue Typographie*' influenced his posters.

American graphic design had, of course, existed long before the 1940s and 1950s. In her book *The Origins of Graphic Design in America (1870—1920)*, the historian Ellen Mazur Thomson observed that the Bureau of the Census listed 'designer' as a job category as early as 1890. The survey described designers as 'professionals, along with dentists, clergymen, actors, and civil engineers.' But it was printers who chose the fonts, set the type and added the decorative embellishments; it was printers, as Thomson noted, who 'designed the business forms, handbills, trade cards, contracts and laws, maps, and books — in short, all the printed material needed by tradespeople and governing officials of the period.'

Technology was the main agent of change: developments in typesetting, printing and even the manufacture of paper (from rag to pulp) allowed graphic designers to begin to practise the craft that we recognize today as professional graphic design.

One of the most important technological advances was the arrival in 1828 of lithography, followed a decade or so later by chromolithography. This purely chemical process allowed designers and illustrators to create vividly appealing packaging for mass-market foodstuffs, promotional

15

16

17

18

19

14

15. Poster for Andrich Minerva, one of the award-winning typefaces in the VGC National Typeface Design Competition. Date: 1965.
16. Poster for the Federation of Jewish Philanthropies of New York. Illustration: Ben Shahn. Hebrew lettering: Tom Carnase. Both posters show Lubalin's interest in Hebrew letterforms.
17. Promotional item for LSC&P, designed by Louise Fili, a Lubalin employee and now a highly respected New York graphic designer. She recalls:

'It all started when Herb had a cold and complained "you can't find good chicken soup in this town." He was a fairly recent widower, so we all mothered him incessantly. I made the soup for him and he said it was the best he had ever tasted, and decided that we should bottle it and send it to our clients. I designed the label ... and made the soup.' Writers: Herb Lubalin and Ernie Smith. Date: c. 1975.
18. Herb Lubalin's son Peter followed his father into advertising. He began as a copywriter, and his first published press

ad won a New York Art Directors award. The art director was Herb Lubalin. It was the only time father and son worked together professionally. Client: CBS Radio Network. Photographer: Irv Bahrt. Agency: Sudler & Hennessey. Date: 1964.
19. Lubalin's entry for the McCandlish outdoor advertising competition. Writing in U&lc, Lubalin wrote 'I won first prize in the student category with a poster for Hires Root Beer. The sparkling, persuasively original copy line was: "It's tops." The graphics displayed this headline in

the sky with the Hires bottle top situated in the "o" of the word "tops." Get it? Evidently, the judges got it. And I got $25.00 plus the enthusiastic handclasp of my graphic design instructor. Spurred on, I decided to become the first designer to not only fill the "o" with every conceivable round graphic symbol, but to exploit the characteristics of all the letters of the alphabet with the goal to replace them, whenever the occasion arose, with a symbol reflecting the nature of the character'. Date: c. 1939.

display cards, illustrated journals and, of course, posters — the TV screens of the 19th century. 'Early posters,' wrote Thomson, 'embodied the boisterous showmanship of the circuses, melodramas, and burlesque shows or nostrums they advertised.'

The arrival of the first mechanical typesetting machine contributed to the further diminution of the role of the printer in the design process. Prior to the Linotype machine (designed by Ottmar Mergenthaler in 1886), all typesetting was done by hand at the printworks using either woodblock or metal type. Mergenthaler's machine spelt the end of hand-compositing and made possible the rapid production of newspapers, journals and handbills. This called for a new sort of designer—one who could direct and shape the appearance of printed material without also being the producer.

The next boundary-shifting development was halftone printing. Dot screen-printing, as it was called, was in use by the 1880s and made possible the deployment of photography, which in turn sparked a huge rise in the circulation of journals and newspapers. It also ushered in a new era of mass advertising based around the photographic image rather than the drawn or engraved image.

With increased control over the methods of reproduction, the designer was now in a position to assert supremacy. Ellen Mazur Thomson quoted one historian's observation that the late 19th-century designer was becoming more like the conductor of an orchestra, 'who by degrees forsook his place at the keyboard and his level with the rest of the orchestra, to acquire a level which was literally and metaphorically above the means of production—the orchestra …'

This description seems to describe an art director rather than a graphic designer. In his book *Graphic Design: A Concise History*, the British design historian Richard Hollis pointed out that art direction preceded the profession of graphic design: 'The Art Directors Club of New York was founded in 1920,' he noted. It was another two years before W.A. Dwiggins coined the term 'graphic design' in his essay 'A New Kind of Printing Calls for New Design'. Hollis goes on to show that it was a group of European émigré art directors working for the new monthly magazines that were to define American commercial graphic expression.

This group was led by Dr. Mehemed Fehmy Agha. Of Turkish extraction, Agha was born in Kiev. In the 1920s, he

was working for the German edition of *Vogue*, where he was spotted by the publisher Condé Nast, who was on a talent-hunting trip to Europe. From 1929 onwards, Agha was based in America and worked on *Vogue, House and Garden* and *Vanity Fair*. He was the first art director to think of the magazine as a series of double-page spreads rather than single pages; he used asymmetric layouts and allowed photographs to bleed. He was also a pioneer of sans serif typefaces. He brought to American magazines some of the best photographers of his era — Edward Steichen, Horst, Edward Weston and Herbert Matter, the Swiss designer and photographer. Hollis quoted Agha as saying that the art director 'plans, coordinates and rehearses, but does not perform; at least not in public.'

Other European giants of art direction followed Agha: Alexey Brodovitch worked at *Harper's Bazaar*, where he became one of the major figures of 20th-century graphic design. Russian-born Brodovitch is widely regarded as the first great designer of the photographic spread. He was an inspired commissioner of artistic talent: Cassandre, Andre Derain and Saul Steinberg all benefited from his finely judged patronage, as did photographers Irving Penn and Richard Avedon.

Also notable was Cipe Pineles, America's first female art director. She arrived in the United States from Austria and became Agha's assistant at *Vogue*. She went on to become the art director of *Glamour, Seventeen, Charm* and *Mademoiselle* magazines. Pineles was the first female member of the New York Art Directors Club. A decade later, Will Burtin, an escapee from Nazi Germany, was to take over the art directorship of *Fortune* magazine, where he brilliantly pioneered the melding of typography, diagrams, illustration, photography and layout, as a way of explaining the rapid growth in economic, scientific and business theory. Burtin married Cipe Pineles after the death of her previous husband, CBS art director William Golden.

Non-editorial graphic design, however, was about to have its moment in the sun. As far back as 1936, Walter Paepcke at Container Corporation of America (CCA) spotted the necessity for high-quality design as U.S. firms jostled for a foothold in a booming industrial marketplace. The producers of consumer goods and their advertisers also recognized the need to be identified in a crowded market. Recognition, promotion and what today would be called 'brand awareness' became as important as possessing a good product or utilizing all the latest manufacturing technology. American graphic design, led mostly by yet more European immigrants, was the lucky recipient of this corporate largesse. Raymond Loewy (France), Herbert Bayer (Austria), Will Burtin (Germany), Ladislav Sutner (Czechoslovakia) and Americans Paul Rand, Lester Beall, Bradbury Thompson and Alvin Lustig all found clients willing to hire them for their radical and sophisticated approach to visual communication.

It was the start of corporate design, which emerged between the wars, and was based on Swiss Modernism, or the International Style as it was also known. Paul Rand created logos for IBM and Westinghouse that have become classics of graphic compression — the sort of visual shorthand that was deemed essential for corporate visibility. In 1956, IBM commissioned one of the first style manuals in an attempt to unify the company's many corporate facets. Rand's work for IBM and Westinghouse was matched by the Modernist rigour of Herbert Bayer for CCA and Atlantic Richfield Company, and Herbert Matter for Knoll Associates and the New Haven Railroad.

But the world of corporate graphic design was not the world into which the young Herb Lubalin launched himself. Instead, he became, firstly, an ad man. Lubalin had great success in advertising, which, like graphic design, was going through its own revolution, and he would continue to design ads for the rest of his life. But eventually he broke away from the advertising world so that he could concentrate on what he did best — pure graphic design.

As an independent graphic designer with his own studio, Lubalin had dealings with the corporate world. However, these encounters were infrequent and did not result in his best work, which was invariably done for small publishers and periodicals with a radical and independent editorial policy. Lubalin was unsympathetic to the Swiss style. In an article for *Print* magazine (March/April 1995), the design historian Philip Meggs recalled attending a lecture in Washington DC in the mid 1970s at which he heard Lubalin lambast Swiss design for its 'sameness and uniformity'. Meggs attributes this to commercial one-upmanship (in other words, Lubalin belittling his competitors), yet it is clear that it was a deeply held conviction and had nothing to do with competitiveness. The Swiss style was simply not suited — ideologically or aesthetically — to the un-dogmatic Lubalin.

In an essay in *Print* ('Herb Lubalin's Typography Issue', May/June 1979), Lubalin explained how his eclectic approach was incompatible with the 'business to business communication of corporate design'. He claimed that what he called his Graphic Expressionism was suited to a mass audience: 'The more intellectual Bauhaus style and the formalized Swiss approach to design has no appeal and did not relate to the rank-and-file American. This work has its validity in the business community and in such special interest groups as the medical profession, and still does.' Even the briefest of encounters with Herb Lubalin's huge body of work reveals the fact that he was no corporate modernist. During the 1950s, as graphic design started to live up to the famous maxim issued by Thomas Watson, Jr. of IBM that 'good design is good business', Herb Lubalin was working as an ad man.

6

The New Advertising

For American graphic designers in the 1940s, advertising was an almost unavoidable first step when beginning a graphic design career. Paul Rand, Saul Bass and Herb Lubalin all worked for ad agencies in the early years of their careers: Rand at the Weintraub Advertising Agency; Bass at Buchanan & Co; and Lubalin at Sudler & Hennessey. Lubalin become a partner at the latter in 1959, leaving in 1964 to start the first of many incarnations of his own studio.

By the 1950s, graphic design had not only become a dominant factor in corporate communications, it had also emerged as a key component of the 'new advertising'. A small group of far-sighted individuals based mainly in New York had grasped a fundamental truth about American life: as the USA entered the Atomic Age and revelled in the great orgy of economic growth that was to turn it into the first global superpower, a new sort of advertising was urgently required. The old-style ads, with their appeal to class

20. Letterhead for Herb Lubalin's first studio, formed after leaving Sudler & Hennessey, the innovative New York ad agency where he learned his craft as typographer and art director. Lettering: John Pistilli. Date: 1964.

21. Inspiration for Lubalin's logotype was derived from this famous example of early American commercial lettering.

snobbery and outdated WASP notions of gentility, were no longer in sync with a newly affluent American public that had money to spend on consumer goods. It was also out of sync with manufacturers who needed to sell vast quantities of goods to a mass market. The new advertising that catered for this cultural shift was sharp, modern and sophisticated, and it came largely from one agency: Doyle Dane Bernbach (DDB).

Herb Lubalin was an admirer of the legendary agency. In an interview in *Idea* in 1969, he said: **'I think the greatest evolution that has happened in advertising can be summed up in the three words, Doyle, Dane and Bernbach. They created a new kind of advertising. They set a whole advertising business on its end. They just showed that there was a completely different way to do advertising and from that point on changes began to take place. Advertising is now entirely different from what it was before.'**

DDB was formed in 1949. Philip Meggs describes the Bernbach approach as descending from Paul Rand's earlier efforts to use visual metaphors and puns in ways that were previously unseen in advertising, and which, crucially, required the receiver to be active rather than passive: in other words, to understand the new ads with their visual gags and smart wordplay, the viewer had to be a participant.

Bernbach and his colleagues took this approach and turned it into a new advertising philosophy. Their creation had various names: The New Advertising; The Creative Revolution; The Big Idea. Meggs wrote that DDB, 'removed the boundaries separating verbal and visual communications and evolved visual/verbal syntax: word and image fused into conceptual expression of an idea so that they became completely interdependent.' Advertising began to reflect the changing culture of post-war America. It was whip-smart and, to quote Lou Dorfsman, utilized 'the language of the street'. Marshall McLuhan, the pioneering media theorist, said: 'Ads are the cave art of the 20th century.'

Bill Bernbach was DDB's creative partner. He hired art director Bob Gage, copywriter Phyllis Robinson, and in 1969 art director Helmut Krone. Krone was responsible for DDB's mould-breaking Volkswagen ads (p.18, figs.22, 24). To contemporary eyes, these minimalist 'pages' look conventional — white space, clever wordplay — but when they

first appeared, they were incendiary. 'It is hard to imagine today the impact that this kind of advertising had in the early sixties,' wrote Pentagram partner and graphic designer Michael Beirut, 'where most cars still had big fins and most ads for them featured polo ponies and people in eveningwear, sipping champagne. The understatement, the conversational tone of voice, the utter lack of glamour all foretold a revolution in the making.'

In his exhaustive book on Krone (*Helmut Krone: The Book, Graphic Design and Art Direction*, 2005), advertising tutor and historian Clive Challis noted that Krone's famous 'Think small' VW Beetle ads offered a genuinely radical solution to the seemingly insoluble problem of how to advertise a tiny, oddly shaped German car to a U.S. public reared on sleek, shark-finned automobiles. Krone expressed reservations about working on the VW account. In an interview filmed many years after he had left DDB, Krone said: 'The car had Nazi connotations; I didn't think it was something we should do.' But he overcame his scruples, and the result was a series of press ads that altered the future course of advertising. His 'pages' were sparsely designed and made use of blunt, no-nonsense copy and imagery. No frills — and no fins.

Krone showed the VW Beetle as a car that never changed and therefore never went out of fashion. Other auto advertisers showed cars with shining bodywork; Krone showed a car with a dent in it to make a point about the availability of spare parts. In a rebuttal of the dominant idea of cars as fetishized objects of streamlined perfection, Krone eulogized the Beetle's bug-like ugliness. This frankness and apparent anti-sell was to appeal to a new latent sensibility in post-war America that came to fruition in the second half of the 1960s, when the counterculture erupted, and when Volkswagen (most especially the VW camper van) became the vehicle of choice for hippies and anti-Vietnam war protesters.

Equally seismic in their impact were Krone's stark mono ads for car hire firm Avis. Second in market share to the giant rental company Hertz, Krone made an asset out of Avis's No.2 status. He ran headlines such as, 'Avis is only No.2 in rent cars. So why go with us?' As Challis pointed out, 'by admitting that they [Avis] were No.2, they gave everybody a reason to believe that they would try harder than the market leader. It had a kind of New York,

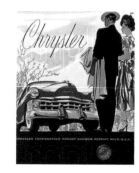

22, 24. Volkswagen press ads by the New York agency Doyle Dane Bernbach (DDB) showing their revolutionary approach to the difficult task of advertising a small, unfashionable German car in the U.S. automobile market. Design by Julian Koenig and Helmut Krone. Krone was to become one of the leading lights in the 'new advertising' and was briefly employed by Herb Lubalin at Sudler & Hennessey. Date: c. 1961.

23. Typical pre-1960s U.S. car ad showing an affluent-looking couple admiring their gleaming new Chrysler.
25. Press ad for RCA Tube division. The verbal/visual construction 'Eye Q' is an example of Lubalin at his most metaphoric. It is advertising that requires the mental participation of the receiver, and is a long way from the conventional aspirational advertising of the time (fig.23). Design by Herb Lubalin. Agency: Sudler & Hennessey. Date: c. 1958.

palms-up, shrugged-shoulder, make-with-the-eyes logic to it: a never-heard-before advertising proposition.'

At DDB, Krone emerged as one of the most forward-thinking ad men of his generation. Prior to his arrival, however, he had worked for Herb Lubalin at Sudler & Hennessey. Lubalin was to claim that Krone was the only person he ever fired, but Challis quoted Krone's version of events; 'I worked for Sudler & Hennessey for three months. Matt Hennessey fired me. Don't blame him, I spent most of my time in the Village … came into work only now and then.'

This was the beginning of the era depicted in the TV series *Mad Men*. It was the start of the boom that established advertising as a key component of modern business culture. And at the heart of it was Herb Lubalin.

7

Sudler & Hennessey

Although overshadowed in advertising mythology by DDB's towering reputation, Sudler & Hennessey nevertheless made a substantial contribution to the formation of the 'new advertising'. S&H was founded by Arthur Sudler and Matt Hennessey. The company was launched as an art studio that worked on pharmaceutical accounts, and this heritage was to remain central to the S&H ethos when it became one of the hottest advertising agencies in the ad boom of the 1960s and 1970s. In addition, S&H achieved a reputation as one of New York's best places to work for ambitious, creative people looking to build a portfolio. Like many talented people of that time, George Lois worked at S&H. Among all the great 'Mad Men' of that period, Lois is the best known beyond the confines of his trade. In an interview I conducted with him, he said: 'Sudler was a beautiful man, but Hennessey was a motherfucker.'

In a film, uploaded to YouTube, titled *The World According to Sudler & Hennessey (Director's Cut)*, various S&H staffers, along with a vigorous-looking Matt Hennessey (Sudler died in 1968, and Hennessey in 2011 at the age of 95), describe the agency's contribution to the evolution

of advertising. Much of the best commentary, however, is provided by Fay Barrows, who had been Herb Lubalin's assistant and had gone on to marry Ernie Smith, a key figure in Lubalin's career as a graphic designer.

Now retired, she provided copious information about her time with Lubalin and her two spells of employment at S&H. In the 1940s, she had studied Literature and Art History at UCLA. Returning to New York in 1949, she joined S&H, where she managed the agency's scheduling of work. Shortly afterwards, she was given the job of Herb Lubalin's assistant; **'My earliest memory of him was his quiet demeanor. He minced few words and literally could do layouts with both hands. I remember when he designed an ad, just by looking at the copy he was able to allow the proper amount of space, selecting the typeface without specimen sheets.'**

As well as her role as Herb Lubalin's assistant, she became the agency's art buyer: **'I hired comp artists to finish work ready for client approval. There were times when Herb handed work to freelancers and if what he got back from them was insufficient, he would say nothing. Those works were placed behind metal files. When we moved to another location, a huge bag of these specimens was dumped. We had what is called a "Swipe File" (no computers then). I collected images from magazines, newspapers, etc, which I filed alphabetically. Each required a separate folder. On occasions, there were phone calls and trips to museums to get approvals to use paintings, sculptures, etc, for use on a folder or mailing. We had an art-book library. Herb purchased books for reference and also because he loved them. Many books had illustrations that we were able to use without a fee.'**

Shortly after Barrows joined S&H, the company lost its biggest client, a pharmaceutical company called Lederle Laboratories that accounted for 50 per cent of the agency's income. An emergency meeting was called at which a decision was made to move away from being an art studio doing ads to become a fully fledged advertising agency. The company started to acquire advertising clients, mostly in the booming pharmaceutical industry. This resulted in mainly trade advertising. Sudler and Lubalin recognized the need to attract 'consumer advertising', and so they set about developing what Barrows called a 'pet project': they formed a division of S&H called Sudler, Hennessey and Lubalin. Having achieved partner status, Herb Lubalin was, in the eyes of many, the dominant creative force in the new agency. But he was wise enough to surround himself with some of the best people in New York. Perhaps his most celebrated hiring was George Lois. The son of a florist from the Bronx, Lois's 1960s covers for *Esquire* — witty visual haikus that defined the zeitgeist for a generation of newly media-literate Americans — have entered the design and advertising canon. In an interview conducted in Lois's Manhattan apartment, he told me the story of how he came to work for 'Herbie': **'When I got back from the army in 1952 — I'd been in Korea — I really wanted to work for CBS. I spoke to Riba Soches, my wonderful teacher at Pratt. She knew Lou Dorfsman. She called him and he said he'd see me. So, two days after getting back from Korea, I'm sitting in Louie's office. He says, "Kid, this is a great portfolio, but I haven't got a job for you." I was about to leave when he said, "Wait, Bill Golden's been looking for someone for two years." Golden was head of the design department at CBS, and I ended up working for him for two years. I loved him. He was great. But I left and went to work for a shitty agency doing ads for American Airlines. I hated it, but I was starting to get stuff in Art Directors Annuals and wanted to work on better ads. I spoke to Louie and he said, "You gotta go see Herbie." And that's how I ended up working for Herb Lubalin at Sudler & Hennessey.'**

Lubalin had been quick to spot Lois's fast-paced genius, and put him to work on the agency's consumer ads. 'He was a sweet man,' recalled Lois. 'He never asked me to do anything that was beneath me. He gave me an office right next to him and we worked on ads together. I loved everything about him. Sure, he was grumpy sometimes, but only about things he had a right to be grumpy about.'

According to Lois, 'S&H was full of talent — Herbie was one of the great talent spotters of all time.' Some, such as Helmut Krone, Bernie Zlotnick and Lois himself, became leading exponents of the new advertising; others, such as Ernie Smith and Tom Carnase, emerged as key members of the Lubalin studios of the next two decades. Another important talent to emerge was the photographer Carl Fischer. Fischer was to become one of the key photographers in the new advertising, but he began his working life as a member of the Lubalin team at S&H. In a privately

published memoir, he wrote about his time at Sudler & Hennessey and his relationship with Herb Lubalin: **'Sudler & Hennessey was one of the first pharmaceutical advertising agencies that began making good design acceptable and their quiet, no-nonsense art director, Herb Lubalin, hired me as his assistant. He liked the fact that I could take photographs as well as design medical ads. One of my first jobs was an album cover and I took a Polaroid picture of a bunch of grapes (can't remember why) and made a Photostat to layout size. But for the finish, I used a large camera and made an exceedingly sharp image. Lubalin liked the softer layout image better. And he was right. The original was more spontaneous than the stilted finish and so I used the Polaroid image.'**

Other names that passed through the breeding ground of S&H include Lester Bookbinder (photographer), Art Kane (leading art and music photographer), Jerome Snyder (later to become art director of *Scientific American* and *Sports Illustrated*) and Jay Maisel (best known for his cover shot of Miles Davis for the album *Kind of Blue*). Even Andy Warhol worked for S&H as a freelance illustrator. He is listed on a poster produced by S&H to show the array of talent they had at their command.

It is fascinating to speculate on the relationship between Lubalin, one of the pre-eminent graphic designers of the 20th century, and Andy Warhol, a prince of the contemporary art aristocracy. Fay Barrows noted: **'Andy Warhol was not on our staff but we hired him to do illustrations for some of our mailers. I certainly met him and gave him those assignments. We both lived on Lexington Ave. He owned a brownstone and lived with his mother. After I left S&H, we would often meet at the local supermarket, me pushing a stroller, he a shopping basket. He was quiet and unassuming. Of course, Herb was the person who made the connection.'**

Warhol's time as an illustrator working on commercial accounts — most famously for various shoe companies — is well documented. Yet despite being a lifelong supporter and commissioner of illustration, Lubalin appears to have never mentioned his connection with the artist in interviews. This was doubly odd, since Warhol's book *The Philosophy of Andy Warhol (From A to B and Back Again)* — described as an 'assemblage of self-consciously ironic "quotable quotes" about love, beauty, fame, work, time, death,

26

27

29

28

30

31

21

32. Lubalin and Fay Barrows at Sudler & Hennessey. Barrows was art buyer for S&H and she and Lubalin were to remain friends until his death in 1981. She married Ernie Smith, who also worked at S&H and was to become one of Lubalin's most important collaborators. Date: 1950s. Photograph courtesy of Fay Barrows.

33, 34. Front and back cover of *Print* magazine (Jan. 1958) showing the famous 'Slinky' that Lubalin used in his celebrated ad for a cure for back spasm

(fig.35). The issue contained an article called 'How Herb Lubalin Creates a Campaign at Sudler & Hennessey.'

35. Creating ads for pharmaceutical companies was the main activity of Sudler & Hennessey. Herb Lubalin designed many of them, often writing the copy too. It was while doing these ads that he refined his theory of 'conceptual lettering' or 'word images', as they were sometimes called. Shown here is one of his most famous ads. The 's' of 'spasm' is replaced by a Slinky:

it stands as a visual metaphor for muscular spasms. Photography: Carl Fischer. Date: c. 1957.

36. House ad for Sudler & Hennessey listing the creative talent that the agency employed either as freelancers or as staff members, many of whom were to remain Lubalin's friends and collaborators throughout his career. It is typical of Lubalin that he would see merit in naming the individuals who contributed to the creative impact of S&H. Andy Warhol is listed under

freelance illustrators. Date: 1957.

37. The Sudler & Hennessey ad team as featured in *Print* magazine article. Lubalin and Barrows can be seen second and third, from left to right. Wearing the slinky is Cal Sacks, an S&H employee and a frequent model for Lubalin ads. Figs.33, 34 and 37 courtesy of *Print*. Date: 1958.

economics, success, and art, among other topics' — had a cover design by Herb Lubalin (p.31, fig.46). S&H marked an important period in the life and work of Herb Lubalin. It was where he made many of the creative alliances that were to prove critical in his development as a pivotal figure in graphic design; and it was where he evolved the creative philosophy that we recognize today as the Lubalin signature style. It was at S&H that Lubalin cultivated his ideas about expressive typography. Ads done at S&H for the pharmaceutical trade allow us to plot his embryonic approach to 'word pictures' and 'conceptual typography' — two phrases that were to be used often to describe work from Lubalin's post-advertising years.

Lubalin's ad for a cough expectorant (Pyribenzamine) uses the headline 'Break up cough' (p.95, fig.23). The word 'cough' is set in a Grotesque font and enlarged to dominate the page: it is then 'broken up' using a trompe l'oeil effect of ripped and torn paper. The message is that if you have bronchial congestion ('tenacious mucus', to quote the body copy), here's the drug that will 'break it up'. Another ad promotes Bentyl, a drug designed to reduce back spasms (p.23, fig.35). Again, the viewer is faced with one big word — in this case, 'spasm'. Lubalin replaces the second 's' with a metallic 'Slinky' coiled into the shape of the missing letter. 'I am accused of having started the whole wordgame in the early 50s,' he said in an interview. 'I became bored with the sameness of all pharmaceutical advertising. It was then that I started playing with words, trying to make them more meaningful than their actual implications.'

Fay Barrows recalled the 'Slinky' ad being made and the improvisatory way this, and other S&H ads, were often conceived and assembled: **'The Slinky idea was Herb's, the design, everything was his. Carl Fischer was working for us as a designer and we set up a small photo studio for his use. That was the beginning of his career as a photographer. Most of us acted as models as required. There were so many mailers done which contained photos of patients. I had more photos of me with all kinds of medical complications...'**

Herb Lubalin's ads may lack the satirical bite of George Lois's or the almost studious literacy of Helmut Krone's, but unlike these two, Lubalin's time in ad land was a stopover on the way to what would become his true calling: graphic design. He was lucky to have found S&H. As an agency

with its roots in design, it always valued the contribution design and designers could make to advertising. Almost uniquely, it gave a platform to Lubalin and many others from which to create advertising that was to have graphic expression at its core.

Today, Sudler & Hennessey works in the health sector with offices around the world. It is part of the giant WPP network of companies.

8

The Break with Advertising

When Rhoda Sparber met her future husband, Herb Lubalin, at a dinner party in the 1970s, he had been out of S&H for nearly a decade. She mentioned to him that her brother was in advertising. Lubalin snapped back: 'I'm not in advertising. I'm a graphic designer.' But long before he set up his first independent studio, in 1964, Lubalin had been considering breaking away from the ad world. When George Lois quit S&H after a violent disagreement with Matt Hennessey, Lubalin suggested that Lois join him and Dorfsman in a new alliance — a creative agency to be called Lubalin, Dorfsman & Lois. 'I envisaged it as the second great creative agency — after DDB,' Lois told me. But despite three months of careful planning, Dorfsman pulled out. 'We even had a letterhead,' remembered Lois. 'I asked each partner to typeset their name. Herbie got John Pistilli to create a Spencerian script version of his name; Dorfsman set his in Bodoni; and I did something like this [scribbles stencil-like letterforms]. It must be somewhere. I'd love to find it.'

But despite creating a letterhead and securing premises, the putative super-agency never got off the ground. This was not the last time that Lubalin and Dorfsman contemplated working together. Indeed, it was proposed on so many occasions that Dorfsman even referred to the fabled on/off nature of their partnership in the address he gave at Lubalin's funeral. As a gesture to the disappointed Lois, Dorfsman helped him get a job at DDB.

32

33

34

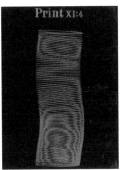 

35

36

37

23

Lubalin finally quit S&H in 1964 to set up Herb Lubalin, Inc. He was following the pattern set by Paul Rand, who had also withdrawn from advertising, leaving the Weintraub agency nearly a decade before. Rand left in disgust with the agency's short-sighted clients, but in Lubalin's case, S&H's design-focused approach and his status as partner had meant that his time in advertising had not been unhappy. However, he knew that he had reached a point where he needed to control his own destiny, and besides, he was not uncritical of the advertising trade.

As a man of liberal sensibilities, it is hardly surprising that Lubalin had some reservations about developments in advertising. Like most educated Americans, he would have been aware of Vance Packard's *Hidden Persuaders*, a famous exposé, published in 1957, of the nefarious side of advertising. The book alerted the American public to ad land's subterfuges and concealed strategies. Today, Packard is often dismissed as a 'pop sensationalist' and a 'puritan', even by commentators who are sympathetic to his anti-advertising stance. Nevertheless, the impact of his book was enormous, and Lubalin shared some of the views contained in this new strand of critical scrutiny directed at advertising.

It is clear from his many statements about advertising in interviews and articles that Lubalin had a degree of moralistic disdain for his trade. But he stops short of outright rejection, and from his published comments, his attitude seems mildly contradictory: on the one hand, he plainly found at least some advertising morally dubious, but on the other, his main complaint seems to stem more from clients preventing him from doing the sort of work he wanted to do, rather than from ethical scruples.

At an advertising conference in Chicago in the 1960s, Lubalin told his audience that, 'Ninety per cent of advertising stinks.' *Advertising Age* ran the comment as a headline. From this fragment, it is not clear whether he thinks it's the rise of sophisticated techniques for mass persuasion that 'stinks', or whether the creative standard of advertising is so poor that he has to hold his nose in mock disgust. In an interview in *Idea* magazine (1962), he came close to spelling out his thoughts about advertising: **'Advertising in the USA is a fairly stupid business. We have made it that way by underestimating the intelligence of the American people. The bulk of our output is devised to appeal to the sub-teenage mentality of that great big consuming monster which we have created.'** He also said: **'I [often] find advertising unrewarding from a moral standpoint. I don't particularly like to advertise products and help clients sell products that I have no particular use for. And very often I turn down a product because I just think it detrimental for people to buy certain products. If you do a beautiful advertising campaign and then a customer walks into the supermarket and picks up the finished product and is completely disappointed, you've wasted a lot of effort to get a dissatisfied customer. The client at point of sale has defeated the whole purpose of your advertising.'**

Another reason for Lubalin's split with advertising is one he also shared with Paul Rand. Both Rand and Lubalin expressed dismay over the way advertising agencies squeezed out the individual. 'At an agency,' said Lubalin, 'there are no individuals ... and all those who stick to it become anonymous.' For designers with the talent — and egos — of Rand and Lubalin, anonymity was not a career option.

Fay Barrows also noted Lubalin's frustration with the increasing dominance of market research in defining creative strategies for advertising: 'He hated the fact that market research was beginning to make inroads in determining what should be said and why.' For a highly intuitive individual such as Herb Lubalin, the rise of the clipboard mentality in advertising must have been hard to swallow.

S&H is the reason Lubalin stayed in advertising longer than his hero Paul Rand. It is also why, for example, he would not have enjoyed as much freedom at DDB, who valued — and utilized — graphic design, but not in the way that S&H did. In her encyclopedia *Typography and Graphic Design*, the historian Roxane Jubert points out that Bob Gage dismissed design as being 'cold, it doesn't move people.' She quotes Krone: **'The thing about DDB was that designers were like poison. Somebody who knew how to draw was poison. A guy who was too good a typographer, we didn't want him. We knew about the Bauhaus, but we weren't after design, we were after advertising. We were interested in reaching people. That's all we were interested in.'**

But by the early 1960s, there was now a schism between design and advertising, and it was clear which side of the divide Herb Lubalin wanted to be on.

38

39

40

9

Independent Graphic Designer

In 1964, the Civil Rights Act abolished racial segregation in the United States; it was the year The Beatles first appeared on *The Ed Sullivan Show*; it was the year when Americans learned to live with what the writer Don DeLillo called the 'confusion and psychic chaos and the sense of randomness' that followed the assassination of President Kennedy the year before. On a more mundane note, it was also the year in which Herb Lubalin opened the door to his first studio — Herb Lubalin, Inc.

Information about the early days of Herb Lubalin, Inc. is scarce. We can speculate, however, that it was characterized by the furious activity that typified Lubalin's entire life. Descriptions of Lubalin in repose are hard to find; on the other hand, there are numerous accounts of his creative fecundity and his remorseless productivity. One colleague described how Lubalin would arrive at the studio at 8am, do the *New York Times* crossword, and from then on it was rare to see him do anything other than work. Fay Barrows recalled that **'except for meetings he rarely left his desk to walk around or relax. No time was wasted between assignments. He had an incredible visual memory and would remember obscure photos or illustrations he had seen in a magazine.'**

Even at home, it seems that the Lubalin machine never switched to idle. His son Peter Lubalin, a successful advertising copywriter, told me that he remembered as a child watching TV while his father sketched tissues: **'We had a TV room and we'd watch a lot of sports — baseball, football, we were big sports fans. My father would bring work home. While we watched, he'd sketch, tear off sheets of tissue paper, crumple them into a ball and throw them on the floor. I remember the sound — scratch, rip, crumple — then it would start all over again. Many decades later, I still remember this.'**

With his name on a bronze nameplate of a studio at 223 East 31st Street, and with a smart letterhead, Herb Lubalin was no longer an ad man; he was a bona fide graphic designer. The outward manifestation of Lubalin's break with advertising could be seen in his clothes and personal grooming habits. While working in advertising, he was clean-shaven and wore a white shirt with a slim tie. But by the time he had made his exit from the world of 'Mad Men', he had grown a beard, taken to wearing open-necked shirts, acquired a pair of aviator glasses and allowed his hair to assume a 1960s waywardness that, if it didn't make him look like a hippy, at least gave him the appearance of a bohemian artist, or perhaps a professor at a progressive university. In the late 1970s, the design writer Steven Heller recalls seeing Lubalin wearing workman's dungarees in the markets around Millerton, an upstate New York village where Lubalin had a weekend home: hardly the uniform of a Mad Man or a New York graphic design demigod.

But it is in his work rather than his sartorial habits that we see the clearest manifestation of Lubalin's break with advertising. The design that Lubalin produced from 1964 onwards in his various studios, with their shifting personnel, shows that he had developed a signature style. His work was varied — an eclectic mix of the vernacular, the modern and the decorative — but it was always identifiably the work of Herb Lubalin. And it flourished because, with the establishment of Herb Lubalin, Inc., he was now free to undertake only the projects that interested him and, most crucially, to take on jobs that allowed him to be an individual creative person rather than an ad agency team player. Paradoxically, as we will see in the following chapter, in order to achieve the individualism he so craved, he needed to surround himself with a great many talented accomplices.

The question of Lubalin's collaborators, and who deserves credit for the work they produced, was to be a feature of his most successful years, and still remains a source of contention decades later. Yet it is one of the great tests of a graphic designer's true worth: can a personal vision be sustained while relying on others to help make that vision come to fruition? In Lubalin's case, the answer is an emphatic yes. He had a signature style — one of the strongest in graphic design history — yet it was made with the help of many hands. Herb Lubalin, the graphic auteur, needed his collaborators in just the same way that the great film directors need to surround themselves with teams of brilliant collaborators.

There is no question that without skilled lettering artists such as Tom Carnase, Tony Di Spigna and John Pistilli, and without the help of people like Ernie Smith and Roger Ferriter, the Lubalin reputation would not be so elevated. But if some of his collaborators claim to have suffered under his shadow, then Lubalin himself is not to blame. The first thing that strikes anyone who makes a close reading of the Lubalin archives is the remarkable efforts he made to ensure that all his senior accomplices received proper credits. Even tiny, throwaway mailers promoting a typeface were scrupulously credited with the names of his co-creators.

This eagerness to acknowledge the contribution of his fellow workers was always a feature of the many interviews he gave to the design press: repeatedly Lubalin praises his collaborators. At the end of a long interview ('Dialogue with Herb Lubalin', *Idea*, 1969) he said: **'... my success in this business is hardly based on my talents alone. All these great people who work for me deserve an incredible and immeasurable amount of credit for their contribution to my success. I would like to give special mention to Ernie Smith, Annegret Beier, Lowell Bodger, G.M. de Lesseps, Fran Elfenbein, Donna Gortinsky, Hans Mauli, Alan Peckolick, Mike Randazzo and Diana Wilko for their design efforts and to Tom Carnase for his contribution of hand lettering.'**

This doesn't strike the reader as a man interested in snaring all the glory. It would be hard to find another figure in graphic design as eminent as Lubalin who was as eager to eulogize his or her collaborators. Anyone who knows the world of graphic design will know that the quest for equitable credits is a ceaseless struggle, which rarely leaves all parties completely satisfied. It is the nature of graphic design — and studio life — that most, if not all work, has an element of collaboration. There is also the question of what aspect of a finished job is the most important: the original idea, or the polish added by a skilled craftsperson? These arguments haunt the annals of graphic design like restless ghosts. They will never go away.

It is significant that in the *Idea* interview quoted above, Lubalin begins and ends the eulogizing of his team with two names: Ernie Smith and Tom Carnase. These two figures, alongside Tony Di Spigna and Alan Peckolick, straddle the Lubalin story, from its beginnings in advertising to its end with the death of Lubalin in 1981. All four would eventually become partners in various Lubalin studios, and all four require close examination in order to establish a fuller understanding of how Herb Lubalin functioned as both a creative and a business person.

10

Partners and Collaborators

Herb Lubalin, Inc., was established in 1964. Two of his associates from his Sudler & Hennessey days, Ernie Smith and Tom Carnase, joined in 1967. Both achieved partner status when Lubalin, Smith, Carnase, Inc. was formed in the same year. Ernie Smith occupied a special place in the Lubalin inner circle. The two men had worked together at S&H for 15 years. Fay Barrows, who was married to Smith, recalled him being hired: 'Ernie had an excellent portfolio and Herb hired him instantly. Ernie and Herb became fast friends. Herb was aware of our relationship and he was the first to learn that we planned to marry.'

In an *Idea* (1969) interview, Lubalin described Smith's role: **'I may contact a client and bring the client in and introduce Ernie Smith. He takes the account and handles everything on the account such as he's doing now for the Coca-Cola Company. In other words, he will share with me the responsibility for the creative output on most of our clients.'** Fay Barrows added that Smith's role involved **'attending meetings with clients. Handling the creative work, layout, design, photography or art to illustrate an ad or package, or folder. He was in total control. He was [Lubalin's] creative partner. His happiest years were working at LSC.'**

Smith left in 1973. His reason for leaving was jocularly referred to as a desire to spend more time fishing. In fact, Smith left to open a resort in upstate New York with his then wife, Fay Barrows. In the inaugural issue of *U&lc*, the ITC house journal that Lubalin edited and art directed (p.60, fig.93), Smith wrote a light-hearted account of his life as a resort owner: **'... after packing away 20 years of accumulated type books, AD Annuals and things like**

42. From left to right: Seymour
Chwast, Herb Lubalin and Bernie
Zlotnick. Date: 1967.
  43. From left to right: Herb Lubalin,
Bernie Zlotnick, Seymour Chwast,
Irwin Rothman (partner in Pioneer
Moss), Gene Federico, unknown winner
of the Pioneer Moss competition,
Stanley Tankel (partner in Pioneer
Moss). Date: 1967. Both pictures
courtesy of Bernie Zlotnick.

furniture, jazz records and my double-vented suits, I packed my family into our new, second-hand station wagon and headed for the New York State Thruway and North! Where? Bolton Landing, New York. Where? Bolton Landing, New York! That's about half-way north on 32-mile-long Lake George about an hour north of Albany.'

Fay Barrows mentioned another reason for her husband's departure: 'One of the reasons he bought the resort was to be able to paint again. Unfortunately, the lack of income forced him to work in the city during the winters. He was also a jazz film historian. He collected jazz films and during our time together many musicians were entertained in our apartment in New York. He had films on jazz dance, lectured for colleges, and lent his expertise to TV. Ernie contributed to The Black Book, which used many of his images and quotations. This book has recently been republished [by Random House].'

In 1993, Smith donated his collection of jazz films to the Smithsonian Institution. He died, aged 79, in 2004.

More than one former employee has mentioned that Lubalin took the departure of staff badly. He was clearly upset when Smith left. Some indication of Smith's importance can be seen in the *Idea* magazine profile of the studio in the special 'Lubalin edition' published in 1969. A page is devoted to individual portraits of the staff at work (p.34, fig.51). A numerical code is provided to allow identification of each studio member: the prime spot — picture No.1 — shows a contemplative, Buddha like Ernie Smith. There is also an affectionately worded press release issued by the studio, announcing Smith's departure. In the hothouse design world, defecting studio members are often treated as pariahs, so it tells us something about Lubalin's fundamental decency that he could say this: 'Ernie Smith, formerly the S in our logo, has left us to go fishing. Alan Peckolick has replaced him as a principal of our company, thus making it possible for Herb Lubalin and Tom Carnase to, occasionally, go fishing with Ernie Smith. If or when you call us (our phone number and address are the same), a delightful voice will say, "LSC&P". Ask for Herb Lubalin, Tom Carnase or Alan Peckolick. If you want Smith, look him up in the Lake George, N.Y. directory. He'll tell you what's biting.'

Tom Carnase was born in 1939. During a long career, he has worked as a typographer, type designer, teacher and graphic designer. Today he runs Carnase, Inc. in Palm Springs, USA. He joined S&H in 1959 and left in 1964 to work as a freelance designer and start the studio Bonder & Carnase, Inc. In 1967, he joined Lubalin, becoming vice-president and partner of Lubalin, Smith, Carnase, Inc. He remained with LSC until 1979, after which he opened the Carnase Computer Typography studio, and became co-founder and president of the World Typeface Center Inc., an independent type-design agency.

Carnase was primarily a lettering artist, but his work includes packaging, exhibitions, corporate identities, logos and typeface design. He was responsible, sometimes jointly, for many important typefaces of the second half of the 20th century. These include: ITC Busorama (1970); WTC Carnase Text; WTC Goudy; WTC Our Bodoni (with Massimo Vignelli); 223 Caslon, LSC Book; WTC Our Futura; and WTC 145.

Carnase is perhaps best known, however, for his pivotal role in the creation of Avant Garde Gothic, a seminal typeface that has come to define an entire decade — the 1970s. The story of Avant Garde Gothic and how it began as a logotype for a masthead and then, due to Carnase, became a full family of typefaces, will be told in a later chapter (p.51). But at this stage, it is worth noting that Carnase is on record as saying that he feels under-recognized and ill-compensated for his contribution to the realization of Avant Garde Gothic as a major typeface, and he has expressed disgruntlement about his treatment by Lubalin.

It is undoubtedly the case that Lubalin owed a huge debt to Carnase. Many of the most famous logotypes and 'wordpictures' attributed to Lubalin were drawn by Carnase from 'sketched tissues' by Lubalin: Mother & Child (1965); the Avant Garde masthead (1967); NY, NY (1959). But Lubalin was never shy about publicly acknowledging the extent of Carnase's contribution, and he made it clear repeatedly that he was in no doubt about Carnase's importance. A 1979 press release stated that: 'In the field of type design, Tom Carnase has few peers.'

In the same year, in his long essay on typography in *Print* magazine ('Herb Lubalin's Typography Issue', May/June 1979), Lubalin referred to Carnase as, 'one of the world's leading letterform designers ... Tom Carnase has long been recognized for his Spencerian script. He is the master craftsman of this particular area of design.'

44. Trade press article in *Graphics: New York* (June, 1966) showing Lubalin's packaging work for Coca-Cola. This work was among the first projects undertaken by the new Lubalin studio. It is barely recognizable as the work of Herb Lubalin, and it is significant that the magazine text refers to it as the 'brainchild of the staff at Lubalin, Inc.'

45. Letter signed by Herb Lubalin inviting Charles and Ray Eames to visit the newly formed Lubalin studio. Date: 1965.

46. During his time at Sudler & Hennessey, Herb Lubalin commissioned Andy Warhol to provide illustrations for pharmaceutical ads. Did Warhol repay the favour by asking Lubalin to design the cover of his book, *The Philosophy of Andy Warhol (From A to B and Back Again)*? Date: 1975.

47, 48. Contact sheets showing Herb Lubalin, Ernie Smith and Tom Carnase around the time that Lubalin, Smith, Carnase, Inc., was formed. Both men joined Lubalin in his independent studio in the late 1960s and both were to play key roles in the Lubalin story. Carnase was a top lettering artist and typographer of the period and was to draw up the typeface Avant Garde Gothic. Date: c. 1967. Photographs courtesy of Fay Barrows.

The frequency with which Lubalin singled out Carnase for praise was remarkable. But as we shall see in a later chapter devoted to Lubalin as a designer of typefaces, it was not praise that Carnase desired, but rather a share in the profits of his typeface-designing skills.

The next great collaboration in Lubalin's professional life was with another lettering wizard, Tony Di Spigna. Di Spigna appears to share none of Carnase's dissatisfaction: 'Tom's contribution to the Lubalin Studio can't be denied,' noted Di Spigna, in an interview I conducted with him via email. 'I think his business relationship to International Typeface Corporation with Aaron Burns was in question. Here I can't help you because I wasn't privy to the arrangement. ITC was a separate business concern from the Lubalin studio.'

Born in Italy in 1943, the Pratt-educated Di Spigna found himself working for Lubalin through his association with Carnase: **'In the same year I graduated, and after four meaningless and not-worthy-of-mention jobs, I was fortunate enough to be hired by Tom Carnase, who then had his own independent studio with Ronnie Bonder. It was in the same building as the Lubalin studio. I knew a great deal about Herb and Tom Carnase long before I met them. As a student, I avidly followed their work through trade publications and shows. Tom Carnase was Herb's principal lettering artist. When he decided to join the Lubalin studio, I went along with him as his assistant designer.'**

Di Spigna joined Lubalin, Smith, Carnase, Inc. in 1969, but left in 1973 to open his own New York studio. He returned to the Lubalin camp in 1978, joining Herb Lubalin Associates as a vice president and partner. 'I had left to do my own thing for a few years,' he recalled, 'until Herb asked me to consider coming back as a partner. For me, to be considered worthy enough as a partner in such a great design firm was a dream come true.'

Younger members of the late-period Lubalin studio recall Di Spigna affectionately as a big, demonstrative, bearded character who filled the studio with expletives and acted as a sort of *yin* to Lubalin's *yang*. As Di Spigna recalls, the Lubalin studio was like, 'a working family, and, like all members of a family, we may not have always agreed business-wise, but design-wise we respected each other's talent and put our best efforts forward. It was a joy to be working with Herb, both personally and professionally. It was a great time for me.'

Together, Lubalin and Di Spigna produced two great typefaces: Serif Gothic and Lubalin Graph (p.52). As with most typefaces developed at the Lubalin studio, they were originally designed for clients in the form of logotypes for corporations, magazine mastheads and other commercial purposes. When they saw unique letterforms that could be developed into entire alphabets, they took advantage of what Di Spigna has called the 'rare waiting periods between assignments' and turned them into fully functioning typefaces. Di Spigna left the Lubalin studio for the last time in 1980, and opened his own design firm, Tony Di Spigna, Inc.

Of all Lubalin's collaborators and business partners, Alan Peckolick was the most enduring. Born in the Bronx in 1940, he was Lubalin's first biographer, and thanks to his famous 'blue' Lubalin monograph of 1985, co-written with Gertrude Snyder, (now out of print, copies can be found on the internet selling for hundreds of dollars), he is seen in the eyes of many as the keeper of the flame. In an interview I conducted with him in his Manhattan apartment, he told me how he first met Lubalin: **'I grew up in a home with no culture, but I could draw better than anyone else in my high school, so when I left, I went to work in ad agencies doing finished art and mechanicals. But I kept getting fired. When I asked why, they said it was because I worried about the look of ads and not enough about selling the client's products. I was also attending evening classes at Pratt and they said to me, look, it's not working, you can't draw. Then someone said, why don't you think about graphic design. I asked what graphic design was, and I was told not to worry about it and to remember that to be a graphic designer you don't have to be able to draw. So I switched over and discovered there was a difference between design and advertising. I started to buy all the magazines and I kept seeing this guy, Herb Lubalin. I wanted to work with the best, so I tried to get hold of him, but couldn't. Then someone I knew saw my work and said, "You should be working for Herb Lubalin." She rang him up and he said he'd see me.'**

Lubalin's willingness to interview the young and untried Peckolick is a recurring feature of his professional life. He seems to have never turned down an opportunity to see a young designer and look at his or her portfolio. In

Sprite's new cartons by Lubalin present 'one-sided' picture as soda pop art

New York: New Sprite cartons, based on a "springtime" theme, use green as their basic color and show, on the "hit" side, what is billed as "a major innovation" in terms of soft drink "tone and artistic treatment"—a waterfall scene meant to suggest spring "serenity." The flip side offers the Sprite logo in alternating dark green and reddish orange letters, with the "It's a natural" slogan below it and, on the bottom, a series of light green S-shaped coil designs. 12-oz. cans and 28- and 32-oz. bottles also "reflect" the new design, which is the brainchild of the staff of Herb Lubalin, Inc.

and Coca-Cola's "brand management for allied products" department (President Herb Lubalin holds the distinction of being the sole U.S. member of the Art Directors Club of Sweden, according to Coke, as well as belonging to many other graphics organizations here and abroad.)

Syndicated cartoonist Mort Walker ("Beetle Bailey," "Hi and Lois," "Boner's Ark") has created a family of giraffes, visually related to his "Boner's Ark" characters, to promote Sprite via the Sunday comics as one part of the Marschalk campaign.

"Take a sip—it's springtime!"

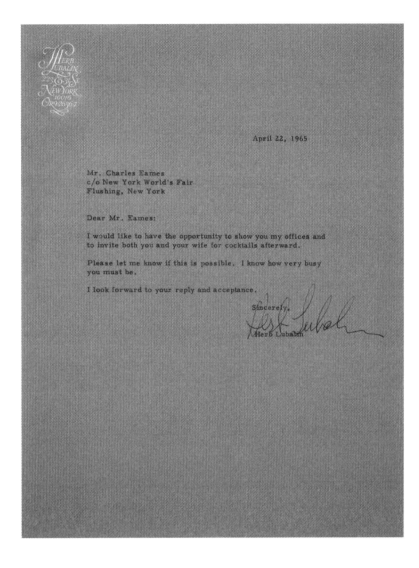

April 22, 1965

Mr. Charles Eames
c/o New York World's Fair
Flushing, New York

Dear Mr. Eames:

I would like to have the opportunity to show you my offices and to invite both you and your wife for cocktails afterward.

Please let me know if this is possible. I know how very busy you must be.

I look forward to your reply and acceptance.

Sincerely,

Herb Lubalin

46

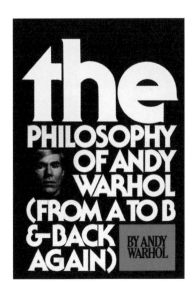

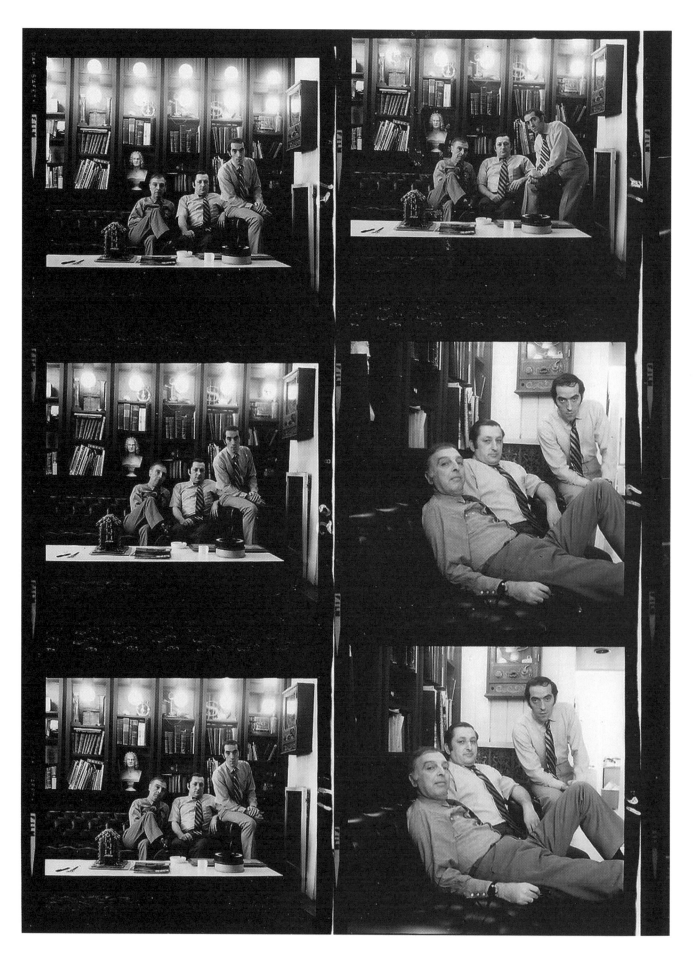

I have long felt the need for a typeface both large and delicate in display sizes. Lightweight text sans serifs cease to be light once they enter the display range; and their weights begin to assume the characteristics of medium or demi-bold. I wanted a typeface that could be dynamic in form, yet unobtrusive...individual in style, yet neutral in form...to be used compatibly with the Futuras, Trade Gothics, Grotesques, and Helveticas, among others. In an attempt to capture this spirit, Tom Carnase and I created L&C Hairline...with alternate characters, light and bold punctuation, modern as well as oldstyle figures, with hopes that it will offer the designer opportunities for creative exploration. Herb Lubalin.

HERB LUBALIN   TOM CARNASE

S&H

BY MARIE CALDERONE WHITE

Around the hallowed halls of Sudler & Hennessey, *John Pistilli's* responsibilities are multi-faceted, including designing new logos for client products; assisting in type styling of ads, folders, and promotional pieces, and even rendering tight comprehensives when called for. But did you know that outside the S&H world, John has carved a deep niche in the world of lettering design?

He is well known for his Pistilli Roman typeface, which he designed originally to promote a nationwide typeface design competition. The poster for this contest was designed by Herb Lubalin, a former executive vice president and art director of Sudler & Hennessey; and Pistilli Roman lettering was used. As soon as the poster was distributed, it became public domain, and as a result Pistilli Roman typeface is now being used all over the world much to John's benefit.

John has created many well-known logos for magazines (*The Saturday Evening Post, Rolling Stone, Reader's Digest*), for products (Schweppes Tonic Water, Nice 'n Easy Shampoo), for restaurants (Zum Zum) and for stores (F.W. Woolworth). He also designed in 1959, along with Herb Lubalin, an airmail stamp in 10¢, 15¢ and 25¢ denominations, for which they both received an award from the Postmaster General.

John especially enjoys telling the story of designing the Zum Zum logo for Restaurant Associates. Since they didn't have any idea of what they wanted, John submitted some rough sketches. The client took one look at the first attempt and decided to go with it...sausage and all!

John's love of "hand lettering" was particularly illustrated in his work with Cutty Sark. It was in the 1700s when the Berry Bros. first distributed Cutty Sark Scotch that the label was designed in the hand lettering of that era, which still exists today. However, it was John Pistilli who designed an entire typeface from the original Cutty Sark label design. It is reminiscent of some of the earliest forms of print: It contains no straight lines, mixes upper- and lowercase letters, and is set with uneven spacing. The typeface generated a tremendous amount of excitement and is currently used in all Cutty Sark ad campaigns...and has become synonymous with the name "Cutty Sark."

John has just completed creating the letter design for a brand-new Columbia Records album...just one more feather in his letter cap!

In addition to having created logos and type designs for most of our present clients, John is always called upon when a new client requests a change in logo or trademark. In fact, the Sudler & Hennessey (S&H) logo was a joint effort of John and a former art director, but the final design bears the signature of John Pistilli.

John Pistilli poses before Cutty Sark type.

Steve Abbruscato, copy supervisor at Sudler & Hennessey, is also an accomplished actor with a long list of credits and favorable reviews. This avocation of Steve's started in the summer of 1977, when he took an acting class in a loft over the Nat Horne Theatre (on Theatre Row). Having attended the class for only about two months, Steve was observed doing a scene and what followed was the goal of every aspiring actor. He was asked to audition for a role (of a harried office manager) in the Nat Horne Theatre production of "War of the Worlds." Steve went into rehearsals shortly after, and, ironically, has never taken an acting class since. His acting schedule averages about two shows a year—usually showcase productions that run from three to four weeks.

Steve is often asked how he finds time for his copywriting responsibilities, acting, and family, consisting of wife and two teenage daughters. He claims that it helps to live in the city, with no time wasted on commuting. Also, he has an

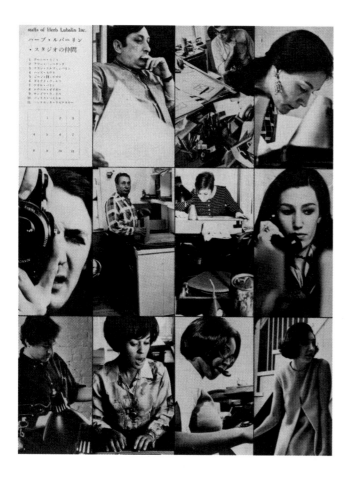

staffs of Herb Lubalin Inc.

ハーブ・ルバーリン
・スタジオの仲間

LUBALIN, SMITH, CARNASE.
223 E. 31 STREET
NEW YORK N.Y. 10016
OR9-2636

HERB LUBALIN
ASSOCIATES, INC.
TONY DISPIGNA
HERB LUBALIN
ALAN PECKOLICK
ERNIE SMITH &
MICHAEL ARON
BILLY BATEMAN
ED BENGUIAT
JASON CALFO
HAU CHEE CHNG
CLAUDIA CLAY
DOUGLAS DILG
TINA ENGHOFF
NANCY PORTER
ANN TURNER
MAGGIE WILLIAMS
& KAREN ZIAMAN
WISH YOU THE
BEST FOR 1980

49. Trade promotion leaflet for L&C Hairline, a typeface designed in 1966 by Herb Lubalin and Tom Carnase. Inset photograph shows Lubalin and Carnase: it is a good example of Lubalin's willingness to publicly share authorship. Date: c. 1966.

50. John Pistilli was one of the most important of Lubalin's many collaborators. Shown here is a Sudler & Hennessey press release. Pistilli worked at S&H as head of lettering design from 1949 onwards. He was born in 1925 and graduated from the Jean Morgan School of Art in New York City, where he studied lettering under the calligrapher J. Albert Cavanaugh. His typeface Pistilli Roman is in the classical French Didot style, and Herb Lubalin is often cited as a co-designer. It currently enjoys cult status among designers attracted to its cool understated refinement. The first time it was used was by Lubalin in his National Typeface Design Competition poster (p.14, fig.15). Lubalin held Pistilli in the highest regard. Date: 1983.

51. Page from *Idea* magazine showing studio personnel. Starting top left: Ernie Smith, Alan Peckolick, Fran Elfenbein, Hans Mauli, Gene H Bigoli, Diana Wilko, Gail Payne, Lowell Bodger, Sandra Willis, Phyllis Battle, Henrietta Lizewski. Date: 1969.

52. New Year greetings card from Herb Lubalin Associates, Inc., listing studio members and partners. Ernie Smith is mentioned despite having left the studio some time before. Date: 1980.

53. Monogram for studio formed by Lubalin's elevation of Ernie Smith and Tom Carnase to full partner status. Lettering: Tom Carnase. Date: 1967.

1966, the English designer David Pocknell travelled to New York with 'my Beatles suit and haircut, and my portfolio of posters done for the Oxford Playhouse.' He contacted the Lubalin studio and, to his astonishment, not only did Herb Lubalin see him, but he also offered him a job. Pocknell reluctantly turned down the offer: 'New York was a dangerous place at that time,' he recalled. 'My then wife was pregnant with our first child and I didn't think it was the place to raise a family. In some ways I regret it now, but I think I was the only person who ever turned Herb Lubalin down.'

Pocknell is not the only British designer who benefited from Lubalin's generosity towards young designers. David Quay, the English typographer and type designer who now lives in Amsterdam, wrote to Tony Di Spigna and sent him some examples of his early work. To the delight of the young Quay, Di Spigna showed his work to Lubalin: 'I received a long letter back with comments from both Tony and Herb,' he recalled. 'Their main comments were to look for my own English models as a basis for my work. They cited George Bickham and the English writing masters. The sign-off on the letter was to remember that, "A well-designed word was worth a thousand pictures." From then on, there was no stopping me!'

When the young Peckolick finally got to see Lubalin, he was offered a job: 'I was so nervous,' recalled Peckolick, 'he had to tell me to sit down six times. He looked at my portfolio, one hand turning the pages, the other working on a layout. He asked me if I wanted to be his assistant.' Peckolick joined the Lubalin studio; it was the beginning of a relationship that was to see him go from Herb Lubalin's assistant to his business partner. Peckolick left in 1968, but returned in 1972 as a full partner.

The two men became friends, yet, as Peckolick noted, Lubalin drew a line in the sand of personal relationships that was hard to cross: **'He was a very private person and that only changed after I left and started my own place. When he asked me to come back and I rejoined, he was much warmer. After a while I said, "I want to have my name on the door." He said "Peckolick! We've got Smith, Carnase — but Peckolick?" After this we became friends. I used to go back with him to his house in MacDougal Alley after work. Sometimes we'd stop at a bar for a drink. On one occasion we had a bit too much to drink,** **and I said I want my name on the door and he said that he would never do that because I was the only one in the studio who could design as well as he could. The next day, I came to work and he was working on a logo with my name in it.'**

In the year of Lubalin's death, 1981, the studio's name was Lubalin, Peckolick Associates Inc., and it indicates the degree to which Lubalin considered Peckolick the most likely candidate to carry on the tradition that he had established over the previous two decades. It's a role that Peckolick has fulfilled by producing his book, but he is not starry-eyed about Lubalin. He has objections to the way work is sometimes credited solely to Lubalin: 'Take the famous Mother & Child logo,' he said. 'I had a hand in that and so did Tom, but Herb gets all the credit. If it's in your head and someone delivers it, then it's a toss-up about who is the real creator.'

After Lubalin's death, Peckolick formed a studio with Seymour Chwast, one of the founders of Push Pin Studios and, to this day, a giant of the New York design and illustration scene. 'It didn't work out,' Peckolick said, 'but it made me realize that I wanted to be on my own.' He then entered a period of successful activity in the booming 1980s design scene. 'I was doing huge annual reports,' he recalled, 'but I fell out of love with it all and started painting.' Today, Alan Peckolick is a successful artist, painting distressed letterforms on giant canvases that he sells in galleries.

Looking at the numerous letterheads that were issued from the various Lubalin studios between 1964 and 1981, it is apparent that Lubalin believed in acknowledging the contribution of his lieutenants. The studio had at least five different names — each acknowledging the elevation of studio members to partner status. What was the reason for this? Was it Lubalin's innate generosity? Was it a fiscal contrivance? Was it his way of keeping ambitious sidekicks happy? The answer may be a combination of all these factors, but judging by the reports that he took departures badly, I tend to favour the generosity explanation. According to Alan Peckolick, there was even a studio joke about it: 'Did you hear about the Lubalin doll? You wind it up and make it a partner.'

54. Double-page spread from *U&lc* (Volume 2. No. 3, 1978), showing the versatility and mutability of the new phototypesetting. The technology allowed Lubalin to indulge his appetite for such effects as the unrestrained mixing of weights of typefaces, minus letter spacing, minimal line spacing, and the dovetailing of blocks of text. The typefaces used are various weights of ITC Cheltenham.

55, 56. Front cover and logotype for the preview issue of *Families*

magazine, a short-lived Reader's Digest Associates, Inc., publication. Shown are the masthead and the preview issue designed by Lubalin's studio. The story of how the masthead was designed is told on p.37. Date: 1980.

11

The Phototypesetting Revolution

Herb Lubalin's Graphic Expressionism (and what the educator and design writer Ellen Lupton has called his ability to create 'textual image') blossomed as a direct result of the technological developments in typesetting of the late 1960s and early 1970s. Typesetting went from metal matrixes to film negatives: it was a revolution almost as monumental as the leap that took place in the 1990s when designers abandoned traditional mechanical or 'paste-up' artwork in favour of digital, print-ready artwork produced on a personal computer. Phototypesetting gave the designer a new freedom of movement, and a new sense of creative control. The industrial-era mechanics of typesetting no longer determined the designer's final product. And no one took greater advantage of this than Herb Lubalin.

What is meant by phototypesetting? During the 1930s, Edward Rondthaler (a future associate of Lubalin's), had helped make the Rutherford photolettering machine, an attempt to create a viable way of generating type photographically rather than mechanically. A decade later, two Frenchmen — René Alphonse Higonnet and Louis Marius Moyroud — developed a successful phototypesetter that used a strobe light and a series of optics to project characters from a spinning disk onto photographic paper. But the duo failed to capitalize on their invention, and by the 1960s their machine was superseded by newer equipment capable of generating typesetting photographically. Economy and efficiency were always the key selling points for the new machines. Film typesetting was quicker and less costly compared to the old and cumbersome machinery used in lead-based type.

New phototypesetting equipment allowed a direct image of letterforms to be made on photosensitive paper or film by exposing the surface to light through transparent matrixes, negative or positive, of the letters and symbols. Body copy could be set in columns and output onto photographic paper. Display text, such as large headlines, for example, were produced using machines such as the Photo Typositor, manufactured by the Visual Graphics Corporation. These machines allowed the designer to instruct the typesetter to position each letter visually and thus exercise complete control over kerning, size and position. The resulting formulations were output on photographic paper, enabling the designer to paste the lettering in position onto boards — this was known as mechanical artwork. Nearly all printed matter — books, newspapers, magazines — was produced in this way, until the method was superseded by print-ready digital files in the 1990s.

Lubalin was a zealous convert to the new phototypesetting. He had felt constrained by the limitations and inflexibility of traditional hot-metal typesetting. In a lecture he gave while still at Sudler & Hennessey, he said that, due to developments in phototypography, it was now possible to 'eliminate the leading between lines, remove space between letterforms and to alter letterforms.' With the new typography, Lubalin argued, the designer was free to present in a single image, 'both the message and the pictorial idea.' He saw this as the reversal of the usual ad procedure of copy dictating the graphic look: 'In many cases the graphic presentation now dictates the copy approach, giving an intimate relationship between copy and design.'

His views on the shortcomings of old metal typesetting were expressed in a comment he made about William Golden, the CBS designer and creator of the timeless CBS eye logo. Golden was one of the designers Lubalin most admired: 'He is one of the very few designers,' Lubalin wrote, 'whose efforts in the early 50s are as apropos today as they were then, with the possible exception of his type handling, which was *dictated by the limits of metal typesetting*.' [Author's italics.]

Phototypesetting freed designers such as Herb Lubalin from the 'limits of metal typesetting', but, as with so many other technological advances, the new technology also brought problems. In a striking parallel with the current issue of instant digital copying, phototypesetting allowed, for the first time, the wholesale and instant copying of fonts. Font piracy was not new — it had existed since the earliest days of printing — but in the metal era it was costly, slow and cumbersome. Now, suddenly, in the phototypesetting era, copying was easy, cheap and fast: and for hard-done-by typeface designers, it was yet another roadblock on

Families

the path to proper remuneration for their efforts. Lubalin was to join the fight against font piracy but, for now, phototypesetting was the technological discovery that allowed his ideas about the pictorial potential within type configurations to be unlocked.

With prescience, Lubalin noted the rise of a new visual culture. **'Television has had its effect on the reading habits of the American people. We are becoming more and more accustomed to looking at pictures and less and less interested in reading lengthy copy. The resulting trend in our advertising has been towards large pictorial elements and short, sparkling headline copy, with much less emphasis on descriptive product identification.'** He also noted, with admirable frankness, that this experimentation sometimes resulted in outcomes that were visually unpleasant or unsettling. He justified this lurch towards the ugly as both a need to create impact and the ability to find 'warmth and charm in deliberate ugliness.' He said: **'One has only to look back to early American design and the subsequent Victorian era. The distorted furniture design, the blatant circus and political posters, the ornate gas lamps are becoming more and more appreciated today as an integral part of our surroundings. One will undoubtedly get accustomed to the appeal of typography that creates a mood through the spectacular — and even the spectacularly ugly.'**

12

Working Methods

Herb Lubalin had a particular way of working and his methodology remained unchanged throughout his life. The first part of the creative process took place in his head: his Cooper Union training, with its emphasis on thinking rather than doing, gave him the ability to visualize complete graphic responses before he lifted a pen or opened up his famous 'tissue' pad.

A story told by Mike Aron, one of Lubalin's most important collaborators in the last years of his life, serves as a splendid example of Lubalin's cerebral way of working. Aron described how he was struggling with a commission to design the masthead for a magazine called *Families* (see above). As the deadline loomed, panic was building. The phone rang. It was Lubalin. He said: 'Dot the "l",' and hung up. Aron duly obliged, and the logo — with its familial visual mnemonic — passed into the Lubalin canon. Like the famous Mother & Child logo (also a masthead; p.40, figs.62—63), it is often held up as Lubalin at his most incisive and virtuosic. Yet to give form to the idea, it seems that he simply passed on a thought. Nothing more.

But he didn't just think work into existence. No examination of Herb Lubalin is possible without coming across references to his sketched 'tissues'. When I talked to people who knew and worked with him, it was invariably the first thing they mentioned. What were these tissues? What part did they play in the Lubalin creative process? And how, considering their roughness, did they result in the highly accomplished and polished graphic design produced by Lubalin's various studios with their shifting personnel?

Lubalin sketched his ideas for logos, typographic formations and entire page layouts on sheets of lightweight, semi-transparent paper that came in 18×24" pads. He reportedly filled a dozen pads each week. He drew his shaky lines with inexpensive, black Pentel pens, and only occasionally used colour. In fact, so famous was he for his freehand approach to lettering at a time when T-squares, set-squares and drawing boards equipped with parallel-motion bars were the universal tools for graphic designers, that his studio colleagues presented him with a specially made 'knotted T-square' as a gift (p.38, fig.57). It was inscribed, 'To Herb Lubalin for successfully ignoring this instrument for so many years.'

Looking at Lubalin's sketches today, with eyes accustomed to the slick, oven-ready outputs produced using a modern computer and smart software, it is impossible not to be struck by their vagueness and sketchiness: it's a wonder that anything ever got made from them. *Idea* magazine noted that, 'all his layout drawings and lettering roughs look as if they were done while riding a stage coach down the side of a mountain.'

In reality, however, a Lubalin tissue was a near-perfect blueprint for the end result: Lubalin's tissues were unattractive grubs that somehow transformed themselves into

57. 'The Knotted T-square' was a gift from Lubalin's staff. It was a light-hearted reference to his habit of drawing freehand without the use of a T-square. It came with the words: 'To Herb Lubalin for successfully ignoring this instrument for so many years.'

58—61. Examples of Lubalin's famous hand-drawn tissues and their final outcomes as pages of *U&lc*. All of Lubalin's work began as a sketched outline, usually in black on white, and done with a cheap Pentel pen. These tissues, as they were called, were then handed to a studio member to be turned into finished artwork. Many of his colleagues and employees have attested to his remarkable ability to sketch accurate letterforms from memory. However, what is not widely known is that he also traced off letterforms from time to time, and then indicated how they could be enlarged to fit the space. Two examples shown. Typeface is various weights of ITC Benguiat. Date: 1978.

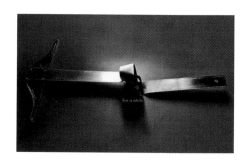

beautiful butterflies. Snyder and Peckolick, Lubalin's biographers, quoted Ernie Smith: **'The art director who got a Lubalin tissue couldn't take credit as the designer. You tightened it up and refined it; but the idea, the major spatial relationships, the elegance, was built into it. Once Herb made the tissue, the ad or booklet was designed.'**

Kevin Gatta, who joined Lubalin's studio in 1979, recalled the remarkable accuracy of these tissues: **'I remember one job — I set the copy to follow the sketch and I said to him, "That's amazing, the type fits the sketch." And he looked at me and said, "No, the sketch fits the type." And he was right, because he knew how to sketch the kerning, how the characters had to be drawn, and he knew the ligatures.'**

When I first saw Lubalin's tissues, I assumed they were tracings. Why would they not be? It was what everyone did at that time, myself included. It was normal in those pre-computer days for designers to 'trace off' words (from type specimen sheets) to gauge their appearance and size, before ordering expensive typesetting. This process was slow and cumbersome; the designer was forever scaling lettering up and down to get the right size. Surely Lubalin did the same? Yet all the people I spoke to assured me that Lubalin didn't trace his letterforms, preferring instead to sketch letters from memory. I was persuaded that this was the case until I decided to make one last check, following a conversation with a sceptical Tony Brook, this book's co-editor. I asked Mike Aron if Lubalin ever traced off letterforms. 'The secret is out,' he said: **'Indeed, Herb traced from alphabets. We always made stats of the newest ITC release in which the cap height was about one inch high. He traced these letterforms at that size. You'll see a diagonal line through some of his sketches. That is his simple way of scaling the design up to the page size. If it was too wide or too narrow, he usually used the remaining space for a caption or block of copy. Very efficient and effective. This, of course, does not diminish his letter-drawing ability. He often chopped, squeezed, overlapped and did other obscene things to these letterforms to achieve the rare combination of art and legibility. He wasn't much for original, free-form lettering. He often did rather clumsy scribbles to represent Spencerian lettering concepts, to be realized by Tom Carnase or Tony Di Spigna. They were the craftsmen,** but the concept behind the design and its tightly compacted words is still evident in the original sketch. The only exception would be the geometric designs, in which the letterforms were based on plain rectangles or circles. These he took great pains to sketch quite tightly, using T-square and triangle. He never used ink, rapidograph, ruling pen, french curves or other final art tools. His favourite pen was a 10-cent Pentel felt tip. And as everyone knows, he was ambidextrous, able to begin a headline sketch with his left hand and, when halfway across the page, he'd switch to his right hand without missing a beat.'

But not everything took place inside Lubalin's head or on his sketchpads. He would also wield a sharp blade when necessary. Philip Meggs wrote: 'Lubalin would cut apart his type proofs with a razor blade and reassemble them. In his hands, type was compressed until letters joined into ligatures and enlarged to unexpected sizes; letterforms were joined, overlapped and enlarged; capital O's became receptacles for images.'

The restless quest for perfection put pressure on his staff and partners. 'When you were working on one of his jobs,' recalled Kevin Gatta, 'all of a sudden you'd feel his presence. He had his own scent. It was the 1970s — he wore an open-necked shirt, chest hair poking out, and his hair was a bit wild. His praise was a grunt and a cough, and you'd know it was okay.' Lubalin's taciturn nature was legendary: his son, Peter, told me that, 'a grunt was probably the highest praise you were ever going to get,' and Carl Fischer tells the story that Lubalin was, 'once berated for not saying good morning to everyone when he came into the office in the morning. He retorted that if he had to say good morning to every employee, he'd never get any work done.'

Another factor in Lubalin's working practices was his colour-blindness. His work — with the possible exception of his 1960s editorial work for *Avant Garde* — is not distinguished by radical colour selection, and it was no accident that many of his most celebrated logos and typographic statements were designed to work only in mono. His taste in colour rarely strayed from a muted palette of autumnal colours and only occasionally erupted into chromatic loudness. Louise Fili, the New York graphic designer, worked for Lubalin in the 1970s and recalled helping him make decisions about colour: **'Choosing colours with him was**

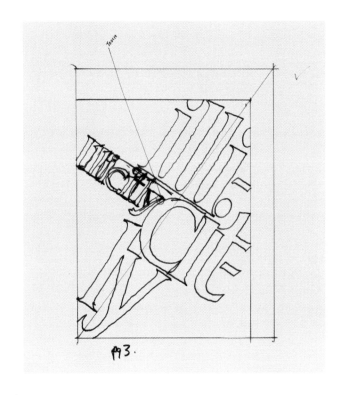

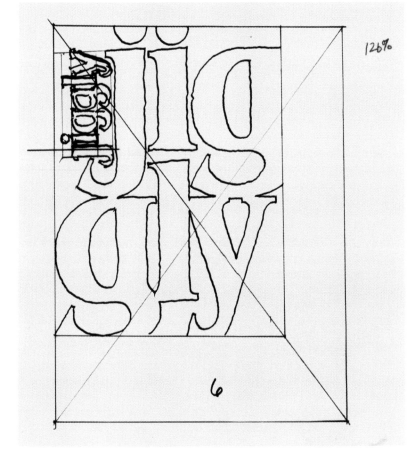

62
63

62, 63. Lubalin's *Mother & Child* logo (1965) was one of his most celebrated pieces of work. It was created as a magazine masthead, but never used. Later, he was to adapt the logotype (to read *Mother & Son*) for use on a book jacket by British author Jeremy Seabrook (1978). Lettering: Tom Carnase.

64—66. Examples of Lubalin's hand-rendered tissues, showing varying degrees of completion.

almost comical; we would leaf through a Pantone book together and he would say, "Let's find a nice red." Unfortunately, we were looking at the green pages. Should I say something, or just let him choose? His preference for muted Pantone 452 [an autumnal yellow and greenish-grey] was a totally neutral shade that allowed type to both surprint and drop out.'

The Lubalin studios of the 1960s and 1970s worked for many household names and large corporations, including Coca-Cola, US Postal Service, CBS, PBS and Mercedes-Benz. Yet even in two studio press releases that have survived from 1979, no clients are mentioned. Instead we are presented with lists of the studio's awards, lectures, and its membership of various U.S. and international design organizations. This is odd because, as Steven Heller has noted, 'With few exceptions, [Lubalin's] experiments were conducted under marketplace conditions, which at once provided certain safeguards and made taking liberties all the more difficult. Lubalin's work was not "design for design", but design for communication.'

Heller's observation is correct. There was nearly always a client behind every job that Lubalin undertook, and even when working on promotional material and logos for his own studios, there is a sense of professionalism and focus that often deserts designers when they are working for themselves. Unlike his hero Paul Rand, or the younger Milton Glaser, there were no paintings or artworks done for pleasure. Lubalin's artistry was channelled into his work as a graphic designer for hire. However, this doesn't mean that he was always a dutiful and subservient designer: Herb Lubalin didn't exactly ignore briefs, but sometimes he had his responses ready so quickly that he was guilty of not giving enough consideration to the clients' needs and wishes.

13

Ignoring the Brief

Like a great many talented and self-assured graphic designers, Herb Lubalin relied on a sure-footed intuition that, more often than not, resulted in a successful outcome. He also had a back catalogue of ideas that he was always keen to find a home for. It is a perennial question facing all graphic designers: what to do with good ideas that get rejected by clients? It's no secret that even the most talented designers occasionally take ideas out of the drawer marked 'rejected' and offer them up as solutions to new briefs. There can't be many graphic designers who haven't been guilty of this 'crime', and Herb Lubalin was no exception.

Perhaps the most notable example of Lubalin's recycling concerned one of the pieces of work for which he is most famous — the Mother & Child logo. This was first created in 1965 for a magazine masthead. It was worked on by Alan Peckolick (from Lubalin tissues) and finalized by Tom Carnase. It was perhaps the finest example of Lubalin's obsession with substituting the letter 'o' with graphic symbols. However, the magazine never appeared, and Lubalin's logo was shelved. But it was not forgotten. Years later, Lubalin was commissioned to design a book jacket for a memoir by Jeremy Seabrook, a British author and journalist who specializes in social, environmental and development issues. The book had the convenient title *Mother & Son*, so Lubalin substituted the word 'Child' with the word 'Son' (see above).

There also comes a time in the life of many graphic designers when their accumulated knowledge and understanding is greater than that of the majority of their clients. Towards the end of his life, this was true of Herb Lubalin. In addition, he had now entered a phase in graphic design history when the professionalization of the discipline was in full swing. As Milton Glaser noted in an interview with Steven Heller: 'The briefings are very different now. The determinations of what's appropriate are very often those of a marketing department, as opposed to the somewhat

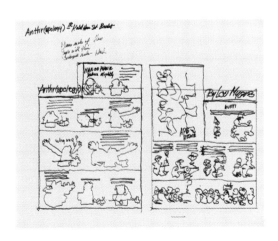

41

67. PBS logo (far right) designed for use on television. The logo first appeared in 1971. The design is widely credited to Ernie Smith. Also shown (near left) are iterations of the logo rejected by the client. They are discussed in a film available on YouTube called 'The origins of the PBS logo.'

68, 69. Attempts by various studio members to design a logo for the newly formed MTV, prior to its launch in 1981. Produced towards the end of Lubalin's life, these attempts reveal how his

approach to logo design — finely drawn, interlocking and formally structured — was beginning to show marked signs of out-datedness. Although it could be argued that the position is now reversed, and that Lubalin's logos are more in sync with current typographic trends. Date: 1980.

70. Original MTV logo designed by Manhattan Design, a collective formed by Frank Olinsky, Pat Gorman and Patti Rogoff. Date: 1981.

casual and random solutions that occurred when people didn't know better.' For a designer like Lubalin, this new way of working was too slow, too cumbersome.

In an interview I conducted with the designer Mike Aron, he spoke about his former employer's approach to clients and their briefs: **'I did not attend many meetings where the client gave us the initial creative brief. However, I was often briefed by Herb immediately after the meetings and was keenly aware that he felt he had a better grasp of the communication problem than the client. Not in all cases, of course. There was a large part of the practice that came from ad agencies who were well versed in the nuances of marketing communications. We took their briefs seriously and often did exactly as asked. There were many clients, though, especially corporate clients, who were less specific in their requests. In those meetings, where Herb had to listen to long diatribes about profit and loss, or product benefits or industry leadership — it was easy to ignore the brief and simply find a clever way to design a solution that would win awards at the next Art Directors Club competition. For example, we designed the annual report for Avnet, where Herb's brother Irwin was the CEO. Their business, electronic parts distribution, was not particularly interesting to Herb. His cover designs were often a typographic riff on the year of the annual report — a rambunctious numeric design. But what Herb missed was important; Avnet was at the nexus of the burgeoning personal computer industry and poised to benefit from the huge groundswell of imported microchips from Asia. That element never really came through in his design solutions.'**

Most of the time, Lubalin's intuitive approach worked well for him and his clients. Sometimes, however, it resulted in meltdown. There are three striking examples of his reluctance to fully grasp a client's brief, all of which show how his creative impetuosity could land him in trouble.

The first of these can be found in a rare filmed interview made towards the end of his life in which Lubalin describes in great detail how the logotype for PBS came to fruition (see above). But as he tells the story, the picture of Lubalin that emerges is of someone who has failed to give the brief close scrutiny. He describes how the logo was shaped — designed, even — by repeated client interventions. We are shown how the configuration of the three

letters goes through a series of weak-looking iterations, and he describes how the client's observations forced him to make numerous alterations to the logotype's appearance. It is important to remember that this film is intended for a non-professional audience and that Lubalin is deliberately exaggerating the often-tortuous journey that designers have to make to satisfy client expectations: he is stating a valuable point that readymade logos don't fall out of the sky. However, to non-designers, it must seem as if the client is the designer, and for fellow professionals it appears as if Lubalin and his team are underresearched, ill-prepared and at the mercy of client whims.

The second example is even more revealing. In 1980, the Lubalin studio was invited to submit proposals for a logo for the newly formed MTV. Lubalin had always been interested in TV graphics and had produced animated onair typography for PBS. But it seems that the MTV brief failed to excite him, and he passed the task on to some of the younger members of the studio. Kevin Gatta and Mike Aron recall working on the project, and it soon became clear to them that Lubalin had failed to appreciate the novelty and groundbreaking nature of MTV's approach to broadcasting. When Gatta quizzed Lubalin on the project, he replied airily, that it was, 'something to do with rock concerts on TV.' He urged them to 'do things' with the 'm' and the 'v' in the style he had perfected over many years.

Of course, Lubalin had failed to grasp the MTV model, with its then revolutionary (in broadcasting terms) new policy of playing back-to-back music videos, only interrupting the flow with the occasional onscreen presence of VJs. This project marked the point in Lubalin's career when his methodology — his creative ethos — suddenly appeared out of date. A new electronic imperative had entered graphic design: as America and the Western world entered an era of wall-to-wall electronic media, the logos of the future would be animated and seen as frequently on TV screens as in print.

The MTV logo was ultimately designed in 1981 by Manhattan Design, a collective formed by Frank Olinsky, Pat Gorman and Patti Rogoff, under the guidance of MTV's Fred Seibert (fig.70). But for Lubalin it represented a moment when, for perhaps the first time in his life, he was out of fashion. It is important to remember, however, that in 1980, Herb Lubalin was at the end of his life.

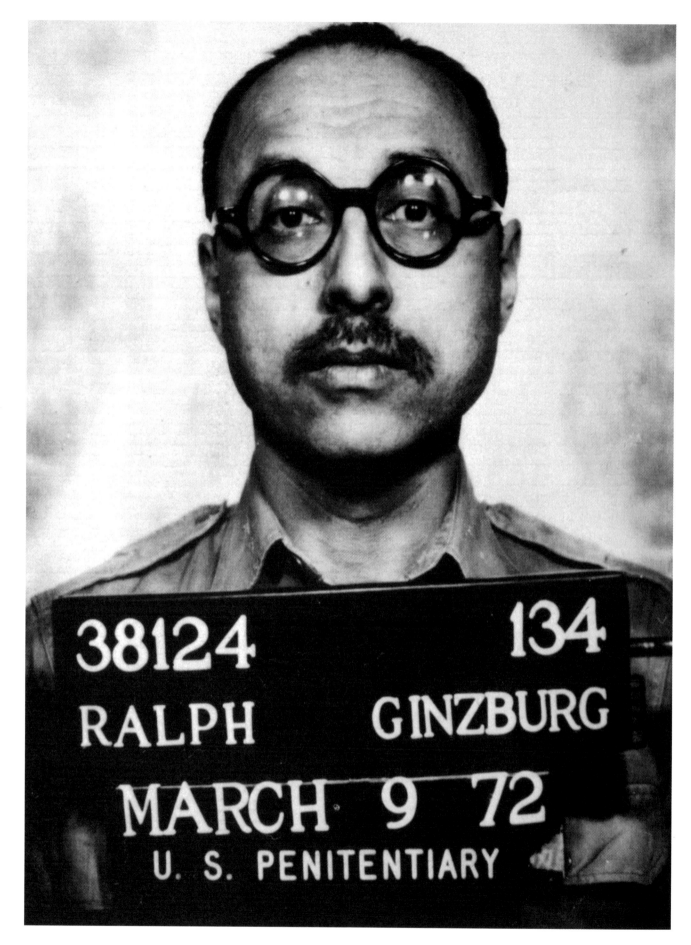

71. Ralph Ginzburg was one of the most important people in the life and work of Herb Lubalin. He was an inspirational client, an enlightened editor and a lifelong friend. As editor of *Eros, Avant Garde* and *Fact* magazines, Ginzburg employed Lubalin as art director on all three publications. He gave his art director ample creative freedom, and in return Lubalin produced some of the finest examples of editorial design of the era. The picture here shows Ginzburg as a prisoner. He was charged with sending obscene materials through the U.S. mail, an offence that related to his editorship and proprietorship of *Eros* magazine. Date: 1972.

72, 73. Front and back cover of *The Best of Fact: Thirty-Two Articles that have made History from America's Most Courageous Magazine*, published by Trident Press. Back cover shows Ginzburg and long-time associate and frequent contributor to *Fact*, Warren Boroson. Date: 1967.

He had contracted cancer, and both Gatta and Aron remembered taking work to his MacDougal Alley home in Greenwich Village when he was too ill to make it into the studio. Another of the younger designers at the time, Jason Calfo, recalled frequent telephone conversations with Lubalin about work when he was too ill to leave his home.

His final illness may have accounted for his failure to comprehend the nature of the MTV brief, but it remains a characteristic of Lubalin's approach that he didn't always study a brief, and relied instead on his ability to intuit a response that, more often than not, was the right one.

The third and most famous instance of Lubalin ignoring a brief is found in his work for the masthead of *Avant Garde* magazine. We'll look at this in detail when we come to discuss his celebrated work for the publication (p.50), and see how it provides an illuminating example of Lubalin's eagerness to jump to solutions. In the case of *Avant Garde*, he was working with his friend Ralph Ginzburg, so he can be excused a certain bullishness, but it is undoubtedly true that he was often guilty of ignoring a brief.

In any examination of Lubalin's working methods, it becomes clear that, above everything else — money, reputation, clients — what he valued most was creative freedom. In Ralph Ginzburg, a man who *The New York Times* called a 'taboo-busting editor and publisher who helped set off the sexual revolution in the 1960s,' Lubalin found his ideal client: a publisher and editor who hired him to design some of the most interesting magazines of the time, and a client who gave him an extraordinary level of freedom.

14

Ralph Ginzburg — The Ideal Client

'He walked into my office one day and said, "How would you like to design a new magazine?" and explained what it was. And I said, "If I am given complete design integrity, I would be happy to do it". He said, "All right", and he gave me the assignment. I think at that time he had selected three art directors and he wanted to pick one of the three, and when he came up and saw the work I was doing, he said, "I want you".'

This was how Herb Lubalin recalled his first encounter with Ralph Ginzburg. The publication was *Eros* — 'a quarterly magazine entirely devoted to Love and Sex' — and although laughably tame by today's standards, in its day (all four issues were published in 1962), it was regarded, at least by one U.S. court of law, as 'obscene'.

Ralph Ginzburg was born in 1929. Like Lubalin, he had Russian ancestry. He studied accountancy before discovering an aptitude for journalism and publishing. After graduation, and with the Korean War in progress, he was drafted into the army and assigned to a base in Virginia. From there he edited the post's newspaper and at night worked as a copy editor for the *Washington Times-Herald*.

After discharge, he was made advertising and promotion director at *Look* magazine. Later, he worked as an editor at *Esquire*. One biographer described him as a 'street-smart striver who talked in the clipped Brooklyn patois of a Coney Island barker.' In later life, he had the bookish appearance of a New York bohemian intellectual — an appearance enhanced by owlish, black-rimmed spectacles and a high-domed forehead. Yet another observer said he had the 'misfortune to look like a pornographer.'

The young, ambitious and idealistic Ginzburg was keen to combine his newly acquired publishing knowledge with social activism. This desire led him to create a series of journals that, in their own way, formed a landmark in radical publishing. Less abrasive and more erudite than the underground press that followed in the mid-1960s, Ginzburg's magazines were precursors of the print revolution that was about to erupt in the years of the counterculture. He tested the limits of authority and questioned social mores with a radical vigour that has rarely been equalled. In so doing he made powerful and vengeful enemies, and was ultimately to pay a high price for his radicalism. In 1972, ten years after he was first charged with obscenity, he was sent to prison. As Steven Heller noted: 'It was the first time in American history that a publisher was sentenced to and served a federal prison term for producing and distributing a magazine that was judged to have abrogated the moral values and standards of society.'

Ginzburg began his publishing journey in 1958. He took an office in Manhattan and set himself up as an independent

74. Front cover of *Fact*, a magazine designed by Herb Lubalin and edited by Ralph Ginzburg. The issue shown features a poll of U.S. psychiatrists invited to speculate on the sanity of right-wing presidential candidate Barry Goldwater. As a result of this survey (conducted by mail), Goldwater sued Ginzburg, and although he won the suit, the jury awarded damages that only covered his legal fees. Nevertheless, this was enough to bring about the financial collapse and closure of *Fact*. Date: 1964.

75. *Eros* was devoted to eroticism. Tame by today's standards, but in the America of the early 1960s, it was regarded as obscene. Puritanical forces within the government and church conspired to have it closed down and its editor jailed. *Eros* was the first collaboration between Ralph Ginzburg and Herb Lubalin. Date: 1962.

76, 77. *Avant Garde* was the apogee of the Lubalin-Ginzburg partnership. It was a tour de force of editorial innovation and graphic flair. In addition, the masthead was to be the starting point for the creation of one of the most important typefaces of the 20th century — Avant Garde Gothic. The image on the front cover is a painting by George Tooker. Date: 1968.

78. Compliment slip for *Moneysworth*, yet another publication by Ralph Ginzburg. The journal used a newspaper format and was an early proponent of consumer protection and rights. Lettering: Tom Carnase. Date: c. 1971.

book publisher. His first title was *100 Years of Lynching*, a book comprising newspaper cuttings cataloguing the extent and viciousness of American racism. He also edited and published a volume called *An Unhurried View of Erotica*, a compendium of erotic literature throughout history. Both books show Ginzburg's canny modus operandi: in his time as an editor he was to commission many top writers, but he also knew that he could fill books and magazines with non-commissioned or 'found' content. It was a technique he was to use many times, and probably enabled him to survive where others failed. *An Unhurried View of Erotica* had an introduction by psychoanalyst Theodor Reik, one of Freud's first students and a pioneer in the application of psychoanalysis to the study of literary works. This book was a precursor to *Eros*.

Although *Eros* was called a magazine, it was, in fact, an ad-free, large-format (13×10") hardback book. Lubalin was at liberty to use a variety of paper stocks and to give assignments to adventurous photographers without worrying about the need to appease advertisers.

For a super-confident designer such as Lubalin, *Eros* was a near-perfect opportunity to put his vision of editorial design into practice. But the publication only lasted four issues before powerful opponents brought it down. And while it is clear that Lubalin supported Ginzburg's desire to publish a magazine promoting a more enlightened attitude to sex, and to demonstrate his opposition to censorship, there is also a sense that it was the number of design awards gathered by the magazine that was of the greatest interest to Lubalin. As he told *Idea*: 'We won more awards for *Eros* during 1963 than any other magazine in the country.'

Ralph Ginzburg died from cancer in 2006, aged 76. He spent his last years as a photographer and produced a number of important photography books. Before he abandoned magazine publishing, he was to publish two more ground-breaking journals, both designed by Herb Lubalin. There is abundant evidence to illustrate how important Ginzburg was to Lubalin. He repeatedly mentioned Ginzburg in interviews and always praised him as an ideal client. Yet there is perhaps no greater proof of Lubalin's affection for Ginzburg than some of the photographs taken at the now famous 'Lubalin roast' in 1974.

A 'roast' is defined as a light-hearted occasion in which an individual — usually someone who has achieved eminence in a particular field — is subjected to a series of comedic insults, lavish praise and witty tributes. The event is a celebration of the roastee's life by friends, family and associates. At Lubalin's roast (which is still talked about by its surviving participants), he sat at the top table while various speakers — fellow designers and colleagues such as Lou Dorfsman, Seymour Chwast and others — took turns to tell their occasionally risqué stories. At a private event such as this, it might have been expected that Lubalin would have chosen a fellow designer or a family member to sit with him at the top table. Instead, he chose his client and friend Ralph Ginzburg (p.48, figs.79—80).

More evidence to illustrate Lubalin's affection and respect for Ginzburg can be found in a revealing comment made by Rhoda Lubalin, Herb's widow and second wife. In an interview I conducted with her, she told me that Lubalin had said that he thought he should have gone to jail with Ginzburg. This is not the remark of someone happy to hide behind his status as a hired hand. He clearly felt that he shared culpability with his 'employer', and that the relationship went beyond the normal definitions of client and designer.

15

Eros and the Price of Sexual Freedom

The story of Ginzburg's prosecution is a dismal tale of prejudice and double standards. Steven Heller has written extensively about the legal case and the cultural baggage surrounding it. Heller has pointed out that *Playboy* had begun publishing in 1955 and used 'partial nudity, particularly women with ample, airbrushed breasts, to lure male readers into its cosmopolitan lifestyle coverage and entertainment. Conversely, *Eros* did not exploit or objectify women in this or any other way. There were no Playmates, pinups, or gatefolds of any kind — no gratuitous nudity whatsoever.'

Today, it is hard to see what caused the furore surrounding *Eros*. Sexually innocuous photographs of Marilyn

74

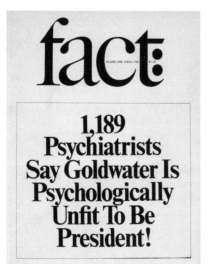

76

77

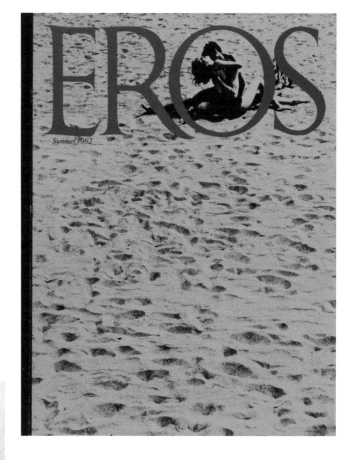

75

78

47

Monroe, taken six weeks before her death by Bert Stern, are suffused with a gentle melancholia that simultaneously reveal Monroe's beauty and her extreme vulnerability — a condition emphasized by Lubalin's decision to reproduce contact sheets that show Monroe's crossing out with bold x's of some perfectly good shots (p.232, fig.19). In an article in *Time* magazine (2006) entitled 'My Favorite Pornographer', the writer Richard Corliss noted: 'It's eerie now to recall that whispers were already connecting her sexually with Jack Kennedy, subject of the lead picture story in *Eros*' previous issue, and with Bobby, who soon would prosecute the magazine.'

Equally mild by modern standards are a series of photographs by Ralph M. Hattersley Jr., a noted photographer, theorist, author and teacher, showing a mixed-race couple (black male, white female) embracing (pp.246—249, figs.31—35). As Corliss noted, the featured couple 'link hands; they kiss, in silhouette; and in the last shot they press against each other. The mood is chaste and a little solemn; no pubic parts go public.' Yet these photographs, reproduced in issue four of *Eros*, were to cause Ginzburg to go to jail. Interracial sex, it seems, was the last taboo in an America that still legally sanctioned racial segregation.

Ginzburg and *Eros* had been in the minds of U.S. prosecutors — and specifically the then attorney general, Robert Kennedy — for some time. With the mixed-race photo shoot in *Eros* No.4, Ginzburg was now in the justice system's crosshairs, and this time they were going to pull the trigger. Ginzburg wrote: **'The New York smut-hunting Catholic priest Morton Hill persuaded US Attorney General Robert Kennedy to have me indicted, as Father Hill later boasted, for distributing "obscene" literature through the mails, a federal crime. The indictment sought punishment of $280,000 in fines and 280 years in prison.'**

Ironically, Ginzburg was not indicted for the sexual content of his magazine, but for 'distributing obscene literature through the mails, in violation of federal anti-obscenity laws.' After a brief trial in June 1963, the U.S. District Court for the Eastern District of Pennsylvania convicted Ginzburg in Philadelphia. The U.S. Court of Appeals affirmed the conviction in 1964, and two years later the U.S. Supreme Court announced its decision to also affirm the conviction. Due to the protracted appeals process, it wasn't until 1972 that Ginzburg finally served his sentence. Immediately after the Supreme Court decision was announced, Ginzburg attracted a great deal of support. The beat poet Allen Ginsberg travelled to Washington and picketed the Supreme Court building as a gesture of solidarity. Writers and intellectuals from around the world voiced their concern and support for Ginzburg. Arthur Miller wrote: **'If it is right that Ralph Ginzburg go to jail, then in all justice the same court that sentenced him should proceed at once to close down ninety per cent of the movies now playing and the newspapers that carry their advertising. Compared to the usual run of entertainment in this country, Ginzburg's publications and his ads are on a par with the National Geographic.'**

As Ralph Ginzburg himself noted, even the U.S. State Department bought copies of *Eros* to exhibit at United States Information Agency libraries overseas as 'exemplars of American periodical publishing'. In a savage irony, the year that Ginzburg finally went to jail was also the year in which the movie *Deep Throat* was shown in cinemas.

He was released after eight months and published a book, *Castrated: My Eight Months in Prison* (Avant-Garde Books, 1973), describing the case and his prison experiences. It was dedicated to Ginzburg's wife, Shoshana, and Herb Lubalin. The book was also designed by Lubalin (pp.198—199, fig.141).

16

Fact — An Antidote to Timidity

While Ginzburg was waiting for the U.S. justice system to deliver a final verdict, he and Lubalin set about their second great collaboration. *Fact* magazine was produced between January 1964 and August 1967. It was a quarterly journal, edited by Ginzburg and Warren Boroson (later a successful financial journalist and author), and designed in a severe and frill-free style by Lubalin. It dealt with contemporary American cultural mores and politics and, as might be expected from a Ginzburg publication, it came with a satiric edge. It was an early example of a new sort of campaigning

81, 82. Front cover and spread from *Nudes of Yesteryear*, a small square-format book published by Eros Books. Originally intended as a feature for *Eros* magazine, this collection of photographs of nude models was published after the suppression of the magazine. Book courtesy of Jessica Rose. Date: 1966.

81
82

and irreverent journalism that was to develop in the 1960s. Some commentators called it muck-raking. Later editions of the magazine carried the slogan: 'An antidote to the timidity and corruption of the American press.'

Unlike the over-designed excesses of the underground press of the 1960s, where the exuberant, day-glo layouts attempted to emulate in print the experience of taking psychedelic drugs, *Fact* was designed with restraint and almost minimalist design values. Unlike *Eros*, it was printed in one colour (black) on cheap uncoated paper stock, and deployed a limited palette of mainly serif typefaces. A different artist was commissioned by Lubalin to handle all illustrations for each issue.

Fact showed a side of Lubalin that was unemotional and understated. His use of typography and layout was conventional — there were none of his vivid, metaphoric word pictures, for example. The covers often featured a block of centered type; the page layouts used a simple two-column grid with centered headlines and standfirsts; the body copy was set in Times Roman. The effect is scholarly and academic, although this impression is subtly subverted by the use of high-quality illustrations by artists such as Charles B. Slackman, Ronald Chereskin, Tom Huffman, Edward Sorel, John Alcorn, Gerry Gersten and Jerome Snyder. Most of the illustrations were executed as sharp line drawings, which gave a quasi-Victorian counterpoint to the typographic severity of the pages and covers. And, as is always the case with Lubalin's work, the technical details are perfect: kerning, line breaks and 'ragging' are all expertly and painstakingly managed.

A typical edition of *Fact* (Volume Four, Issue Four, July—Aug 1967) featured an article by the late Tuli Kupferberg (of 1960s outrage rock group The Fugs) about the rise of the counterculture and the anti-war movement. This was followed by an article by Auberon Waugh (the son of English novelist Evelyn Waugh) on the sex lives of air hostesses. The same issue features responses by famous cultural figures of the 1960s to the question: 'Who are the heroes in the age of non-heroes?' Answers are supplied by, among others, poet Allen Ginsberg, writer Paddy Chayefsky, folk singer Tom Paxton and crime novelist Agatha Christie.

Fact was the first journal to publish a young Harvard student called Ralph Nader, the person widely credited with starting the modern consumer-protection movement.

Nader first came to notice in the 1960s, when he confronted the poor safety record of the U.S. car industry. In 1965, he wrote *Unsafe at Any Speed*, a book claiming that many American automobiles were deathtraps. Today, however, he is best known for his failed and divisive presidential bids in four U.S. election campaigns from 1996 to 2008. He is blamed in Democratic circles for splitting the vote in the 2000 election in which George W. Bush defeated Al Gore by the slimmest of margins.

But it was a much earlier presidential election that was to be the undoing of *Fact*. In the election of 1964, the right-winger Barry Goldwater stood as the Republican candidate against the Democrat, and eventual winner, Lyndon Johnson. Goldwater was a despised figure among Democrats and liberals in 1960s America. Prior to the election, *Fact* ran an edition entitled 'The Unconscious of a Conservative: A Special Issue on the Mind of Barry Goldwater'.

The magazine contended that Goldwater was mentally unfit to be president. This view was reached by polling 12,356 psychiatrists by mail. Over a thousand responders stated that Goldwater was clearly psychologically unfit to be president. The front cover bore the stark legend (in well-kerned Times Roman): '1,189 Psychiatrists Say Goldwater Is Psychologically Unfit To Be President!' (p.47, fig.74).

Half of the magazine was taken up with verbatim quotes from named psychiatrists: Goldwater was referred to as 'paranoid', 'emotionally unstable and mentally immature', 'weak, insecure, confused'. Ginzburg, to his credit, also printed replies from psychiatrists who supported Goldwater. Others expressed reservations about undertaking public psychoanalysis on subjects not examined in person.

After the election, Goldwater sued the publisher, the editor and the magazine for libel. In the case Goldwater v. Ginzburg, the jury awarded Goldwater only $1 in compensatory damages against all three defendants. But it also awarded him punitive damages of $25,000 against Ginzburg and $50,000 against Fact Magazine, Inc.

There were two significant consequences of this case. The first was that The American Psychiatric Association issued what it called The Goldwater Rule. This reaffirmed medical privacy and forbade commenting on a patient whom an individual psychiatrist had not examined personally. The second was that *Fact* went out of business.

49

83, 84. *The Saturday Evening Post* was published weekly from 1897 until 1969, since then it has existed in various incarnations. It was the first U.S. magazine to sell a million copies, and is perhaps best remembered for its famous Norman Rockwell covers depicting an idealized version of American life. Herb Lubalin made two attempts to redesign the magazine, first in 1961 (fig.83), and then again in 1968 (fig.84). Neither outcome can be said to have been successful. Compared to his other editorial work, his attempts to revivify the *Evening Post* appear constrained and half-hearted. It is interesting to note, however, that in seven years, the magazine's front covers went from Rockwell's cosy illustrations to a photograph of hardline right-wing politician George Wallace (by Vernon Merritt III). The illustration by Rockwell (fig.83) is said to be a portrait of Lubalin redesigning the *Post* logo. It is hard to detect a likeness, although the hip 'Mad Men' look that Rockwell has conferred on Lubalin is a fine example of his ability to romanticize. Lettering (fig.83): John Pistilli.

85. Front cover of *Moment*, described as 'The New Magazine for America's Jew.' Co-founded by Leonard Fein and Nobel Peace Prize-winner Elie Wiesel, the magazine was designed by Herb Lubalin. Also shown are alternative masthead designs revealing Lubalin's abiding interest in Hebrew letterforms. Lettering: Tom Carnase. Magazine Illustration: Gerry Gersten. Date: 1975.

17

Avant Garde — The Magazine

Ralph Ginzburg described the designing of the masthead for his magazine *Avant Garde* as 'the single most difficult collaboration we had — [Lubalin's] first logo was in Hebrew. He thought that was funny. Then he did it in Coca-Cola script. We went through a dozen logos, masterfully executed.' Herb Lubalin remembered it slightly differently. Four years after the demise of *Avant Garde*, in the inaugural edition of *U&lc*, Lubalin wrote: **'I submitted Avant Garde [the masthead] in Old English, Bank Script, Cartoon Bold, Balloon Bold, Dom Casual, Flash Italics, Wedding Text, Monastic, Buffalo Bill and a last-ditch effort reflective of Coca-Cola. Ginzburg said, "Stop kidding around!" I then tried to dazzle him with a multitude of ornate swashes, which usually does the trick with less knowing clients. He said, "Cut it out!" When a man is as graphically astute as Ralph Ginzburg, one is hard put to dazzle him with anything but something completely out of the ordinary. Ligatures! Nobody knows about ligatures. Not lower case ligatures, not upper and lower case ligatures. But cap ligatures. To my knowledge, nobody had ever fooled around with cap ligatures. And that's how the logotype for Avant Garde magazine was born. I created an AV ligature, a VA ligature, an AN ligature and a GA ligature. Ralph said: "It's illegible but great. I'll buy it".'**

Lubalin omitted two important details from his account of designing a masthead for *Avant Garde*: he neglects to tell us that he had 'misread' the brief; and also that he received some crucial assistance from Ralph Ginzburg's wife, Shoshana Ginzburg. He can perhaps be excused for not telling the full story since he was writing a 'promotional' article aimed at selling his expertise as a professional practitioner. But the two omissions tell us a great deal about Herb Lubalin as a designer.

Writer and design historian Steven Heller has revealed more background to this incident. It seems that after so many failed attempts, Shoshana Ginzburg went to Lubalin's studio in a final attempt to find a satisfactory outcome. As we have previously noted, Lubalin was sometimes guilty of not fully absorbing a brief. The story of how the *Avant Garde* masthead came about illustrates his impetuousness to leap to solutions. Writing in an essay called 'Crimes Against Typography' (available on the AIGA website), Heller noted that Lubalin's early efforts were based on a misreading of the magazine's intention. Lubalin approached the task of designing a masthead for the magazine under the misapprehension that its subject matter was, to quote Ralph Ginzburg, 'the nihilistic avant-garde school of art of the early 20th century.' Ginzburg pointed out that this was a wrong assumption and that *Avant Garde* was, in fact, a publication for, 'intellectuals who might also possess a sense of humor.'

Heller has given Shoshana Ginzburg's first-hand account of what happened when she went to see Lubalin: **'I asked him to picture a very modern, clean European airport (or the TWA terminal), with signs in stark black and white. Then I told him to imagine a jet taking off the runway into the future. I used my hand to describe an upward diagonal of the plane climbing skyward. He had me do that several times. I explained that the logos he had offered us for this project, so far, could have been on any magazine but that Avant Garde (adventuring into unknown territory) by its very name was something nobody had seen before. We needed something singular and entirely new.'**

Equipped with this new brief, and clearly inspired by Shoshana Ginzburg's dramatic mime, Lubalin set to work again. As Ralph Ginzburg recalled: 'The next morning, driving to work from his home in Woodmere [New York] he pulled over to the side of the road and phoned me (the first time he ever did that). "Ralph, I've got it. You'll see". And the rest is design history.'

The resulting logogram has indeed passed into design history. It has the compactness and graphic simplicity of all great logos, and it also imparts the attributes of upward modernity that Shoshana Ginzburg was so keen to incorporate. Yet in his published account of how the logo came to fruition, Lubalin makes no mention of her contribution.

With the new masthead in place, Ralph Ginzburg launched *Avant Garde* in 1968; it lasted until 1971. For Ginzburg, it was to prove a much less controversial undertaking than

either *Eros* or *Fact*; for Lubalin, it was to represent one of the most complete and highly accomplished statements he ever made as an editorial graphic designer. His work on *Avant Garde* was only equalled by *U&lc*, the newspaper-format journal that Lubalin edited, art directed and co-published in the 1970s. But *U&lc* was produced for a design audience: *Avant Garde* was for the general reader.

According to Lubalin, editorial design was, 'almost a vacation.' In an article by his friend Marilyn Hoffner, published in *Graphis* in 1964, Lubalin said that editorial design was an opportunity to, 'create an entity, a whole package. You sustain interest from page to page, create a look, a style.' While at Sudler & Hennessey, Lubalin had redesigned *The Saturday Evening Post* (see above). The contrast between his cautious improvements to the venerable *Post* and the more expressive, uninhibited design of *Avant Garde* could not have been greater and give a clear indication of his growth as an editorial designer.

The inaugural issue of *Avant Garde* opened with the words: 'As most of the world's ills are traceable to old imperatives, old superstitions, and old fools, this magazine is exuberantly dedicated to the future.' This declamatory statement was set, uncharacteristically for Lubalin, in the early Modernist typeface Futura. The sentiment encapsulated the ethos of the magazine's design (exuberance), and its editorial ethos (the rejection of the old). The visual content of the publication was richer and more dynamic than that of *Eros* or *Fact*: the editorial content, although less provocative and adversarial than Ginzburg's previous two journals, nevertheless had a familiar caustic and anti-establishment tone that was the hallmark of all Ginzburg's three great publishing triumphs.

Avant Garde ran articles on LeRoi Jones ('The Laureate of Black Revolts'); on Andy Warhol ('Warhol's Girls'); and on scandals in the American medical profession ('The Doctor Who Called the A.M.A. The American Murder Association'). It published essays by Arthur Miller and Norman Mailer. It reprinted erotic poetry by D.H. Lawrence and W.H. Auden. It featured photography by Bert Stern, Carl Fischer and Alwyn Scott Turner. It had illustrations by Seymour Chwast, John Alcorn, James Spanfeller, drawings by John Lennon and Yoko Ono, and sketches by Muhammad Ali. It devoted an entire issue to the rarely seen erotic engravings of Pablo Picasso.

Avant Garde had all the flair and waywardness of the 1960s underground press, but it was distinguished by sophisticated (and legible) typography. Restrained body text was paired with startling headlines set in a variety of vernacular and oddball typefaces: Black Letter, Wild West and Hairline type were used with judgment and precision. *Avant Garde* gave free reign to Lubalin's famous eclecticism, and the result was vibrant, unrestrained and engaging.

When *Avant Garde* is mentioned today, it is not the writing that is recalled, rather it is Lubalin's ground-breaking design and art direction. Yet even this is eclipsed by the era-defining typeface that came out of his work on the magazine's masthead. Avant Garde Gothic was to become a seminal typeface and would eventually take its place as one of the leading typefaces of the past 50 years: the story of its creation reveals a great deal about Lubalin, his working methods, and his place in design history.

18

Herb Lubalin: Typeface Designer

Herb Lubalin's reputation as a graphic designer and typographer is secure. He is accorded top-table status by encyclopedias and surveys of 20th-century graphic design, and even among those who are unsympathetic to his 'conceptual typography', or find his work over-wrought and over-decorative, there is no dispute about his position as a graphic innovator and seminal figure in American design. But what about his position as a designer of typefaces? Can he be considered in the same breath as other great figures of American typography? Is he, for instance, the equal of Frederic Goudy, Morris Benton or Oswald Cooper? And what about recent generations of American font designers: Ed Benguiat, Jonathan Hoefler, Tobias Frere-Jones, Matthew Carter (not American by birth, but worked mainly in the USA)? It's a glittering array of talent. Goudy designed more than 100 typefaces including Copperplate Gothic and Goudy Old Style; he wrote extensively about type and taught the young William Addison Dwiggins. Benton designed Franklin Gothic and News Gothic. Cooper designed Cooper Black. Ed Benguiat designed Souvenir, Benguiat and Bookman.

Lubalin's claim to a place among the elite rests with a trio of classic typefaces: Avant Garde Gothic, Serif Gothic and Lubalin Graph. But his reputation as a major figure in American type design is also based on his contribution to the International Typeface Corporation (ITC), one of the most influential type houses of the modern era, and with his role as editor and art director of U&lc, which was published by ITC, and for a period influenced an entire generation.

It is important to note that all of the typographic giants named above are typeface designers rather than graphic designers. Lubalin, however, was both. This made him unusual: his contemporaries — Paul Rand, Saul Bass and Lou Dorfsman — did not design typefaces. Only Milton Glaser, a younger man, can match Lubalin's combination of professional graphic design assignments with a commitment to font creation. In Glaser's case, however, his approach to type design is far more illustrative than Lubalin's: Baby Teeth, Baby Fat and Glaser Stencil are visually arresting display fonts, but unlike Lubalin's typefaces, do not work as fully functioning typeface families; nobody ever set a book in Baby Teeth.

Far from considering himself a great type designer, Lubalin didn't even rate himself as an outstanding typographer: 'From a classic sense,' he once wrote, 'I don't feel I am a great typographer. In fact, from this standpoint, I'm terrible, because I don't follow the rules. I use razor blades, cut out spaces between letterforms and join type together in a kind of design unity.' Yet Herb Lubalin was the first major designer to emerge on the back of photocomposition in typesetting. He foresaw the potential for a new typography that was flexible and malleable, and more than anyone else at the time (1960s—70s), Lubalin understood that it was possible, via new photomechanical technology, to deploy an array of visually arresting effects: minus letter-spacing, overlapping letters, back-slanting letters, and controlled distortion. He also saw the need for typefaces that could be used to exploit the new typesetting technology; few typefaces fulfill this need better than Avant Garde Gothic.

Controversy has always surrounded this remarkable typeface. Its geometric, almost mechanical, perfection offended some purists raised in the classical tradition; and the forest of ligatures, which encouraged rampant misuse by undiscerning designers, has enraged typographers (Lubalin included) in a way that no comparable typeface can match. On top of this, there was also the question of authorship and who should benefit from Avant Garde Gothic's success as a best-selling commercial typeface.

Lubalin's longtime associate, Tom Carnase, drew the font from sketches made by Lubalin. Steven Heller quoted Carnase: 'Herb was a scribbler, but his scribbles were very readable.' This brings to mind Ernie Smith's earlier comment that, 'The art director who got a Lubalin tissue couldn't take credit as the designer.' But the typeface Avant Garde Gothic wasn't a logo or a page layout for a magazine; it was an entire font, and Lubalin did not make sketches for every character and every weight — or for the notorious ligatures. For these, he had to turn to someone else. That someone was Tom Carnase.

Carnase has said that he alone designed the additional characters and created all the ligatures. As Heller noted: 'After making a handful of these headlines, he [Carnase] further realized there were almost enough characters to complete an entire alphabet, which he eventually drew, and from which a prototype film font was made for the studio's use.'

Lubalin never denied the role Carnase played in the creation of the font. On leaflets promoting the face, Lubalin and Carnase are credited as the joint designers. As was noted previously, Lubalin was scrupulous in his crediting of work: in this regard he was far more generous than most of his contemporaries. But in the case of font design, there is also the question of who gets the money. Heller wrote: **'Carnase recalls that Photolettering Inc. illicitly copied many of the letters and ligatures and sold them without permission. So, to counteract this and other unauthorized use, Carnase produced a specimen card pack that offered custom settings to Lubalin, Smith, Carnase's clients. Given the high volume of requests, it was clear to Lubalin, and his soon-to-be partner, type director Aaron Burns, that Avant Garde should be released as a commercial font. Lubalin Burns was founded to produce and sell typefaces.'**

Lubalin Burns was an important entity in Lubalin's career. It lasted from 1964 until 1970, when it was superseded

by the International Typeface Corporation (ITC), which released Avant Garde Gothic in a fully working version in
1970. Although Carnase made, and retains ownership of,
all the original drawings for the light, medium and demi-
bold weights (at a later date, other designers at ITC designed the additional weights), he did not share in the
profits. Steve Heller quoted him as having said: 'I resen-
ted it highly. This was no way to treat a partner.'

No discussion of the typeface can avoid the subject of
the ligatures: ligatures had existed in typography for centuries, but what was different about those found in Avant
Garde Gothic was that they were formed from capital letters. This was new, and newness — especially in typography — invariably divides people. For some, Avant Garde
Gothic's geometric precision defined graphic coolness and
modernity; for others, the typeface was 'a poor fusion of
Helvetica and Futura', and the abundant supply of ligatures only encouraged misuse by sensation-seeking graphic
designers. Lubalin's partner, Tony Di Spigna, commented:
'The first time Avant Garde was used was one of the few
times it was used correctly. It's become the most abused
typeface in the world.' Ed Benguiat, a friend and colleague
of Lubalin's for many years, said: 'The only place Avant
Garde looks good is in the words Avant Garde. Everybody
ruins it. They lean the letters the wrong way.'

None of this stopped Avant Garde Gothic becoming a
global smash-hit typeface. During the 1970s, it was ubiquitous: its use in 1976 as the typeface of choice for the signage of Las Vegas airport by designer John Follis (who also
designed signage for San Diego Wild Animal Park, Sea
World in Florida, and the J. Paul Getty Museum in Malibu)
confirmed it as both a major style statement and a highly
functional typeface with many practical uses.

A serifed version of Avant Garde, called Lubalin Graph,
was designed by Herb Lubalin and drawn by Tony Di
Spigna and Joe Sundwall (yet another fine lettering artist
of the 1970s). The bold face was created especially for the
Public Broadcasting Service (PBS) for their 1974—75 promotion program. It was made available to ITC by PBS for
release to all ITC subscribers. Like an updated Rockwell,
this Slab Serif typeface retains many similarities to Avant
Garde Gothic. It has the same large x-height, a set of ligatures,
and variance characters in the cap letters. The design of
this typeface grew out of the need for a more flexible

Egyptian alphabet, one that would be more acceptable to
the requirements of the contemporary graphic designer,
and more suitable for the new technology. Oblique versions and small caps were designed by Lubalin and drawn
by Ed Benguiat.

Tony Di Spigna and Lubalin also designed Serif Gothic.
The letterforms were originally conceived as a logotype
— by Lubalin and Carnase — for a French shirt company,
but the work was rejected. During what he called a 'slow
period', Tony Di Spigna decided to see if it could be expanded into a full-blown typeface. 'We thought it was an interesting idea,' he said in an interview in *The Typographer*
(1984), 'to take a sans serif letterform and add minute serifs
to it, but at the same time to give it a different twist, a
different character and identity of its own.' The entire
family was produced in what the article calls a 'deadline-
pressuring nine months'. Other notable typefaces were
L&C Stymie Hairline and L&C Hairline Gothic (loosely
modelled on Rudolf Koch's Kabel). Herb Lubalin and
Tom Carnase are both credited as the designers.

But it is by Avant Garde Gothic that Herb Lubalin's reputation as a type designer will always be measured. He created
— in partnership with Carnase — a font that has endured,
and that has a strong following among young designers
who prize its well-tooled compactness. It turns up everywhere;
in trendy magazines, on record covers, on book jackets,
on chic packaging. Just as Template Gothic (designed by
Barry Deck) stands as the typeface of the 1990s digital generation, Avant Garde Gothic is the great typeface of the
phototypesetting era.

One world-beating typeface, however, isn't enough to
put Lubalin among the immortals. Indeed, it may be that
his greatest contribution to type design was the part he
played in the formation of a company that was to transform
the way type was created, set and paid for. The International
Typeface Corporation (ITC) offered a radical alternative to
the past: a past that was rooted in industrial-era machinery
and rife with font piracy; a past where typeface designers
went largely unrewarded.

19

ITC (International Typeface Corporation)

ITC was one of the world's first type foundries to emerge without a past in hot metal. Founded in 1970 by Aaron Burns, Edward Rondthaler and Herb Lubalin, it blew in on the winds of change that swept through typography and typesetting at that time.

Aaron Burns was a graphic designer. He had been an assistant to Lubalin in the 1940s at Sudler & Hennessey, and in the 1950s he was a director of The Composing Room, a company that set and sold type commercially. He claimed to have been the first graphic designer to work for a type shop. His book *Typography* (Rheinhold, 1961), was the first to show how the expressive power of type could be unleashed when unyoked from its past in hot-metal setting. He also put forward the notion that typography was an 'attitude' — a remarkably prescient view that would find many adherents in the years that were to follow, as typography moved from a mainly functional and impersonal discipline to one that could be used for personal expression. Yet one of his most important achievements was the way in which his almost evangelical zeal for type, in all its manifestations, helped bridge the divide that traditionally separated designers from typesetters. Having spent long periods in type shops, overseeing the production of his work, Burns foresaw the benefits that would accrue from both sides knowing more about each other. Through ITC and his writings, he worked assiduously to improve the dialogue between the two groups. Nowhere was Burns more effective in this than in his proprietorship of *U&lc*.

As was noted earlier, Ed Rondthaler was a pioneer of phototypesetting. In the mid-1930s, he had built a phototypesetting machine that revolutionized traditional typesetting. Known as the Rutherford photolettering machine, it was one of the first such devices in commercial use. Rondthaler also had a lifelong commitment to the promotion of literacy through the adoption of a simplified English spelling system, and was a past president of the American Literacy Council. The three ITC directors set about the task of transforming contemporary typography from top to bottom. They sought to control the design, licensing and marketing of typefaces for filmsetting, and later for computerized setting. But first they had to find a way of avoiding the piracy of fonts. This did not prove to be easy. Typeface design has never had legal protection in the USA, and an editorial in *U&lc* spelt out the problem: **'When a thief takes pennies from a newsstand, it's called stealing. But when a duplicator lifts design material without paying for it, it is folly to condone the act with the half-excuse "It's not illegal". Under our present laws it's not illegal, but it's highly unethical. Protecting a type design from piracy is a problem as old as typefounding itself. The alphabet has never enjoyed much legal status. Type designer and manufacturer have long been victims of this unfortunate situation.'**

In the days of metal type, piracy was slow and expensive, but in the age of phototypesetting, when fonts were mastered on film, copying fonts became much easier. Typesetting houses could duplicate film negatives in minutes and offer them to their customers without paying for the rights. For the type designer, there was no financial incentive to design new typefaces. The situation was explained in *U&lc*: **'Unauthorized film font duplicators — also known as "contact-copiers" — were hard at work. From a co-conspirator the copier borrows or buys an original font negative upon which many thousands of dollars have been spent in creative design, in microscopic placement of letters, in unit modification and fit, in grid pattern and technical layout. With one quick flash he duplicates everything. It is a highly lucrative business since each contact copy — made for pennies — is sold for twenty or even fifty dollars to the unwitting typographer.'**

Burns, Rondthaler and Lubalin set about offering a properly regulated and accountable scheme for the licensing of fonts to typesetting houses and printers. In the ITC scheme, the master font of each ITC typeface was licensed — not sold — to different phototypesetting firms. ITC then acted as a middleman between type designers and type houses: it collected royalties from type houses and distributed a portion of this income to type designers.

The trio constituted a formidable team with which to fight the growing piracy threat, but ITC also allied itself with some heavyweight talent to bolster the ethical crusade in favour of properly licensed fonts. George Lois said in support: **'There's enough illegality, unethicality and immorality in the world without having to condone the legalized plagiarism that has invaded the typographic field, which I have always regarded as being curiously honest!'**

Saul Bass said: **'I don't have time to investigate who is ethical and who isn't in our business. I have faith in the integrity of my suppliers and would be sorely disappointed if I found out otherwise. I sincerely hope my typographers are not buying contact-copied fonts!'**

It wasn't only the question of piracy that ITC addressed. Up until the arrival of ITC, type was set on expensive proprietary typesetting machines. Different manufacturers offered type libraries that only worked on their machines: they used their type libraries to sell the machines. Burns saw that the new booming market for typefaces required that every manufacturer of typesetting machines should have every typeface. Writing about Burns in *U&lc*, Ed Gottschall (author and vice chairman of ITC) spelt out the methodology ITC employed: **'Without exclusive type libraries, the machines would have to compete on their own merits. This was a revolutionary concept, and it was a key basis for the founding of ITC. In addition to the policy of non-exclusivity, by which ITC licensed the identical typeface to all its customers, Aaron reinvented typeface marketing to keep pace with the technological changes. ITC subscribers (as its customers — the manufacturers of typesetting machines — were known in the early days) were given the art for ITC typeface designs without charge. They paid monthly royalties to ITC, based on how many ITC fonts they sold to their customers, the type composition shops. In other words, the subscribers paid nothing until they were assured of a profit.'**

But ITC offered more than a smart fiscal arrangement to sell fonts and protect the designers of typefaces: it also had a fully fledged typographic ethos that was to prove hugely influential throughout the world in the 1970s and into the 1980s. There was an ITC typographic style, and it briefly conquered the world. In its impact, ITC can be compared to many of the great type houses of Europe, such as Deberny & Peignot, Berthold and Monotype.

The most salient characteristic of ITC fonts was their large x-heights. They also had short ascenders and descenders. They were designed to be tightly spaced and to work with minimum leading. Advertising designers loved them; they were legible and compact and their compactness dominated the page and commanded attention. It was Lubalin who provided the most cogent rational for the ITC 'style'. In an essay, he wrote: **'The most significant change in type stylization was the decrease in letter-spacing, word-spacing, and leading, and a simultaneous increase in type size due to the larger x-heights of lower case letters. I remember an incident when a client chastised me severely for using "illegible typography". My answer to him was that ever since Gutenberg invented movable type, with its built-in drawbacks caused by the metal shoulders surrounding the letterforms, people have been reading illegible type. Now, for the first time, type could be set the right way, the way people speak — in a steady flow, without interruptions between letters, words, sentences and paragraphs. I told him that he would have to accommodate his reading habits to the new typography, for that was the wave of the future. He was hard to convince at that time; now, he's a true believer.'**

Throughout its most successful years, ITC had legions of 'true believers'. Many of the fonts were new cuts of classic typefaces: ITC Garamond and ITC Caslon, for example. The company was widely praised for its commitment to reviving forgotten typefaces and making them fit for use in the new 'hot' media landscape that included television, a medium where the old spindly typefaces looked especially outmoded and ill-suited. Two fonts were to epitomize the 'new typography': Avant Garde Gothic and Souvenir. The latter, designed by Ed Benguiat, has lasted less well than Avant Garde, but for a period, they both dominated graphic communication in the Western world.

ITC also has its detractors. Neville Brody — the star of the 1980s typographic revolution — was not an ITC admirer. In his 1988 book, *The Graphic Language of Neville Brody*, he told interviewer and co-author, Jon Wozencroft: **'I dislike the ITC cuts of typefaces ... Really, I don't know what they think they're doing — in a way, it's an attempt to create an American typographic tradition out of European type. The ITC typefaces have a very Seventies' look, too, and if you use them large, this colours what you are trying to communicate so completely that it**

91

57

92. Front cover of *U&lc* (Volume 4, No.3, September 1977). *U&lc* was a quarterly journal, published by ITC, and edited and designed by Herb Lubalin. The magazine, printed on newspaper stock, included an eclectic mix of articles and features about graphic design, illustration and typography, combined with the promotion of ITC typefaces. As editor, Lubalin maintained a sophisticated balance between the advertising of typefaces and ITC's desire to increase knowledge of type and typesetting at a time of rapid change, and his own recondite taste in vernacular design and various antique styles. As editor, designer and co-publisher, Lubalin was at last in a position to shape a publication to his own liking.

overrides your intentions. ITC faces don't have the kind of anonymity that a good colour has in painting. If you use one, then what you're doing is revealing a part of the painting that you haven't created.'

Graphic designer and Pentagram partner Paula Scher was not an admirer either. At a type conference in New York (Type 1987), Scher and the magazine designer Roger Black debated the effect of ITC on typography. In an account of the discussion subsequently published in *Metropolis* magazine, the writer and editor Karrie Jacobs described the two viewpoints. Roger Black, she wrote, 'lauded ITC's type library, the almost universal availability of ITC faces, their publication of the quarterly magazine *U&lc*, and even their interpretations of historic faces. "ITC's Garamond is a peculiarly contemporary Garamond", Black opined. "It's not a bookish Garamond."'

Jacobs then described Scher's view: 'She showed two slides, one of ITC Garamond and the other of a Garamond out of a Linotype book. Two of Garamond's hallmarks, the peculiarly high waist of the lowercase 'e' and the dainty loop of the lowercase 'a', had been normalized a bit, rounded out slightly, by ITC for their Garamond. "The problem with the new form is it's called Garamond and it's not Garamond", argued Scher.'

By the late 1980s and 1990s, the tightly spaced ITC aesthetic was no longer fashionable. This was caused by a number of factors: a taste for a more widely spaced typographic aesthetic; the widespread rediscovery of Swiss typographic modernism; and a corresponding appetite for outlandish, digitally modified letterforms. ITC typefaces were on the wane.

The debate about ITC's contribution to the history of type continues: did they invent a new typography for the McLuhanesque 'hot' media age, or did they denude a series of near-perfect typefaces of their charm and originality? For those who lived through the era of ITC's triumphant years, the typefaces now look dated and are forever associated with a particular strand of wordy advertising. Paradoxically for a younger generation of designers — many of them growing up in the second great coming of Helvetica in the 1990s — ITC fonts (particularly those by Lubalin) have a strong attraction, especially the more eccentric ones. You can see this in the current obsession with Avant Garde Gothic and, to a lesser extent, in Lubalin Graph, but also in the typefaces of Ed Benguiat and others from the ITC boom years.

Herb Lubalin's role in ITC is hard to fully assess. He sat on committees to vet typefaces, but, as a number of people who knew him have confirmed, he had no great interest in the minutiae of typesetting. He appears to have reserved his contribution to the design and editorship of *U&lc*, where he relished the opportunity to be editor, designer and publisher. *U&lc* was Lubalin's baby and he was free to raise his offspring any way he chose.

Both Burns and Rondthaler outlived Lubalin and survived long enough to see the second great typographic revolution of the 20th century — the domination of typography by the personal computer and the DTP explosion. Burns in particular was a zealous enthusiast for computerized typesetting. He died in 1991, age 69; Rondthaler lived to be 104, dying in 2009.

In 1986, ITC was bought by Esselte Letraset. Ironically, a few years before this date, when Letraset was a highly successful independent company, selling sheets of rub-down lettering, they foresaw the end of dry transfer lettering and wanted to make the move into photo and computerized typesetting. According to Mike Daines, the British designer and a former employee of Letraset who had regular dealings with Lubalin, their initial efforts to acquire the company, were rebuffed by ITC — although Daines suspects that Lubalin was sympathetic to the idea of a sale. In 2000, Agfa Monotype Corporation announced the acquisition of ITC and its library of more than 1,600 typefaces. From then on, ITC ceased to operate as an independent entity. It is now owned by Monotype Imaging. But for a few years, ITC ruled the world of typesetting and type design, and Herb Lubalin was a vital part of that all-conquering era.

AaBbCcDdEeFfGgHhIiJjKkLlMmNnOoPp   QqRrSsTtUuVvWwXxYyZz1234567890&ÆŒ$¢£%!?()[]

UPPER AND LOWER CASE, THE INTERNATIONAL JOURNAL OF TYPOGRAPHICS   PUBLISHED BY INTERNATIONAL TYPEFACE CORPORATION. VOLUME FOUR, NUMBER THREE, SEPT. 1977

An exploration of the new and merging word processing and typesetting technologies and what they offer the designer, buyer, specifier and other users of printed communications.

Vision'77, a three-day conference sponsored by the International Typeface Corporation and hosted by the Rochester Institute of Technology May 16-19, 1977, addressed itself to the ultimate consumers who work with type. Newspapers, book and magazine publishers, and commercial graphic arts services have been flooded with seminars, exhibits and trade paper reportage, but the ultimate consumers—such as art and production managers, graphic designers, type directors, printing buyers, advertising and sales promotion managers, marketing directors and some editors and publishers—have been under-informed.

Vision'77 attempted to fill this void. U&lc offers in this and its next issue heavy coverage of the information and thinking exchanged at Vision'77. It is impossible, even in the large number of pages of U&lc is devoting to Vision'77, to produce verbatim coverage. Some 1500 slides plus films and even videotapes were needed for the intensive 3-day "crash course." U&lc has edited down the presentations and, in so doing, captured not just Vision'77's highlights but the major viewpoints and conclusions, together with considerable supportive detail. The bulk of U&lc's report is in the words of each speaker. Vision'77, Part I, starts on Page 2. Vision'77, Part II will appear in the next issue of U&lc.

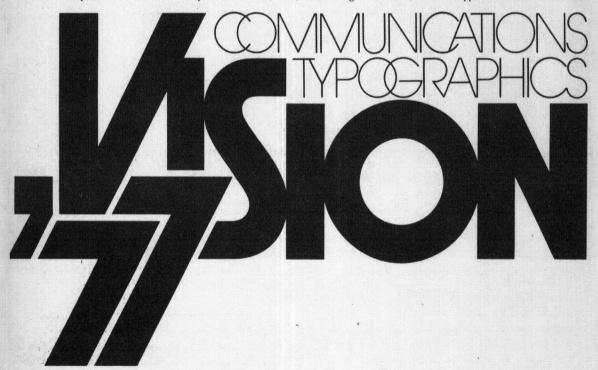

93. Cover of *U&lc* (Volume 6, No.3, Sept 1979); a typographic portrait of Pablo Picasso by Paul Siemsen. The idea was conceived, designed, researched and written by Siemsen as a promotion poster for The Graphic Corporation, a studio-print house in Des Moines, Iowa. It uses four different sizes and weight combinations of ITC Korinna.
    94—96. Sculptures by Rhoda Sparber. Limericks by Herb Lubalin. Photography: Carl Fischer.

20

U&lc — The International Journal of Typographics

Leafing through old copies of *U&lc* from the 1970s — the pages now an age-revealing yellow — the contemporary reader comes across an eclectic mix of vintage and contemporary subject matter: an article by Norman Mailer on graffiti sits next to one on Spencerian scripts. Yet, despite the diversity of subject matter, *U&lc* was a nakedly commercial enterprise. As Richard Hollis has noted: 'To advertise their designs, ITC launched a large-format tabloid journal, *U&lc*, unmistakably American from its logo to its layout. Under Lubalin's direction it was more like a women's weekly than a technical newssheet.'

It is true that Lubalin's design did not give the journal the appearance of a 'technical newssheet', but ITC's aim — as well as to encourage the licensing of their fonts — was to promote technical knowledge of typesetting and typography in a fast-changing world. As one editorial put it: **'The world of graphic arts is alive today with new technological advances, so vast and difficult to comprehend, that they strain the imagination of even the most knowledgeable and creatively gifted among us. New materials, new tools, new ways to plan work are becoming mandatory for efficiency, quality, economy — presenting problems for all — printers, typesetters, artists, writers, advertisers, publishers — all the creative people who have anything to do with preparation of the visual word. How to keep up? How to stay in touch with what is current? How to plan for tomorrow? To envision a future essential to decision making today?'**

Alongside promoting fonts and boosting technical know-how, Herb Lubalin introduced a third element: a joyous celebration of graphic design culture. His choice of subject matter encompassed the new and the old; the vernacular and the professional; the witty and the serious. Humour was a recurring element: the work of cartoonist Lou Myers was a regular feature, as were the sharp-brained satires of illustrators such as Ed Sorel and Charles B. Slackman. An issue from 1979 (Volume 6, No.3) features sculptures by Lubalin's second wife, Rhoda Sparber (figs.94—96). She produced sculpture-portraits of Saul Bass, Lou Dorfsman, Gene Federico, Milton Glaser, George Lois, Cipe Pineles and Henry Wolf, each accompanied by a limerick written by Lubalin. His limerick-writing capabilities can be judged by this effort, produced to accompany a sculpture of Lou Dorfsman's face bursting out of a cardboard TV set.

A clever designer named Lou,
Alumnus of famed Cooper U;
With the cheers of his peers
In his ears all these years,
his motto: 'So what else is new?'
When Lou was a budding young teen,
His efforts were heard but not seen;
An inadequate drummer,
He ruined people's summer —
This scourge of the borscht circuit scene.
Now creative VP in TV,
His CBS confreres all agree:
There is no debate
That Lou Dorfsman is great,
As far as their eye can see.

The original idea to publish the magazine came from Aaron Burns. *U&lc* first appeared in 1973. It was quarterly and distributed by direct mail, free to anyone who signed up to receive it. By the end of the 1970s, it had a controlled circulation of more than 250,000, and an international readership, according to ITC, of one million.

In the first issue, Herb Lubalin is listed as Editorial & Design Director. The inaugural issue featured, among other articles: a scathing indictment of type piracy by Edward Rondthaler; an article on Robert Indiana by *New York Times* art critic, John Canaday; Willem Sandberg on the function of the artist in society; Lubalin's account of the story behind Avant Garde Gothic (see p.50); Tom Carnase demonstrating the lush beauty of Spencerian script; and a round-up of new typefaces offered by ITC.

For Lubalin, *U&lc* represented a defining moment in his career. Here at last was the freedom he craved. He was designer, editor and co-proprietor. It is also abundantly

clear that he relished the task. He often had as many as three issues on the go at once; hand-rendered layouts from that period have an exuberance and virtuosity that is plain to see (p.39, figs.58—61). And while he was self-evidently not a conventional editor — his interest was fundamentally visual, not textual — he made sure that there was always a high degree of textual content in each issue, a mixture of the intellectually rigorous and the frothily ephemeral.

U&lc covered a wide range of subject matter, from hieroglyphics and calligraphy, to computerized typesetting and TV graphics. Although politics was largely missing from U&lc there was, nevertheless, a discernible ethical position to be found in the journal's pages. The publication championed typographic excellence across the realm of graphic design, and not just from the perspective of ITC fonts; there was a strong voice (fuelled by self-interest, admittedly) for the need for a new ethical approach to typography. And while Lubalin was editor, the magazine eschewed the boosterism of graphic design as the friend of big business, and instead promoted a mildly iconoclastic atmosphere that put craft, ideas and an undogmatic eclecticism at the heart of the publication.

As a young designer in the late 1970s, I can remember copies of U&lc kicking around every studio, every printworks and every typesetting house I visited. Back then, type catalogues and the sales literature of type foundries and typesetters were only just beginning to throw off the musty air of men who smoked pipes and wore tweed jackets with leather elbow patches. But nothing looked like U&lc. Here was a publication that showed the kinetic energy of the new typography, but was also an informative and helpful guide through the trackless terrain of the new visual communication landscape.

Looking at U&lc today, with its ads for typesetting machines, it seems like a relic from a distant age. But the viewer can still sense Lubalin's love of typographic expression and his mastery of contrast; it's the incisiveness of the page layouts that most captivate the contemporary viewer. It may have been a consequence of his colour-blindness, but newsprint was one of Lubalin's natural habitats. He was clearly at home in the mono terrain of absorbent newsprint.

21

Foreign Affairs

In the boom years of the late 1970s and 1980s, there was a vogue for international expansion among design groups. A network of offices in the capitals of the world was regarded as the macho way to capitalize on the worldwide demand for corporate design. The received wisdom was that if designers' paymasters — the big corporations — were spreading across the globe, then designers should follow. Even the desk-bound, work-addicted Herb Lubalin was stung by the bug of global expansion, although as we shall see, his reasons were not to do with global domination or corporate servicing.

Information about the satellite Lubalin studios is hard to come by. The studio press releases listed these 'foreign' offices like trophies in a cabinet, and when they were mentioned in promotional material they were usually listed alongside the awards and professional accolades. Nowhere does Lubalin go into detail about the creative or fiscal reasons why his name was attached to offices in Paris, London and Hawaii.

It seems, however, that in all three cases, Lubalin's involvement was minimal. The French and UK design offices were formed in 1971. The Hawaiian office, Aki, Lubalin, Inc., was formed in 1974. In Lubalin's Art Directors Club biography, dated 1977, it is stated that he had 'just recently found out he had a thriving Hawaiian operation called Aki, Lubalin, Inc.' This hardly makes Lubalin sound like an active member of the studio. How had this situation arisen? None of his former employees or partners that I interviewed could offer an explanation. Was it perhaps another example of Lubalin's generosity? Had Aki asked him if he could open a Hawaiian office and use Lubalin's name, and the ever-amenable Lubalin simply said yes?

Lubalin's precise role in his Paris operation — Lubalin, Delpire & Cie — is only slightly less mysterious. His 'partner' Robert Delpire was, and still is, well known in French and international publishing and photographic

97. Stationery and logotype for Playstreet Inc. Design by Angaret Beier while working at Lubalin, Smith, Carnase. See text below for more information about one of Herb Lubalin's favourite designers.

circles. He was born in 1926 and, as a medical student, started a magazine called *Neuf*, an art review designed for doctors. He published works by artists, writers and photographers including Doisneau, Breton, Capa, Picasso, Sartre and Cartier-Bresson. 'People sometimes say I discovered Cartier-Bresson,' he wrote, 'but that's just not true: he had already been published. I approached him, we got on immediately, and he remained one of my greatest friends. I organized as many exhibitions as I could for him, I've lost count of how many, and published about 15 of his books.' In 1958, Delpire was the first to publish one of the most famous books in photographic history — *Les Américains* by Robert Frank, the Swiss-born photographer.

To help finance his ambitious projects, Delpire set up an advertising agency and produced campaigns for clients such as Citroën, L'Oréal and Habitat, and the famous Cacharel ads, photographed by Sarah Moon. He was also involved in film and produced two classics of radical cinema by the American director William Klein (*Muhammad Ali the Great* and *Who Are You Polly Maggoo?*). He directed a film about the work of Cartier-Bresson, and in 1982 was appointed head of the National Center for Photography in France. He also created and published the series *Photo Poche*, the first pocket collection of books dedicated to photography.

Lubalin, however, was unforthcoming about his Paris operation in interviews. Even Robert Delpire's current website (www.delpire.com) has no mention of his alliance with Lubalin, although the site has a strong echo of Lubalin's typographic aesthetic — especially in the treatment of the Delpire logotype. In his exhaustive study of French graphic design (*The Story of Graphic Design in France*, 2005), Michel Wlassikoff noted only that a meeting between Delpire and Lubalin led to the 'founding of the Lubalin, Delpire & Cie agency, which distinguished itself for its virtuoso use of letterforms in the initials and logos it designed for L'Oréal, BSN, Air France, Sheila Hicks, and Daniel Hechter.' He further noted that: **'France began to catch up in the field of brand images in the early 1970s. Innovative typefaces and techniques (such as photolettering) were marketed ... American models were spread thanks to the U&lc journal (launched in 1973) and the first Paris exhibitions by Herb Lubalin and Push Pin Studios. Design agencies created specialist departments, and a number of studios (including Excoffon Conseil and Lubalin, Delpire & Cie) offered their design services to companies for the creation of brand images. Many long-lasting logos were designed in this period.'**

However, in *U&lc* (Vol.1, No.3, 1974), there is a less grandiose explanation for Lubalin's willingness to set up a Paris operation. No writer is credited with the article, but it seems likely that it was Lubalin who wrote it as part of his role as the journal's editor. The article is titled 'Ms', and is described as, 'The first of a new series of articles devoted to the many talented women in communications, the kick-off being devoted to the superior work of Annegret Beier of the Paris office of Lubalin, Delpire et Cie, and one of Europe's finest graphic designers.' That's a pretty tall claim, but it is known that Lubalin admired Beier enormously, and it provides a further incentive to believe that he was the author of the short article.

Beier was born in Germany in 1940. She worked as a freelance designer for several publishing companies, and in 1963 moved to Paris. In 1967, she turned up in New York and took a job at Lubalin, Smith, Carnase, Inc. According to the *U&lc* article, it was Beier who provided the incentive to open a Paris office: **'She developed a simultaneous love for LSC and a hatred for NYC. Her determination to return to Paris made it imperative for LSC to open an office there, rather than to lose her services. She became the guiding light of Lubalin, Delpire et Cie, where she created innovative designs for the European market.'** So, rather than a grand plan to dominate the European design scene by opening an office in Paris, it appears that Lubalin was simply locking in the services of a designer he rated highly.

Lubalin, Maxwell, Ltd., London, also has its share of mystery. No one associated with Lubalin that I spoke to knew anything about it. It is referenced in all the press releases, studio promo leaflets and biographies of Lubalin, but not even the British designers I spoke to who were around in the 1970s and who knew Lubalin and the local design scene were aware of its existence. Only David Pocknell was able to fill in a few blanks, although he knew nothing about the studio's make-up, or what work it produced. But he knew that, in 1971, Doug Maxwell was a well-respected UK designer who was making a name for himself as a talented art director. According to Pocknell, Maxwell

98—100. Details of the *Gastrotypo-graphicalassemblage*. This was a 35-foot-long wall of carved wooden words, erected in the CBS building in New York. Herb Lubalin and Tom Carnase worked extensively on this famous installation.

worked for Wolff Olins, and was also art director of Island Records, one of the most important labels of the period. A handful of album covers bear his name as designer and art director. Pocknell also knew that Maxwell spent some time in New York, where it is likely that he met Lubalin.

Again, it is easy to be persuaded that here was yet another example of Lubalin's generosity. We can imagine a young British designer (much like Pocknell himself did earlier, p.35) turning up on the Lubalin doorstep in New York. He's ambitious and talented, and Lubalin wants to recruit him. What better way to do it than form a London office, and create the impression that the Lubalin empire had roots in another of the great design capitals of the world? It is known that Lubalin visited London regularly. Mike Daines, who worked for Letraset, invited Lubalin to London three times a year to sit on a panel that chose typefaces for Letraset's high-end range — Lettragraphica. Whether he used these visits to develop his London business arm is not known, but the Lubalin Maxwell studio appears short-lived and left no body of work by which to measure it. In an odd coda, it transpires that in 1983 Douglas Maxwell was the designer of the logo of TV-am, the UK's first breakfast TV channel. The logo uses Avant Garde Gothic.

If, as seems likely, all three of Lubalin's forays into overseas expansion were whims on his part to maintain links with designers he thought important, only the Paris office produced work that we can evaluate today — thanks mostly to the efforts of Annegret Beier. Of course, there may be another simpler reason for Lubalin's empire-building. According to Fay Barrows, Herb Lubalin loved to travel.

22

Lou Dorfsman — Friend and Collaborator

It is hard to evaluate the life and work of Herb Lubalin without considering his relationship with Lou Dorfsman. Lubalin had many other close friendships and alliances: his relationships with his various business partners, Aaron Burns, Ernie Smith, Tony Di Spigna, Tom Carnase and Alan Peckolick; his mentor-like relationship with George Lois; and the special bond that existed between Lubalin and Ralph Ginzburg. But none of these relationships come close to matching the durability and depth of his friendship with Dorfsman. As well as being lifelong friends, they were also two giants of the mid-20th-century New York design scene.

The young Dorfsman might have joined his father's sign-painting business but instead, like Lubalin, he enrolled at Cooper Union. There he was attracted to courses in architecture, decorative art, painting and lettering, and as his biographers Dick Hess and Marion Muller note, it was often his extra-curricular activities that excited him most. Along with his friend Lubalin, Dorfsman was a frequent visitor to the Apollo in Harlem, where he saw the greats of jazz perform. Fay Barrows, Lubalin's assistant at Sudler & Hennessey, recalled Lubalin and Dorfsman going to a club on 52nd Street where they met Billie Holiday and, 'ended up bar hopping with her.'

After Cooper Union, the two men lived together — both married Cooper Union sweethearts, both shared a portfolio, and both helped each other to find jobs. Lubalin eventually went into advertising and later worked as an independent designer. Dorfsman, on the other hand, spent his entire career as an art director, and later as design director, at CBS.

As a World War II army recruit, Dorfsman had filled his spare time browsing Art Directors Annuals, and it was in their pages that he saw the work for the nascent Columbia Broadcasting System. CBS was a network broadcaster with an Olympian view of its role in American cultural life. Under William S. Paley, a titan of U.S. broadcasting, CBS became

101. Lubalin in Paris: photograph from the press kit of Herb Lubalin's exhibition of his work in Paris (p.148).

102. Portrait of Herb Lubalin towards the end of his life. The designer Kevin Gatta, who worked for Lubalin in the late 1970s, recalls his employer's appearance: 'He wore an open-necked shirt, chest hairs poking out, and his hair was a bit wild.' Photograph kindly supplied by Bernie Zlotnick.

one of the largest radio networks in the United States and then, alongside NBC and ABC, one of the big three U.S. television networks.

CBS was committed to quality in all areas of the company's operations: radio dramas were commissioned from W.H. Auden, Dorothy Parker and William Saroyan; during World War II, CBS correspondents broadcast from the battle zones of Europe; when television arrived, programs such as *I Love Lucy* and *The Ed Sullivan Show* were balanced with documentaries and shows such as *60 Minutes* and *Face the Nation*. CBS was also the home of *The Waltons*, *M*A*S*H* and countless sports specials. It spawned a world-class record label (CBS), and various publishing arms. A flavour of life in a mid-20th-century U.S. TV network can be gleaned from watching the George Clooney-directed movie of 2005, *Good Night, and Good Luck*. The film is based on the life of Edward R. Murrow, who worked for CBS and was one of the first household names of broadcasting.

In its most successful years, the company was a commissioner and public champion of high-quality design in its advertising, promotional materials, and even in its architecture. The first great art director of CBS was William Golden — a figure greatly admired by Herb Lubalin. It was Golden who hired Dorfsman as his assistant, and after Golden's sudden death in 1959, Dorfsman succeeded him. William S. Paley is on record as having said: 'CBS has a corporate commitment to excellence in design and Lou Dorfsman is the one whose genius has translated that commitment into reality.'

As the design director of CBS, Dorfsman oversaw the use of the iconic CBS eye logo (designed by Golden), produced annual reports and other promotional materials, and designed the interior signage and graphics of the entire CBS building, famously designed by architect Eero Saarinen. One of his most celebrated works was the *Gastrotypographicalassemblage*, a 35-foot-long wall of carved wooden words, created for the dining area in the building, which Herb Lubalin and Tom Carnase worked on extensively (p.63).

Lubalin and Dorfsman remained friends throughout Lubalin's life. They met frequently on design juries and in their roles as grandees of the 1960s and 1970s American design scene. As men, they were radically different — Lubalin, small and taciturn; Dorfsman tall, moustachioed

and verbose. Dorfsman hired Lubalin to do work for CBS, and on numerous occasions, as has already been noted, they contemplated going into business together. However, their commercial marriage was never to take place, although it was even referred to by Dorfsman in his memorial address at his old friend's funeral in 1981: 'I feel sure we'll meet sometime in the future and at last we'll pull off our business partnership. And when we do ... we're going to redesign the hell out of heaven.'

Due to remaining 'in house' all his working life, it is arguable that Dorfsman did not receive the acclaim that is more readily accorded to independent designers such as Paul Rand, Saul Bass and Herb Lubalin. Among graphic designers, the independent designer is usually, and somewhat lazily, regarded as inhabiting a higher plane than the in-house designer, but in Dorfsman's case, this assessment does not apply. At CBS, he had the support of an enlightened regime, healthy budgets and a corporate ethos that paid more than lip service to good design. In 1977, he told his biographers that if the CBS Broadcast Group's Advertising and Design Department was measured by billings, it would be the 11th largest agency in the USA. To occupy that position and still manage to produce vast amounts of high-quality work is a remarkable achievement, and goes a long way to explaining why, despite his friendship with Lubalin, Dorfsman never left CBS.

Dorfsman's graphics for television, literature design, advertising and environmental design has dated less than many of his contemporaries. There's a sharp-eyed precision to everything produced under his direction. Unlike Lubalin, Dorfsman was more of a creative director and design director than a working designer. He employed many fine designers to work at CBS. And again, unlike Lubalin, Dorfsman appears to have kept at least a toehold in the Modernist camp. The crispness and matter-of-factness that characterizes much of his work sets him apart from the more humanist and eclectic output of Herb Lubalin.

The friendship between the two men was deep and enduring. It lasted until Lubalin's death in 1981. When both Lubalin and Dorfsman were established figures on the international design scene, jetting off to conferences and lecturing gigs, Dorfsman is on record as having said that if Lubalin hadn't got his first wife [Sylvia Kushner] pregnant, they might still be living together. Dorfsman died in 2008.

103—5. Three magazines with political agendas. As a man of liberal sensibilities, Lubalin was always happy to support liberal causes by reducing his fees, but only if his gesture guaranteed creative freedom. Dates: various.

106. A spread from *McGraphic*, a tabloid newspaper produced in support of the doomed presidential campaign of George McGovern, who advocated withdrawal from the Vietnam War in exchange for the return of American prisoners of war. Described as a pro-McGovern/anti-Nixon/anti-Vietnam War publication, the *McGraphic* was published and paid for by Graphic Artists and Writers for McGovern. The issue was designed and edited by Lubalin, Seymour Chwast, Bill Maloney and Ellen Shapiro. In a note to the author of this book, Steven Heller wrote: 'I was toiling, as they say, for McGovern, designing flyers on a shoestring. When I saw *McGraphic* at a fundraising party, I split a gut. I was so angry that these smarmy uptown ad men were making pretty design in the guise of McGovern support. Only years and years later did I appreciate what they had done. Or I became more tolerant of their efforts. Incidentally, all it did was make supporters content with themselves. We had no chance in hell of beating Nixon.' Date: 1972.

23

Political Beliefs and Activities

The huge number of Eastern European Jews who arrived in America between 1880 and World War I came mostly from Russia and what is now modern Poland, Lithuania, Belarus, Ukraine and Moldova. They were fleeing the pogroms (a term applied to attacks on Jews in the Russian empire in the late 19th and early 20th centuries), and they were mostly of liberal or left-wing persuasions. They read Jewish newspapers such as *Forverts*, a publication loosely affiliated with the Socialist Party of America, and *Morgen Freiheit*, a daily Yiddish-language newspaper affiliated with the Communist Party of the USA. Many Jews occupied leading positions in the early 20th-century American labour movement and helped found unions that played a major role in left-wing politics. As the son of Jewish immigrants, the young Lubalin would have been raised in a home that supported left-wing causes in such matters as workers' rights and social justice, and which voted Democrat. In other words, Lubalin would have had a liberal political upbringing, and he was to remain committed to a liberal viewpoint for the rest of his life.

In the 1960s, when Herb Lubalin entered his most productive years, America was undergoing perhaps its greatest political upheaval since the crash of the 1930s. The USA was locked in a deadly war in Vietnam, and back home it was fighting a different sort of war against students and anti-war demonstrators. It was the era of the counterculture, when, for the first time in the modern age, American hegemony was threatened, and a significant number of its citizens emerged who didn't share the American dream of unlimited wealth and imperial power.

As we have already seen, Lubalin was a close collaborator and friend of Ralph Ginzburg, a radical in a peculiarly 1960s sense of the word (he championed sexual liberation, freedom of speech, consumer rights and an end to censorship). So it is perhaps tempting to see Lubalin as a radical, too. But his son, Peter, was adamant when he told me: 'My father was a liberal, not a radical.' Nor does he have any recollection of political discussions at home, or even of his father voicing political views. Rhoda Lubalin, Herb Lubalin's second wife and widow, agreed with this assessment of her late husband's political views; he was not a shout-out-loud liberal, she said, but she confirmed that they both shared liberal views.

Looking through the vast archive of Lubalin's work, we find a number of instances of him designing for politically liberal causes. The most famous example — apart from his work with Ralph Ginzburg — was the *McGraphic* (fig.106), an eight-page tabloid newspaper produced in support of the presidential campaign of George McGovern and his running mate, Sargent Shriver, brother-in-law of John F. Kennedy. McGovern advocated withdrawal from the Vietnam War in exchange for the return of American prisoners of war, and an amnesty for draft evaders who had gone abroad to escape conscription. He has remained a pillar of the American left: in 1998, the journalist and broadcaster Tom Brokaw wrote that McGovern 'is one of the country's most decent and thoughtful public servants.' He stood against Richard Nixon, the famously reactionary U.S. president, who was ultimately brought down by the Watergate scandal of the 1970s.

The *McGraphic* has been described as a pro-McGovern/anti-Nixon/anti-Vietnam War publication. It was published and paid for in 1972 by Graphic Artists And Writers For McGovern/Shriver. The solitary issue was designed and edited by Lubalin, Seymour Chwast, Bill Maloney and Ellen Shapiro. Contributing illustrators included Marshall Arisman, Jules Feiffer, Paul Giovanopoulos, Norman Green, Robert Grossman, David Levine, James McMullan, Ed Renfro, Burt Silverman and Ed Sorel.

The publication was serious-minded, well written, elegantly designed and handsomely produced. It did the rounds of New York art direction shows and awards ceremonies, where it was admired by other designers and illustrators. However, it failed to help McGovern in his bid to defeat Nixon and become president of the USA.

Lubalin designed other liberal and progressive political literature. *The New Leader* (fig.103) began in 1924 as a weekly newspaper 'devoted to the interests of the Socialist and Labor movements.' Over the years, the publication evolved: in the 1940s, it was regarded as an important

source of information on events in the Soviet Union; to such a degree, in fact, that even the Kremlin subscribed to it. Its writers included Albert Camus, Arthur Koestler, George Orwell, Stephen Spender and Alberto Moravia.

When Myron Kolatch took over the editorship of the *New Leader* in 1961, one of his primary aims was to have the magazine redesigned. He was advised to contact Herb Lubalin, who, he was told, would recommend a suitable designer. In an editorial in the final issue of *The New Leader* (2006), Kolatch described his meeting with Lubalin: **'When I phoned him for an appointment, he seemed reticent but agreed to see me. I arrived at his office with half a dozen issues, told him about the magazine while people kept marching in to show him their work. Lubalin, a slight, youthful-looking man in his 40s, with a soft voice and a poker face, said simply: "Leave the copies here. If I like what's in them I'll do it myself". As I began to reiterate our financial condition, he waved me out. The next week he informed me that he was going ahead, and a month later he phoned to say, "I've got a new magazine for you". Lubalin became devoted to the NL, designed all of its full-size special issues, "freshened up" (as he put it) the basic design in 1969, and was supportive in various ways until his death in 1981.'** After Lubalin's death, the work was carried on by Alan Peckolick and Mike Aron. The magazine closed in 2006.

The New Leader described itself in its final incarnation as an 'independent, democratic, liberal journal of news analysis and opinion'. So what was the attraction for Lubalin? Intelligent content that engaged his political sympathies? Or an opportunity to enjoy creative freedom? Most likely, it was a combination of both — plus the simple realization that projects that are based on ideological grounds, rather than commercial imperatives, usually have greater leeway for visual experimentation and a reduced incidence of editorial interference.

Whatever the reason, it wasn't the money. It's doubtful whether the fees for designing *The New Leader*, or the one or two other political journals that Lubalin designed, such as *Change Magazine* (full title *Change in Higher Education*) (fig.104), and *Africa Report* (fig.105), which was published by the African-American Institute (three issues, 1970—71), would have shown a profit. But as we have seen, profit was not Lubalin's primary motivation.

One of the most celebrated projects undertaken by Lubalin was his ad campaign for *Ebony* magazine. Founded by John H. Johnson and published continuously since 1945, *Ebony* is a monthly publication aimed at the African-American population. The poet Langston Hughes wrote in the magazine in 1965: **'Though America was slow to realize it, the world was not entirely white. It was predominantly colored — and what is right for the white nations is not always right for the colored nations. Indeed, in 1945 America was being forced for the first time to carefully examine the values of human dignity proclaimed in its own constitution, and to begin practicing, however grudgingly, those ideals to which it had been giving lip service for generations. As to that world within a world of Black-Americans, new understandings had to be developed. At this crucial period, fortunately, along came Ebony, whose very name means Black, to help America better understand ourselves and itself.'**

In 1968, four years after he left Sudler & Hennessey, Lubalin produced a scintillating ad campaign to encourage corporations and advertisers to book ad space in *Ebony* (pp.98—101). Despite the magazine's vast readership, and the growing economic power of black America, big corporate spenders failed to include *Ebony* in their advertising plans.

Lubalin adopted a confrontational approach. He art-directed and co-wrote a series of ads that used gripping photography and provocative headlines to address entrenched views on race in post-war America. A portrait of a caricature, cigar-chomping white supremacist (his eyes obliterated by reflections on his spectacles and his wide-brimmed, black hat imparting a sense of judgmental dread) is accompanied by the headline, 'Some of our best friends are bigots' (p.99). Another ad shows a handsome African-American man with thick, black-rimmed spectacles; draped over his shoulder in a patronizing manner is a large, white hand with a cigar wedged between two fingers. The headline reads, 'You don't have to love us. Just give us your business' (p.98).

To modern eyes, the *Ebony* ads exhibit Lubalin's customary precision and balance. Image and type sit in dovetailed harmony. The viewer's eye is obediently directed around the page as if choreographed by the designer himself. The photography by Irv Barht — a longtime associate

107. On behalf of the American
Heritage Foundation, Grey Advertising
invited Herb Lubalin to design a poster
to encourage voter registration in
time for the 1964 presidential election.
Lubalin said that he designed the
poster using a 'nostalgic type treatment,
trying to recapture the good old days
when Election Day and Fourth of July
were exciting holidays, with bands and
firecrackers … I wanted to capture
that 1920s feeling.' Lubalin and Grey
liked the poster, but it was rejected by
the Foundation on the grounds that it
was 'killing the words and producing
something too old-fashioned that would
not interest anyone.' Lubalin decided
to run the ad as a public service ad. It
was picked up by a printer and inserted
in graphic design magazines. Lettering:
Tom Carnase. Date c. 1968.

of Lubalin — is particularly striking. The copy's eagerness to show how black people are really 'just like us', reveals a mildly patronizing tone that would be unacceptable today, yet for the time they show a remarkable bravery.

The *Ebony* ads were produced in 1968, the year in which Dr. Martin Luther King was assassinated, and against the backdrop of the Civil Rights movement. The Civil Rights Act had been passed four years earlier, but race was still a contentious issue, so this was not a normal, run-of-the-mill ad campaign. By taking it on, Lubalin was risking disapproval from more conventional clients.

Herb Lubalin's political sensibility was formed out of his familial and social upbringing, the times he lived in, and his innate sense of fairness and probity. There are many examples of acts of personal kindness (an odd and unexpected accompaniment to his famous brusqueness). The American graphic designer and biographer of Lou Dorfsman, Dick Hess, opened his studio in 1965. He had a variety of corporate and editorial clients, and tells a story that shows Lubalin in an interesting and benign light: **'A client and I had a disagreement. It was something I felt strongly about and could not in all conscience do what I was asked to do. The client went to see Herb and he heard her story. "Just a moment", he asked, "isn't Dick Hess designing for you?" — at which point he picked up the phone and called me. I explained that if she's in his office, she wasn't my client any more. Instead, he turned to her and said: "You're damn lucky that Dick is designing for you and it's my advice that you go back and apologize to him". I had a $40,000-a-year guarantee with this client, and I don't know anyone else who would have done that.'**

24

The Final Years

Herb Lubalin's notoriously gruff demeanour meant that he found it difficult to give praise to junior staff — a significant failing in a profession where encouragement and recognition are the food that gives sustenance to frail creative egos. Even his son, Peter, said that it was unusual to have conversations with his taciturn father. When I set out to interview people for this book, I wondered if I might find hostility among the people who knew him, or at best, indifference. Not so. In fact, I've rarely encountered anyone as universally loved as Herb Lubalin, and although people who knew him are quick to point out his shortcomings, these views are always delivered with a palpable sense of affection and respect.

The younger designers who joined his studio in the final years of Lubalin's life regarded him as a benign, if somewhat remote, father figure who they were proud to work for. An incident recalled by Kevin Gatta, a designer who worked in the Lubalin studio from 1979 onwards, illustrates this aspect of Lubalin's character: **'He took us on a studio trip to the country, near Millerton where he lived with Rhoda, his wife. It was a private development with a clubhouse you could hire. Wives and partners were invited, too. We had dinner, went for walks in the snow and hung out. It wasn't boring but there was nothing to do. The only entertainment we had was an early Betamax player and in the evening we could watch movies — this was really something back then. Movies at home — amazing. Then someone lit up some pot. I'm sitting on the floor next to Herb. When it gets passed to me I say no — I never was a pot smoker — and I pass it to Herb. He passes it straight on to the person next to him without smoking it himself. Then he turns to me and says "Wise choice, my boy".'**

Lubalin's paternalism didn't extend only to the young men he employed; he was also an active recruiter of female designers and administrative staff, and in this respect,

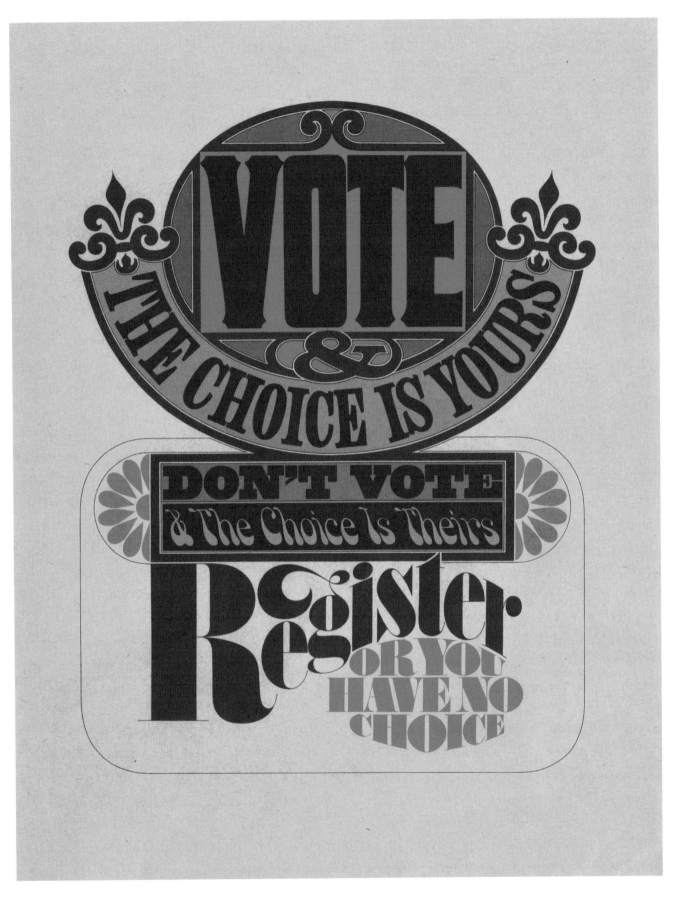

108. Promotional item for *Diners Club* magazine. Shown is a special one-off edition produced to attract advertising. Herb Lubalin (top right) can be seen holding the 'twisted T-square' he was given as a gift by his staff in recognition of his refusal to use this essential tool from the pre-computerized era of design. Also shown is Roger Ferriter (bottom right), another key Lubalin collaborator over the years. Ferriter is widely credited with devising the name, logo and packaging design for the L'eggs dispenser that he developed while working for Lubalin, Smith, Carnase. Later he became art director at Burson-Marsteller and taught graphic design at the School of Visual Arts in New York. Photographer: Irv Bahrt. Client: Diners Club. Date: 1970.

109. An unusually formal portrait of Herb Lubalin. Photographer and date unknown.

too, he inspired affection. In a profile written by Marion Muller and published in *U&lc* (while Lubalin was still editor), it is noted that: **'Lubalin operates from a code of decency few people understand: he was an "equal-opportunity employer" long before those words were invented. He hired women designers, artists and administrators before any one of them had her consciousness raised. He initiated the Ms. section of U&lc as a showcase for women in graphics. But don't, unless you enjoy severe indigestion, get him started on Women's Lib in the midst of a nice quiet dinner.'**

Lubalin may not have been a champion of feminism, and he had a reputation as an ardent admirer of feminine beauty and female sexual attraction, yet he inspired great affection from the women in his working life. As we have seen, his advocacy of the designer Annegret Beier went beyond mere tokenism. The designer Louise Fili speaks fondly of her time with Lubalin, and the legacy of his decorative, virtuoso style can be seen today in her highly cultured work. But of all the professional female relationships in his life, none seem to have deeper roots than the bond he formed with Fay Barrows, his assistant from Sudler & Hennessey days. She was privy to a side of Lubalin's life and character that few others saw: **'When I left S&H, our relationship continued. We spent many weekends at his home (p.77, fig.123). His wife Sylvia attended Cooper Union and was an extremely talented painter. My girls spent time splashing in the pool with their third child, who had cerebral palsy. He died when he was around 20. Herb would leave the office most evenings on time to help with his son, whom he adored.'**

All of the former Lubalin employees that I spoke to — male and female — claim to have learned a great deal about design from him, but mostly by osmosis rather than direct instruction. For much of his adult life, Lubalin taught design as well as practised it. According to New York designer Carin Goldberg, however, he was an unsatisfactory teacher: **'We met for class at Herb's office once a week and sat around a large mahogany table feeling a bit like we were at the doctor's office waiting for a checkup. Herb was not a chatty guy. He wasn't necessarily intimidating or cold, but he lacked the ability to connect with us. I recall one assignment — design something about "color". Looking back, that assignment was kind**

of vague. I recall that most of us were a bit lost and Herb wasn't the kind of guy to take us through the process. I guess Herb might be considered one of those great designers who shouldn't teach.'**

He may not have been a great teacher, but as with so many smart human beings, Lubalin realized one of the fundamental truths of teaching: it is a two-way process, and teachers learn from pupils as much as pupils learn from teachers. In 1969, writer John Durniak sat in on one of Lubalin's classes. It was called Graphic Arts for the Architect. He wrote: **'Of all the things that go on during the week, Lubalin is most intrigued with his college class. "I learn more from them than they do from me," he states about the architectural students. Lubalin does not hide the fact that he is a frustrated architect.'**

By the late 1970s, Lubalin had reached the top rung on the ladder of design success: he was the recipient of many awards and accolades; a principal in a number of successful businesses; a star turn on the international lecture circuit; and globally recognized as a leading figure in typography and graphic design. His death at 63 cut short a career that was in its prime. He had been a lifelong smoker, and was described as a 'reluctant walker'. Apart from a fondness for swimming, he lived a sedentary existence crouched over his worktable. He died of cancer in the spring of 1981.

25

Herb Lubalin — The Legacy

Today, Herb Lubalin's work is disliked in some circles and venerated in others. His detractors dismiss his output as too decorative, or view him as a drily conventional figure, purely concerned with commercial norms. He did not write books or produce manifestos, and his early career in advertising, coupled with his relative lack of interest in European avant-garde art and design, did not endear him to critics and commentators in the 1990s, when 20th-century graphic design went under the critical microscope.

110. Visual identity, bespoke typefaces and graphic design by A2/SW/HK Scott Williams and Henrik Kubel. Typefaces are A2 Beckett and Monday, designed by Henrik Kubel (A2-TYPE). Kubel is an admirer of Lubalin and cites him as an influence. Date: 2008 www.a2swhk.co.uk

111. British designer Rick Banks designed the typeface Bella in the classical French Didot style with what he describes as an added 'geometric twist'. The typeface is based on

'letterforms of American typographers: John Pistilli and Herb Lubalin, and Swiss typographer Jan Tschichold.' The layout is also reminiscent of the composition in Avant Garde #1, (page 272 in this book). www.face37.com

112. The December 2009 issue of Creative Review posed the question, was Lubalin 'behind the current predilection for elaborately decorative typography?' http://bit.ly/x3Y7ww

110

As a consequence, there weren't any profiles of him in the journals offering historical and critical appraisals of graphic design such as *Eye* or *Émigré*. Lubalin became the Norman Rockwell of graphic design, respected but also neglected by design's commentariat.

During the 1990s, if Lubalin was mentioned at all, it was as a representative of the best tradition of ideas-led and craft-based commercial graphic design. He was championed by conventional designers unimpressed with the new, computerized generation of designers who, in their eyes, were heretics threatening to tear down the citadel of professionalism and decorum. Typical of this viewpoint was an article written by British designer Mark Wickens, a partner in a successful mainstream UK design group called Wickens Tutt Southgate. Writing in *Campaign* (August 1990), the British advertising journal, he eulogized Lubalin's dedication to craft and his high-powered conceptual skills, but then added: **'It is a pity I cannot say the same of today's design efforts where computers have been used, I often felt that the computer has been used for the computer's sake alone and to hell with everything, including the message and the client.'**

In sharp contrast to Lubalin stood the archetypal 1990s designer Tibor Kalman, the hero of a new generation of radical designers who publicly questioned the role of design in culture. The designer Paula Scher recalls meeting Kalman shortly after Lubalin's death. It was clear to her that Kalman regarded Lubalin as an outdated figure barely worthy of consideration and an object of derision.

In the years after his death, Lubalin fell out of fashion. His imagistic approach to typography and his strong emphasis on craft and meticulous execution were elbowed aside by the onrush of computerized design that allowed designers to create instantly many of the effects that he and his accomplices took months to painstakingly achieve.

Yet even as his fashionability waned, Lubalin had influential supporters. Steven Heller, who knew him personally, and Ellen Lupton, who curated a Lubalin show at Cooper Union in 1987, both wrote perceptively about him during periods when he was out of vogue. And today, Lubalin is venerated by a new generation of young, type-obsessed graphic designers who see him as the father of conceptual typography and a grand master of American Graphic Expressionism.

The Lubalin revival started at the beginning of the new millennium. Avant Garde Gothic began to appear with perplexing frequency. Hip young designers in Europe were using Lubalin typefaces again. Spencerian script became fashionable once more as a new generation of designers made elegant, quasi-Baroque typographic concoctions, reminiscent of Lubalin at his most exuberant (foremost in this group were Marian Bantjes and Alex Trochut). A number of mainly English design groups, such as Made Thought and Non-Format, revived a strand of Lubalin's work that had lain untouched during the digital upheaval of the previous decade — namely, his almost classical use of serif typefaces and his highly stylized and articulate use of typographic contrast. Suddenly, black letterforms on white backgrounds were everywhere; thick lines were partnered with ultra-thin lines; the Lubalin revival was on.

Among younger type designers, Lubalin appears to have retained his allure. The designer and type designer Henrik Kubel runs the much-admired London design studio A2/SW/HK and the type foundry A2-TYPE. For him, Lubalin is: **'A designer and letterer supreme! Ultimate master of curves. Creator of the tightest letter spacing ever done by hand. Scripts that make you green with envy. Inventor of never seen before ligatures. Swashes galore, and numerals so well designed that one has to sit down. Herb's work is a lesson in originality and craft on the highest level. If you want to learn the art of type and lettering — look here first.'** (fig. 110)

British type designer Rick Banks designed the typeface Bella, which he described as **'based on letterforms of American typographers: John Pistilli and Herb Lubalin, and Swiss typographer Jan Tschichold. Lubalin is important for many reasons. It's his sheer simplicity, mixed with playfulness, that's always underpinned by a concise and brilliant idea. Something I always try and aim for.'** (fig. 111)

U.S. designers also rediscovered the well-schooled typographic aesthetic of Lubalin. Elegant serifs and tight letterspacing have made a comeback. A member of the LA design group AdamsMorioka wrote on their *Burning Settlers* blog: **'When I was in school, I was told that Herb Lubalin, one of ITC's founders, was rotting in hell for ITC Garamond. And I've walked around with a snobby disdain for all ITC fonts since then. Like this, "Well, I'm sure they**

work for some people, but I could never". Something, however, has gone horribly wrong. I look at Lubalin and Tom Carnase's work and find myself loving the flamboyant thicks and thins, swashes, and extreme x-height. I have a strong desire to use ITC Firenze on everything, including body copy.

The New York-based designer, Justin Thomas Kay, has produced work that owes a debt to Lubalin's pioneering efforts in the 1970s. In 2009, he told the magazine *Creative Review*: 'I had a professor who saw my background in illustration as well as my obsession with learning as much as I possibly could about working with type. He gave me a copy of the "blue Lubalin bible" [Peckolick and Snyder: Herb Lubalin] and I became immediately enthralled with the way he made type speak as the main illustrated element in his work.'

In the early years of the new millennium, the Lubalin Study Center at Cooper Union started to be talked about as a fashionable destination for designers visiting New York, and I was repeatedly struck by the number of students I met in European design schools — not to mention their tutors — who held Lubalin in the highest regard. What was the attraction to a younger generation?

It was an attraction I had once shared, but that had been eclipsed by the forces that shaped 1990s graphic design: Swiss neo-modernism; the rise of a new sort of 'critical' designer typified by Tibor Kalman; a new mutant strain that had grown out of postmodern theory. I remember throwing away my yellowing copies of *U&lc*, and replacing them with editions of *Eye* and *Émigré*. April Greiman seemed more interesting than Paul Rand; Wolfgang Weingart preferable to Herb Lubalin.

So I went back hesitantly to the work of Lubalin, and began a journey of rediscovery that resulted in the book you are currently holding. It has been an odd journey — a journey back into my own past and the formative days of my life as a graphic designer, but also a journey into the private life of a private man.

I discovered many things on this journey. I discovered that Lubalin was a far more intriguing and unconventional figure than I had imagined. His reputation as a purely commercial designer turned out to be largely false. In fact, much to the despair of his many studio partners, Lubalin repeatedly took on work for love not money. The

proprietors of small, penniless left-wing journals were astonished to find him willing not only to design their publications himself, but also to work within their measly budgets. His political views were not those of a curmudgeonly graphic designer resentful of new trends and new designers. He was a champion of young talent, even if he didn't always remember to tell them what he thought was good about their work. His association with his friend, the editor and publisher Ralph Ginzburg, resulted in a body of work that has few equals in the history of radical 20th-century publishing. Lubalin was the designer and art director of a trio of iconoclastic magazines — *Eros*, *Fact* and *Avant Garde* — that flouted the moral codes of repressive pre-counterculture America, and resulted in Ginzburg's imprisonment. On closer inspection of his life and work, Herb Lubalin turns out to be, if not exactly a revolutionary figure, then a much more progressive individual than his reputation encourages us to believe.

But in the final analysis, Herb Lubalin was happy to be known as just a graphic designer. He was not enslaved to dogma, and he believed in a form of typographic design that required the active participation of his audience. It is almost impossible to find examples of his work that are not technically perfect, both in execution and construction, and as the story of his rather short life unfolds, it is plain to see why he inspired such loyalty and affection among those who knew him, and why today he has a new following made up of thousands of people who were born after his death.

Coda

Herb Lubalin's widow Rhoda told me a story about her husband that surprised me, and has surprised his former associates who I have told it to. He turned to her one day and said: 'As soon as I retire, I want to paint'. Who would have guessed that this virtuoso performer of commercial graphic design had a secret desire to paint? He was remarkable among leading figures in American graphic design for his apparent lack of interest in fine art. But it seems that the skinny kid who impressed his tutors at the Cooper Union with his skill as a calligrapher had other reservoirs of passion and interest that he kept to himself.

113—5. Family portraits of Herb Lubalin and his twin brother Irwin as children. The brothers maintained a close relationship throughout their lives, but they were temperamentally different. Herb was quiet and taciturn; Irwin extrovert and talkative. Irwin went into business and became a successful executive at Avnet, a distributor of computer equipment. Herb became one of the most celebrated graphic designers of his generation. All photographs kindly supplied by Peter Lubalin.

116. Labor Day weekend, 1959. From left to right: Peter Lubalin; Sylvia Lubalin, Herb Lubalin's first wife; David

Lubalin, Herb Lubalin's youngest son; Herb Lubalin (with paddle); Ceil and Milt Ackoff with their two children; Carl Fischer with wife Marilyn and children Kim and Douglas; Ernie Smith (with paddle) and Fay (Smith) Barrows (with umbrella). Photograph kindly supplied by Carl Fischer.

117. Standing, back row: Sylvia Lubalin, Carl Fischer (in mask), Herb Lubalin, Fay Smith Barrows, Robert Lubalin, unknown person, unknown person, Ceil Ackoff, Milt Ackoff. Seated, middle row: David Lubalin, Marilyn Fischer, Ernie Smith. Photograph kindly supplied by Carl Fischer.

118

119

120

76

118. 'The Gladiators' — a self-named group of friends in the advertising business. According to Carl Fischer, the group met on Wednesday nights at a Russian baths off Times Square for 'very minor gym work, a swim, a steam room, and a massage. Afterwards the group had dinner at a different place each week. The best part, of course, was the shop-talk and gossip and complaints about clients. We talked ceaselessly about work; we were all fascinated by what we were doing. There was a special camaraderie in that group. There would seem to be an instinctive need for men to get together without women.

The meetings continued for many years.' Standing, left to right: Dan Wynn, Roy Kuhlman, Lorenzo Arranz, Ernie Smith, Pete Palazzo. Seated, left to right: Carl Fischer, Herb Lubalin, Milt Ackoff.

119. 'The Gladiators Golden Jock Award'. Carl Fischer notes: 'Ernie Smith dreamed up this award, which was given out each month for almost any reason.' Photographs kindly supplied by Carl Fischer.

120. Advert on the front page of *The New York Times*, paid for by Lubalin studio staff to celebrate his 59th birthday. Note the phonetic spelling of Lubalin's name: 'Loobalin.'

121. Herb Lubalin and staff in front of the 223 East 31st Street office (c. 1976). From left to right: Eloise Coleman, Herb Lubalin, Ann Turner, Glenda Spencer, Louise Fili. Photograph kindly supplied by Louise Fili.

122. Letterhead for Herb Lubalin's private address, No. 9, MacDougal Alley, Greenwich Village, New York City.

123. The Lubalin residence in MacDougal Alley today. Built in the 1830s to house the horses of the gentry living in nearby Washington Square Park, a century later these buildings were turned into artists' studios. The house was extensively renovated and

redesigned by Lubalin. Jackson Pollock was a previous occupant. Photograph by Alexander Tochilovsky.

124. A photograph of Herb Lubalin in casual attire, probably taken at his country home. Photographer unknown.

let's talk type

let's talk type
let's talk type

ADV
ERTIS
ING

nationally advertised
ca shorts, fabulous
straw and vinyl bags,
nationally advertised
Miss and Half-Size
Cannon printed beach towels,
18" charcoal broilers, 10 lb.
bags of charcoal briquettes
and, for all the extra things
you bought, stand-up or folding zipper travel bags, Dart's
has everything you need for
fun, at prices it's fun to pay.
For your holiday pleasure,
we'll be open all day July 4th.

let's talk type let type talk

Some ads must whisper, some must shout. But whatever the tone of voice, creative typography speaks with a distinction that sets your advertising above the clamor of competing messages. If you share our interest in good typography, and the other creative tools that work with it, we would welcome the opportunity to show you how we at Sudler & Hennessey ● ● ●

In wooing a woman or a customer no single technique has yet been invented that, to our knowledge, is infallible. And yet the advertising business seems to develop periodic passions for a single font of wisdom. Unfortunately, when all products are dressed alike in a single advertising style and their messages addressed alike to all customers, their individual notes of me-me-me become indistinguishable in the chorus of me-toos. We don't believe in this kind of type-casting. To us, the heart of each ad is a simple, vital, selling idea. To convey it, our illustration can be art, photography or type: our sell can be soft or hard, our copy long or short. It takes all types. Call SH&L

IT TAKES ALL TYPES

1. Let's Talk Type, Let Type Talk
Trade journal ad promoting the advertising agency Sudler & Hennessey, where Herb Lubalin worked from 1945 until 1964. As well as being the agency's art director, Lubalin frequently wrote copy for the ads he designed. The concept of 'talking type' encapsulates his typographic ethos. Lettering: John Pistilli. Date: 1959.

2. It Takes All Types
Trade press ad eulogizing the benefits of commissioning Sudler, Hennessey & Lubalin. Herb Lubalin was made a partner in the 'consumer advertising arm' of S&H (p.86, fig.8). In this ad, Lubalin demonstrates the conceptual power inherent in typography. The message is: don't be typecast. The ad shows Lubalin's love of Victoriana, illustration and humour. Typographic illustrations: Gerry Gersten. Date: 1962.

NOVEMBER/DECEMBER **ca'62** PRICE: SIX DOLLARS

The Distinguished Jury for the Third Annual Exhibition of Communication Art

Bob Blanchard

Lou Dorfsman

Allan Fleming

Bob Freeman

Herb Lubalin

Fred Papert

Art Paul

Jack Roberts

HERB LUBALIN/CARL FISCHER

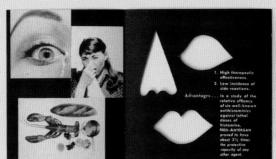

A highly effective antihistaminic agent

3. CA'62
Front cover of magazine titled 'The Journal of Commercial Art' (now 'Communication Arts') showing jury members for 'Third Annual Exhibition of Communication Art.' The police 'mugshot' approach is typical of Lubalin's irreverent wit. Jury members include: Lou Dorfsman, Allan Fleming, Art Paul, and a seedy looking Herb Lubalin. Design: Herb Lubalin. Photography: Carl Fischer. Date: 1962.

4. A highly effective antihistaminic ...
Front cover and opened-out reverse of die-cut folder for Neo-Antergan, an antihistamine. Agency: Sudler & Hennessey. Client: Sharpe & Dohme. Date: 1954.

5. Holiday New York
Typographic magazine cover. Agency: Sudler & Hennessey. Date: 1959.

6. When the appetite is in control ...
Front of mailer for Altepose, a product designed to suppress the appetite. Model is Fay Barrows. Photographer: Carl Fischer. Agency: Sudler & Hennessey. Client: Sharpe & Dohme. Date: 1950s.

7. Urecoline Chloride
Cover and pages for 6-page mailer for Urecoline Chloride. Yet again Fay Barrows is the model. Agency: Sudler & Hennessey. Client: Sharpe & Dohme. Date: 1950s.

8

SH&L Expanded-redesign of
a familiar face. A more flexible version of S&H, long
a favorite of people who
work with fine design.
You can specify SH&L for
a wide range of uses from small
space campaigns to large corporate image projects. We
offer a Bold Face (for impact), Oblique (new ways of viewing old problems), and Casual (no straining for mere effect).
For a full showing, call Herb Lubalin at Plaza 1 4250, or
write him c/o SH&L, 130 E. 59th Street, New York 22, N.Y.

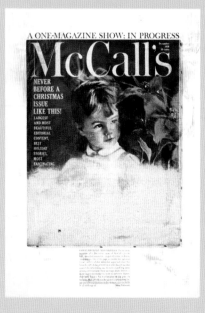

10

11

12

13

8. Expanded redesign of ...
Trade press ad announcing arrival of Sudler, Hennessey & Lubalin. The text wittily promotes SH&L using the language of typeface specification. The design incorporates many familiar Lubalin stylistic devices: ornate ampersands; contrast between thick and thin lines; blocks of type engineered to fit unusual spaces. The lettering is by John Pistilli, head of lettering design at S&H. Born in 1925, Pistilli graduated from the Jean Morgan School of Art in New York, where he studied lettering under J. Albert Cavanaugh (author of the book *Lettering & Alphabets*, Dover, 1955). Pistilli died in 2003. He was one of Herb Lubalin's most important collaborators. Date: 1959.

9. McCall's
Advertisement designed to attract advertisers to Christmas issue of *McCall's* magazine, a monthly women's journal that enjoyed huge popularity in the United States throughout the first half of the 20th century, peaking at a readership of 8.4 million in the early 1960s. Design: Herb Lubalin and Bernie Zlotnick. Photographer: Irv Bahrt. Agency: Sudler & Hennessey. Date: 1959.

10. Leap year
Press ad for *McCall's* magazine. Lubalin's use of 'leaping' type expresses the notion of a 'leap year'; note the characteristic way he allows both words to be formed from the same letters. Photographer: Irv Bahrt. Agency: Sudler & Hennessey. Date: 1959.

11. S&H, Design and Art Division of ...
Trade ad announcing the addition of Lubalin's name to the Sudler & Hennessey name, and offering a 'personalized design service for special Advertising'. By listing the names of his co-workers, Lubalin goes against the prevailing trend in advertising to downgrade the importance of the individual, a trend he abhorred. Date: c. 1959.

12. Awards are nice. Sales are nicer
Trade press ad for Sudler & Hennessey. Design: Herb Lubalin and George Lois. Date: 1958.

13. The language of ...
Trade press ad for Sudler & Hennessey. Date: 1958.

If advertising isn't men

norable, it doesn't sell!

What makes it memorable?
Creative people! What makes
it sell? Fresh ideas! Who
makes it their business?...

SH&L!

Design and Art Division of
Sudler & Hennessey, Inc.
Telephone: PLaza 1-1250

14. If advertising isn't memorable ...
Trade journal ad promoting SH&L,
the design and art division of Sudler &
Hennessey. It was customary to use
S&H personnel as models in press ads.
The model is Clarence O. Sacks, an
artist and illustrator employed in the
S&H 'bull-pen'. During the 1950s, 'Cal'
Sacks was frequently used as a model
for many self-promotion ads for S&H,
and in ads for clients. According to Fay
Barrows, Lubalin's assistant at the time,
Sacks had a droll sense of humour. He
can be seen playing with a Slinky on
his head (p. 23, fig.37). Photographer:
Irv Bahrt. Date: c. 1959.

The Fourth of July means picnics and parks, beaches and boating, the whole family going places together. Of course you'll go by car, and of course you'll drive carefully. But the other fellow might not be so smart. So tomorrow, no matter where you go and no matter what you do, do it with that extra touch of caution. You'll like the leisurely pace, and you'll come home as happy as you left. And by the way, when you're on your way, stop in at Carr's to buy whatever you forgot to pack: men's nationally advertised bathing trunks, tots' and girls' swim suits, Banlon knit men's sportshirts, men's nationally advertised Jamaica shorts, fabulous summer straw and vinyl handbags, nationally advertised Junior Miss and Half-Size dresses, Cannon printed beach towels, 18" charcoal braziers, 10 lb. bags of charcoal briquettes and, for all the extra things you bought, stand-up or folding zipper travel bags. Carr's has everything you need for fun, at prices it's fun to pay. For your holiday pleasure, we'll be open all day July 4th.

GOES ANYWHERE: the world's best 4-wheel drive takes the Land-Rover over any terrain, up and down incredible 45°-plus grades, through brush, swamp and desert. Yet on the highway, it cruises easily and comfortably at touring speeds. **DOES ANYTHING:** hauls, tows, operates portable and stationary machinery from three power take-off points. The Land-Rover has proved indispensable in agriculture, industry and private use around the world, in the armed services of over 23 countries and the police forces of 31. **LAND-ROVER** offers a wide range of body styles in two chassis lengths, plus a choice of gasoline or diesel engines. High and low gear ratios give a total of eight speeds forward and two reverse. Test-drive the Land-Rover to see for yourself why it is called "the world's most versatile vehicle."

THE ROVER MOTOR COMPANY OF NORTH AMERICA LIMITED, 373 SHAW ROAD, SOUTH SAN FRANCISCO, CALIFORNIA

15. The fourth of July means picnics ...
Newspaper ad informing customers that Carr's department store is open on 4th July, a U.S. national holiday. Carr's was an imaginative and bold commissioner of design. The Czech-born designer Ladislav Sutnar worked for them. Photograph: Carl Fischer. Agency: Sudler & Hennessey. Client: Carr's Department Store. Date: c. 1958.

16. Goes anywhere
Newspaper ad announcing the versatility of Land Rover vehicles. Note the trademark Lubalin block of justified type. The effect is effortless and typifies his meticulous approach to typographic craft. Photographer: Michael Burns. Agency: Sudler & Hennessey. Client: Rover Motor Company of North America. Date: 1960.

**"But he cuts off his nose
to spite his face!"**

"Why does he do it, Doctor? That man is
obsessed with his corporate image and
yet he continually presents less than his
best face to the public.

"He spends millions of dollars for advertising space and as little as he can for
what fills that space. We come up with
great ideas. He buys them. We present
estimates. He slashes them. Between the
great ideas and the great ads a great deal
gets lost in the translation.

"He's actually more concerned with the
charge for photostats than the charge
people will get from his advertising. In
television, the syndrome is the same
with the symptoms on a much larger
scale. And in point-of-sale and direct
mail, his company appearance is even
more embarrassing.

"Sure, I realize that he has a strong urge
for self-destruction. I know it's his problem but what can be done to help him?"

Psychiatry might help. But it's probably
too late. You will have to get him to face
the facts of life. That there's nothing as
expensive as advertising that just misses.
SH&L has helped convince men like this
to take a new look at their advertising.
Call Dr. Lubalin at PL 1-1250 or leave
a message with his nurse.

A straight line is the shortest distance between advertiser and consumer...

Sudler & Hennessey, Inc.,
130 East 59th Street,
New York City, U.S.A.
PLaza 1-1250

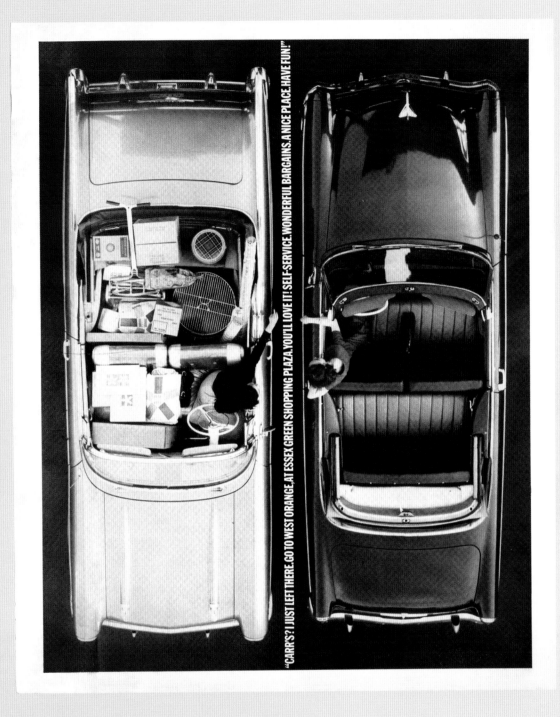

"CARR'S? I JUST LEFT THERE. GO TO WEST ORANGE, AT ESSEX GREEN SHOPPING PLAZA. YOU'LL LOVE IT! SELF-SERVICE. WONDERFUL BARGAINS. A NICE PLACE. HAVE FUN!"

17. But he cuts off his nose ...
Magazine ad promoting Sudler,
Hennessey & Lubalin. Witty text makes
fun of blinkered clients who fail to
promote themselves by diluting creativity and choosing to concentrate on
the 'charge for photostats' rather than
paying for creativity: this is a familiar
refrain that runs throughout Lubalin's
career. Clients who are convinced by
the ads' argument are invited to contact
'Dr Lubalin... or leave a message with
his nurse.' The model was Lazar (Louie)
Lenov, an employee of Sudler &
Hennessey. Photography: Carl Fischer.
Copywriting: Larry Muller. Date: 1963.

18. A straight line ...
Magazine ad illustrating the importance
of straight talking and immediacy,
a salient feature of the 'new advertising',
as practised by Sudler & Hennessey,
in contrast to the more flowery and
allusive advertising of previous decades.
Photography: Carl Fischer. Date: 1956.

19. Carr's? I just left there
Newspaper ad giving location of New
Jersey department store. Photographer:
Carl Fischer. Designers: Herb Lubalin
and George Lois. Agency: Sudler &
Hennessey. Client: Carr's Department
Store. Date: c. 1958.

21
22

20. Bentyl puts a quick stop to SPASM
One of the most famous Lubalin ads from his time at Sudler & Hennessey. It typifies his approach to expressive typography. Client: William S. Merrell Company. Photography: Carl Fischer. Agency: Sudler & Hennessey. Date: 1958.

21. Carr's has a clearance!
Newspaper ad. Designers: Herb Lubalin and George Lois. Agency: Sudler & Hennessey. Client: Carr's Department Store. Date: c. 1958.

22. 10/7/'61/1:50/880/hike!
Press ad for Ivy League Football on the radio. The drawing is by American illustrator John Groth, known for his depiction of combat. Agency: Sudler & Hennessey. Client: CBS. Date: 1960.

23. Break up cough
Another seminal Lubalin ad showing his trademark use of metaphoric type: in Lubalin's hands, the word 'cough' is shown disintegrating in a literal depiction of the medicine's ability to 'break up' congestion. Agency: Sudler & Hennessey. Client: Ciba Pharmaceuticals. Date: 1956.

break up cough

relax bronchioles, reduce histamine-induced congestion and irritation throughout the respiratory tract, liquefy thick, tenacious mucus. **PYRIBENZAMINE EXPECTORANT** with Ephedrine

ALSO AVAILABLE: PYRIBENZAMINE EXPECTORANT WITH CODEINE AND EPHEDRINE (EXEMPT NARCOTICS). PYRIBENZAMINE CITRATE (TRIPELENNAMINE CITRATE CIBA)

15 picas SQ HT.

24

25
26

96

Mother Brown
has survived
the Civil War, the
Spanish-American War,
World War I,
World War II,
the Korean War, and
the Vietnam War.

We hope
Mother Brown
lives long enough
to see peace.
But time
is running out.
Mother Brown
is 116 years old.

ZEBRA ASSOCIATES INC. ADVERTISING
1180 AVENUE OF THE AMERICAS
NEW YORK, N.Y. 10036

24. Hey mom, I want ...
Magazine ad for Tetrex. Agency Sudler &
Hennessey. Client: Bristol Laboratories.
Date: c. 1956.

25. A big fish story
Newspaper ad. Illustration: Bettman
Archive/Cal Sacks. Copywriting:
Florence Goodman. Agency: Sudler &
Hennessey. Client: CBS. Date: 1964.

26. He should have been a mother
Magazine ad promoting the CBS radio
show of Arthur Godfrey. When he
moved to television, Godfrey became
one of TV's most valuable stars,
generating millions of dollars in advertising each year. Godfrey's head is
superimposed on a reproduction
of Whistler's Mother, to emphasize his
homely radio persona. Copywriting:
Florence Goldman. Agency: Sudler &
Hennessey. Client: CBS. Date: 1964.

27. Mother Brown has survived ...
Magazine ad promoting Zebra
Associates Inc, the first U.S. advertising
agency formed by African-American and
white American owners. Photography:
Hugh Bell. Copywriting: Byron Barclay.
Agency: Lubalin, Smith, Carnase Inc.
Client: Zebra Associates. Date: 1970.

You don't have to love us.
Just give us your business.

The "us" we're talking about is Ebony. A magazine that reaches 43% of all Negro households in the country. 2,500,000 households every month. People with a median income of $6648 a year. Consumers who spend more of their income on food, liquor, home furnishings and personal-care items than white people of comparable income do.

Some advertisers have two things against us: First, Ebony doesn't whitewash any aspect of the Civil Rights struggle. We call it as *we* see it. Which is why the Negro

believes what he reads in Ebony.

And second, since some advertisers mistakenly consider the Ebony reader to be part of a mass market, they think they can reach him without us.

They're wrong. Take Lifebuoy, Dove and Dial. 3.9% of total homemakers buy Lifebuoy. 10.9% buy Dove. And 17.7% buy Dial. All three are advertised on television. But only Dial uses Ebony. The result is interesting. 1.6% of Ebony homemakers use Lifebuoy. 4.5% use Dove. But 21.3% use Dial.

What about print advertising? Well, no magazine on Campbell Soup's list reaches more than 8% of the nation's 23 million Negroes. And 82% of Ebony readers never see a copy of one of the most widely circulated magazines in the country. That's Life.

Today the Negro makes up 28% of the central-city aggregate population in 78 key cities. Today the Negro represents an estimated 45% of Rich's customers in Atlanta. 35% of Lit Brothers in Philadelphia. 45% of J. L. Hudson's in Detroit. 40% of Hecht's in Washington D.C. And he's being reached and persuaded by Ebony.

So don't let your personal feelings about Ebony color your business judgment. Add Ebony to your schedule. Not for love. But for money.

Ebony.
The magazine that gets to the heart of the Negro market.

Some of our best friends are bigots.

For years the American bigot has loudly defended his Jim Crow-given right to persecute the Negro. For years the bigot has gotten away with murder. But thanks to a Supreme Court that believes in liberty and justice for all, the bigot is at the end of his rope. Every day he finds it tougher to practice what he preaches. Maybe that's why he's screaming louder than ever.

Or maybe it's because 20,000,000 Negroes earn $30 billion a year, and make up 28% of the central city aggregate population in 78 key cities, and represent huge percentages of the customers in downtown stores and retail outlets all over the country.

Whatever the reason, we consider it pretty white of the bigot to sound off. Because the more he rants, the more he calls attention to the growing affluence and size of the Negro market. And who are we to feel unkindly about a rave review? Ebony gets to the heart of the Negro market.

For example, every month Ebony reaches 13% of the Negro households in the country: 2,500,000 households. Of which 34.1% of the male heads earn more than $10,000 a year. An audience that includes a large percentage of professional people, managers, and business owners. People with a median income of $6,648 a year. Consumers who spend more of their income on food, home furnishings, and personal-care items than white people of comparable income do.

Ebony does more than reach the Negro. It gets to him in a way that no white-oriented mass media could: with reports on Negro Masons, Negro Elks, Negro weddings, with editorials on separate-but-unequal school systems, white-only jobs, and black-only ghettoes. In other words, Ebony gives the Negro what he hungers for: identification and recognition as a person.

That's why advertising in Ebony moves goods and services. Can any businessman be prejudiced against that?

Ebony.
The magazine that gets to the heart of the Negro market.

28. You don't have to love us
Newspaper ad, part of a campaign for *Ebony* magazine, designed to encourage businesses to advertise in the magazine, a publication for African-Americans. These hard-hitting, full-page ads have a confrontational tone that seeks to challenge inherent prejudice and deeply rooted notions of discrimination. As well as acting as designer and art director, Herb Lubalin contributed to the copywriting; his acerbic wit can be detected in the provocative headlines. This was advertising done after Lubalin had left Sudler & Hennessey. By 1968, when these ads were published, Lubalin had been running his own studio for four years. Photography: Irv Bahrt/ Culver Pictures. Copywriting: Byron Barclay/Herb Lubalin. Client: *Ebony* Magazine/Wyse Advertising. Date: 1968.

29. Some of our best friends ...
Newspaper ad. Photography: Irv Bahrt/ Culver Pictures. Copywriting: Byron Barclay/Herb Lubalin. Client: *Ebony* Magazine/Wyse Advertising. Date: 1968.

Whatsamatta, don't you trust us?

For more than 25 years, Ebony has been getting to the heart of the Negro market: Business owners, managers, professionals, just people—people who buy razor blades.

To shave with.

Yet in Ebony's entire publishing history, we've never carried a page of advertising for a certain razor-blade manufacturer. White-oriented mass media has gotten all of the action.

That's a mistake. The Negro doesn't belong to a mass market. He's separate. As separate as centuries of Southern hospitality and Northern justice can make him. He thinks black, feels black, lives black. No lily-white commercial has much to say to him.

Neither do all-white print ads. The Negro ignores the publications they run in, because these publications ignore the Negro. Sure, the "First Negro Ever To…" rates an article in the slicks. But the *average* Negro is neither recognized nor understood.

Ebony understands Negroes. The kind who sit on the Supreme Court as well as the kind who sit on the front steps.

Because Ebony gives the Negro what he hungers for—status and recognition and understanding and the truth—Ebony reaches 2,500,000 households every month: People who live where 2 out of 3 of all retail sales are made. People who spend more of their income on personal-care items than white people of comparable income do.

With this kind of an audience, it's hard to understand why our razor-blade prospect—who never passes up a chance to look sharp, feel sharp, and be sharp—has never tried to reach the Negro. Maybe he thinks the heart of a $30-billion-a-year market isn't worth talking to. Or maybe he's afraid that anything he advertises in Ebony will be used against him.

Ebony. The magazine that gets to the heart of the Negro market.

When was the last time you saw a cotton-pickin' Negro?

Some advertisers' idea of the American Negro comes right out of Old Man River. Well, the Negro doesn't plant many taters or chop much cotton anymore. He cuts meat. He bakes bread. He makes automobiles. He practices medicine and law. He's changed. He's changing.

Despite these changes the Negro still lives differently from white people. Mostly because lots of white people still feel the same about the Negro.

For example, operators of restaurants and nightclubs aren't exactly putting out the red carpet for black patrons. So the Negro does most of his entertaining at home. That's why the Negro spends a greater percentage of his $30-billion-a-year income on food, alcoholic beverages, and home furnishings.

And because he isn't welcome in the suburbs—suburbanites have a colorful way to resort to choosing their neighbors—the Negro on the move heads for the city. The result: Negroes make up 28% of the central-city aggregate population in 25 key cities. In fact, 95% of the entire Negro population lives where 63% of all retail sales are made.

The Negro also responds differently to advertising. White-oriented advertising doesn't get to first base with him. But it's a different ball game with Negro-oriented advertising in a magazine written solely for Negroes: Ebony.

Every month Ebony reaches 2,500,000 households, of which 34.1% earn more than $10,000 a year. People with a median income of $6,648 a year. People who last year bought a greater percentage of home freezers than the readers of Life, Look, Holiday, Reader's Digest, Time, and The New Yorker. People who believe in Ebony because Ebony doesn't tell white lies about black problems. Ebony tells it like it is.

If you doubt the power and separateness of the Negro market, the extra buying power of the Ebony audience, the advantages of advertising the Negro in a medium that offers him recognition and identification, call Ebony. (New York, Wm. P. Grayson, V.P., 1270 Avenue of the Americas, JUdson 6-2911; Los Angeles, LeRoy Jeffries, V.P., 3600 Wilshire Boulevard, DUnkirk 3-5181; Chicago, Lincoln Hudson, Ad Mgr., 1820 S. Michigan Ave., CAlumet 5-1000.)

We'll send you some persuasive statistics in black and white.

Ebony.
The magazine that gets to the heart of the Negro market.

This Advertisement appeared in the
NEW YORK TIMES—October 19, 1967
and will also appear in
AD AGE—October 30, 1967

30. Whatsamatta, don't you trust us?
Produced in the same year that Dr. Martin Luther King Jr was assassinated and just four years after the Civil Rights Act had been passed, these ads have lost none of their original potency and still succeed in confronting ingrained bias. Photography: Irv Bahrt/Culver Pictures. Copywriting: Byron Barclay/Herb Lubalin. Client: *Ebony* Magazine/Wyse Advertising. Date: 1968.

31. When was the last …
Newspaper ad. Copywriting: Byron Barclay/Herb Lubalin. Client: *Ebony* Magazine/Wyse Advertising. Date: 1968.

TYPOGRAPHY

In the beginning God created the heaven and the earth.

genesis

1965 NATIONAL TYPE FACE DESIGN COMPETITION AWARD-WINNING TYPE FACE: BAKER SIGNET BY ARTHUR BAKER / SPONSORED BY: VISUAL GRAPHICS CORPORATION (MANUFACTURER OF THE PHOTO TYPOSITOR) / POSTER DESIGN: HERB LUBALIN / TYPOSITOR TYPOGRAPHY: AARON BURNS & COMPANY, DIVISION OF RAPID TYPOGRAPHERS, INC. / PRINTING: DRUM LITHOGRAPHERS, INC.

THIRTY DAYS HATH SEPTEMBER ( ),

APRIL ( ),JUNE AND ( )

NOVEMBER ( ); ALL THE REST HAVE

THIRTY-ONE ( ),( ),( ),

( ),( ),( ),( ),

EXCEPTING FEBRUARY ALONE ( ),

WHICH HATH BUT TWENTY-EIGHT, IN FINE,

TILL LEAP YEAR GIVES IT TWENTY-NINE.

Fair summer gently fades away.
And withering flowers foretel her doom.
Thus will earth's joys decay.
And bear us on to the tomb.

Though Nature smiles when comes her time,
And decks the fields in verdant green,
Yet in our cold New England clime
Few pleasant days this month are seen.

Fair Summer reigns o'er all the land
How mild and gentle is her sway.
She scatters with a liberal hand
Choice blessings round us every day.

Now sumber clouds o'erspread the skies,
And cast a gloom o'er hill and lea,
Cold is the wind, bleak storms arise,
And tune their mournful minstrelsy.

How fierce the wintry tempests howl,
How cheerless is the naked grove,
The skies assume an angry scowl,
And lakes and streamlets cease to move.

The dreary winter months are gone.
And Sol prolongs the hours of day.
But yet no music hails the morn,
No verdure clothes the leafless spring.

The blooming beauties of the spring
With balmy odors fill the air,
And birds with cheerful music sing,
To drive away corroding care.

How grateful is the cooling shade
To those who toil or roam the plain,
When Sol, in glowing robes arrayed,
Resumes o'er all his sultry reign.

Now leave the scenes of pampered wealth,
Nor breathe the city's noxious air,
And seek for vigor and for health
In verdant fields and woodlands fair.

Though blooming verdure smiles no more,
And dreary is the landscape round.
Yet autumn's rich and bounteous store
Cause joy and gladness to abound.

Another year its course has run.
And all its scenes forever fled.
How soon will mortal life be done
And we all numbered with the dead!

Yet time so rapidly moves on.
That snowy fields and wintry skies
Will like a phantom soon be gone,
And other scenes before us rise.

1965 NATIONAL TYPE FACE DESIGN COMPETITION AWARD WINNING TYPE FACE. JANA BY RICHARD D. JUENGER / SPONSORED BY: VISUAL GRAPHICS CORPORATION (MANUFACTURER OF THE PHOTO TYPOSITOR) / POSTER DESIGN: HERB LUBALIN / TYPOSITOR TYPOGRAPHY: AARON BURNS & COMPANY, DIVISION OF ANRIO TYPOGRAPHERS, INC. / PRINTING: DRUM LITHOGRAPHERS, INC.

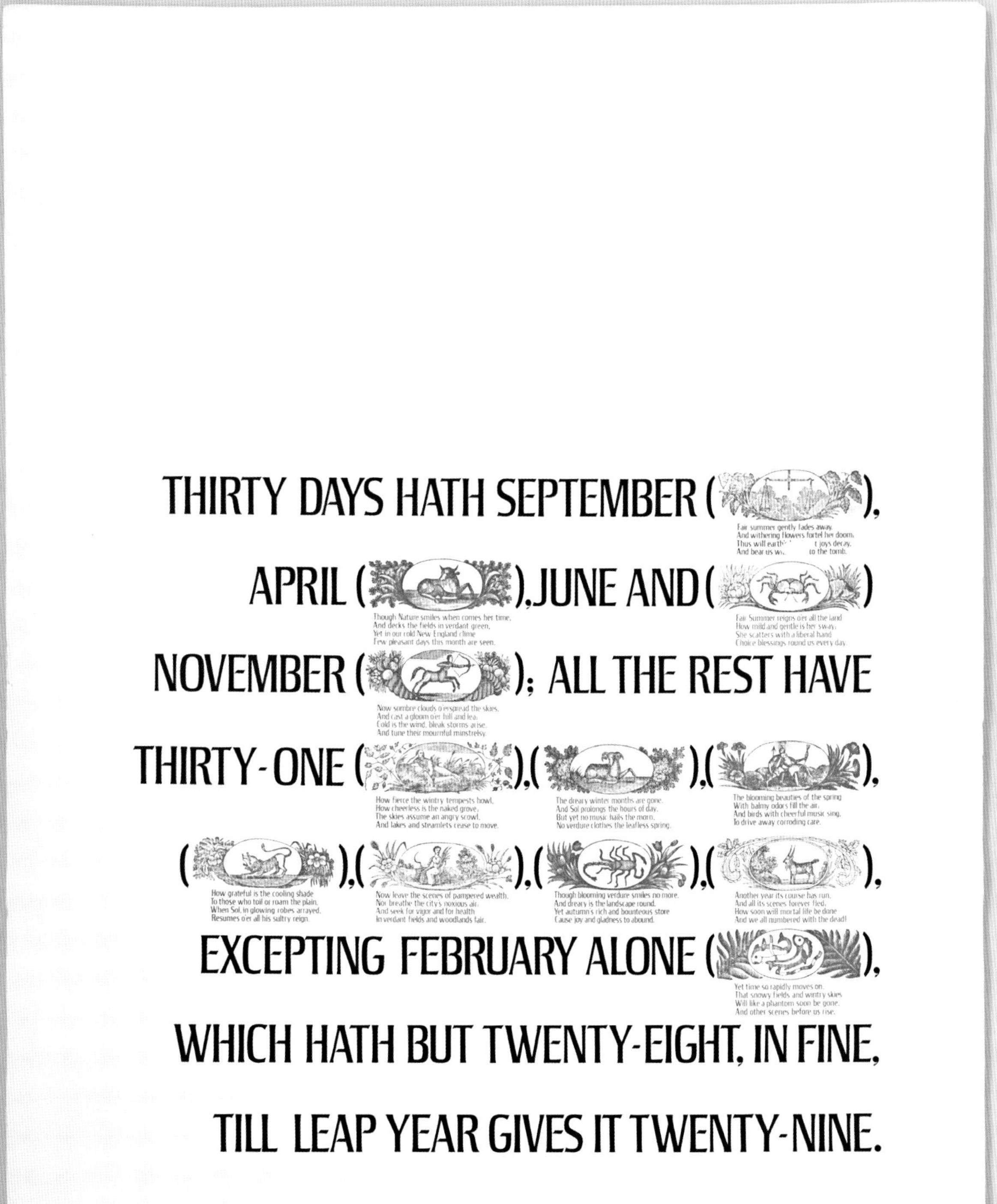

1. In the beginning ...

In 1965, and again in 1966, Herb Lubalin was commissioned to design a series of posters based on typefaces that had won the National Typeface Design Competition, an award scheme sponsored by Visual Graphics Corporation. VGC was a prominent US type foundry and typesetting machine manufacturer in the 1960s and 70s. VGC was created in 1963/4. It manufactured the PhotoTypositor, a popular headline phototypesetting machine. Herb Lubalin designed the VGC logo. The typeface competition served to create a library of unique VGC typefaces intended for the PhotoTypositor. The 1965 jury comprised Arnold Bank, Lucian Bernhard, Will Burtin, Alvin Eisenman, Paul Rand, Klaus Schmidt, Bradbury Thompson, Carl Zahn, and Herb Lubalin, Lubalin used the poster commission to show the versatility of contemporary typefaces, and how, with his various signature techniques such as use of contrast, scale, asymmetry, and manipulation, it was possible to create dynamic posters that used type as their main component. Poster shown here uses Baker Signet, a typeface designed by Arthur Baker, USA. Client: VSG. Date: 1965.

2. Thirty days hath September

Poster using Jana, a typeface by Richard D. Juenger, USA. Illustrations: Uncredited. Client: VGC. Date: 1965.

MARRIAGE

DON JUAN

THIS NATIONAL TYPE FACE DESIGN COMPETITION AWARD WINNING TYPE FACE, STETTLER BY MARTIN J. STETTLER. / SPONSORED BY: VISUAL GRAPHICS CORPORATION (MANUFACTURER OF THE PHOTO TYPOSITOR) / POSTER DESIGN: HERB LUBALIN / TYPOSITOR TYPOGRAPHY: AARON BURNS & COMPANY, DIVISION OF RAPID TYPOGRAPHERS, INC. / PRINTING: BRUM LITHOGRAPHERS, INC.

עדטמבבם עדםם םעז
ראז רעדם בעז.*

* Eat first, talk(ʿAaBbCcDdEeFfGgHhIiJjKkLlMmNnOoPpQqRrSsTtUuVvWwXxYyZz&\$1234567890°‰?!")later

1965 NATIONAL TYPE FACE DESIGN COMPETITION AWARD WINNING TYPE FACE: ANDRICH MINERVA BY VLADIMIR M. ANDRICH | SPONSORED BY: VISUAL GRAPHICS CORPORATION (MANUFACTURER OF THE PHOTO TYPOSITOR.) | POSTER DESIGN: HERB LUBALIN / TYPOSITOR TYPOGRAPHY: AARON BURNS & COMPANY, DIVISION OF RAPID TYPOGRAPHERS, INC. / PRINTING: DRUM LITHOGRAPHERS, INC.

3. Marriage

Poster using Stettler, an Optima-like typeface designed by Wayne J. Stettler, who also designed Neil Bold, a popular face in the 1970s (p.112, fig.12). Lubalin conveys the idea of marriage by flipping the second 'R' in marriage to face the first 'R'. This stylized use of visual metaphor is a Lubalin trademark, and this is one of the most celebrated uses of his approach. Client: VGC. Date: 1965.

4. Eat first, talk... later

Poster using Andrich Minerva, a typeface designed by Vladimir Andrich, who was also responsible for the fonts Cremona (1982) and Vladimir Script (1995). Unusually in this series of posters, Lubalin does not use the awarded typeface as his main typographic element; instead, he uses a bold version of a popular 19th-century Ashkenazi Hebrew type style, commonly referred to as 'Meruba'. Client: VGC. Date: 1965.

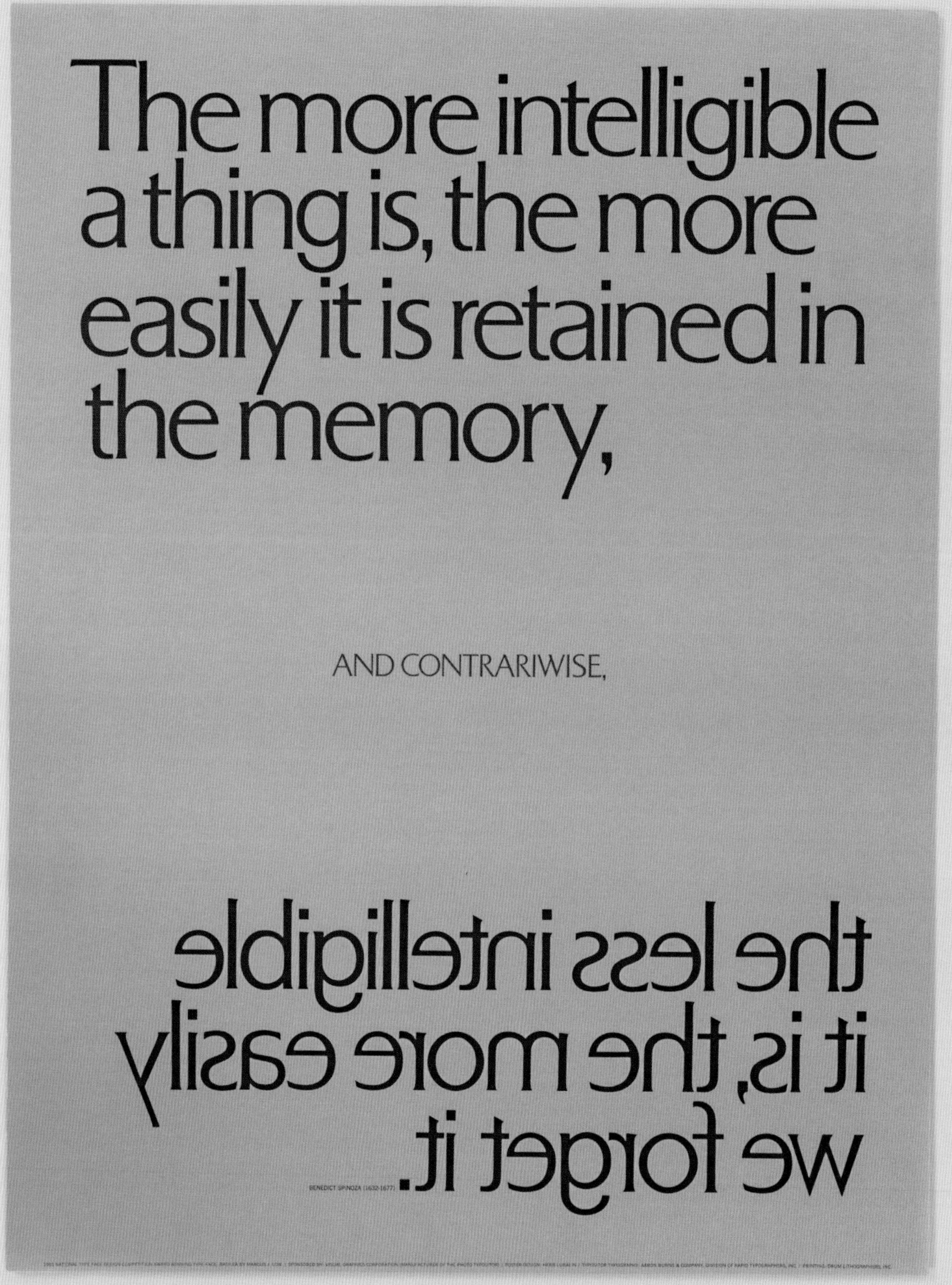

The more intelligible
a thing is, the more
easily it is retained in
the memory,

AND CONTRARIWISE,

the less intelligible
it is, the more easily
we forget it.

BENEDICT SPINOZA (1632-1677)

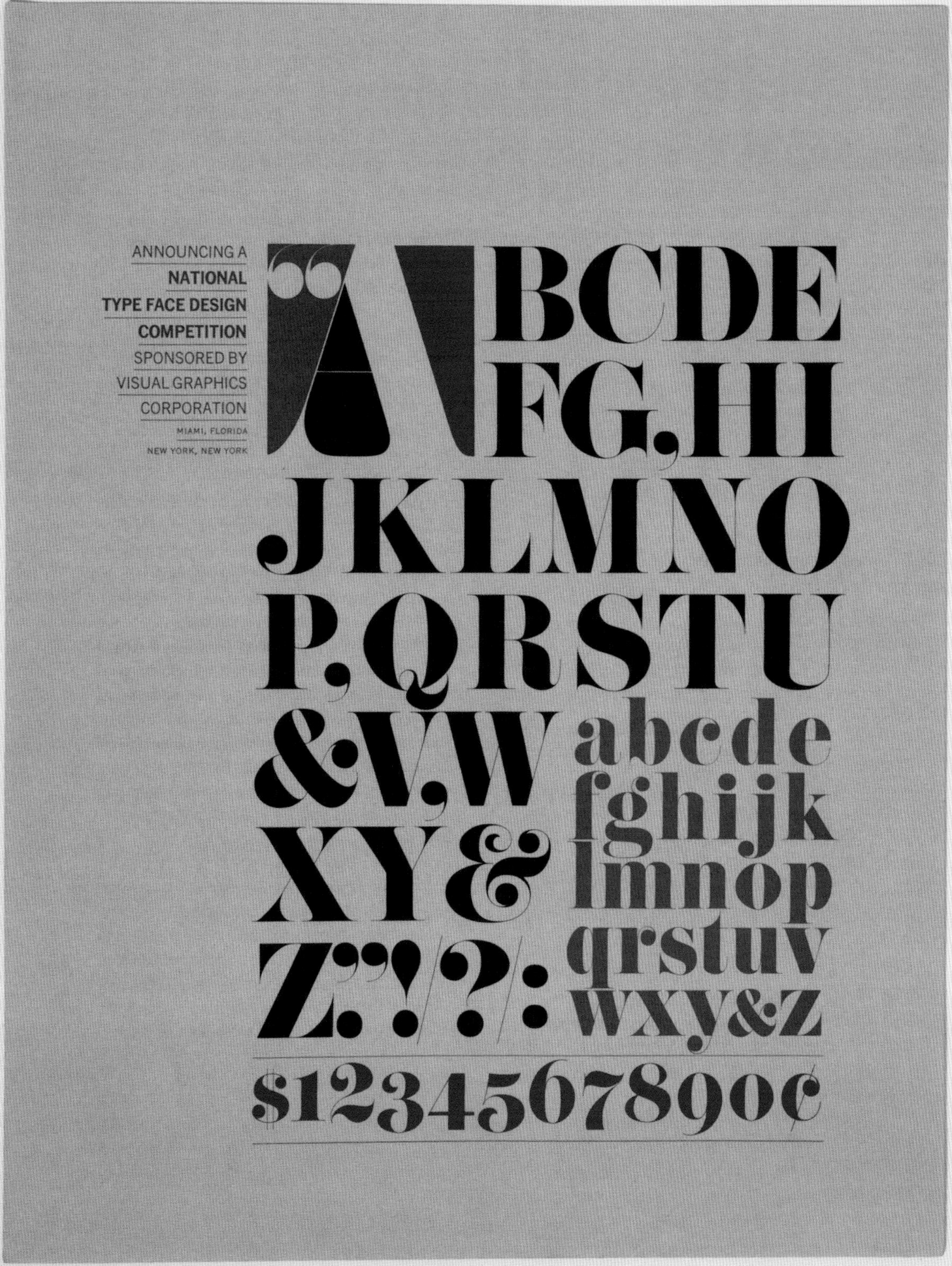

ANNOUNCING A
NATIONAL
TYPE FACE DESIGN
COMPETITION
SPONSORED BY
VISUAL GRAPHICS
CORPORATION
MIAMI, FLORIDA
NEW YORK, NEW YORK

"ABCDE
FG.HI
JKLMNO
P.QRSTU
&V.W abcde
fghijk
XY& lmnop
qrstuv
Z"!?: wxy&z
$1234567890¢

5. The more intelligible a thing is...
Poster using Basilea, a typeface
designed by Marcus J. Low. Client:
VGC. Date: 1965.

6. Poster announcing typeface ...
The display typeface is Pistilli Roman,
a face that has cult status among
modern typographers. Despite its name,
it is widely credited to both Herb
Lubalin and John Pistilli. Pistilli Roman
was produced for use on a typositor
machine. Client: VGC. Date: 1964.

FOR MOST MEN LIFE IS A SEARCH FOR THE PROPER MANILA ENVELOPE IN WHICH TO GET THEMSELVES FILED.
CLIFTON FADIMAN

1966 INTERNATIONAL TYPE FACE DESIGN COMPETITION / AWARD WINNING TYPE FACE : GIORGIO BY GIORGIO GAIOTTO, ITALY / SPONSORED BY VISUAL GRAPHICS CORPORATION /
POSTER DESIGN : HERB LUBALIN / PHOTOGRAPHY : IRV BAHRT /TYPOSITOR TYPOGRAPHY: TYPOGRAPHICS COMMUNICATIONS, INC. / PRINTING: DRUM LITHOGRAPHERS, INC. / PUBLISHER: HARLIN QUIST, INC.

Edmund Gosse

THE GIRLS NOWADAYS DISPLAY A SHOCKING FREEDOM; BUT THEY WERE PARTLY LED INTO IT BY THE RELATIVE LAXITY OF THEIR MOTHERS, WHO, IN THEIR TURN, GAVE GREAT ANXIETY TO AN EARLIER GENERATION.

1966 INTERNATIONAL TYPE FACE DESIGN COMPETITION. AWARD WINNING TYPE FACE: WOLF ANTIQUA BY HANS-JURGEN WOLF, GERMANY / SPONSORED BY VISUAL GRAPHICS CORPORATION.
POSTER DESIGN: HERB LUBALIN / PHOTOGRAPHY: IRV BAHRT, TYPOSITOR TYPOGRAPHY: TYPOGRAPHICS COMMUNICATIONS, INC. / PRINTING: DRUM LITHOGRAPHERS INC. / PUBLISHER: HARLIN QUIST, INC.

7. For most men life is a search...
Poster using Giorgio, a woodblock-style typeface designed by Giorgio Giaiotto, Italy. The reclining model is Cal Sacks, a regular choice for Lubalin as a model during his time at Sudler & Hennessey, where Sacks also worked. Photography: Irv Bahrt. Client: VGC. Date: 1966.

8. The girls nowadays display...
Poster using Wolf Antiqua, a typeface designed by Hans-Jurgen Wolf. Photography: Irv Bahrt. Client: VGC. Date: 1966.

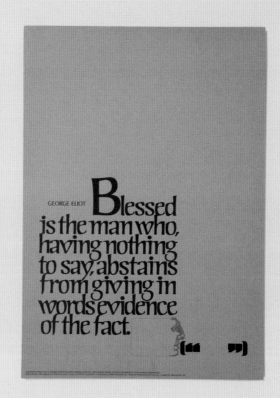

9. The Devil's Dictionary
Poster using Egyptian 505, a typeface designed by students of Allgemeine Gewerbeschule, Switzerland. Illustrations: students, School of Visual Arts, New York. Client: VGC. Date: 1966.

10. Blessed is the man ...
Poster using York, a typeface designed by Georg Salden, Germany. York is used by the cosmetic brand Clinique as the typeface of their logo. Illustration: Shelley Sacks. Client: VGC. Date: 1966.

11. Few have heard of ...
Poster using Deutsch Black, a typeface designed by Barry Deutsch, USA. This typeface and versions of it became popular in the 1980s among graphic designers looking to make use of its retro jazzy stylishness. Client: VGC. Date: 1966.

12. The bizarre world of cards ...
Poster using Neil Bold by Wayne J. Stettler, USA. Stettler was also the designer of Stettler (p.106, fig.3). Client: VGC. Date: 1966.

MAURICE CHEVALIER **Old Age Isn't So Bad When You Consider the Alternat_ve**

The world's a theatre in which some of the worst people have the best seats. ANONYMOUS

Nothing exceeds like excesss.
Robert Moses

HENRY FORD **A bore is a fellow who opens his mouth**

13. Old age isn't so bad ...
Poster using Visa, a typeface designed by Raphael Boguslav, USA. This poster is characterized by two familiar Lubalin graphic strategies: he infills the letter 'O', and allows the 'i' of 'Alternative' to lie on its side, thus signifying death. Photography: Irv Bahrt. Client: VGC. Date: 1966.

14. The world's a theatre in which ...
Poster using Jay Gothic, a typeface designed by Jay H. Schechter, USA. Photography: Irv Bahrt. Client: VGC. Date:1966.

15. Nothing exceeds like excesss
Poster using Antikva Margaret by Zoltan Nagy, Hungary. One of the giants of Hungarian typography, Nagy's typeface Antikva Margaret is used on the pages

of Hungarian passports. Illustration: Shelley Sacks. Client: VGC. Date: 1966.

16. A bore is a fellow who ...
Poster using Domning Antiqua, a type-face designed by Karl-Heinz Domning, Germany. Domning also designed the slab serif typeface Quadra 57 BQ for the Berthold AG Typefoundry. Client: VGC. Date: 1966.

Benjamin Franklin

I WISH THE BALD EAGLE HAD NOT BEEN CHOSEN AS THE REPRESENTATIVE OF OUR COUNTRY; HE IS A BIRD OF BAD MORAL CHARACTER; LIKE THOSE AMONG MEN WHO LIVE BY SHARPING AND ROB-BING, HE IS GENERALLY POOR, AND OFTEN VERY LOUSY~~THE TURKEY IS A MUCH MORE RESPECT-ABLE BIRD, AND WITHAL A TRUE ORIGINAL NATIVE OF AMERICA

1966 INTERNATIONAL TYPE FACE DESIGN COMPETITION./AWARD WINNING TYPE FACE: FRIZ QUADRATA BY ERNST FRIZ, SWITZERLAND./SPONSORED BY VISUAL GRAPHICS CORPORATION./
POSTER DESIGN: HERB LUBALIN./ILLUSTRATION: SHELLEY SACKS/TYPOSITOR TYPOGRAPHY: TYPOGRAPHICS COMMUNICATIONS, INC./PRINTING: DRUM LITHOGRAPHERS, INC./PUBLISHER: HARLIN QUIST, INC.

Oscar Fingal O'Flahertie Wills Wilde **A POET CAN SURVIVE EVERYTHING BUT A MISSPRINT.**

17. I wish the bald eagle ...
Poster using Friz Quadrata, a typeface designed by Ernst Friz, Switzerland. The typeface shown here is the first weight of Friz Quadrata. Later, ITC added a bold weight, and in 1992, French designer Thierry Puyfoulhoux designed italic weights for both the original and bold weights. Illustration: Shelley Sacks. Client: VGC. Date: 1966.

18. A poet can survive anything ...
Poster using Arrow, a typeface designed by Walter J. Diethelm, Switzerland. Diethelm was the author of *Signet Signal Symbol* (Hastings House Publishing, 1976), an important book in the literature of graphic design. Photography: Irv Bahrt. Client: VGC. Date: 1966.

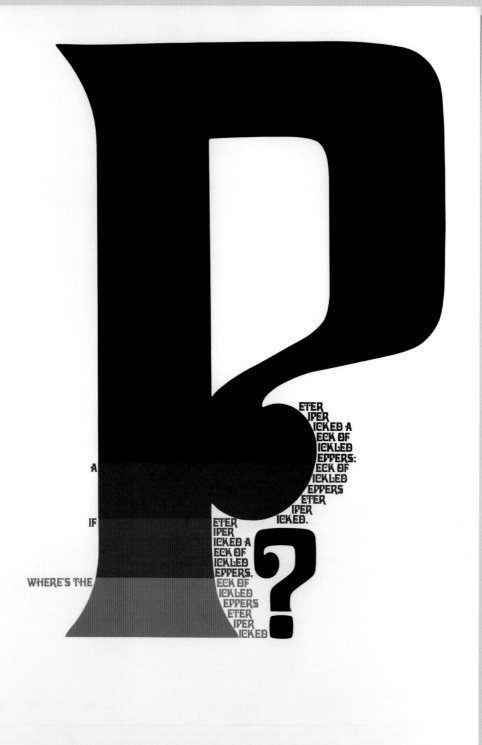

1966 NATIONAL TYPE FACE DESIGN COMPETITION AWARD WINNING TYPE FACE: DAVIDA BOLD BY LOUIS MINOTT. / SPONSORED BY: VISUAL GRAPHICS CORPORATION (MANUFACTURER OF THE PHOTO TYPOSITOR) / POSTER DESIGN: HERB LUBALIN / TYPOSITON TYPOGRAPHY: AARON BURNS & COMPANY, DIVISION OF RAPID TYPOGRAPHERS, INC. / PRINTING: DRUM LITHOGRAPHERS, INC.

19. Peter Piper picked a peck of ...
Poster using Davida Bold, a typeface
designed by Louis Minott, USA. This
typeface enjoyed a huge vogue in the
UK in the 1970s. Its neo-Victorian
flavour caught the wave of nostalgia
and retroism that swept through Britain
at that time. After his retirement, Minott
became a silversmith. Client: VGC.
Date: 1965.

20. No More War?
This 'call for entries' announcement
is pure Lubalin: he juggles Victorian
playbill typography with a sly reference
to the U.S. flag, yet the graphic formul-
ation is late 1960s modern. The list of
judges is an unusual fusion of design
and art world luminaries. Here shown
in recreated poster format. Client:
Avant Garde. Date: 1967.

THE NEXT WAR WILL DETERMINE NOT WHAT IS RIGHT BUT WHAT IS LEFT.

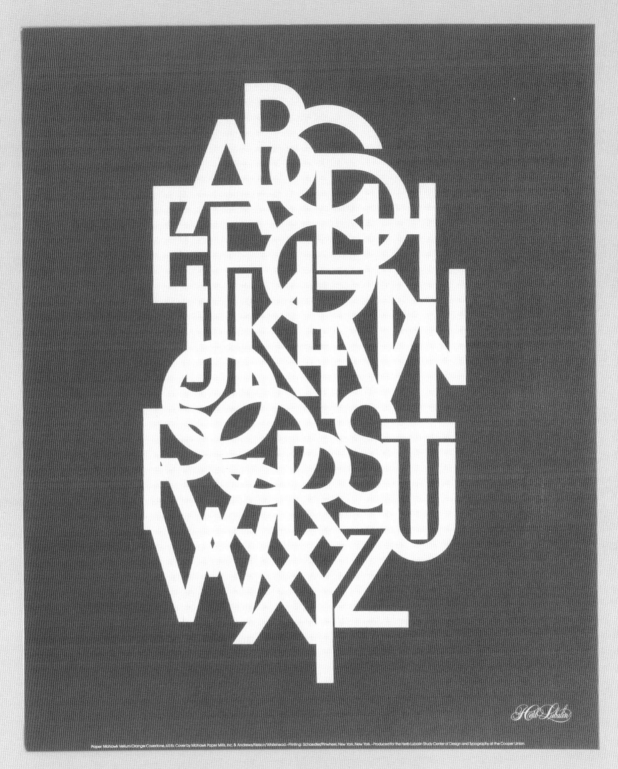

21. The next war
Politically charged anti-war poster. Lubalin both designed the poster and wrote the text for an AIGA exhibition called 'Survival'. According to Ed Benguiat, the cockroaches were frozen in order to get the shot. Here shown in recreated poster format. Date: 1972.

22. ABCDEFG ...
All 26 letters of the alphabet set in Avant Garde Gothic, designed by Herb Lubalin and Tom Carnase. This typically Lubalin-esque arrangement of interlocking and overlapping letterforms was originally commissioned by the Type Directors Club (New York) as an illustration to an essay Lubalin wrote for *Typography 1 — The Annual of the Type Directors Club*. Here shown in recreated poster format. Date: 1979.

MILTON GLASER

HERB LUBALIN

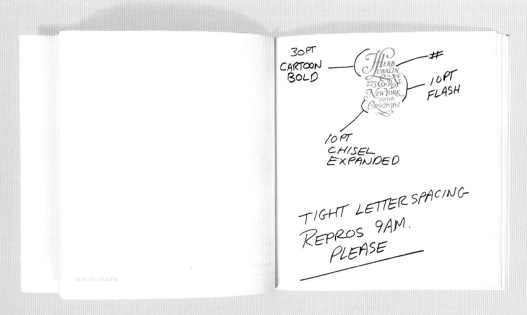

ALAN PECKOLICK

It says here, somewhere: "Peace on earth, good will to all men." Let's get it together.

23. Herb Lubalin Inc. (p.120—21)
Book advertising an exhibition of work
by the newly formed studio of Herb
Lubalin. *Idea* magazine cites Ernie Smith
as the book's designer. Text reads: 'This
book began as a series of spontaneous
doodles around our memo pad by
members of Herb Lubalin, Inc. and
blossomed into an idea. Our graphics
begin the same way. We would like to
invite you to an exhibition of some of
our ads, folders, trademarks, packaging,
TV spots, letterheads, etc., which have
grown out of our doodles. In case you
can't make it, this booklet will serve as
a memo of how we feel about creativity.'
Illustrations shown are by (top to bottom): Milton Glaser, Herb Lubalin and
Alan Peckolick. Date: 1964.

24. Somewhere in here it says ...
Holiday poster for second incarnation of
Lubalin studio caused by the elevation
to partner status of long-time Lubalin
associate Ernie Smith and lettering
wizard Tom Carnase. The jumble of
letterforms, presumably a Victorian
assemblage found in one of the old
copyright-free graphic ephemera books
that Lubalin treasured, is accompanied
by the words: 'Somewhere in here it
says, Peace on earth, good will to all
men. Let's get it together.' Date: c.1967.

25. Typography pack
Promotional typeface pack offering the
LSC signature typefaces for use. The
design features the distinctive monogram of the LSC studio. Note how in this
symbol Lubalin refrains from his normal
habit of fusing thick and thin lines:
the line work here is almost uniform in
width. According to Tom Carnase, this
pack was originally designed by him for
his company Bonder & Carnase. It was
repurposed for LSC. Client: Lubalin,
Smith, Carnase, Inc. Date: c. 1967.

26—39. The First Typo-Graphics ...
Cover and spreads of booklet containing
over 75 black and white illustrations.
Lubalin Burns & Co. was a joint venture
between Herb Lubalin and Aaron Burns.
It offered a new way to supply type to
clients, which it called 'Typo-Graphics'.
The intro text reads: 'Do you know that
we can overlap, join or interlock letters?
This is a Lubalin Burns & Co., speciality.'
Previously this work was done with razor
blades and a high degree of manual
skill. Now it could be ordered via the
telephone. The contents of the booklet
include a summary of services and
brief biographies of principals Lubalin
and Burns, and illustrated sections
on trademarks and logos, corporate

design, annual reports, package design,
architectural graphics, advertising
design, promotion, poster design, editorial design, books, book jackets,
typeface design, and film and television.
On show is the versatility and sheer
prolificness of Lubalin and his collaborators. Few printed items give a greater
insight into Lubalin as he emerged
from the 1960s into the boom years for
print and visual communication. Herb
Lubalin, as his friend Lou Dorfsman
noted, was the 'typographic impresario
of our time. [He] profoundly influenced
and changed our vision and perception
of letterforms, words and language.'
All script lettering: Tom Carnase. Client:
Lubalin Burns & Co., Inc. Date: 1970.

WORDS-IN-GALLEY Do you know that we set headlines for
as little as $3.00 a word?

The price includes (at your request)
joined serifs, close-fit characters and other
Lubalin, Burns & Company touches.

Did you ever think you could buy anything
from Lubalin, Burns & Co.,Inc. for $3.00?

Well you can.

Please read the fine print on page 52

We can help you.
Because we're a Typo-Graphics Agency.

10

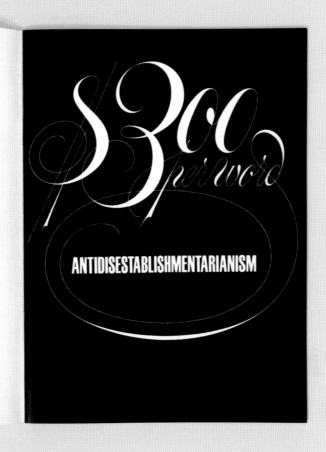

ANTIDISESTABLISHMENTARIANISM

NORMAL HEADLINES Do you know that we arrange "words-in-galley"
into headlines? For $5.00 a word.

The price includes the cost of each word and
the pasteup.

This headline is considered "Normal."
There are no unusual spacing requirements and
no extra costs for camera enlargements.

The price for the composition is $30.00.
Six words at $5.00 per word.

Please read the fine print on page 52.

We can help you.
Because we're a Typo-Graphics Agency.

12

26 GOOD REASONS TO USE LBC

13

126

Top spread

ADVERTISING AND PROMOTION

Newspaper Ads
Magazine Ads
TV Commercials
Posters
Car Cards
Booklets
Brochures
Catalogs
Product Research
Sales Presentations

EDITORIAL DESIGN

General Magazines
Trade Magazines
Newspaper Formats
Newsletters

FILM & TELEVISION

TV Commercials
Educational
Documentary
Industrial
Sales Training
Sales Promotion
Slide Presentations
Multi-Media
Set Design

COMPANY IDENTIFICATION

Logotypes
Trademarks
Official Type Styling
Annual Reports
Employee Information
Directories
House Organs
Notices & Bulletins
Stockholder Reports
Trucks
Uniforms
Corporate Films
Business Forms:
Letterheads
Envelopes
Checks
Calling Cards
Invoices
Statements
Memo Pads

ARCHITECTURAL GRAPHICS

Information Signage
3-D Displays
Interior Design
Typographic Murals
Information Booths

PUBLISHING

Book Creation & Design
Book Jackets

PRODUCT DESIGN, PACKAGING AND POINT-OF-SALE

New Product Ideas
Product Naming
Product Forms
Boxes
Cans
Cartons
Drums
Bottles
Labels
Stickers
Tags
Wrappings
Bags
Toy Creation & Design
Point-of-Sale:
Window Displays
Counter Cards
Display Cartons
Record Albums
Record Jackets
Record Labels

Graphics

Bottom spread

BOOKS

HOLT RINEHART & WINSTON, INC.

CROWELL COLLIER & MACMILLAN, INC.

THE WORLD PUBLISHING COMPANY

RANDOM HOUSE

44

45

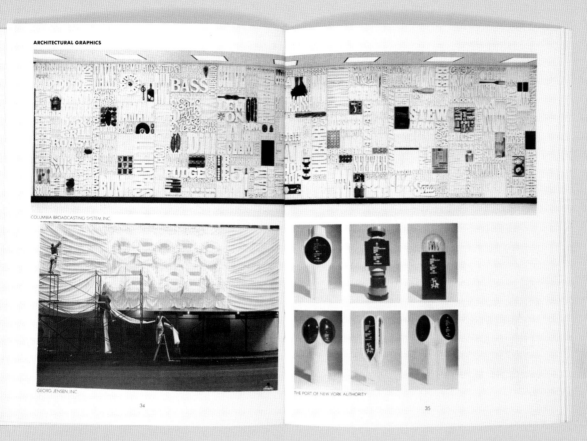

COLUMBIA BROADCASTING SYSTEM, INC.

GEORG JENSEN, INC.

THE PORT OF NEW YORK AUTHORITY

34

35

AMERICAN CAN COMPANY

HERALD TRIBUNE

CULVER PICTURES INC.

THE COUNTRY WIFE

THE REPERTORY THEATER OF LINCOLN CENTER

1-MINUTE CURE FOR AMERICAS NUMBER 2 HEADACHE

ROTOPARK CORPORATION

AMERICAN EXPRESS CARD DIRECTORY

UNITED STATES
BERMUDA
CANADA
THE CARIBBEAN
CENTRAL AMERICA
MEXICO
SOUTH AMERICA

AMERICAN EXPRESS COMPANY

SPECTRUM COSMETICS, INC.

38

39

POSTER DESIGN

AVANT GARDE MAGAZINE

LUBALIN, SMITH, CARNASE, INC.

VISUAL GRAPHICS CORPORATION

VISUAL GRAPHICS CORPORATION

VISUAL GRAPHICS CORPORATION

LUBALIN, SMITH, CARNASE, INC. / DRUM LITHOGRAPHERS, INC.

VISUAL GRAPHICS CORPORATION

VISUAL GRAPHICS CORPORATION

40

41

TYPEFACE DESIGN

48

49

40. Typeface Directory
Cover and spreads of booklet promoting
range of more than 500 typefaces
offered by Lubalin Burns & Co. They
offered typesetting fit for purpose in the
new phototypesetting era. The intro
notes: 'Our normal is like most people's
tight. Of course we can give you tighter
spacing and we can also set headlines
to match your layout.' The address
of Lubalin Burns & Co. was 223 East
31st Street. At this time Lubalin was
operating both his design company
and his 'Typo-Graphics' business under
one roof. Client: Lubalin Burns & Co.,
Inc. All script lettering: Tom Carnase.
Date: 1970.

Lubalin, Burns & Co. Inc.

We offer more than 500 faces.

Faces from film, metal and electronic composing processes.

For this book, we've chosen film typefaces that seem to us to work well for today's display purposes. To help you visualize them at work, we set them as headlines.

The spacing between letters, words and lines is the standard for headlines at Lubalin, Burns & Company.

(Our normal is like most people's tight.)

Of course we can give you even tighter spacing, and we can also set headlines to match your layout.

At the back of the book is a section listing faces for text use, with a guide to processes and sizes.

To learn what else we can do for you, call us at (212) OR 9-2636 or write to: Lubalin, Burns & Co., Inc., 223 East 31st St., New York, N.Y. 10016.

3

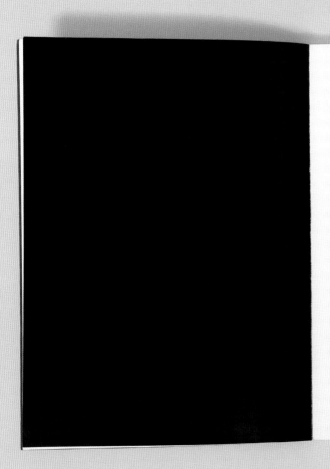

Headline Visuals

135

41—45. LSC typefaces
Cover and spreads of booklet showing
'43 LSC typefaces that take advantage
of film, as never before.' Note the boast
that Avant Garde Gothic is 'so flexible it
actually has more ligatures than characters.' The text also provides a rationale
for redrawing Caslon, Bodoni and
Garamond for the new era: this was a
practice that was to prove wildly successful in commercial terms, but was
attacked on aesthetic grounds by many
practitioners who saw it as a desecration
of time-honoured typefaces. Shown
here are: Avant Garde X-Light, Bernase
Roman, Busorama Light, Machine
and LSC Manhattan. Client: Lubalin
Burns & Co., Inc. All script lettering:
Tom Carnase. Date: 1970.

Caslon, Bodoni and Garamond were
trapped by metal.

Lubalin, Smith, Carnase aren't.

When Caslon designed his italic, for
instance, he was stuck with the width of
a standard character and the clumsiness
of the metal. So he had to condense his
letters. And make his thins a little thick.

Lubalin, Smith, Carnase took a new look
at Caslon. The way Mr. Caslon would have
done if he had a chance to design for film.

Result: the first Caslon italic that goes
with Caslon roman. With hairline delicacy.

This book shows 43 LSC faces that take
advantage of film. As never before.

Look, for example, at Avant Garde Gothic.

It's so flexible it actually has more
ligatures and alternates than characters.

Look at the other faces, too.

You've never seen the like.

These faces are available in display sizes
from Lubalin, Burns & Co., Inc.

And soon, many will be available in
text sizes. The first, ready now, is the exciting
Avant Garde Gothic.

These faces and a steady flow of new
faces from Lubalin, Burns & Co., Inc.
will soon be available worldwide for use in
all typesetting processes.

For more information, write or phone
Lubalin, Burns & Co., Inc., 223 East 31st Street,
New York, N.Y. 10016, (212) OR 9-2636.

4

26 good reasons to use:

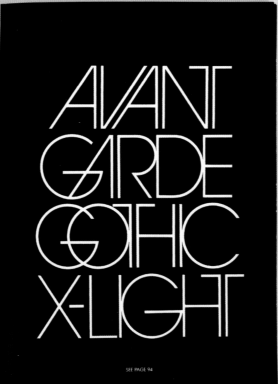

SEE PAGE 94

26
good
reasons
to use:

Bernase
Roman

SEE PAGE 112

26
good
reasons
to use:

ISC
Manhattan

SEE PAGE 120

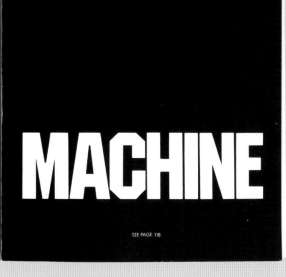

26 GOOD REASONS TO USE:

MACHINE

SEE PAGE 118

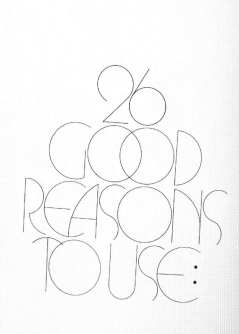

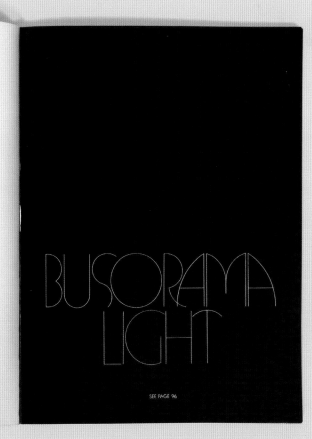

BUSORAMA LIGHT

SEE PAGE 96

46

46—58. Typo-Graphics
Cover and spreads of booklet promoting
a complete Typo-Graphics service.'Typo'
is supplied by Lubalin, Burns & Co;
'Graphics' by Lubalin Smith Carnase,
Inc. This offering is backed up by pages
of striking work, much of it the best
graphic design Lubalin produced. Note,
however, how credit is given to 'the
staff of Lubalin, Smith, Carnase.' Trademarks and logos can be identified by
the listing on 'table of contents' (see
over). Client: Lubalin Burns & Co.,
Inc. All script lettering on this page:
Tom Carnase. Page 143, fig.49, left hand,
lettering: Tom Carnase. Page 146, fig.55,
56, lettering: Tom Carnase. Page 147,
fig.58, lettering: Tom Carnase.
Date: 1970.

TABLE OF CONTENTS:

Typo: Lubalin, Burns & Co., Inc.
Graphics: Lubalin, Smith, Carnase, Inc.
We've put it together. The art and
industry of typography.
One example: trademarks and
logotypes using letterforms designed by
the staff of Lubalin, Smith, Carnase.
Typo-Graphics are now available
through Lubalin, Burns & Company.
Call us at (212) OR 9-2636 or write
to: Lubalin, Burns & Co., Inc., 223 East
31st Street, New York, New York 10016.

47

48

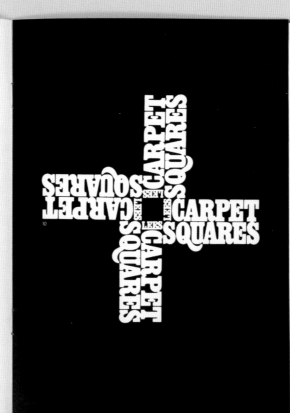

ad1234567890 11

AVANT GARDE ® 12

Family Circle 13

fact: 14

STAR 15

The Saturday Evening Post 16

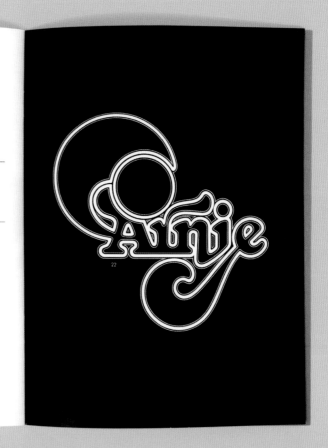

57

Pocket Coffee
25

L'Aiglon
26

L'eggs
27

28

58

32

PRINTED IN USA 1970 BY GLENN PRINTING CO., INC., NORTH KANSAS CITY, MISSOURI
COVER ENGRAVED BY SIEGRIST ENGRAVING COMPANY, KANSAS CITY, MISSOURI
PAPER: MEAD 80 LB. BLACK AND WHITE OFFSET DULL, WITH FABRIANO COVER 214 BY ANDREWS/NELSON/WHITEHEAD

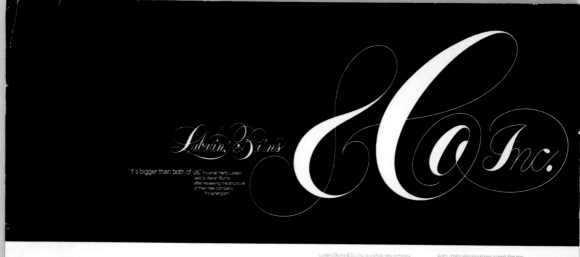

Lubalin, Burns & Co., Inc. is a whole new company, based on a whole new idea, which should have been thought of years ago but wasn't.

Which is just fine with Lubalin, Burns & Co.

Put together in one company the very best people who work in the two different kinds of companies that make up the art and industry of typography.

The creative. The technological.

So, Herb Lubalin, who may well be one of the most influential and innovative designers in our times, and Aaron Burns, who for twenty years has been a prime mover in the aesthetics and technology of typography, got together.

Two men. Two minds. Four hands.

Maybe enough to ignite a revolution, but not enough to keep it going.

They needed help. Hands and minds.

So Burns turned to Bob Farber.

Which makes sense because there's an old saying in type circles that "What Burns doesn't know about typography Farber does."

And Lubalin, who also knows a good alter ego, and who will trade away a piece of the action for brains and talent, any day, turned to Ernie Smith, the only designer he ever trusted to mind the store.

Tom Carnase, whose fresh new type faces have launched a thousand ad campaigns and Roger Ferriter, whose adaptations of type to printed matter have been making trends and influencing people for years.

Plus three floors full of the loosest, free-thinkingest designers, typographic craftsmen, consultants and boardmen that money and the promise of glory could buy.

Put them all together and they spell trouble for traditions.

The world's first typo-graphics "agency".

A marriage of convenience between art and technology which will provide new graphic dynamics for the client with imagination.

Synergism.

If you want to know more about it get in touch with Aaron Burns, Herb Lubalin, Ernie Smith, Tom Carnase, Roger Ferriter, Bob Farber at 223 East 31st Street, New York, N.Y. 10016. 679-9330.

Or look it up in your Funk & Wagnalls.

INVITATION

LUBALIN IN PARIS

LUBALIN IN PARIS

MECANORMA A LE PLAISIR DE VOUS INVITER A RENCONTRER LE CELEBRE CREATEUR AMERICAIN A LA PREMIERE DE L'EXPOSITION DE SON OEUVRE GRAPHIQUE & TYPOGRAPHIQUE, MARDI 23 MAI 78 A 18 HEURES. GALERIE ROBERT CLARENCE 57 RUE SAINT LOUIS EN L'ILE PARIS 4° DU 23 MAI AU 3 JUIN, DE 10 HEURES A 18 HEURES. FERME LE DIMANCHE

ONE BICENTENNIAL TH∶54∶74

You are cordially invited to attend
"1/10th of a bicentennial,"* a retrospective
exhibition of the old work of Herb Lubalin
which includes his new work which is now
old. Please show up at the opening and meet
Mr. Lubalin in person Friday April 25, 1975
5∶30 pm. Ryder Gallery, 500 No. Dearborn
Chicago. Show continues through May 23
Open from 11∶00 am to 5∶00 pm Monday to
Friday or by special appointment · 467-7117

BEFORE AFTER

*1/10TH OF 200=20 YEARS AT HARD LABOR 1954 1974

59. Lubalin Burns & Co. Inc.
Flyer promoting the commercial marriage of 'the creative and the technological.' Note the importance given to Ernie Smith, Tom Carnase and Roger Ferriter — at this point, Lubalin's most important and valued accomplices. This item was found in the Lubalin Study Center archive: note the use of odd line breaks to emphasize the names. Client: Lubalin Burns & Co., Inc. Date: 1970.

60. Lubalin in Paris
Printed invitation to an exhibition of Lubalin's work in Paris. By the late 1970s, Herb Lubalin was at the height

of his fame. In May 1978, he held an exhibition in Paris. It was sponsored by the French company Mecanorma, the only serious rival to Letraset in the production of rub-down lettering sheets. The wording of the invitation translates as: 'Mecanorma has the pleasure of inviting you to meet the famous American designer at the opening of an exhibition of his graphic and typographic works. Tues 23rd May 78 at 6pm. Gallery Robert Clarence, 57 Rue Saint Louis on the Ile Saint Louis, 4th Arrondissement, from 23rd May to 3rd June from 10am to 6pm, closed Sundays.' The following year, Lubalin

held another exhibition, this time at Centre Georges Pompidou in Paris. In 1980, he held a show at the ITC Center in New York. Client: Mecanorma. Illustartion: John Alcorn. Date: 1978.

61. 1/10ᵗʰ of a Bicentennial
Front and back of a witty invitation to attend a 'retrospective exhibition of the old work of Herb Lubalin which includes his new work which is now old.' Postage-stamp-sized pictures of Lubalin purport to show the effects of 20 years' hard labour ('1/10th of 200=20 years'). The exhibition was held in Chicago. Date: 1974.

62. Love & Joy
Christmas card from Lubalin, Smith,
Carnase. The AIGA archives cite Herb
Lubalin as art director, Alan Peckolick
as designer and Tom Carnase as artist.
Client: Lubalin, Smith, Carnase Inc.
Date: 1975.

63. Seasons Greetings '72
Christmas and New Year card from
Lubalin, Burns & Co. Note that the 7
and 2 are the same letterform. Client:
Lubalin Burns & Co., Inc. Date: 1972.

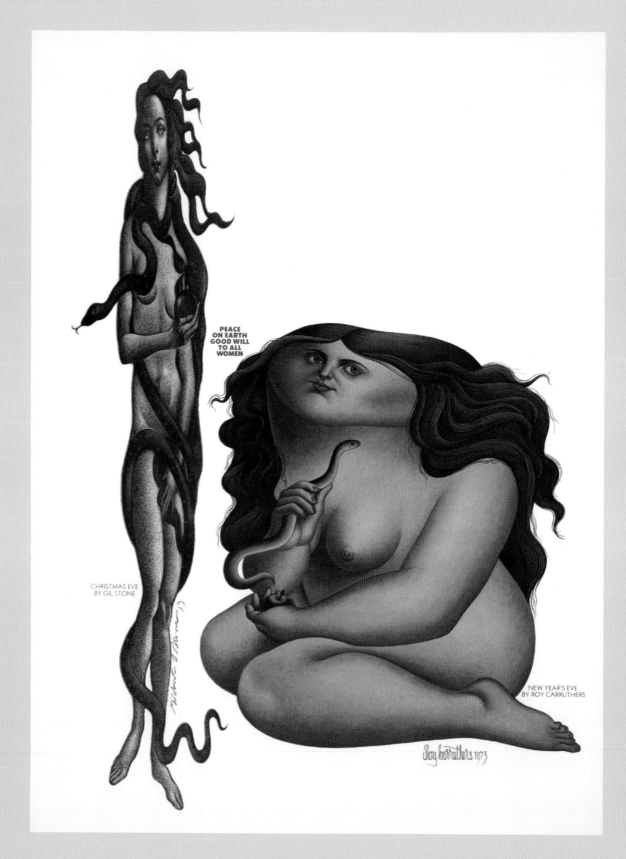

PEACE
ON EARTH
GOOD WILL
TO ALL
WOMEN

CHRISTMAS EVE
BY GIL STONE

NEW YEAR'S EVE
BY ROY CARRUTHERS

Happy Holidays **1976**

64. Peace on Earth ...
Seasonal greetings card from Lubalin, Smith, Carnase, retelling the Adam and Eve story — without Adam. Instead we see 'Christmas Eve' (drawn by Gil Stone) and 'New Year's Eve' (by Roy Carruthers). Date: 1973.

65. Happy Holidays 1976
Folding calendar showing key American public holidays for the year 1976. Lubalin uses this as an opportunity to indulge his taste for old American woodcut illustrations, and his predilection for the patriotic colour palette of red, white and blue. The entry for 17th March is explained thus: 'In lieu of an adequate picture of St Patrick we have substituted an inadequate picture of Herb Lubalin, whose birthday, on March 17th, is honored by a grand parade up 5th Avenue, after which he gets appropriately bombed.' Client: *U&lc.* Date: 1975.

L&C HAIRLINE
a new typeface
designed by
Herb Lubalin and
Tom Carnase.
Now available in
Typositor Typography
at TGC.

TypoGraphics Communications, Inc. 305 East 46th Street, New York, N.Y. 10017 (212) 688-2445

68
69
70

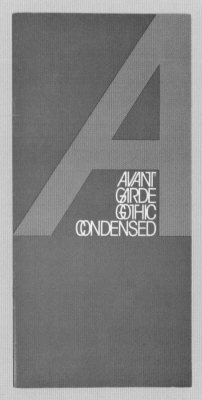

ITC SERIF GOTHIC & BOLD
ALTERNATE CHARACTERS

This is twenty-four point ITC Serif Gothic. It is shown here in a series of point sizes that will shortly be available on a variety of photo typesetting machines sold by ITC Subscribers. Larger sizes, with alternate characters, will also be available e for headline use on photo display typesetting machines and as dry transfer letters. ITC Serif Gothic is an original typeface designed by Herb Lubalin and Tony DiSpigna for International Typeface Corporation. It combines gothic si mplicity together with traditional roman elegance. **This is twenty-four point ITC Serif Gothic Bold. It is shown here in a series of point sizes that will shortly b e available on a variety of photo typesetting machines sold by ITC Subscribe rs. Larger sizes, with alternate characters, will also be available for headline use on photo display typesetting machines and as dry transfer letters. This is**

abcdefghijklmnopqrstuvwxyzABCDEFGHIJKLMNOPQRSTUVWXYZ1234567890
abcdefghijklmnopqrstuvwxyzABCDEFGHIJKLMNOPQRSTUVWXYZ1234567890
abcdefghijklmnopqrstuvwxyzABCDEFGHIJKLMNOPQRSTUVWXYZ1234567890
abcdefghijklmnopqrstuvwxyzABCDEFGHIJKLMNOPQRSTUVWXYZ1234567890
abcdefghijklmnopqrstuvwxyzABCDEFGHIJKLMNOPQRSTUVWXYZ1234567890
abcdefghijklmnopqrstuvwxyzABCDEFGHIJKLMNOPQRSTUVWXYZ1234567890

JOHN ALCORN VIA DEI SERRAGLI 132·50124 FIRENZE ITALIA TEL:(055) 220033 PEACE ON EARTH GOOD WILL TO ALL MEN & JOY TO THE WORLD

TRUMAN CAPOTE'S OTHER VOICES, OTHER ROOMS

ITC Serif Gothic with bold is also available for headline use on our photo display typesetting machines. Several alternate characters have been designed but unless specifically requested normal font characters will always be used.

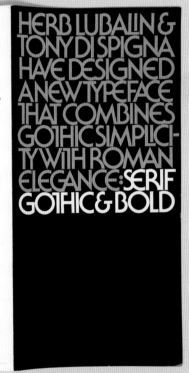

HERB LUBALIN & TONY DI SPIGNA HAVE DESIGNED A NEW TYPEFACE THAT COMBINES GOTHIC SIMPLICITY WITH ROMAN ELEGANCE: SERIF GOTHIC & BOLD

INTERNATIONAL
TYPEFACE
CORPORATION
PRESENTS
A COLLECTION
OF 43 NEW
PHOTO-DISPLAY
TYPEFACES
DESIGNED BY
HERB LUBALIN &
TOM CARNASE

AVANT GARDE GOTHIC X-LIGHT

AVANT GARDE GOTHIC MEDIUM

AVANT GARDE GOTHIC DEMI

Bernase Roman

Bolt Bold

LSC Book Regular Roman

LSC Book Bold Roman

LSC Book X-Bold Roman

LSC Book Regular Italic

LSC Book Bold Italic

LSC Book X-Bold Italic

BUSORAMA MEDIUM | BUSORAMA BOLD | Caslon Headline

LSC Caslon Light No223 | LSC Caslon Regular No223 | LSC Caslon Bold No223 | LSC Caslon X-Bold No223

LSC Caslon Light No223 Italic | LSC Caslon Regular No223 Italic | LSC Caslon Bold No223 Italic | LSC Caslon X-Bold No223 Italic

Condensed | Condensed Italic | Didi | Fat Face

Firenze | Gorilla | Grizzly | Grouch

Honda | MACHINE | MACHINE BOLD | Machine Medium

Milano Roman | NEON | PIONEER | Ronda

Ronda Light | Ronda Bold | L&C Stymie Hairline | Tom's Roman

66. Avant Garde Gothic

Leaflet front promoting Avant Garde Gothic — the typeface Lubalin designed with Tom Carnase — in various weights and in an Oblique version. International Typeface Corporation, Inc. Date: c. 1971.

67. L&C Hairline

Promotional leaflet for the remarkable 'hairline' typeface designed by Lubalin and Carnase. This typeface and its sister face, L&C Stymie Hairline (1972), were hugely popular in the 1970s, when phototypesetting and improved printing technology meant that ultra-thin letter-forms could be reproduced effectively. Another page of this document can be seen on p.34. Client: Typo-Graphics Communications Inc. Date: c. 1966.

68. Avant Garde Gothic Cond...

A promotional leaflet for the condensed version of Avant Garde Gothic. This version was drawn by Ed Benguiat, who is responsible for more than 600 typefaces including Souvenir, Tiffany, Bookman, Benguiat and Benguiat Gothic. Client: International Typeface Corporation, Inc. Date: c. 1974.

69. Serif Gothic

Promotional leaflet for ITC Serif Gothic, the typeface designed by Lubalin and Tony Di Spigna. See p.52 for more information on this typeface. Client: International Typeface Corporation, Inc. Date: c. 1974.

70. Lubalin Graph

Promotional leaflet for Lubalin Graph, the only typeface where Lubalin's name is part of the typeface's name. It was designed by Lubalin, Tony Di Spigna and Joe Sundwall. It is Avant Garde Gothic with slab serifs. Client: International Typeface Corporation, Inc. Date: c. 1974.

71. Serif Gothic & Bold

Both sides of Concertina leaflet with gold metallic ink, promoting ITC Serif Gothic. The design of the leaflet is credited to Herb Lubalin. The documents still bears the imprint of Lubalin Burns & Co., although ITC, formed the year before, had largely replaced this venture. Client: International Typeface Corporation, Inc. Date: 1972.

72. International Typeface ...

Promotional literature for '43 New Photo-Display Typefaces designed by Herb Lubalin and Tom Carnase.' Not all the typefaces on show here were designed jointly by Lubalin and Carnase. Attributions are hard to pin down. Some sources cite Busorama as a Lubalin-designed typeface; others give it to Carnase. All that we can be sure about is that ITC fonts were to revolutionize typography in the 1970s, and Herb Lubalin and Tom Carnase were key players in that revolution (p.51). Client: International Typeface Corporation, Inc. Date: c. 1971.

AMPERSAND
PRODUCTIONS INC.
424 WEST 33RD STREET
NEW YORK 10001
LO 5-2080

STATEMENT NO.

0091

TO:

DATE

DATE	INVOICE NO

NOTE: TERMS ARE 10 DAYS

AMPERSAND
PRODUCTIONS
INC. 424 WEST
33RD STREET
NEW YORK 10001
LO 5-2080

AMPERSAND
PRODUCTIONS
INC 14 EAST
52ND STREET
NEW YORK 10022
PL 1-1580

73. Ampersand Productions, Inc.
Stationery range and logotype with
film-strip business card for Ampersand
Productions. The flowing ampersand,
with its extreme thick and thin lines,
is Lubalin at his most characteristic and
refined. Lettering artist: Tom Carnase.
Client: Ampersand Productions Inc.
Date: 1972.

74

74. VPI
Letterhead and logotype for VPI,
a division of Electrographic Corporation.
Lettering: Tom Carnase. Date: unknown.

75. 285
Letterhead and logo for the Design
Division of Young & Rubicon, Inc. The
agency's address was 285 Madison
Avenue. Art direction: Herb Lubalin and
Bernie Zlotnick (Zlotnick was creative
director of 285 at the time). Designer:
Annegret Beier. Lettering artist: Tom
Carnase. Client: Young & Rubicam, Inc.
Date: 1969.

76. Ah!
Stationery for photographer Anthony
Hyde, Jr. The logo represents the
client's initials, and the onomatopoeic
expression of delight by anyone
receiving one of Hyde's photographs.
Lettering: Tom Carnase. Client: Anthony
Hyde, Jr. Date: 1964.

77. Typographic Innovations, Inc.
Stationery range. Note the familiar
Lubalin graphic device of mixing
extreme thickness with extreme thin-
ness. The compact, almost symmetrical
nature of the TGI logotype, and the
highly crafted yet subtle modifications
to the letterforms create a distinctive
customized marque. Lettering: Tom
Carnase. Date: 1969.

78. Zebra
Logo and stationery for Zebra Associates, the first U.S. advertising agency
formed by African-American and white
American owners. Yet again, Lubalin
introduces a conceptual note, this
time signifying the agency's dual-race
ownership: the letterforms alternate
between black and white, and the logo
itself works equally well on a white or
black background. Lubalin worked with
the designer Mike Randazzo on this
project. Client: Zebra Associates Inc.
Lettering: Tom Carnase. Date: 1970.

79. Vern Associates
This logo has been likened to Alan
Fletcher's famous V&A logo, but
Lubalin's composition is even more
minimalist than Fletcher's logotype.
It was done for Ike Vern, a freelance
magazine photographer and docum-
entary filmmaker. Vern worked for
Look, Life and *Collier's* magazines in
the 1940s and 1950s. Client: Ike Vern
& Associates, Inc. Lettering: Tom
Carnase. Date: unknown.

75

76

TYPOGRAPHIC
INNOVATIONS,INC.
221 PARK AVE.SOUTH
NEW YORK 10003
PHONE:777-3900

ZEBRA ASSOCIATES INC. ADVERTISING
1180 AVENUE OF THE AMERICAS
NEW YORK, N.Y. 10036   586-2160

DIANE GREATHEART
RESEARCH ASSISTANT

IKE VERN & ASSOCIATES INC. PHOTOGRAPHY. 808 SEVENTH AVENUE. NEW YORK 10019. CI 5-4730

Spectrum Cosmetics Inc.

80. Steelograph Company
Logo and letterhead for New York
steel-engraving company celebrated for
the quality of its work. This is Lubalin
at his most unrestrained. To modern
eyes, his love of Spencerian script is
somewhat overwrought, but here he
uses it to express the high level of
workmanship offered by the specialist
engraving company. Lettering: Tom
Carnase. Client: Steelograph Company.
Date:1965.

81. Spectrum Cosmetics
More Caslon Swash. Note the care with
which Lubalin assembles the type on
this business card. No matter how large
or small the project, Lubalin's work
was always distinguished by its unstinting
craftsmanship. Client: Spectrum
Cosmetics Inc. Date: Unknown.

82. Jody
Monogram and letterhead.
Date: unknown.

80

81

Spectrum Cosmetics, Inc.
Six East Forty-Fifth Street
New York, New York 10017
212·972·0530

René Plessner
President

82

83. Waring & LaRosa
Letterhead for New York advertising
agency. Typeface is Bernase Roman,
designed by Tom Carnase and Ronne
Bonder. Client: Waring & LaRosa Inc.
Date: 1970s.

84. Herb Lubalin, Inc
Letterhead and logotype for the first
independent Lubalin studio at 223 East
31st Street, New York. Both John Pistilli
and Tom Carnase are widely credited as
the lettering artists for this famous logo.
Inspiration was derived from the New
York, New Haven and Hartford Railroad
logo — a classic example of early
American commercial lettering design
(p.17, fig.21). Client: Herb Lubalin, Inc.
Date: 1964.

85. Oak Tree Press
Traditional-looking letterhead using
Caslon Swash. Lubalin at his least
adventurous, yet characterized by
his habit of dovetailing words and
letterforms to make arresting shapes.
Client: Oak Tree Press. Date: c. 1965.

86. Rhoda Sparber
Envelope with typography for Rhoda
Sparber, Herb Lubalin's second wife.
She is an art teacher and practising
artist. Some of her work can be seen
on p.61. Date: 1970s.

87. Jack Arkin
Logo and letterhead. Conventional
design using modified version of Caslon
Old Style Swash. Jack Arkin was
a New York furrier. Date: unknown.

164

85

OakTree Press 54 W. 40th Street, New York, N.Y. 10018, 212-279-2545

86

*Rhoda Sparber
One Thirty One
Prince Street
New York 10012*

87

150 WEST 30th STREET, NEW YORK, NEW YORK 10001

88. Cooper Union ...
Textbook example of Herb Lubalin's meticulous use of lettering to create a stacked block of type that is seemingly natural and unforced, but which on closer inspection is revealed as an example of adroit typographic engineering. Countless 'tricks' are employed to ensure the perfect block: the 'V' and 'A' of 'Advancement' are conjoined, and the ampersand in 'Art & Architecture' extends downwards to fill the gap in the line below. Minimal line spacing ensures a compactness that is offset by the ultra-light weight of Futura. It is widely reported that Lubalin set this project as a competition for his students. He entered the competition and failed to win. It was only later that his entry was accepted. Lettering: Tony Di Spigna. Date: c. 1975.

89. Good Book
Logo and business card for publishing venture between Herb Lubalin and Swiss-born illustrator Etienne Delessert, a frequent Lubalin collaborator throughout the 1960s, especially on *Avant Garde* magazine. Good Book was described in Lubalin's 1977 Art Directors Club biography as 'a highly unsuccessful publishing venture'. The book *How the Mouse Was Hit on the Head by a Stone and So Discovered the World* was written and illustrated by Delessert and designed by Lubalin. It is a children's story developed in close co-operation with a team of psychologists who tested each sentence and each picture for comprehension by five- and six-year-olds. Designer: Annegret Beier. Client: Good Book Inc. Date: c. 1969.

90. The Directors Center
Ultra-thin type, 'kiss-tight' letter spacing and minimal line spacing make for an archetypal Lubalin logo and letterhead. Client: The Associated Directors Center Inc. Date: Unknown.

166

THE COOPER UNION FOR THE ADVANCE-MENT OF SCIENCE AND ART

SCHOOL OF ART & ARCHI-TECTURE

COOPER SQUARE
NEW YORK NY 10003
(212) 254-3600

GOOD BOOK INC. SWITZERLAND

BERTIL GALLAND
CENTRE D'INFORMATION
ET D'ARTS GRAPHIQUES
33 AVENUE DE LA GARE
1000 LAUSANNE
SWITZERLAND
234444

THE DIRECTORS CENTER

THE
ASSOCIATED
DIRECTORS
CENTER INC
74 EAST 96 ST
NEW YORK
N.Y. 10022
(212) 838-3900

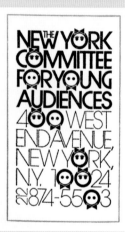

91. Peter Blake Architect
Peter Blake was an architect, critic and editor-in-chief of *Architectural Forum*. He was born in Germany in 1920; to avoid the rise of Nazism, his parents sent him to England to be educated. He became an American citizen in 1944, and soon found himself at the heart of American artistic life. He knew all the leading architects of his day as well as having a keen eye for graphic design. He worked with Alexey Brodovitch (p.15) on two book projects. In his autobiography, he refers to Herb Lubalin as an 'extra-ordinary graphic designer.' He died age 86. Client: Peter Blake Architect. Date: 1970s.

92. New York Committee for ...
Logo and stationery for committee promoting theatre to the young. An example of Herb Lubalin at his most playful and excessive: to modern eyes, the typography is over-embellished and over-cooked. Client: New York Committee for Young Audiences. Date: unknown.

93. Kathleen Benveniste ...
Letterhead showing accomplished and customized (note subtle kerning of key letter combinations) use of Serif Gothic, the typeface that Lubalin designed with Tony Di Spigna. Client: Kathleen Benveniste. Date: c. 1974.

94. Gerry Gersten
Letterhead for one of Lubalin's favourite illustrators, and one of his most frequent collaborators. Yet another Cooper Union alumnus, Gersten has worked for *Newsweek, Harpers, Rolling Stone, Esquire, Playboy* and *MAD Magazine*. The drawings beneath the logotype came in the form of a sticker. Lubalin left a blank space and Gersten inserted a new illustration each month. Client: Gerry Gersten. Date: 1965.

169

95. Avant Garde
Logo and stationery. The story of this logo and subsequent typeface is told elsewhere (p.50). Client: *Avant Garde* Magazine. Date: 1968.

96. VGC
Visual Graphics Corporation was established in 1964. It designed and manufactured the Photo Typositor, a film typesetting machine that allowed letters to be visually selected, sized and spaced. It was a predecessor of photographic computer typesetting equipment. VGC also offered a library of display fonts, including many original designs. As well as designing the corporation's logo, Herb Lubalin designed the now famous set of posters that promoted the annual type design competition run by VGC (p.105) Client: Visual Graphics Corporation. Date: 1964.

97. Warner Paperback Library
Logo and stationery for Warner Paperback Library (which was originally called Paperback Library, but changed after acquisition by Warner Communications). Client: Warner Paperback Library. Date: 1970.

AVANT GARDE
110 WEST 40TH STREET
NEW YORK, N.Y. 10018

Visual Graphics Corporation

305 EAST 46TH STREET, NEW YORK,

NEW YORK 10017,CABLE:VISCO

TELEPHONE:212-PLAZA 2-5247

WARNER PAPERBACK LIBRARY

MEMO FROM BOB ABEL,
EXECUTIVE EDITOR

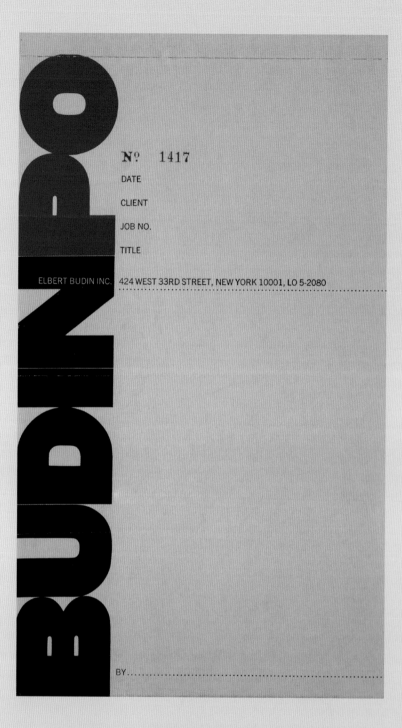

98. Elbert Budin
Logo, letterhead and stationery for
Elbert Budin, a famous 'table-top
photographer.' He shot food and other
still-life set-ups. Client: Elbert Budin
Inc. Date: Unknown.

99. America Unlimited
Letterhead and logo design for a
charitable organization dedicated to
research and education. Herb Lubalin
frequently used the American flag as
a recurring motif in his work. For more
on this project see p.202. Date: c. 1968.

100. Design Processing International
Hermann Zapf, Aaron Burns and Herb
Lubalin founded Design Processing
International to develop typographical
computer software. After Lubalin's
death, the company became Zapf,
Burns & Company. Date: 1977.

AMERICA
UNLIMITED
THE AMERICA FUND
303 LEXINGTON AVE.
NEW YORK, N.Y. 10016
MURRAY HILL 5-1780-1-2

DESIGN PROCESSING
INTERNATIONAL, INC.
2 HAMMARSKJOLD PLAZA
NEW YORK, NEW YORK 10017
(212) 371-0699

HERB LUBALIN
CHAIRMAN
217 EAST 28TH STREET
NEW YORK, N.Y. 10016
(212) 679-2636

101. Videa1
Logo showing one of Lubalin's most favoured typographic strategies: overlapping and colliding letterforms. The use of a TV screen in place of a dot over the 'i' suggests that the activity of this company is television-related. Client: Videa. Date: 1966.

102. Training Systems
Stationery and logo. Unusually brutal logo design. Client: Training Systems, Inc. Date: unknown.

103. World Trade Center
Letterhead for The World Trade Center in the Port of New York. Lubalin's logo has a geometric simplicity — a Cubist-like construction — that reminds the viewer of the best European logos. In the aftermath of the 9/11 tragedy, this marque assumes added poignancy. Client: World Trade Center. Date: 1968.

174

WINTER 1966 / $25.00   52 PARK AVENUE, NEW YORK, N.Y. 10016, PHONE 683-0710   THE STUDIOS

TRAINING SYSTEMS, INC.
200 PARK AVENUE
SUITE 303 EAST
NEW YORK, N.Y. 10017
(212) 986-2515

VICTOR M. PAGAN
EXEC. VICE PRESIDENT

THE
WORLD
TRADE
CENTER
IN THE
PORT OF
NEW
YORK

104. Art Kane Studio
Letterhead for Art Kane's studio. Kane
was a leading New York photographer.
He studied with Alexey Brodovitch, and
Herb Lubalin worked with him on many
occasions, most memorably on *Avant
Garde* magazine. He committed suicide,
aged 69, in 1995. Lettering artist: Tom
Carnase. Client: Art Kane Studio, Inc.
Date: 1971.

105. Art Kane
Personal letterhead for Art Kane.
Sprockets are die-cut. Date: 1962.

105

106. Eve Cigarettes
Eve Filter Cigarettes were launched
as a rival to Virginia Slims, the world's
first cigarette marketed specifically to
women. The packaging was designed
by Herb Lubalin and Ernie Smith. The
on-pack illustration — highly unexpected
in the context of cigarette packaging —
is by Lubalin stalwart John Alcorn.
Client: Liggett Group. Date: 1971.

107. Reemtsma Erste Sorte
Mock-ups of packs for German cigarette
brand Reemtsma Erste Sorte. Reemtsma
is one of the biggest cigarette companies
in Europe. It is a subsidiary of Imperial
Tobacco. Client: Reemtsma Cigarettenfabriken GMBH. Date: c. 1968.

108. Reemtsma Erste Sorte
Final versions of the packaging. The
design is unusually conventional and
restrained for Lubalin, although his
signature can be seen in the way he
infills the 'O' of 'SORTE' with the
cigarette company's symbol. German-
language ads for this product can be
found on the internet dated between
1968 and 1970. Client: Reemtsma
Cigarettenfabriken GMBH. Date: c. 1968.

109. Jug-O-Glug
Spoof Christmas promotional item
for Lubalin, Smith, Carnase. The copy
on the label indicates that the 'contents'
were brewed by Annegret Beier, one
of Herb Lubalin's favourite employees.
The story of Lubalin's respect for this
German-born graphic designer is told
on p.62. Client: Lubalin, Smith, Carnase,
Inc. Lettering: Tom Carnase. Date: 1973.

110. Dr Brown's
Dr. Brown's dates all the way back to
1869, when Dr. Brown's Cel-Ray Tonic
was sold in Jewish New York delicat-
essens. In the early 1930s, before Coca-
Cola received kosher certification, many
Jewish people drank the flavoured soda
that had been created as a beverage
for immigrant children. Herb Lubalin
redesigned the cans using engravings
of historic New York scenes and events.
Client: New York American Beverage
Company. Date: 1975.

110

Inspired Typography '56 An exhibition of the typographically outstanding pieces produced during the past year, coast to coast. The 128 pieces shown are the winners of the Certificate of Typographic Excellence awarded by the Type Directors Club. This exhibition is sponsored by the American Institute of Graphic Arts. Open from 1 to 5 weekdays, now and through June 29th at Wilkie Memorial Building, Freedom House, 20 West 40th Street, N.Y.C. Admission is Free

DESIGN: HERB LUBALIN——————TYPOGRAPHY: THE COMPOSING ROOM, INC.——————PRINTING: THE LENMORE PRESS——————PAPER: REINHOLD-GOULD INC.

111. Inspired Typography '56
Promotional literature announcing the
exhibition of work by winners of the
Certificate of Typographic Excellence
awarded by Type Directors Club and
sponsored by AIGA. Herb Lubalin is
credited as the sole designer (he was
an employee of Sudler & Hennessey
at this time); the typesetting is by The
Composing Room, the typesetting
house where Aaron Burns worked.
Client: Type Directors Club. Date: 1956.

112

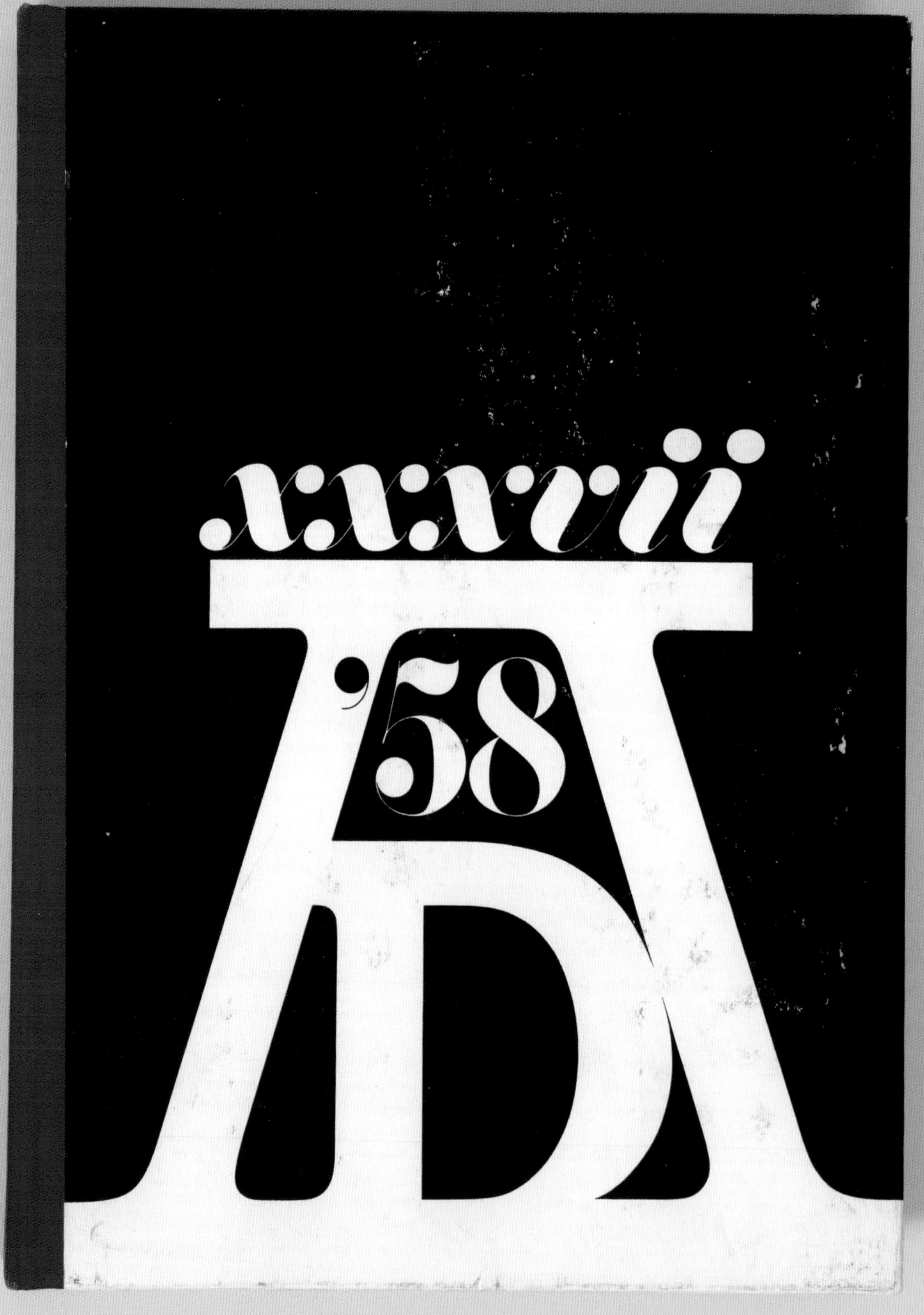

THIRTY-SEVENTH ANNUAL OF ADVERTISING AND EDITORIAL ART AND DESIGN OF THE NEW YORK ART DIRECTORS CLUB

112. The 37th Annual of Advertising ...
Book design for awards annual.
Designers credited are Herb Lubalin
and George Lois, both employees of
Sudler & Hennessey at the time. The
relationship between Lubalin and Lois
is described elsewhere (p.20). Shown
are front and back cover of hardback
book, plus inner spreads. Client: Art
Directors Club of New York. Date: 1958.

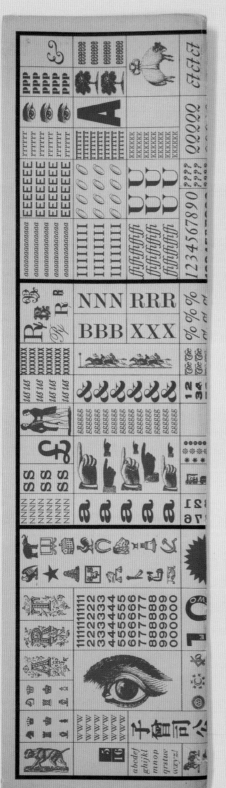
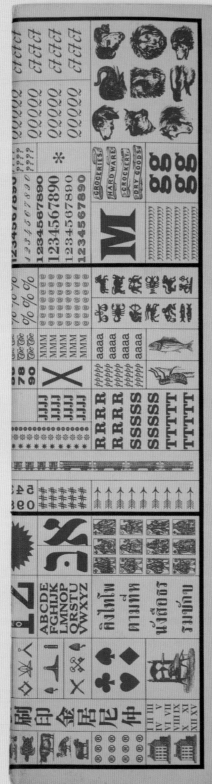

113, 114. TDC 26—66
12-page concertina leaflet for event
organized by Type Directors Club.
Fig.113 is front and back cover.
Fig.114 is opening spread. Client:
Type Directors Club. Date: 1966.

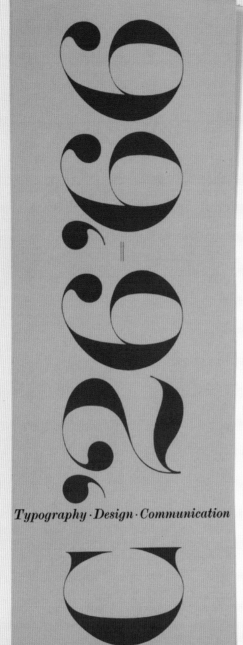

TDC 26-66

Typography · Design · Communication

Why?...

That is the key question
behind all four evenings of
TDC 26-66. Each evening's
analyst will show carefully
selected, specially
prepared slides to visually
explain what was done in
the decades reviewed.
His comments will shed light
on how and why the
designers arrived at the
solutions shown.

Inspired Typography

Emphasis throughout TDC-26-66
will be on the most
exciting, most significant
work. The cumulative
result of the series will be
a clear, revealing,
stimulating picture of how
today's design developed,
where it is leading us in the
immediate future, and why.

Aaron Burns

AARON BURNS
CHAIRMAN, EDUCATIONAL COMMITTEE
TYPE DIRECTORS CLUB

d a

VOLUME LI, NUMBER 4

FOURTH QUARTER 1965

Typahgrrphy

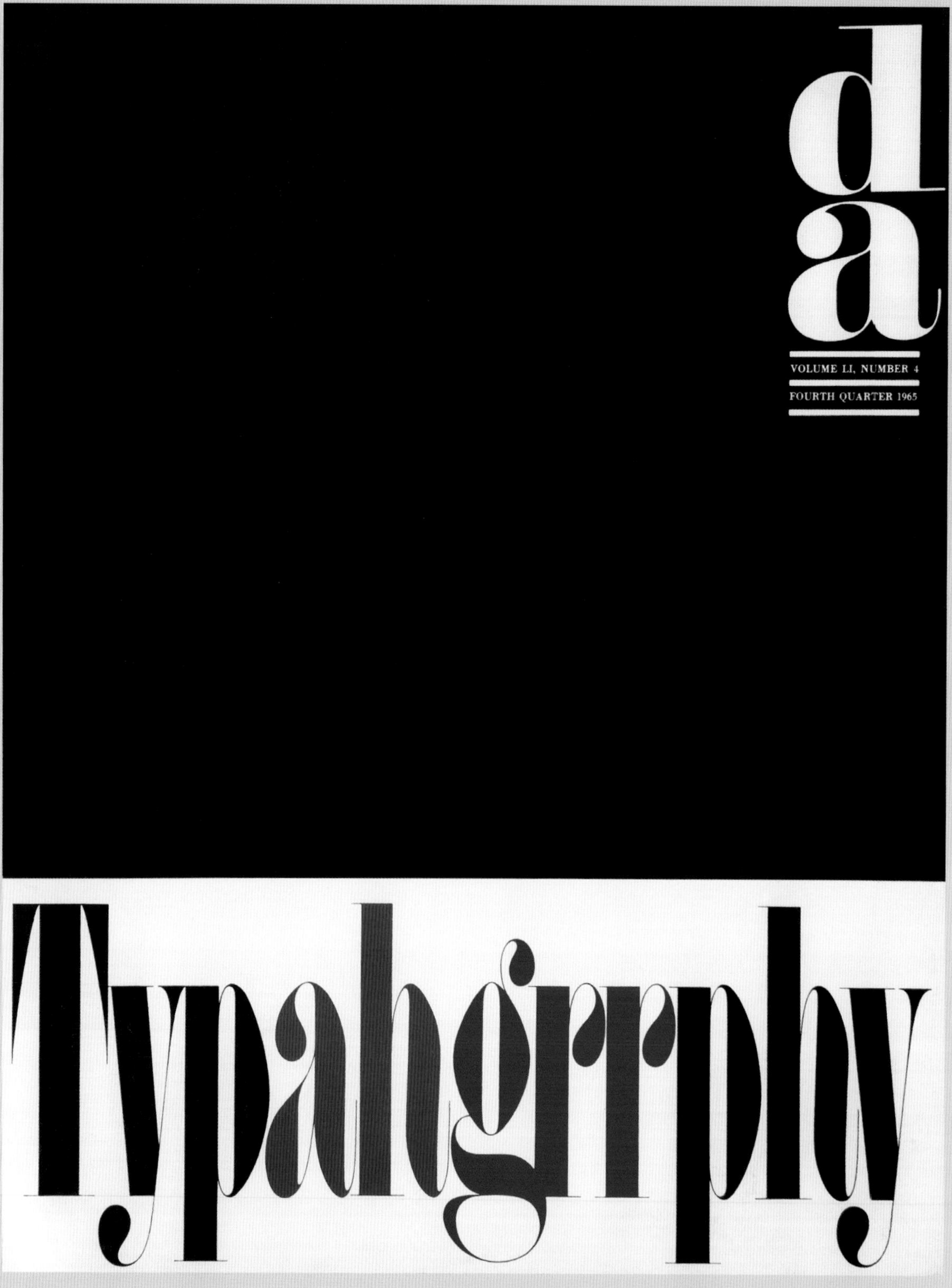

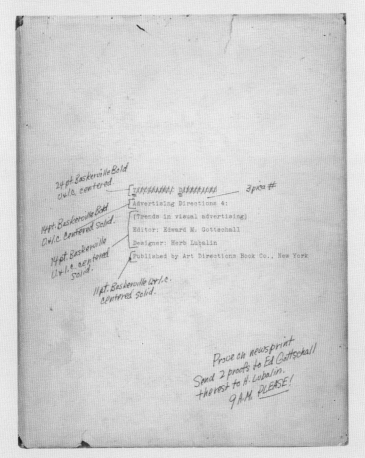

115. Typ-ah-grr-phy
Front cover design for graphic arts
quarterly. Issue shown is devoted to
'good and bad' typography. Note
the onomatopoeic rendering of the
word 'Typography.' Lettering: Tom
Carnase. Client: Unknown. Date: 1965.

116. Graphis Annual Reports
Cover for dust jacket for Swiss
publisher's annual survey of Annual
Reports. Client: Graphis. Date: 1971.

117. Typographic Directions 4
Dust jacket for survey of design in
advertising; described in the introduction as 'the only book of its kind ever
published devoted entirely to advertising typography — its past, present
and future explored by 30 outstanding
authorities.' Front cover design is in the
style of old-fashioned type mark-up that
was sent to typesetters with instructions
handwritten by the designer. Cover
and inside designed by Herb Lubalin.
Publication edited by Edward Gottschall,
who would take over as editor of
U&lc after Lubalin's death. Client: Art
Directions Book Co. Date: 1964.

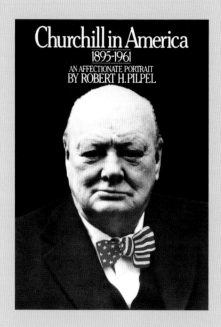

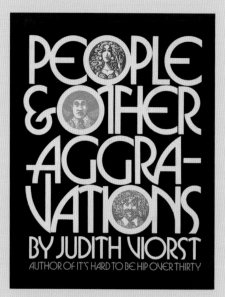

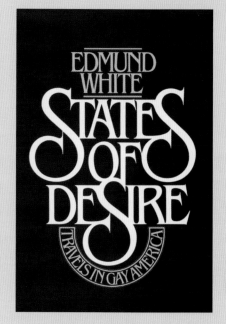

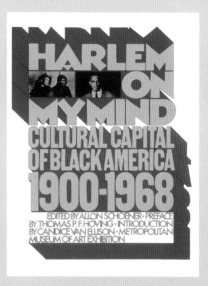

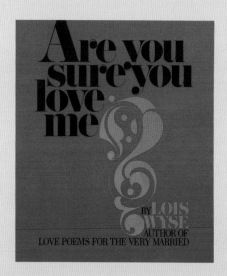

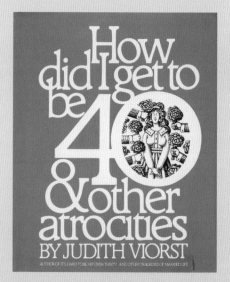

118. Churchill in America
Conventional dust jacket design for hardback book. The introduction of a bow tie rendered in the colours and pattern of the U.S. flag is a typical Lubalin gesture; more witty than subversive, but nevertheless hardly reverential. Client: Harcourt Brace Jovanovich. Date: 1976.

119. People & Other Aggravations
Dust jacket for first edition of non-fiction work by Judith Viorst. Born in 1931, Viorst is an author and journalist with an interest in psychoanalysis. In 1968, she signed the 'Writers' and Editors' War Tax Protest' pledging to refuse to pay tax in protest against the Vietnam War. The design uses modified Busorama, and yet again shows Lubalin's fixation with o-filling. Illustrations are by longstanding Lubalin collaborator John Alcorn. Client: World Publishing Company. Date: 1971.

120. States of Desire
Typographically symmetrical design for dust jacket for book by Edmund White. Subtitled *Travels in Gay America*, the book is a city-by-city description of the way homosexual men lived in the late 1970s. Even at this late period in the 20th century when the book was published (1980), homosexuality was a taboo subject in many circles, yet the liberal-minded Lubalin was not deterred from designing the cover of White's 'travelogue of pre-AIDS gay America.' Lettering is based on extensively modified ITC Benguiat. Client: Dutton Adult. Date: 1980.

121. Harlem on My Mind
Book cover. Art director: Harris Lewine. Designers: Herb Lubalin, Ernie Smith. Client: Random House. Date: 1968.

122. Are You Sure You Love Me?
Cover design for book by 'wordsmith' Lois Wyse, co-founder of the advertising agency Wyse Advertising. The agency was a client of Lubalin's, hiring him to design, among other things, a campaign for the drink Angostura ('A little Angostura goes a long way', 1967). Client: World Publishing. Date: 1971.

123. How did I get to be 40 ...
Densely packed, interlocking typographic construction for another book by Judith Viorst. Illustrator John Alcorn is employed to infill the zero of '40'. Lubalin and Alcorn were to work on other books by Viorst. Client: Simon & Schuster. Date: 1976.

124. Moscow Summer
Dust jacket for book by Yugoslavian writer and dissenter Mihajlo Mihajlov. His book *Moscow Summer* is critical of the Soviet Union. In 1966 he was arrested and sentenced to jail by the Soviet authorities. The book has a foreword by Myron Kolatch, the editor of the *New Leader*, a publication that Lubalin designed (p.67). The design of *Moscow Summer* relies on the monumental power of a block of tightly spaced typography redolent of prison bars, and in its utilization of an unusually vibrant colour palette. Client: Farrar, Straus and Giroux. Date: 1965.

125

American Institute of Architects, New York Chapter

AIA
GUIDE
TO
NEW
YORK
CITY

Norval White / Elliot Willensky

125. AIA Guide to New York City
Book cover and end papers for visitors' guide to New York City. Art directors and designers are given as Fran Elfenbein and Herb Lubalin. Elfenbein was hired by Lubalin at Sudler & Hennessey shortly after graduating from Pratt in 1957. She first worked as Ernie Smith's assistant, and after a spell away from the agency, returned as Lubalin's design assistant. In 1965 she went to work for Lubalin in his newly formed design studio as a senior designer/art director. 'The work was varied, interesting and always had the Lubalin touch,' she recalls. She retired in 1999. Client: Committee for AIA Guide Book to New York City. Date: 1967.

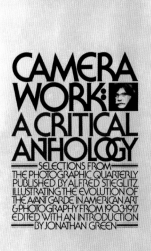

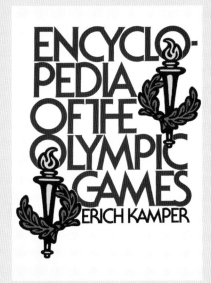

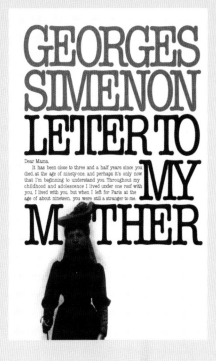

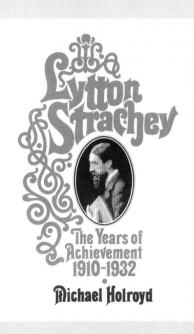

126. Camera Work ...
Typical Lubalin design for the cover for an anthology of articles culled from *Camera Work*, the quarterly photographic journal published by Alfred Stieglitz from 1903 to 1917. Editor Jonathan Green was associate editor of *Aperture Quarterly*, 1974—1976. To ensure his trademark block of type, Lubalin modifies the lettering in places. Note the way he dispenses with the letter 'T' in the word 'Anthology'. Text prints black on gold foil background. Client: Alfred Stieglitz/Aperture Inc. Date: 1973.

127. Encyclopedia ... Olympic Games
Jacket design for hardcover version of book by Erich Kamper, the distinguished lexicographer of the modern Olympic Games. Kemper wrote a number of books about the Games. Again, Lubalin modifies and conjoins letters to create the desired type block. Client: McGraw-Hill. Date: 1972.

128. Letter to my Mother
Jacket design for book by prolific Belgian writer Georges Simenon, best known for his novels about the detective Maigret. Lubalin uses the then-newish typeface ITC American Typewriter Condensed (designed by Joel Kaden and Tony Stan, 1974). Client: Harcourt Brace Jovanovich. Date: 1976.

129. The Penguin Companion to ...
Unremarkable design for compendium of literature. Typeface is Bernase Roman, attributed to Ronne Bonder and Tom Carnase. Bonder was a former business partner of Carnase's, and the designer of many popular typefaces including ITC Machine and ITC Pioneer. Client: McGraw-Hill. Date: 1971.

130. The Silent Syndicate
Cover design for book by Hank Messick, an author and investigative journalist who wrote extensively about organized crime. Ellen Lupton has written about this cover: '[it] uses a field of text as a direct "illustration" or sample of the book's interior content. As in his designs for *Fact*, Lubalin suggests that a book can be judged by its cover; the text has an air of frank literalness that a conventional illustration might lack.' Client: Macmillan. Date: 1967.

131. Lytton Strachey
Dust jacket for book about Lytton Strachey, one of the pioneers of 20th-century biography. He was a member of the Bloomsbury Set. The florid and highly decorative design is credited to 'Herb Lubalin, Inc./Alan Peckolick (illustrator)'. Client: Holt, Rinehart and Winston. Date: 1968.

NEW YORK JEW

ALFRED KAZIN

132. New York Jew
Austere dust jacket for book by Alfred
Kazin, an American writer and critic,
who wrote mainly about the immigrant
experience in early 20th-century
America. The stark type-only design
makes use of the popular typeface
ITC Benguiat, with slight modifications
— although fewer than is customary
in Lubalin's book designs of this period.
This highly successful typeface is descended from Kleukens, the Art Nouveau
font designed by German type designer
Friedrich Wilhelm Kleukens. Benguiat
adheres to the ITC style of large x-height
and closely fitting letters. Client:
Random House Inc. Date: 1978.

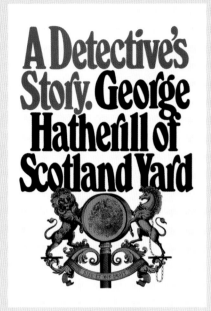

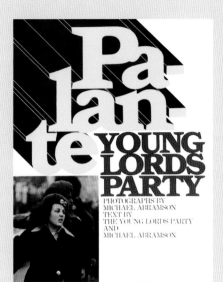

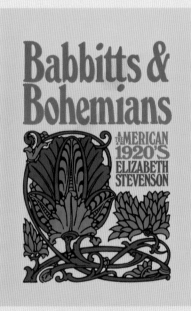

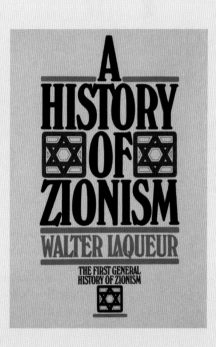

133. A Detective's Story
Faux-heraldic cover design for book by George Hatherill, an ex-Commander of New Scotland Yard. Typeface is Windsor Elongated, with compressed letter spacing so that letters touch or merge, and with other modifications. The illustration is a mild lampoon of the coat of arms of the United Kingdom. 'Dieu et mon droit' (God and my right) is the motto of the British Monarch in England. Note fingerprint in circle. Illustration: unknown. Client: McGraw-Hill. Date: 1971.

134. Palante
Cover for book about Young Lords Party, a Puerto Rican nationalist group found in several US cities, notably New York City. Client: McGraw-Hill Book Company Date: 1971.

135. Yes, Married
Book jacket with another outing for Lubalin's liking for arranging the two "R's"in the word 'married' to face each other. It was a graphic trope he used on a number of occasions (p.106). It is also another book cover that Lubalin designed for writer Judith Viorst. The lettering is slightly modified Souvenir (designed by Ed Benguiat). Client: Saturday Review Press. Date: 1972.

136. Portal to America
Jacket design for a book about the harsh reality of life in New York City for immigrants: 'As a portal, the Lower East Side — the area bounded by the Brooklyn Bridge on the south, Fourteenth Street on the north, Broadway on the west, and the East River on the east — prepared Jews, Italians, Irish, Chinese, and Poles for the greater America that lay beyond its boundaries.' Client: Henry Holt & Co. Date: 1967.

137. Babbitts & Bohemians
Dust jacket for a book about two conflicting views of America in the 1920s. Elizabeth Stevenson describes how the citizenry of mainstream America embraced conventional life, while at the same time, bohemians in Greenwich Village and expatriates in Paris scorned it. Client: Transaction Publishers. Date: 1967.

138. A History of Zionism
A typically impacted typographic design for a book by historian Walter Laqueur. The typeface, Windsor Elongated, is combined with graphic renderings of the Star of David. Although Lubalin was Jewish by birth, he was not religious. His son Peter remembers the family celebrating Christmas. Client: Holt Rinehart and Winston. Date: 1972.

AMERICAN SHOWCASE OF PHOTOGRAPHY AND ILLUSTRATION

139. American Showcase
Jacket design for compendium of photography and illustration. Once more, we see the Lubalin device of referencing the American flag, both graphically (its rectangular proportions) and its colours (red, white and blue). Design is credited to Herb Lubalin and Michael Aron, an important member of the Lubalin team in the late 1970s. Client: American Showcase Inc. Date: 1979.

140. A Women's Liberation ...
Another book by Judith Viorst. Illustration: John Alcorn. Designers: Herb Lubalin and Annegret Beier. Client: World Publishing Company. Date: 1971.

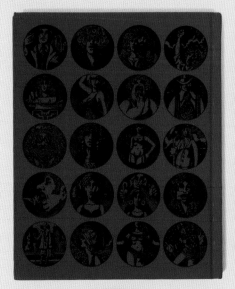

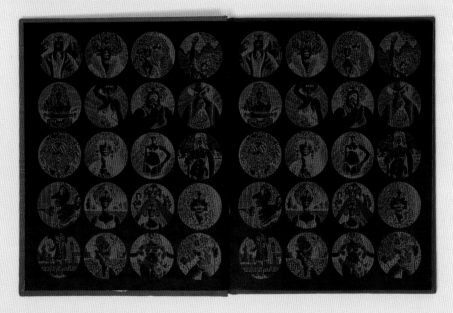

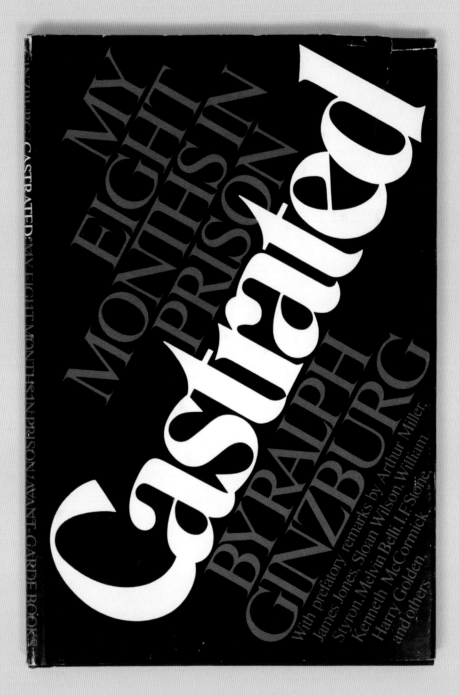

Ralph Ginzburg's imprisonment climaxed a ten-year literary cause célèbre stemming from the United States Supreme Court's suppression of his quarterly *Eros*. The Court found *Eros* "obscene." The Court's decision, in turn, has been denounced as obscene by leading professors, civil libertarians and students of constitutional law. One member of the Court itself, the conservative Mr. Justice Potter Stewart (who voted for overturning Ginzburg's conviction), declared that the decision in *Ginzburg vs. United States* was the worst since he had been on the Court. Ralph Ginzburg's account of his imprisonment is both an historical document and a profoundly moving, unabashedly intimate personal narrative.

141. Castrated

Dust jacket and spreads for Ralph Ginzburg's account of his time in prison as a result of obscenity charges. The designer is Herb Lubalin. From Ginzburg's handwritten note (written 16 years after Lubalin's death), we can glimpse the warmth and depth of the relationship between the two men. The account of their time working together is told in detail elsewhere (p.48).
Client: Avant-Garde Books. Date: 1973.

To Harlie, where-
ever you are!
Still, after all
these years, I
miss you so.
Ralph Ginzburg
12/97

Castrated
MY EIGHT
MONTHS
IN PRISON
BY RALPH
GINZBURG
DESIGNED BY HERB LUBALIN

AVANT
GARDE
BOOKS

FEDERAL PRISON
CAMP

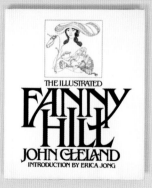

142. The Illustrated Fanny Hill
A tour de force of book design for John
Cleland's erotic novel of 1748. The book
has a long history of suppression and
controversy due to the sexual nature of
its subject matter. The designer is Herb
Lubalin and the illustrator is Zevi Blum,
who worked with Lubalin on other
projects. Blum was born in Paris in 1933;
his work has been described as 'gothic
whimsy'. Lettering is by Tony Di Spigna,
and the typeface is ITC Benguiat. Erica
Jong wrote the introduction and the
book's editor is Shoshana Ginzburg,
the wife of Ralph Ginzburg and a key
figure in the development of *Avant
Garde* magazine. Client: The Erotic Art
Book Society. Date: 1978.

ISBN 0-915566-26-0

NE PLUS ULTRA

INTRODUCTION
WRITTEN BY
ERICA JONG.
DESIGNED BY
HERB LUBALIN.
ILLUSTRATED
BY ZEVI BLUM.

JOHN CLELAND FANNY HILL

THE EROTIC ART BOOK SOCIETY
1775 BROADWAY NYC 10019

ISBN 0-915566-26-0

NE PLUS U

I concluded that I had fallen into the hands of the kindest mistress in the world

---

Letter the First

M

ADAM: I sit down to give you an undeniable proof of my considering your desires as indispensable orders. Ungracious then as the task may be, I shall recall to view those scandalous stages of my life, out of which I emerg'd, at length, to the enjoyment of every blessing in the power of love, health, and fortune to bestow; whilst yet in the flower of youth, and not too late to employ the leisure afforded me by great ease and affluence, to cultivate an understanding, naturally not a despicable one, and which had, even amidst the whirl of loose pleasures I had been tost in, exerted more observation on the characters and manners of the world than what is common to those of my unhappy profession, who looking on all thought or reflection as their capital enemy, keep it at as great a distance as they can, or destroy it without mercy.

Hating, as I mortally do, all long unnecessary preface, I shall give you good quarter in this, and use no farther apology, than to prepare you for seeing the loose part of my life, wrote with the same liberty that I led it.

Truth! stark, naked truth, is the word; and I will not so much as take the pains to bestow the strip of a gauze wrapper on it, but paint situations such as they actually rose to me in nature, careless of violating those laws of decency that were never made for such unreserved intimacies as ours; and you have too much sense, too much knowledge of the *originals* themselves, to sniff prudishly and out of character at the *pictures* of them. The greatest men, those of the first and most leading taste, will not scruple adorning their private closets with nudities, though, in compliance with vulgar prejudices, they may not think them decent decorations of the staircase, or salon.

This, and enough, premised, I go souse into my personal history. My maiden name was *Frances Hill*. I was born at a small village near *Liverpool*, in *Lancashire*, of parents extremely poor, and, I piously believe, extremely honest.

My father, who had received a maim on his limbs that disabled him from following the more laborious branches of country-drudgery, got, by making of nets, a scanty subsistence, which was not much enlarg'd by my mother's keeping a little day-school for the girls in her neighbourhood. They had had several children; but none lived to any age except myself, who had received from nature a constitution perfectly healthy.

My education, till past fourteen, was no better than very vulgar; reading, or rather spelling, an illegible scrawl, and a little ordinary plain work composed the whole system of it; and

AMERICA UNLIMITED
THE AMERICA FUND
303 LEXINGTON AVE., NEW YORK, N.Y. 10016

AIRMAIL

Number *338*   *338*

AMERICA UNLIMITED
THE AMERICA FUND
303 LEXINGTON AVE.
NEW YORK, N.Y. 10016
MURRAY HILL 5-17801-2

Founding Patrons Membership Reservation

I support the goals and purposes of **America Unlimited** and would like my name entered on the permanent Roster of Founding Patrons. I understand that I will receive a Founders Certificate suitable for framing, a Founding Patrons Identification Card for convenience in using **America Unlimited** facilities, regular issues of the *Bulletin*, and a subscription to the beautifully-illustrated publication, *American Monthly Magazine*.

Like John Steinbeck, I am concerned about the character of the American environment—its physical, cultural, social and technological aspects—and about the welfare and dignity of Americans living in that environment. I want to be one of those doing something today to make the American tomorrow a more beautiful one.

I would like to help launch the National Campaign to raise funds, coordinate sponsorship and institute the practical programs of **America Unlimited**.

Enclosed is my contribution made payable to **The America Fund** in the amount of $_____

I understand this donation to the general fund of **America Unlimited, Inc.**, will be fully tax-deductible, and that it will be used solely to maintain and promote **America Unlimited** and its charitable programs. As a Founding Patron I understand that I will be kept personally informed about the work of the organization and about my opportunities to participate actively in its exciting and worthwhile projects.

I look forward to receiving my personal set of *America and Americans*, by John Steinbeck, *In Wildness is the Preservation of the World*, by Eliot Porter, and *God's Own Junkyard*, by Peter Blake.

☐ I can also use some extra copies of *America, the Beautiful*, brochure and songsheet.

Signed _____

Date _____

143. America Unlimited
Patriotic design for America Unlimited, a charitable organization dedicated to research and education. Shown is envelope and fund-raising letter. Client: America Unlimited Inc. Date: c. 1968.

144. Postage stamps
Rejected designs for U.S. postage stamps. To modern eyes, these designs appear sharply contemporary. Ironically, the US Postal Service was to play another role in Lubalin's life when a court action was brought against Ralph Ginzburg for sending obscene material through the mail resulted in the closure of *Eros* magazine and the eventual imprisonment of Ginzburg. Client: US Postal Service. Lettering: Tom Carnase. Date: c. 1978.

145. Postage stamps
Design for series of Air Mail postage stamps exhibiting Lubalin's trademark love of blocks of justified type and vernacular illustration. Stamps shown: Liberty Bell, 10c and 13c; Statue of Liberty, 15c; Abraham Lincoln, 25c. Designers: Herb Lubalin and John Pistilli. Illustrator: Joseph Lombardero. Client: US Postal Service. Date: 1959—1961.

146. Our Best Wishes ...
Spread from *U&lc*. In the table of
contents for that issue it states: 'Happy
New Year. *U&lc* expresses its best
wishes in a handsome greeting created
by Tom Carnase.' Date: Dec 1979.

147. Marge & Jeff
Highly stylized card announcing the
birth of a baby girl. This simple item
exhibits many of Lubalin's trademark
typographic mannerisms. Date: 1973.

148. Art Kane Announces ...
Another instantly recognizable block
of expertly dovetailed Lubalin type.
Font: Avant Garde Gothic Extra Light.
Client: Art Kane. Date. c. 1970.

ART KANE ANNOUNCES THE OPENING OF HIS NEW STUDIO AT 1181 BROADWAY, NEW YORK, N.Y. 10001. (212) 582-0780 REPRESENTED BY BILL RABIN, 944-6655

149

150

149—151. Gastrotypographical ...
This famous wall is now part of graphic design history. It spanned more than 35 feet in width, and more than 8 feet in height, and was situated in the canteen at CBS headquarters, 51 West 52nd Street, New York City. The wall was envisaged by Lou Dorfsman, CBS's director of design at the time. Dorfsman resisted the idea of a photographic blow-up, opting instead to treat the wall like a giant typesetter's case, with a lock-up of words and objects on the theme of food. Dorfsman enlisted the support of his friend Herb Lubalin. Along with Tom Carnase, Lubalin crafted the typography. The wall was created in nine panels. Most of the words were jigsawed out of wood. Gaps were filled with specially made food props, and the entire installation was spray-painted with white enamel. The installation is reported to have cost $14,000. It was dismantled in the 1990s, but the constituent parts were saved and the wall is being restored by The Center for Design Study. Figs.149 and 150 show preliminary drawings. Fig.151 shows Lou Dorfsman standing in front of the finished work. Client: CBS. Date: 1966.

THE MARILYN MONROE TRIP:
A PORTFOLIO OF SERIGRAPHIC
PRINTS BY BERT STERN

AVANT
GARDE 12

U&lc.

SCARAB
SCARAB
SCARAB
SCARAB

EDI TOR IAL

fact

American Cars Are Death Traps
This issue reveals which car makes are the most dangerous of all

EROS

Spring, 1962

"Before"
An engraving by William Hogarth, 1798

1. Eros, Number 1

Eros was a quarterly 'magazine' devoted to erotica. It was the first time Herb Lubalin and editor Ralph Ginzburg worked together. *Eros* boasted an eclectic mix of articles and imagery. The inaugural issue contained a range of articles including: 'A Plea for Polygamy' by Dr. Albert Ellis; poems by the Earl of Rochester (born 1647); and a photographic essay on male prostitutes in Bombay by Art Kane. This was sexual enquiry at its most diverse. The publication styled itself as a magazine, but in truth it was a hardback book with high-level production values. It carried no advertising, leaving Lubalin free to mix paper stocks and use sophisticated layout techniques. The playing card on the front cover is tipped in.
Date: Spring 1962.

2. Endpapers

Heavy yellow stock is used for front and back endpapers. The engraving is by William Hogarth and is titled 'Before'. The book ends with Hogarth's 'After' (not shown here).

3. Who Was Eros?

Generous opening spread for the inaugural issue of *Eros*. Note that even here, in this elegant typographic construction, Lubalin cannot resist filling in the 'O' of the word 'Eros' — a Lubalin trope that began with one of his first pieces of published work (p.14).

4. Love in the Subway

Photographic essay by Garry Winogrand, a celebrated street photographer, who studied painting and photography at Columbia University in New York in 1948, and attended a photojournalism class taught by Alexey Brodovitch. These atmospheric shots of romantic encounters on the New York subway are presented without commentary — a tactic Lubalin and Ginzburg were to repeat many times when they worked together on *Avant Garde* magazine. Lubalin fills the pages with Winogrand's images, creating an impression of subterranean claustrophobia.

5, 6. Depictions of Eros

Top, left-hand page: *Venus and Cupid* by Paris Bordone. Right-hand page: *The Education of Cupid* by Correggio. Bottom, left-hand page: *Adonis Discovers Venus* by Annibale Carracci. Right-hand page: *Cupid and Psyche* by François Gérard.

7, 8. Me & the Male Prostitutes ...

Photo-essay with text by the photographer Art Kane. Born in New York City, Kane became best known for his work in fashion and music. He made many portraits of musicians, including Bob Dylan, The Who and the Rolling Stones. Kane took his remarkable portraits of male prostitutes and transvestites while on an assignment in India in the 1960s. Lubalin's bold layout and his use of hot colours (fig.7) forces the viewer to confront the reality of these marginalized people. Courtesy of The Art Kane Archive: www.artkane.com.

WHO WAS EROS?

Eros was the Greek god of love. In early myths he is portrayed by storytellers and artists as a beautiful and serious youth who brings harmony out of chaos. Later stories picture him as a mischievous little boy with golden wings, often blindfolded, indiscriminately setting hearts afire with his torch or piercing the stoutest barriers to love with his arrows. He was never admitted to Mount Olympus because of his capriciousness. Most accounts call Aphrodite the mother of Eros, but we do not know whether his father was Hermes, Ares or Zeus. Hermes, a phallic deity, would have been a fitting lover for Aphrodite, to whom the Fates assigned only one divine duty—making love. Ares, the brawny god of war, may have worn the first uniform that ever turned an impressionable female's head. And Zeus, Aphrodite's own father, may have demonstrated that flaming passion need not stop short of incest. More than two millennia separate Aeschylus from Tennessee Williams, but love is pretty much the same. Eros brings both delight and vexation, both joy and grief. To him we have dedicated our magazine. On balance, we feel as Plato did when he wrote: "Love—Eros—makes his home in men's hearts, but not in every heart, for where there is hardness he departs...and he whom Love touches not walks in darkness." On the following pages we present six masterpieces of painting in which Eros has been depicted. Their titles use the Latin names of the gods: Cupid for the Greek Eros, Venus for Aphrodite, Mercury for Hermes and Mars for Ares.

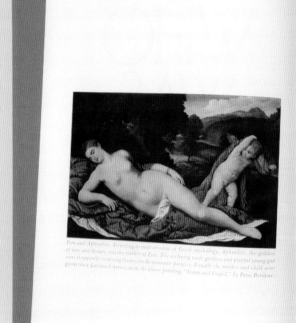

Eros and Aphrodite. According to most versions of Greek mythology, Aphrodite, the goddess of love and beauty, was the mother of Eros. The reclining nude goddess and playful young god were frequently recurring themes for Renaissance painters. Usually the mother and child were given their Latinized names, as in the above painting, "Venus and Cupid," by Paris Bordone.

Eros receives his education from Hermes. A master thief on one hand and the inventor of the lyre on the other, Hermes was able to impart a great number of useful skills to the young god of love. The painting, titled "The Education of Cupid," is by Correggio.

Aphrodite turns upon Aphrodite's command. The stirring was engineered by young Eros. Ares, a jealous lover of Aphrodite, first disguised himself as a wild boar and gored Adonis to death, to Aphrodite's everlasting grief. This is Annibale Carracci's "Adonis Discovers Venus."

Eros, approaching manhood, with Psyche. His mother, Aphrodite, had tried to discourage their romance which culminated, nevertheless, in their marriage, symbolizing the union of Passion and Soul. The painting is François Gérard's "Cupid and Psyche."

The Push-button Test

Only the Festive

photographs & text by Art Kane

me & the male prostitutes of Bombay

EROS

Summer, 1962

Summer,1962

9, 10, 18. Eros, Number 2
Cover and endpapers for second edition of *Eros*. The social mores of 1962 did not permit Ginzburg and Lubalin the freedom they would enjoy when they came to publish the raunchier *Avant Garde* in 1969. But *Eros* was pushing the boundaries of what was permissible. Cover and endpapers show photographs by Donald Snyder. Snyder published the book *Aquarian Odyssey* in 1980. By printing Snyder's images onto coloured stock, Lubalin creates a powerful opening and closing statement. Date: Summer 1962.

11, 12. We All Love Jack
Double-page spreads for essay analyzing the pop-star-like appeal of John F. Kennedy in his bid to become the next U.S. president. Lubalin uses press shots to suggest the attraction of Kennedy to a young, mainly female, audience. As usual, his pacing is immaculate; tiny pictures on the opening spread are followed by a full-bleed image.

13—16. Les Mesdemoiselles
Double-page spreads for daring photo-essay on Parisian prostitutes. Here again, no text accompanies the images. Lubalin and Ginzburg were pioneers of the photo-essay and the ability of a new visually literate generation to follow pictorial narratives. Photography is by Marvin E. Newman. A successful photojournalist, Newman contributed to *Sports Illustrated*, *Life*, *Look* and *Newsweek*. His moody shots of life on the streets of Paris have a contemporary flavour of understated realism. Like stills from a 1960s *nouvelle vague* movie, these images are not sensationalist. Lubalin's masterly layout gives the sequence pace and grandeur. The only colour shot is printed on gloss art paper; the remaining black and white images sit on matt stock, divided by thin white borders.

17. Letters
In advance of publishing the first issue of *Eros*, the publishers had sent three million letters inviting the recipients to become subscribers. 10,000 replies were received. About 20 per cent were hostile: *Eros* published 16 pages of these hostile responses. They note: 'All together, the critical letters presented a candid view of present-day puritanism in the United States ... so valuable do we believe these letters to be as sociological and psychological artefacts that we are presenting them to the Institute for Sex Research at the University of Indiana ...' A *Monty Python*-esque quality is evident in some of the more agitated responses. Lubalin has replicated the original perforations from the questionnaire in the pages of *Eros*, however the handwriting was extensively faked by Tom Carnase.

222

WE ALL LOVE JACK

by Faye Emerson

First there were the "jumpers." It began with the primaries, when John F. Kennedy was fighting desperately for the nomination a lot of Americans thought he was too young, too Catholic, and too rich to deserve. His political advisers and the press, alert to any straw in the wind, began to notice an odd reaction in the crowds. An increasing number of young women seemed to be traveling by pogo sticks and when Mr. Kennedy approached, they bounced in the air like lady jumping jacks. They shrieked ecstatically, threw kisses and waved madly at their hero.

Then there were the "touchers." These were for the most part respectable, mature women who, with incredible determination and stamina, fought their way close to Mr. Kennedy, patted him gently and retired dazed and happy. They didn't even ask for his autograph.

As the phenomenon of female reaction to the candidate became more pronounced, there was a good deal of discussion as to just what it all meant. The political wise men shook their heads gravely and the press viewed with suspicion, if not outright alarm. No one had seen anything quite like it before in politics. This was not the fond father figure of Eisenhower. It wasn't even like the "friend-protector" magic of F. D. R. No, this was much more personal. And there was something for all the girls. His boyish appeal made mothers and grandmothers want to look after him, see that he got a haircut and a good meal. Wives all over the country daydreamed themselves into Jackie's shoes. Teen-agers forgot about Fabian, and the very young set thought Caroline was the luckiest little girl in the world. Glamorous movie stars stumbled over their sables to stand near him, even when there wasn't a camera in sight. An astonishing number of ladies in café society suddenly recalled intimate little friendships with "Jack," and a few hinted discreetly at even more tender relationships—pre-Jackie, of course.

The press and the politicians were puzzled. What did it mean to the candidate? "It's nice to be loved," they said, "but is it dignified?" What would it do to the so-called "image" that had been so carefully presented? Were the women voters listening with cool intelligence to Mr. Kennedy speak of taxes, tariffs and treaties? Were they moved by the call of the New Frontier, or was it just "that old feeling"? And most important of all, would this surge of emotion sweep the ladies into the voting booths? Would love pull the right lever?

Well, the answers to all these questions are now purely academic. How much influence the lovelorn ladies had on the election will be found in the history books eventually, but in the meantime, the romance is still on. The females of this country have a crush on J.F.K. They dig him. His shining armor may be a little battered, but it doesn't hide his sex appeal.

5

La patience, c'est la vertu.

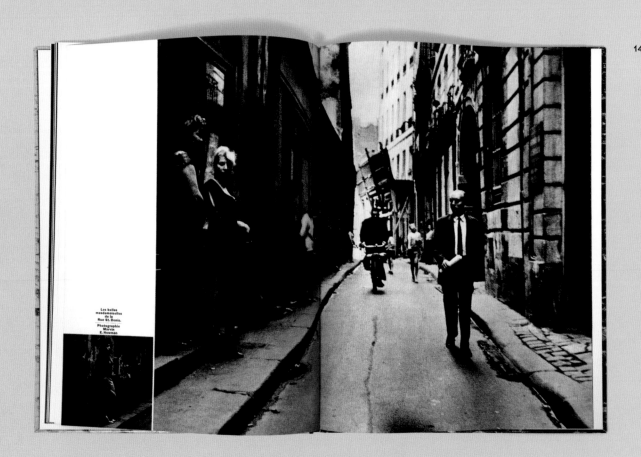

Les belles
mesdemoiselles
de la
Rue St. Denis.
Photographie
Marvin
E. Newman

227

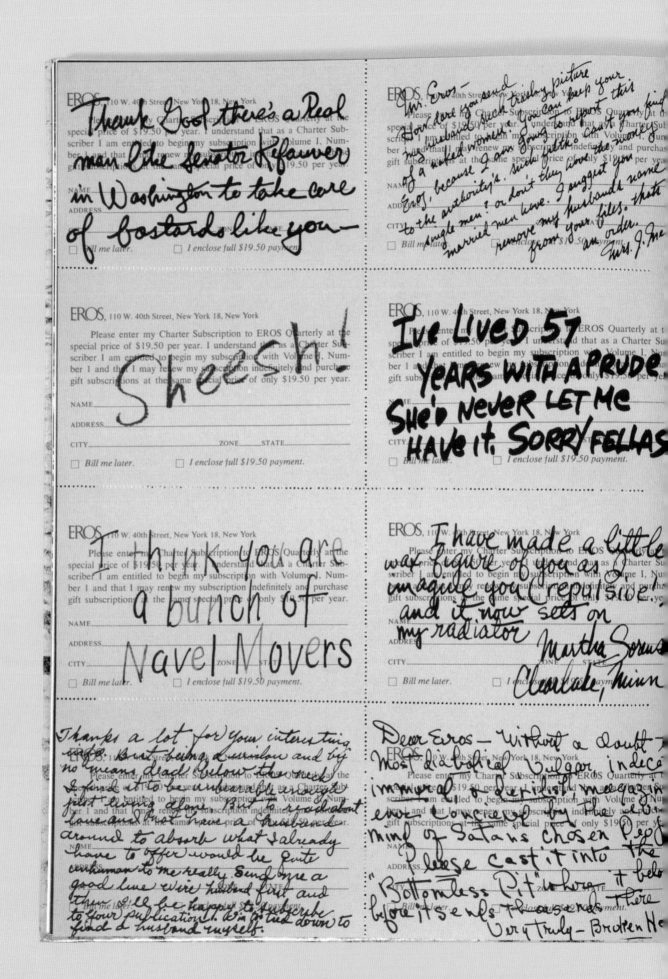

It is a well known fact that it is part of the Communist
Master Plan to undermine the people through sex and dope, before they take over a country. You may fool some stupid people,
but most will see through your sinister plan.

Sending this obscene literature to clergymen shows your
utter disdain for this group. More proof of your Communist
backing.

Your statement that the country is ready for this magazine
is the understatement of the year. You may think you are ready
for a takeover, but there are still a lot of people who are
ready to fight.

Everyone I know of who received your insulting offer is up
in arms. They are bombarding their Congressmen and Senators to
protest your vile action. They will keep on until they obtain a
reversal of the laws.

I predict that your plan won't get off the ground. Financial
ruin is letting you off too easily. We plan to see you prosecuted
and put in prison where you belong.

                                        Americans For Decency

                                                    April 3, 1962

FIRST BAPTIST CHURCH / WEST PALM BEACH, FLORIDA / DR. JESS C. MOODY, SENIOR MINISTER / TE 3-3622

Editor
Eros
110 W. 40th Street
New York, 18, New York

Dear Sir:

Thanks for doing your best to break the moral
foundations of our nation. I intend to give
straightforward comment concerning your publication on my daily TV show. I will not dignify
your publication by mentioning its name, however.

Please put your country and its survival above
the almighty dollar.

Sincerely,

Jess Moody

Jess Moody

JM:k

EROS

On June 21, 1962, Bert Stern took the last studio portraits of Marilyn Monroe. That was six weeks before her tragic death. A portfolio of these photographs begins on page three.

19. Eros, Number 3
In June 1962, Bert Stern photographed Marilyn Monroe. It was the first time Stern had photographed her, and it was to be the last time she entered a photographic studio: she died six weeks later. The three-day session, conducted on behalf of *Vogue*, yielded nearly 2,600 pictures. Lubalin's cover uses unedited strips of film, showing how Stern has captured the chaste eroticism that was Monroe's hallmark. Her most salient quality, besides her natural beauty, was innocence. Stern published the photographs later in a book called *Marilyn Monroe: The Complete Last Sitting* (Schirmer/Mosel, 2006). Date: Autumn 1962.

20. Endpapers
Lubalin makes dramatic use of Monroe's face. By using the portrait full-bleed, he maximizes its psychological impact: we sense that we are seeing the real Monroe.

21. The passing of time ...
Exquisitely framed and posed pictures of the star in a black evening gown. Lubalin's retention of the black photo frames gives the images added graphic impact and imparts a sense of isolation.

22. Underappreciated ...
In a postmodern gesture of openness, Lubalin retains the original scratches and rejection crosses made by Monroe herself. His bold use of this rejected shot gives this sequence a transgressive quality. Not only is the picture crossed out with an emphatic X, but Monroe is also naked (clad only in jewels, echoing her famous song 'Diamonds Are a Girl's Best Friend' from the film *Gentlemen Prefer Blondes*; her half-open eyes suggest someone lost in the throes of erotic pleasure. The film strip on the right-hand page shows the value of retaining the hard black frames of transparencies.

23—26. Various double-page spreads
The sessions produced a wide variety of poses, costumes and stylings. In a short editorial fore-note to introduce the photographs, it is stated that: 'Marilyn became a fantastic model right before Stern's eyes. She would work until two and three in the morning, playing her favourite Frank Sinatra records to help her react before the camera, while the improvised studio at the Bel Air Hotel in Los Angeles became littered with rolls of film, lights, trays of food, and bottles of champagne.' Text is used sparingly, and set in old-style Garamond Italic. The session is spread over 18 pages.

"The passing of time is making it clear that the peak of Marilyn Monroe's trage...

...t she never knew how much people everywhere loved her." Richard Watts Jr., critic.

"She was one of the most unappreciated people in the world."
Joshua Logan, director.

15

"I never quite understood it, this sex symbol. But if I'm going to be a symbol of something, I'd rather have it sex than some of the other things they've got symbols for." Marilyn Monroe.

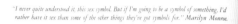

"Marilyn was a phenomenon of nature, like Niagara Falls and the Grand Canyon. You couldn't talk to it. It couldn't talk back to you. All you could do was stand back and be awed by it." Nunnally Johnson, producer.

"Gosh, there were a lot of people who loved her. There were no pretenses about Marilyn Monroe." Carl Sandburg

"She represents to man something we all want in our unfulfilled dreams. She's the girl you'd like to double-cross your wife with." Jean Negulesco, director.

EROS

And the Lord God caused a deep
sleep to fall upon Adam...and he
took one of his ribs. Genesis 2·21
And the rib, which the Lord God
had taken from man, made he a woman, and brought her unto the man 2·22
Of every tree of the garden
thou mayest freely eat. 2·16
But of the tree of the knowledge of good and evil, thou shalt
not eat. 2·17
She took of the fruit thereof, and
did eat, and gave also unto her husband with her, and he did eat. 3·6

27. Eros, Number 4
Despite its dark quasi-Biblical cover, *Eros* No. 4 was to prove the most controversial, indeed ruinous, of all four editions of the publication. Editor and publisher Ralph Ginzburg's ambitious libertarian plans for a sophisticated journal devoted to erotic art and literature was to prove too advanced for its time. The story is told in detail elsewhere (p.46), but the consequences of Ginzburg's ambitions were to result in his imprisonment in an American jail. Date: Winter 1962.

28. Unto the pure, all things are pure
The exuberant calligraphy is uncredited, but it is almost certainly by Hal Fiedler. Lubalin himself had learned calligraphy as a student at the Cooper Union. In fact, it was his early proficiency in calligraphy (an accomplishment greatly aided by his legendary ambidextrousness) that Lubalin found the confidence to become a graphic designer. The story is told in detail elsewhere (p.8).

29. Love in the Bible
Opening pages for main feature devoted to sexual content found in the Bible. The engraving of Adam and Eve is by Albrecht Dürer.

30. Was Shakespeare a Homosexual?
Opening spread for feature on the likelihood of Shakespeare being homosexual. Illustration is by Lionel Kalish — like Lubalin, a graduate of the Cooper Union.

31—34. Black and White in Colour
The opening spread (fig.31) announces: 'On the following eight pages, *Eros* proudly presents a photographic tone poem on the subject of interracial love.' The photographs, laughably tame by today's standards, were taken by Ralph M. Hattersley Jr. The disastrous outcome of these photographs is told elsewhere (p.48), but it is worth noting that they were far less 'revealing' than many of the erotic photographs used in the previous three editions of *Eros*. However, in pre-Civil Rights Act America, the sight of a naked, interracial couple embracing was a step too far. Although Ginzburg was to pay a heavy price for incurring the wrath of conservative forces in America, he did not suffer in vain. According to the journalist Nat Hentoff, the cultural historian, novelist and jazz critic, Ginzburg's efforts helped move the U.S. justice system towards the recognition of sexual content as free speech. Lubalin's layout shows his skill at placing images on a page, and his love of contrast — big pictures sit next to small ones — creates a taut, easy-to-navigate layout.

35. Lysistrata
Left-hand page shows final shot of 'Black and White' series. It was this image, where the couple's unseen genitals are pressed together, that caused Ginzburg's opponents the greatest anger. The right-hand page is the opening page for a 'free adaptation' of *Lysistrata*, a Greek masterpiece by Aristophanes. First performed in 411 BCE, it is a comic account of Lysistrata's efforts to end the Peloponnesian War. She persuades the women of Greece to withhold sexual favours as a way of persuading their menfolk to stop fighting. On this spread, Lubalin switches from gloss stock to matt stock; this deft gear change is satisfying to both the eye and the touch.

36—38. The Jewel Box Review
A photographic essay by Raymond Jacobs, a New York photographer who had work published in *Harper's Bazaar*, *Esquire* and *Picture Post*. The pictures document the life of a then-popular troupe of female impersonators called the Jewel Box Revue. Lubalin makes good use of mono, duotone and full-colour versions of the photographs. His layout uses his familiar technique of mixing large and small images.

39. Memoirs of a Male Chaperone
Illustrations are by Milton Glaser. Like Lubalin, Glaser was a Cooper Union alumnus, although he attended after Lubalin's time. As two giants of the New York graphic design scene, it is surprising that the two men did not work together more frequently.

Adam and Eve

Now the serpent was more subtil than any beast of the field which the LORD God had made. And
God said, Ye shall not eat of every tree of the garden? And the woman said unto the serpent, We
the garden: But of the fruit of the tree which is in the midst of the garden, God hath said, Ye sh

Love in the Bible

In 1895, John B. Wise of Clay Center, Kansas, was convicted of sending obscene material through the mail—material that consisted entirely of excerpts from the King James version of the Holy Bible.

At his trial, it must have struck Wise as ironic that *Exhibit A* in the case against him was also the book upon which the accusing postal authorities swore their oaths. Wise was hardly the first to discover this irony. At least twice before in American history, obscenity prosecutions had been based upon the Holy Bible, once in Maryland and once in New York.

So the Bible is obscene?

By the moral and social standards of postal officials in nineteenth century America, the answer is yes. For those postal officials, the Bible's countless descriptions of rape, incest, sexual sadism, fetishism, homosexuality, masturbation, castration, adultery, prostitution, and phallic worship were too much to take. What is more, these acts are seldom deplored in the Bible—they are in most cases related without comment.

In the Bible, sex begins in the Beginning. Adam seeks a mate in the animal kingdom (Genesis 2:20) and only when he fails to find one does God create Eve from Adam's rib. That the man "gives birth" to the woman here, contrary to both natural law and to the mythology patterns of most other cultures, is a reflection of one of the most interesting psychological phenomena in the Bible, the superinflated importance of the male role in life— a function no doubt of the strong patriarchal influence in ancient Hebrew life. Obviously, the incident implies, the more important sex came first. We shall see further examples of this strong patriarchal point of view as we proceed.

That the rib in this story is a phallic symbol is apparent to mythologists as well as to psychologists. Aphrodite, in a less inhibited Greek version of this same story, was created from the cut-off

Was Shakespeare a Homosexual?

BY JOHN ERNO RUSSELL

Shall I compare thee to a summer's day?
Thou art more lovely and more temperate...

The world knows this as one of its best-loved and most tender love poems. The world, for the most part, does not know that the lovely party on the other end of Shakespeare's line was not a demure, beauteous maiden at all. The lovely party in this case—and in 126 of Shakespeare's 154 sonnets—was a rich, spoiled, but irresistibly beauteous boy.

Two loves have I ...
The better angel is a man right fair
The worser spirit is a woman, colour'd ill.

The world in general may neither know nor care about Shakespeare's amorous preferences, but the literary world seems both to know and to care very much indeed. In the three and one half centuries since Shakespeare's death, no aspect of his personality has provoked more acrimonious controversy than the question of his homosexuality.

Nearly 2000 books, articles, and treatises, embodying the opinions of such august literary personalities as Coleridge, Keats, Goethe, Wilde, Butler, Shaw, Joyce, and Gide, have been published on the subject. And no work of Shakespeare's—with the possible exception of *Hamlet*—has received greater attention than the opus that brought forth all this trouble: his sonnets.

27

black & white in color

A PHOTOGRAPHIC TONE POEM BY RALPH M. HATTERSLEY JR.

On the following eight pages, EROS proudly presents a photographic tone poem on the subject of interracial love. This is presented with the conviction that love between a man and a woman, no matter what their races, is beautiful. Interracial couples of today bear the indignity of having to defend their love to a questioning world. Tomorrow these couples will be recognized as the pioneers of an enlightened age in which prejudice will be dead and the only race will be the human race.

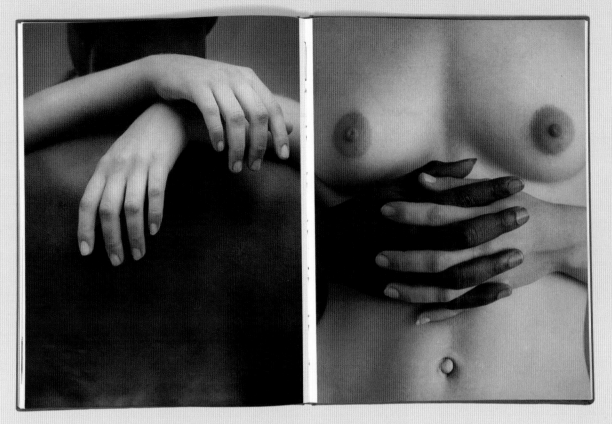

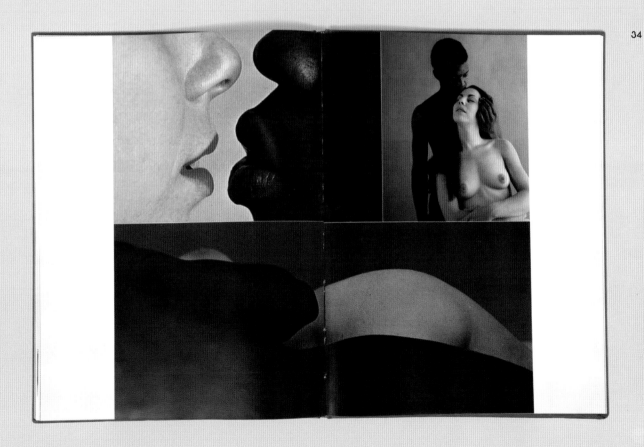

LYSISTRATA
BY ARISTOPHANES
IN A FREE ADAPTATION BY IVAN GRAZNI

CAST OF CHARACTERS

LYSISTRATA
a frustrated woman of Athens

KALONIKE }
MYRRHINE }
women friends of Lysistrata

LAMPITO
a Spartan woman

A BOEOTIAN NOBLEWOMAN

A CORINTHIAN WOMAN

KINESIAS
Myrrhine's husband

LITTLE BOY
their son

ATHENIAN POLICE CHIEF

CONSTABLES

SPARTAN HERALD

SPARTAN AMBASSADORS

CHORUSES OF OLD MEN, OLD WOMEN, AND YOUNG WOMEN

ASTERISKES
a walking footnote

Danny Brown, left, co-director of the Jewel Box Revue, guides a rehearsal at the Bal Tabarin, New York. The Jewel Box Revue is America's best-known company of female-impersonators. Below, the men present their stylized version of the cancan.

THE JEWEL BOX REVUE

A photographic essay by Raymond Jacobs

The most unexplainable phenomenon of show business in the year 1962 was the sudden increase in the popularity of that highly specialized branch of entertainment known as female-impersonation. Very simply, female-impersonation consists of men who dress like women, sing and dance like women, and even beguile and titillate like women. Several dozen companies of these female-impersonators are presently touring the nation's theaters and clubs, playing to record crowds.

By far the most popular troupe of female-impersonators is also the oldest and best-known, the Jewel Box Revue. It consists of some thirty men who present a two-and-a-half hour vaudeville routine, including elaborate choreography, music, and skits, and who are adorned with even more elaborate costuming and make-up. The men chirp in falsetto voices, flutter their false eyelashes, and sashay and wiggle their foam-rubber bosoms and behinds. And just as Liza Doolittle, in her strenuous efforts to acquire the poise of a lady, came closer to resembling a princess, so members of the Jewel Box Revue, in striving to attain femininity, don't just resemble women—but superwomen. This

helps explain why ninety per cent of their audiences—by actual survey—are made up not of other men, but of women. Dowdy housewives, antiseptic secretaries, and nostalgic old maids are bewitched by the glamour that these men, using standard cosmetic equipment, are able to project. Often Jewel Box performers are asked to appear on women's beauty-tip shows on TV and to act as make-up consultants to certain well-known show business figures. A number of Rockettes from Radio City Music Hall regularly bring their beauty problems to men of the Jewel Box Revue.

Creators and directors of the troupe are Danny Brown and Doc Benner, who organized it in 1932. Mr. Brown was then a master of ceremonies and Mr. Benner a dancer in a night club in Youngstown, Ohio. They started the review as a road show, later made it a resident company at a night club in Miami, and have since moved it to the Bal Tabarin in New York City (where the pictures on the following pages were taken).

"The show caught on right from the start," says Mr. Brown, "and the reason was that we took the degeneracy out of female-impersonation. Way back, in ancient China and in Shakespeare's time, all female roles were played by men. But during the early part of this century female-impersonation took on an unsavory character and fell out of popularity. We revived the art by staffing our company with actors of unimpeachable moral standards. Our players lead lives that are as normal as any in show business. Nine out of our thirty players are married, and the wife of one of them is our wardrobe mistress. Several of the married men have children and they bring their families along with them when we're on the road. They have no qualms about letting their kids see their act. The Jewel Box Revue is just a clean, family-type show."

15

38

39

MEMOIRS OF A MALE CHAPERON
BY JOHN SACK
The official escort of 21 Miss Universe contestants answers such questions as: Are bathing beauties beautiful but dumb? Do bathing beauties bathe? And what happened when one of the contestants entered his motel room late one night?

fact:

JANUARY-FEBRUARY 1964   VOLUME ONE, ISSUE ONE • $1.25

Bertrand Russell considers *Time* magazine to be "scurrilous and utterly shameless in its willingness to distort." **Ralph Ingersoll:** "In ethics, integrity, and responsibility, *Time* is a monumental failure." **Irwin Shaw:** *Time* is "nastier than any other magazine of the day." **Sloan Wilson:** "Any enemy of *Time* is a friend of mine." **Igor Stravinsky:** "Every music column I have read in *Time* has been distorted and inaccurate." **Tallulah Bankhead:** "Dirt is too clean a word for *Time*." **Mary McCarthy:** "*Time*'s falsifications are numerous." **Dwight Macdonald:** "The degree of credence one gives to *Time* is inverse to one's degree of knowledge of the situation being reported on." **David Merrick:** "There is not a single word of truth in *Time*." **P. G. Wodehouse:** "*Time* is about the most inaccurate magazine in existence." **Rockwell Kent:** *Time* "is inclined to value smartness above truth." **Eugene Burdick:** *Time* employs "dishonest tactics." **Conrad Aiken:** "*Time* slants its news." **Howard Fast:** *Time* provides "distortions and inaccuracies by the bushel." **James Gould Cozzens:** "My knowledge of inaccuracies in *Time* is first-hand." **Walter Winchell:** "*Time*'s inaccuracies are a staple of my column." **John Osborne:** "*Time* is a vicious, dehumanizing institution." **Eric Bentley:** "More pervasive than *Time*'s outright errors is its misuse of truth." **Vincent Price:** "Fortunately, most people read *Time* for laughs and not for facts." **H. Allen Smith:** "*Time*'s inaccuracies are as numerous as the sands of the Sahara." **Taylor Caldwell:** "I could write a whole book about *Time* inaccuracies." **Sen. John McClellan:** "*Time* is prejudiced and unfair."

40. Bertrand Russell considers ...
The inaugural issue of *Fact*. The publication was launched in January 1964 and appeared quarterly until August 1967. Ralph Ginzburg started the magazine after the closure of *Eros*, and in many ways, despite its conservative appearance, *Fact* was as revolutionary as *Eros*. It was a Ginzburgian mix of investigative journalism (or 'muckraking', as his detractors called it), and the beginnings of consumer advocacy. As with *Eros*, Herb Lubalin was the art director. And as before, Lubalin's role went beyond mere art direction and the layout of the pages: he was an active partner in setting the style and tone of the publication. Ginzburg said: 'Lubalin and I worked together like Siamese twins. It was a rare and remarkable relationship. I had no experience or training as a graphic designer. Herb brought a graphic impact. I never tried to overrule him and almost never disagreed with him.' Date: January—February, 1964.

fact:

VOLUME ONE, ISSUE FOUR $1.25

"Bobby Kennedy is the most vicious, evil _ _ _ _ in American politics today," says lawyer Melvin Belli.

41. Bobby Kennedy is the most ...
A typical example of a *Fact* cover: Lubalin's covers were stark, black and white, and mostly typographic. They appear guileless and almost bereft of 'design'. However, Lubalin introduced many subtle flourishes; for example, his use of the colon at the end of the word 'fact' and the way he incorporates it into the bowl of the 't'. As always with Lubalin, the kerning, leading and line breaks are handled with consummate skill. *Fact* covers used coated stock: inner pages were inexpensive pulp stock. As U.S. Attorney General, Bobby Kennedy had led the attack to close down *Eros* and prosecute Ginzburg. This cover ran while Ginzburg's trial was on-going. Date: July—August, 1964.

fact:

VOLUME ONE, ISSUE SIX $1.25

Coca-Cola can cause tooth decay, headaches, acne, nephritis, nausea, delirium, heart disease, emotional disturbances, constipation, insomnia, indigestion, diarrhea and mutated offspring.

42. The Case Against Coca-Cola
In each issue of *Fact*, Herb Lubalin made use of a single illustrator: in this case, the highly respected Paul Davis, one of the titans of American editorial illustration in the 1970s. His satiric depiction of a Coke bottle as a syringe set the critical tone for an eight-page article by contributing editor Warren Boroson, pointing out that Coca-Cola was not the harmless elixir of the American popular imagination. The front cover shows Lubalin's mastery of justified type.
Date: November—December, 1964.

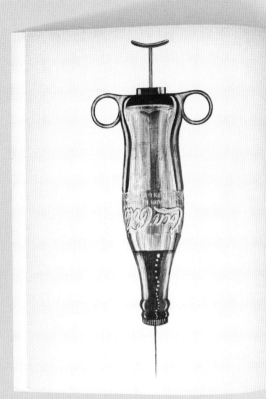

The Case
Against Coca-Cola
By Warren Boroson

The "pause that refreshes"? Many medical men think it would more aptly be called "the refreshment that poisons"

Coca-Cola is the best-known and most widely distributed commercial product in the world. Just in the United States alone, 40,000,000 drinks are consumed every day, which averages out so that every man, woman, and child could swizzle a Coke over 70 times a year. Abroad, the Big Daddy of soda pop is made in 129 countries at 1900 licensed bottling plants—understandably, many foreigners honestly believe that the object held aloft by the Statue of Liberty is a Coca-Cola bottle. But even though everyone from Adolf Hitler to Richard Nixon has tasted and enjoyed Coca-Cola, even though our Astronauts and Olympic Team members swill Coke regularly, even though records show that one baby imbibed Coke before milk and survived and one woman lived into her late 90s after having drunk a Coke a day for 60 years, even though hordes of people warmly agree with the *Life* Magazine man who called Coke "the sublimated essence of all that America stands for," even though Coke is served throughout our nation's hospitals and schools, and even though a Coca-Cola P.R. man has boasted of receiving "many letters from leading physicians, surgeons, and pediatricians who tell of their use of Coca-Cola professionally in their practice," there is nonetheless a massive dossier of medical evidence indicting Coca-Cola as one of the most poisonous beverages ever found in a bottle that doesn't bear a skull and crossbones.

Most people probably know that the dental profession has long damned Coke, Pepsi-Cola, and the hundreds of other cola drinks as among the worst enemies our teeth have. Coke and cavities go together, like cigarettes and cancer. But how many Americans know that an American Medical Association committee has urged our public schools to ban the sale of Coke and kindred cola drinks? How many Americans know that the leading association of nutritionists, the American Dietetic Association, refuses to run Coke ads in its official journal and forbids Coca-Cola exhibits at its conventions? Or that Coca-Cola contains caffeine—and because the caffeine is *cold*, it may be more harmful than the caffeine in coffee? Or that Coca-Cola has been implicated as a cause of palpitation, insomnia, nausea, vomiting, headache, dizziness, restlessness, anxiety, high blood pressure, delirium, acne, nephritis, emotional disturbances, and juvenile delinquency?

The answer, of course, is very few, but for that matter very few Americans even know what the ingredients of Coke are (they're not listed on the bottle because of a Food and Drug Administration screw-up). Over the years there's been an awful lot of brouhaha about the ingredients of Coke, but there's really no mystery. Analyses of Coca-Cola have been made

3

The Huckster
As Headshrinker
By Fredric Wertham, M.D.

Misuse of psychology by advertising men is creating cynicism, passivity, and a sense of inadequacy in the American people, says a noted psychiatrist

The successful advertiser, according to a widely read book, "sends his thoughts through all the instincts and passions of men; he knows their desires and their regrets; he knows every human weakness and is sure decoy."

This reference to a deep study of human nature for promotional purposes is not from a recent book. It was published almost a half-century ago. Since then, mass advertising has made tremendous strides. It has become all-pervasive and inescapable; it is not only part of business but part of our life. It faces us on the TV screens in our living rooms and in the landscape we view from our automobiles. And yet the basic purpose of advertising has remained the same. Industry produces the commodities, advertising produces the needs.

Now, there is no doubt that advertising can be beneficial. What is *not* sufficiently recognized is that large areas of modern advertising are harmful to the individual, both physically and mentally.

Actually, what is at issue is not advertising but *over*-advertising. The difference is like that between drinking and over-drinking. We may not know precisely at what point a man drinks enough to become an alcoholic—but we do know there are too many alcoholics.

Confronted with the ubiquitous pressure of advertising, the average individual feels—and rightly so—that he is exposed to a superior power. This contributes to his sense of isolation and alienation. Advertising does not appeal to our strength; it exploits our weaknesses. People are asked to believe that they choose when they are really being manipulated, to believe that they are buying when they are really being sold. If a lot of current advertising would cease, people would have more chance to act normally, to be themselves. The pressure of over-advertising helps to create the supposed antagonism between the individual and society.

How does the individual react to over-advertising? There are two ways: resistance and submission.

Resistance, the attempt to protect ourselves from being too gullible, has led—especially among the young—to a general attitude of cynicism: not only ads, but *everything* is "hooey."

In the second—submissive—type of reaction, individuals respond with compliance. They have been conditioned to jump for the product if the bell rings often enough. They have learned from childhood on that singing commercials are a basic form of communication, and they have difficulty giving their attention to any sober exposition that takes more than two minutes. They don't want to be told; they want to be sold. Many have been processed so well that they even accept absurdities—that perspiration

29

43. Marilyn Monroe by Bert Stern
A rare photographic cover. This issue
of *Fact* contains an essay by Ralph
Ginzburg recounting the 'true story' of
Eros, as well as a portfolio of images
from all four issues of *Eros*, including
the images that led to Ginzburg's
prosecution on obscenity charges and
the closure of *Eros*. The guest illustrator
was Barry Geller (work not shown).
Date: May—June, 1965.

The cover itself reads:

fact:

VOLUME TWO, ISSUE THREE $1.25

This issue contains a portfolio of the most beautiful art from Eros
together with the <u>true</u> story of how the magazine was suppressed

MARILYN MONROE, FROM THE MEMORABLE PHOTOGRAPHIC ESSAY IN EROS BY BERT STERN

43

fact:

$1.25
VOLUME THREE
ISSUE FOUR

A physician says, "Circumcision is unnecessary and barbaric. It cripples children, physically and mentally, for their whole lives."

44. Circumcision
Another rare photographic cover. The main feature is a study into circumcision. Also, a prophetic article by Beat poet and critic Kenneth Rexroth bemoans the fact that 'Books in America are commodities, no different from Rice Krispies and Thunderbirds.' The guest illustrator is Carl Fischer, who provides a series of photographic tableaux (work not shown).
Date: July—August, 1966.

fact:

VOLUME THREE, ISSUE ONE $1.25

Interracial marriage: in this issue Mort Sahl, the KKK's Robert Shelton, Godfrey Cambridge, Nat Hentoff, Judy Collins, Arthur Krock, Rudy Vallee, Ralph Ellison, Murray Kempton, Lillian Smith, Rona Jaffe, Paul Goodman, Harper Lee, Dave Garroway, Dore Schary, Harry Golden, Dr. Kenneth Clark, Gov. Ross Barnett of Mississippi and others give their personal views.

45. Interracial marriage
Interracial marriage was a recurring subject for Ginzburg and Lubalin. It was a topic famously tackled in *Eros* No.4 and revisited in *Avant Garde*. Sparse cover design with uncredited illustration. Date: January—February, 1966.

46. Vietnam
Issue contains British left-wing historian Arnold Toynbee's solution to the war in Vietnam; a compendium of LBJ jokes; and a survey describing the inroads made by homosexuals into the world of TV. Date: January—February, 1967.

47. Arnold Toynbee Excoriates ...
Another contribution from Arnold Toynbee. The anti-American sentiment expressed in the front cover display text is daring for the time. Ginzburg and Lubalin were not courting popularity. Illustration by Jim Spanfeller. Date: September—October, 1965.

48. Police brutality
Another topic — police brutality — unlikely to make *Fact* appeal to the leaders of conservative early 1960s America. Illustration by Richard Smith. Date: November—December, 1965.

49. Ophthalmology
Lubalin did not restrict himself to a rigid layout for *Fact* front covers. When the subject matter dictated, he was not averse to moving the masthead and changing the typeface. Here he incorporates photographic elements to give added impact. Date: September—October, 1966.

fact:

$1.25
VOLUME FOUR
ISSUE ONE

Vietnam: a way out, by Arnold Toynbee. Those hush-hush jokes about LBJ: what Americans really think about their president. **The fag-jag on the boob-tube: homosexual inroads into TV.**

fact:

VOLUME TWO, ISSUE FIVE $1.25

Arnold Toynbee Excoriates U.S. Policy in Viet Nam:

"THE USA IS BECOMING THE WORLD'S NUMBER ONE AGGRESSOR AND BULLY"

fact:

VOLUME TWO, ISSUE SIX $1.25

*"Police brutality" is **not** a myth. Experts say 7 out of 10 cops will use violence when it isn't needed.*

---

fact:

$1.25
VOLUME THREE
ISSUE FIVE

A professor of ophthalmology says, "Everybody who puts on contact lenses will experience eye damage, and in many cases the damage will be permanent."

259

fact:

VOLUME TWO, ISSUE ONE $1.25

"The Star Spangled Banner is just so much trash. -Joan Baez" Westbrook Pegler: "I think The Star-Spangled Banner is just terrible." Louis Untermeyer: "The poets and composers of America could come up with something much better." Richard Rodgers: "It's impossible to sing." Marya Mannes: "Any musician will tell you it's a lousy piece of music." Meredith Willson: "It violates every single principle of song writing." Elmer Bernstein: "In today's world, we could do without warlike anthems like The Star-Spangled Banner." Godfrey Cambridge: "It has no meaning for the black man." LeRoi Jones: "It's pompous, hypocritical, vapid, and sterile." Fannie Hurst: "The Star-Spangled Banner, long may it <u>not</u> wave!"

50. The Star-Spangled Banner ...
An all-typographic cover with the unusual introduction of colour — albeit Lubalin's favourite red, white and blue. Visual riffs on the American flag and the patriotic U.S. colours are recurring themes throughout Lubalin's work. Date: January—February, 1965.

fact:

VOLUME TWO, ISSUE FOUR $1.25

Obesity

It's incurable – SO relax and enjoy it

51. Obesity
Once more, colour makes a rare
appearance on a *Fact* cover. A novelty
typeface is sculpted to fit around an
illustration by guest illustrator Jerome
Snyder, a frequent Lubalin collaborator.
Date: July—August, 1965.

fact:

VOLUME ONE, ISSUE FIVE. $1.25

1,189 Psychiatrists Say Goldwater Is Psychologically Unfit To Be President!

52. 1,189 Psychiatrists Say ...
Yet another landmark publication in
the life and work of Ralph Ginzburg and
Herb Lubalin. As a result of the story
announced on the cover, Ginzburg was
sued by right-wing presidential candidate Barry Goldwater, and as a result,
Fact was eventually closed. The story
is told on p.49. Guest illustrator:
Rick Schreiter. Date: September—
October, 1964.

What Psychiatrists
Say About Goldwater

By Warren Boroson

In a national poll by FACT, 1189 psychiatrists said the Republican candidate was not psychologically fit to be President; only [...] thought that he was

On July 24, one week after Barry Goldwater received the Republican nomination, FACT sent a questionnaire to all of the nation's 12,356 psychiatrists asking, "Do you believe Barry Goldwater is psychologically fit to serve as President of the United States?" (The names were supplied by the American Medical Association.)

In all, 2417 psychiatrists responded. Of these, 571 said they did not know enough about Goldwater to answer the question; 657 said they thought Goldwater was psychologically fit; and 1189 said that he was not. (It might be pointed out that the majority of those who thought Goldwater was psychologically fit nevertheless said they were not voting for him.)

FACT's questionnaire left room for "Comments" and over a quarter of a million words of professional opinion were received. On the next 41 pages we present a sampling of these comments, which, all together, constitute the most intensive character analysis ever made of a living human being.

Senator Barry Goldwater gives the *superficial* appearance of solidity, stability, and honesty. However, my impression is of a brittle, rigid personality structure, based on a soft-spoken continuous demand for power and authority and capable of either shattering like crystal glass or bolstering itself by the assumption of a paranoid stance and more persecution of others. In his book, *The Conscience of a Conservative*, his position is one of anachronistic authoritarianism, using the Constitution in a litigious way. . . . He seems unaware that modern nationwide transportation and communication have increased identification of the populace with the nation as a whole—rather than the states—and that people generally want national standardization of law, welfare, and education.

In allowing you to quote me, what can I rely on the protection of Goldwater's defeat at the polls in November; for if Goldwater wins the Presidency, both you and I will be among the first into the concentration camps.

G. Temple[...]
Director, Community Hospital Men[...]
Glen Cov[...]

The main factors which make me [...] Goldwater is unfit to be President are:

(1) His impulsive, impetuous behavior. Such behavior in this age could result in world destruction. This behavior reflects an emotionally immature, unstable personality.

(2) His inability to dissociate himself from vituperative, sick extremists. This [...] reflects his desire for support from any[...]

gests paranoid tendencies in the candidate or his advisers.

[Name Withheld], M.D.
Santa Monica, Calif.

I do not think two nervous breakdowns, if he had them, is against Goldwater's being President. Such illnesses do not, of themselves, alter judgment or insight or ability to reason.

R. B. Mershon, M.D.
Chief of Psychiatric Service,
Mobile General Hospital
Mobile, Ala.

What has been said about Mr. Goldwater's emotional state could be said about Mr. Johnson's. They are equally sane. One might add that Johnson has sadistic tendencies. Didn't he pick up his dogs by their ears?

Anonymous
Stockton, Calif.

Being a psychiatrist I feel renders me perhaps more sensitive to mental illness by inference than can be considered fair to the object of such intuition. However, the little I have heard about and from Mr. Goldwater concerns me. I feel he has large areas of personality that are immature and not well enough integrated to render him fit for the multiplex job of President. I refer in particular to his judgment. I feel he is often swayed by his emotions more than by his reason.

Although I am a staunch Republican,

Goldwater's nomination has brought me to my own political "moment of truth." I plan to vote for Johnson.

D.J. Bennington, M.D.
Seattle

Goldwater reminds me of Forrestal who, fortunately, had no access to the *button.*

Anonymous
Galveston, Texas

Politically, I heartily disapprove of Goldwater. In fact, I find him somewhat frightening. Yet I do not feel I can honestly say he is psychologically unfit to serve as President. . . . I don't believe emotional disorder in the past or even the diagnosis of schizophrenia is prima facie evidence of unfitness to govern. . . . Abraham Lincoln was repeatedly subject to severe depressions. It is conceivable to me that a compensated schizophrenic could be a brightly creative administrator.

Joseph Schachter, M.D.
New York

I believe Goldwater to be suffering from a chronic psychosis. It is usually in remission but he is maintaining a rather marginal adjustment.

My fear of his destructive acting-out is so great that I am seriously considering moving to another country should Goldwater be elected.

The prospect of his becoming President is

the most frightening thing I've felt since the A-bomb.

Anonymous
New Orleans

Mr. Goldwater seems psychologically naive at times, e.g., when offended by a Negro on the Platform Committee he said, in effect, that he should be annoyed but he was not going to be. This assumption that one can choose one's feelings may account for his outbursts which seem to reflect feelings he tries to deny within himself that break through explosively at times.

Calvin S. Drayer, M.D.
Philadelphia

Mr. Goldwater's emotionalism and concreteness have an appeal to the primitive instinctual feelings which are generally suppressed. One danger is that he, as a national leader, gives a legitimacy to these destructive impulses and thereby encourages their expression by others. History is filled with unstable leaders like Mr. Goldwater who for a time are able to mobilize the primitive hate and destruction that resides in some form in all human beings.

[Name Withheld], M.D.
Washington, D.C.

Goldwater reminds me in his psychological make-up and political success of Hitler. I witnessed Hitler's early rise with anxiety. . . . Even

the fact that psychiatrists recognized Hitler's power drive as they now recognize Goldwater's is comparable. . . . Goldwater may for personal glory sacrifice the future of the world.

Otto J. Metzger, M.D.
New York

To me Senator Goldwater appears an angry, frightened, intemperate man, whose speeches and public remarks have sadistic overtones. Descriptions of his early life that I have read indicate to me that his mother assumed the masculine role in his family background. My impression was that she was domineering and considerably lacking in her ability to provide affection and interest in her children. The picture, therefore, is of a domineering, emasculating mother and a somewhat withdrawn, passive, narcissistic father. It would appear that Harry had a stronger identification with his mother than with his father. This would provide a fertile background for sado-masochistic temperament, such as is seen in paranoid states.

My conclusion is that this man is temperamentally unsuited to carry out the responsibilities of the Presidency. The likelihood of his being overly militant, suspicious, and impulsive would create a constant state of tension and apprehension.

[Name Withheld], M.D.
Reading, Pa.

It is my opinion that Goldwater's so-called

fact:

VOLUME TWO, ISSUE TWO $1.25

New evidence proves Dag Hammarskjöld committed

suicide!

53. Dag Hammarskjöld
The death in an air crash in 1961 of the
Secretary-General of the United Nations,
Dag Hammarskjöld, is one of the great
enigmas of 20th-century political life,
and a source of continuing speculation.
Unusually, Lubalin here makes use of
a black background with reversed-out
type. Illustration by Charles B. Slackman.
Date: March—April, 1965.

fact:

VOLUME ONE, ISSUE THREE $1.25

American Cars Are Death Traps

This issue reveals which car makes are the most dangerous of all

54. American Cars Are Death Traps
This issue marked one of the first
appearances in print of Ralph Nader —
a pioneer of consumer rights and
a future presidential candidate. Date:
May—June, 1964.

Why I Am [For] [Against] Pornography

28 Famous Americans answer these questions: Is pornography bad or good? If bad, should it be censored?

Introduction. For years and years, philosophers, linguists, sociologists, psychiatrists, historians, lawyers, judges, writers, and politicians have been trying their damnedest to come up with a proper definition of the word "pornography."

Now the quest is finally over.

Because now an unchallengeable, irrefutable definition has been found.

Pornography is whatever five members of the U.S. Supreme Court consider pornography.

The next step, of course, is to stop sex crimes—which is, supposedly, why everybody was so concerned about pornography in the first place.

Now, for a long time people labored under the misimpression that sex + lust = sex crime. But, obviously, normal people like you and us *Fact* editors are occasionally lustful and sensuous, yet we don't go out raping every girl we see, or even every other girl.

No, sex criminals don't read pornography—studies have shown as much. But sex criminals *are* disturbed. So the new equation is, sex + disturbance = sex crime.

If you're mathematically minded, and you examine the two aforementioned equations carefully, you will see that they have one factor in common. That factor is *sex.*

Sex causes sex crimes!

Obviously, what our Government must do is stop worrying about pornography and start eradicating sex. It won't be nearly as difficult as it sounds. The Government could put up posters around the country saying, "Reach for a sweet instead of a sweetheart," or "Better Red than wed." Engraved on every contraceptive pill could be the words: "Caution: Sex may be hazardous to your health." (It *can* be, especially if you smoke in bed.) The John Birch Society could launch a campaign to make every patriotic American aware that Mao Tse-tung, General Eisenhower, and many other Commies and Comsymps are married—and have children, to boot. The American Legion might point out how few nuns and priests have defected. If we really want to get serious about the whole thing, of course, we could simply pass a law banning sexual intercourse.

In the meantime, to find out what distinguished Americans in all walks of life think about pornography, censorship, and sex, we solicited their opinions, which follow. If the opinions seem to be loaded against censorship, it is not due to bias on our part. On the contrary, we went out of our way to solicit as many pro-censorship replies as we could. But, alack, Ronald Reagan, Cardinal Spellman, Billy Graham, Everett Dirksen, Rep. Glenn Cunningham, et al., wouldn't answer the phone when we called. Making statements in favor of censorship seems to be quite unpopular

The Women's Army Corps: Life Among the Funny-Bunnies

By Gloria Dippolitino

An ex-WAC describes how her feelings about the Lesbians she met in the service changed from disgust and fear to genuine pity

In 1962 I was 18 years old, and had never been anywhere outside my small home town in the Midwest. Also, as the only daughter of a religious Catholic family, I had led a particularly sheltered life. That year, therefore, when a WAC recruiter came to our high school to talk to us seniors about careers in the U.S. Army, I was positively enthralled.

The recruiter's spiel was worthy of Madison Avenue. In a private interview, he told me that as a member of the Women's Army Corps I would be well-fed and properly housed and smartly clothed. I would meet brilliant women and fascinating men. And (the key to my heart) I would travel. All I had to do in return was serve my country for 3 years.

I was so enthusiastic that I spent hours in the public library reading up on the WACs. Among other things, I learned that while the WAVES (Women Accepted for Voluntary Emergency Service) have declined since World War II, and the SPARS are just about out of existence (they now have 9 officers and 34 enlisted women), the Women's Army Corps—as well as the WAFS (Women's Air Corps) and the Women Marines—are still thriving. An outgrowth of the Women's Army Auxiliary Corps of World War II, the WACS today have 3700 officers and 8625 enlisted women.

I was so eager to enter this new life that,

with my parents' blessing, the day after I graduated I went to the nearest recruiting station. There I was informed that I would have to be interviewed by a psychiatrist. This made me a little nervous—none of my friends had ever been to a psychiatrist, and I didn't know what to expect. I certainly didn't expect to spend a mere 5 minutes explaining why I bite my nails and the way I feel about my parents to an unimpressive little man. On the other hand, I had to take a barrage of aptitude tests. The Army spends hours giving and marking aptitude tests, but only 5 minutes evaluating the mental health of its candidates.

Well, the Army decided I was mentally healthy. And within 2 hours after I'd said "I do" to Uncle Sam, I was whisked onto a train heading for a fort in Alabama.

Despite some misgivings, I was still so starry-eyed about my new life that I stayed awake throughout the whole 5-hour trainride imagining my future: my fashionable uniform, my important and glamorous job, the friends I would make, the places I would visit. At my destination, Fort McClellan, home of the Women's Army Corps Center and School, I was furnished a bed in a room with 40 other women, given linen, assigned a wall and foot locker, and told, "You're in the Army now!"

And so I was.

It was a letdown from the very beginning. I

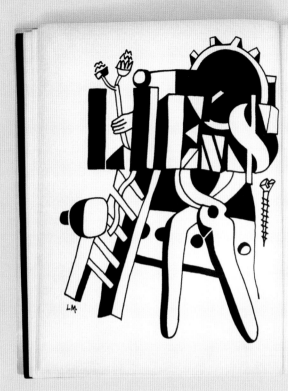

Man Against Repairman
By Phyllis Jay

The garage's bill was $120, but the car was still on the fritz. To pay or not to pay? One daring couple decided not to—and quickly learned the unpleasant consequences

Repairmen—those fellows who fix refrigerators, TV sets, typewriters, cars, and so forth—are, as everybody knows, getting increasingly cussed and ornery. The causes are perfectly clear. There are fewer and fewer repairmen around today (for example, the Bureau of the Census reports that from 1950 to 1960, the number of auto mechanics rose only 3% , and the number of apprentice mechanics declined 51%). But there are many, many more cars and TV sets that have to be repaired. Since demand exceeds supply, unskilled, cloddish mechanics are sometimes pressed into service; once working, they rush like fiends to finish the flood of jobs they have, and, since the occupation of repairman isn't exactly prestigious, repairmen may overcharge—to prove they're better than those who look down on them, and to get rich quick so as to assume a more impressive role in life.

Now, shrewd, suspicious customers may be able to protect themselves against untrustworthy repairmen. But what can the customer do when he's *already* been had? When the TV set comes back from the factory with presumably $75 worth of repairs and the picture still flip flops hysterically? Well, I may have some sound advice to offer, advice that comes from personal experience.

My story begins on an October day 2 years ago. My husband, John, is a 35-year-old junior executive for a large pharmaceutical company.

He had been assigned to visit South America for 3 weeks on business, and was almost all packed and ready. Just 5 hours before he was to leave, he was driving our 3-year-old Volkswagen through the choked streets of the little New Jersey town we live in. He stopped the car for a light, and when the light changed, John pressed down the clutch, shifted into first, stepped on the gas, and nothing happened. As horns from cars behind him blared, John gave the pedal a hard shove, and the car managed to creep through the intersection like a wounded animal. There was no Volkswagen agency in town, and the nearest one, considering how little time he had, was just too far away. There was still laundry to be picked up, more packing to do, and a long trip by bus to Kennedy International Airport. Down the block, though, John saw an independent garage. He had read its ads in the newspapers, and knew it repaired all kinds of cars. So he began coaxing the car into the station.

A young mechanic trotted up. He listened to the motor, test-drove the car around the compound, and then announced what was wrong: the transmission and clutch assemblies were shot, and completely beyond repair. He had not only the diagnosis, but the cure: used parts, good as new, from a Volkswagen that had been in an accident but whose clutch and transmission had been unscathed. The job would take 5 days, and would

---

The Failure
of American Foreign Policy
By Arnold J. Toynbee

The century's foremost historian accuses President Johnson of bringing back colonialism, driving Russia and Communist China back together, and turning America into the world's No. 1 bully

The Administration at Washington is showing signs that it resents criticism of its foreign policy, a foreign policy that is causing increased anxiety all over the world.

From an American's point of view, however, if the Administration is claiming the right to make life-and-death decisions in private, this is a new departure in American political life. The publication of political facts and the public discussion of political issues seem to be key parts of the American political tradition, and it seems improbable that the American people are going to renounce traditional rights that are the essence of democracy.

But what about *world* opinion?

Probably there are many Americans, besides President Johnson and his advisers, who feel that United States policy is exclusively the American people's affair. This too is a traditional attitude, one not confined to the United States. It is bound up with the concept of local sovereign independence. A sovereign country has been held to have a right to go its own way as it chooses. But today every country in the world, including the most powerful, is dependent on the behavior of other countries. And this means that no country any longer has a moral right (if it ever had one) to act just according to its own sovereign will and power. And therefore an enormous degree of responsi-

bility rests upon the two countries—the United States and the Soviet Union—that now possess effective atomic armaments. Deliberately to escalate a "conventional" war is knowingly to increase the risk of this ranking into an atomic war. And the threat of an atomic war legitimately concerns the whole human race.

Naturally, America's and Russia's allies and satellites would all try to jump clear of entangling alliances before any Russo-American duel started. And we would be morally justified, because we should have had no voice in the decisions that had led up to the catastrophe. We might or might not succeed in avoiding belligerency, but none of us could escape the damage that a Russo-American war would do. In other words, such a war would not be just a Russian and American catastrophe; it would be a *world-wide* catastrophe.

This is a point Americans ought to bear in mind if they find themselves resenting foreign criticism of the United States Government's policies. The 85% of the human race that are neither Russians nor Americans have the same life-and-death interest that the Russians and the Americans have in the consequences of Russian and American policy. And we do not even have a vote. The American voters do have a say, if only a rather small one, in decisions about their own fate. *The rest of us have no say.*

55—58. Various spreads
Examples of Lubalin's restrained and formal two-column page layouts from various issues, and his use of a variety of illustrators with strong graphic styles capable of working on *Fact*'s cheap pulp stock. Illustrators shown: fig.55, Etienne Delessert; figs.56 and 57, Louis LoMonaco; fig.58 Jim Spanfeller.

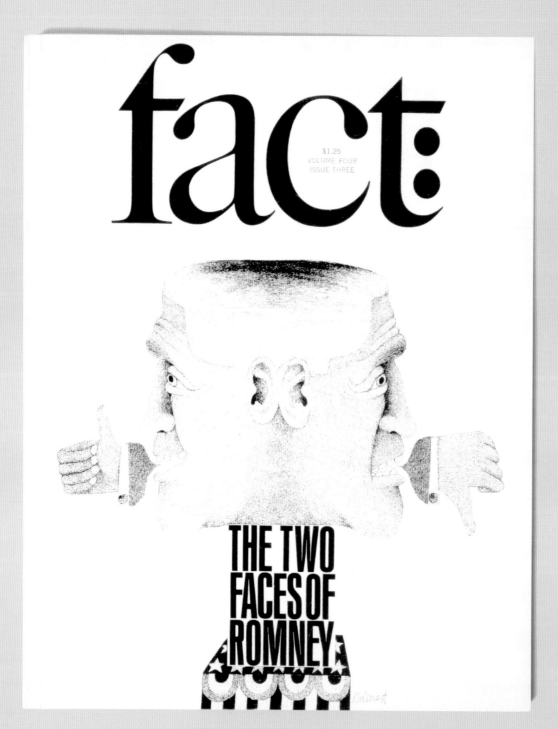

59. The Two Faces of Romney
Illustrated cover for issue featuring an
article on Republican politician George
Romney, father of Mitt Romney, a
candidate for the 2012 Republican
Party presidential nomination. The issue
also features responses from leading
figures of the 1960s to the question: 'Is
pornography bad or good?' Replies
are received from Marshall McLuhan,
Woody Allen, J. Edgar Hoover, Andy
Warhol, and others. Illustrator: Etienne
Delessert. Date: May—June, 1967.

fact:

VOLUME FOUR, ISSUE FOUR $1.25

CIVIL WAR!

AMERICA IS SPLITTING IN TWO

Hippie poet Tuli Kupferberg says, "On one side are the hawks, most of the millionaires, the old-line politicos, the gray-haired mothers, the retired Army officers, the Spellmans of the ecclesia castrata, the sadistic police, the poor stupid soldiers, the rednecks, the frustrated, the Madison Avenue alcoholics, the suicidal Marines, the robotteachers, the Fundamentalist boondockers —the forces we used to call 'reactionary.'

"On the other side are the youth, the doves, the beatniks, the poets and artists, the professors, the protesting students, the minorities, the singers, the rock 'n' rollers, the psychedelics, the young parents crying for the fullness of their lives—whatever remains of the old humanism, liberalism and idealism of America."

60. Civil War
Another cover dominated by an illustration, this time signalling an article by Fugs founder Tuli Kupferberg on the split between hawks and doves in American public life. This was the last issue of *Fact*. The following year Lubalin and Ginzburg reunited to start *Avant Garde* magazine. Illustration by Tom Huffman. Date: July—August, 1967.

61. Avant Garde #1

Front cover. The geometric construction of artist Richard Linder's painting, the magazine's square format (11×11"), and the machine-like precision of the masthead typography, make a dramatic visual statement for the inaugural edition of the magazine founded by Ralph Ginzburg and art directed by Herb Lubalin. As the following pages will show, Lubalin's design, layout and typography was as much part of the ethos of *Avant Garde* as the editorial content. It is why, when talking about this revolutionary publication, it is hard not to refer to it as Ginzburg and Lubalin's magazine. Date: January 1968.

62. Richard Nixon

Double-page spread with essay on Nixon, then a U.S. presidential hopeful, written by long-time Ginzburg associate Warren Boroson. Nixon is referred to as 'obnoxious'. Boroson was to become a successful financial journalist and writer. Illustrations by Rick Schreiter.

63. The Case for Retiring

The left-hand page has the credit: 'Illustration is by Etienne Delessert'. Swiss-born Delessert is responsible for the magenta-coloured line drawings of heads in profile; the typographical arrangement of punctuation marks is pure Lubalin. Set in Pistilli Roman.

64. The Fugs

Photograph shows original members of the Fugs — Ed Sanders, Tuli Kupferberg and Ken Weaver. The band was named after the euphemism that Norman Mailer used in his novel, *The Naked and the Dead*. The Fugs mixed on-stage outrage with political activism. While protesting against the Vietnam War, they famously attempted to 'levitate' the Pentagon by chanting. Lubalin uses the somewhat incongruous typeface Amelia, designed by Stan Davis in 1964. It is used famously as the typeface for the title of The Beatles film *Yellow Submarine*. Note Lubalin's trademark use of overlapping letterforms: the dot of the 'i' forms the counter of the 'g'. See also how he indicates the fact that the Fugs were a trio, by highlighting of the letter 'i' three times. Photograph of the Fugs by Peter Hujar. A book of Hujar's work, *Portraits in Life and Death*, was published in 1976, with an introduction by Susan Sontag.

65. Galahad's Pad

Survey of 1960s communal living in New York's East Village. The uncredited writer quotes a Tufts University academic observer: 'If this communal life-style continues, marriage and family life will be obsolete in the 21st Century.' The grungy documentary-style photographs are by Julio Mitchel, who was to become a regular contributor to *Avant Garde*. Lubalin's use of Gothic lettering is a reference to the medieval Arthurian legends of Sir Galahad. The photographer Julio Mitchel has graciously given us permission to print his photographs, which were used in Herb Lubalin's *Avant Garde* page designs. Mitchel notes that he is not a 'square photographer'; the images were cropped by Lubalin without his consent. More of Julio Mitchel's work can be seen at: www.juliomitchel.com.

66, 67. Richard Lindner

Richard Lindner was a German-American painter. In his later work (shown here), he creates a quintessentially 1960s vision of sexual pleasure and machine-age modernity. It is not hard to see how his sexual explicitness and his graphic use of geometric forms would appeal to both Ginzburg and Lubalin respectively.

THE CASE
FOR RETIRING OUR
MOST OVERWORKED
FOUR-LETTER WORD
BY PROFESSOR L. ERIC HOTALING

ne day when I was considerably younger than I am now, my
mother prodded me up the stairs
to her bedroom, where she slept
on and off with my father. On
her face was the Old Testament
, that, from experience, I had come to rec-
ze as a storm warning. "Mrs. Powell," she
n, naming a white-haired neighbor who
d radishes, "heard you say a certain word."
"What word was that?" I asked.
"You know perfectly well what word," my
her replied. And that was true. I did. It
also true that I had no idea what the word
fied, or understood much of anything else
it it. Gordon Brazen, a friend who grew up
er a name other than the one I have here
ned him, introduced it to me in Mrs.
ell's garden. We were stealing her radishes.
don turned to me and uttered a word that
d never heard before. Actually, he uttered
words: "Fuck you."
I identified this vaguely as a command, al-
ugh the imperative rang no semantic bells.
what action was he suggesting that I take?
d not know then, and I do not know now,
n though the passage of 30 years has en-
ed my cultural understanding of that mus-
r, four-letter transitive verb. At the time,
nsed only that Gordon's proposition was
ntially jocular, and that if he ever repeated
o his father, who had a very short fuse, he
ld probably get his mouth washed out with
p. A response seemed indicated, but my for-
education, which was then in the sun-baked
uum between fourth and fifth grade, fur-
hed no clue. So I took the easy way out, one
t I have re-traveled many times since. I re-
d: "Fuck you, too."
My comment was accepted with impassive
sfaction; apparently I had said the right
ng. And for the next few minutes, Gordon
I improvised a dialogue that gave star bill-
to the new word. No one recorded it, unless
s. Powell did, but as I remember it went
nething like this:
I: Gordon: Okay. Fuck you back.
I: What does fuck mean?
Gordon: I don't know. It's a dirty word.
hink.
I: Like what?
Gordon: I don't know. Like—well, like shit.
I: Shit you.
Gordon: Shit you back.

RATION BY ETIENNE DELESSERT

I: Shit fuck you.
Gordon: I'm sick of radishes. Let's go.
The whole exchange conveyed so little
meaning to me that, on climbing the stairs
ahead of mother, I felt sure that she was about
to arraign me on quite a different rap. After
parting company with Gordon that particular
afternoon, I had spent the better part of a
quarter-hour, with my older brother Alfred,
examining the sexual equipment of our twin
sisters, who were seven. It proved to be dull if
licentious sport; none of us showed any inclin-
ation to do it again. But my sisters were notorious ratters. They told mother everything. And
I suspected that Alfred and I had not heard the
last of the incident.

So it was with an agreeable shock of relief,
the same perhaps that a murderer feels when his
sentence is commuted to rape, that I learned the
true nature of my offense. In mother's statute
book profanity was not a capital crime. I re-
solved, as usual, to plead guilty and throw
myself on the mercy of the court, which was
unlimited.

"I said a bad word," I confessed.

"It was a very bad word," agreed my mother. "Nice people don't use it." Then followed a
sermon on the manifold transgressions of mothers' sons, the great anguish thereby suffered by
mothers, the urgent need to reform, etc. I tuned
out automatically, having audited the sermon
countless times before, and while mother solilo-
quized, I set about embossing the word, in
Second-Coming type, on my brain. If two female grown-ups could work up such a lather
about it, it was obviously of gem value to small
boys, one of those forbidden lexicological treas-
ures that are stubbornly suppressed by the
taste-setters of every generation but that nevertheless stubbornly survive. I decided then and
there, as mother gently massaged my shins with
a yardstick, that I would henceforth embellish
my social discourse with this remarkable find.

But as anyone knows who has ever tried to
do the same, it can be a vexing business. To begin with, the word fuck does not always mean
what it should mean; the possibilities for mis-
interpretation are endless. Dictionaries are not
helpful. Most of them ignore the word entirely,
and the few that list it tend to be coy. "To
cheat, trick, take advantage of, deceive, or treat
someone unfairly," begins the definition of
fuck in the Dictionary of American Slang (Sup-
plemented Edition, 1967); and it ends, some

100 words later, without once mentioning
fuck's fundamental linguistic function, which
is—putting it as chastely as possible—to conjoin
the fucker and the fuckee.

To make up for this bashful omission, the
Dictionary of American Slang catalogues fuck's
other conversational possibilities, such as fuck
a duck ("an expression of surprise, disbelief,
dismissal, or rejection"), fuck off ("to refuse
to work or think seriously"), fuck it ("stop
nagging, or the like"), and fuck up ("to waste
time"). They all seemed somewhat less useful
to me than the words I found surrounding the
fuck entries: fu, for instance ("marijuana"),
fuff ("A reply to an unnecessary statement:
'Oh, willy-nilly and fiddle-faddle; fuff too'"),
and furp ("to escort a girl on a date"). It goes
without saying that the opportunities to furp,
or even fuff, vastly outnumber the opportunities to fuck in this life.

The reticence of the dictionaries probably
accounts for the fact that most people don't
know how to use fuck properly. I discovered
this in the army, among other places. My first
sergeant, a brutish Texan who took a quarter
from every pot in pay-day poker games, would
have been rendered mute had he been denied
the use of the word. "All right, you fuckers,"
he would bark at Reveille, "get your fucking
asses out of your fucking bunks and fuck out
to the fucking company street for fucking roll
call." From the waters of Long Lake, where we
sometimes spent a Sunday, his hook extracted
nothing but copulating trout. Or so he said
anyway: "Look hey, I got me another fucking
fish." His lips lent the word both poetic and
sentimental value. What are you doing, Sarge?
"Writing a fucking letter to my fucking mother." Where are you going, Sarge? "Out to see
that fucking sunset."*

The Sarge was one of several thousand soldiers—none of them WAVEs, WACs or enemies,
I might add—who punctuated my military career with indecent proposals. Fuck you, they
all said, in a variety of circumstances; that was
not what they meant, of course. But it was,
after all, what they said, and it is a common
example of the dangers that await the unwary,

*The military mind, it should be noted, is sometimes just as
shy as the etymological mind about using the word. Witness
the constructions snafu, fubar, fubb, fumtu, and fubis, all
euphemisms coined during World War II and no longer in circulation. We all know what snafu stands for. Here are the
others: fucked up beyond all recognition; fucked up beyond
belief; fucked up more than usual; fuck you, buddy, I'm ship-
ping (out).

FUGS ED SANDERS, KEN WEAVER, AND TULI KUPFERBERG, PHOTOGRAPHED BY PETER HUJAR.

The Fugs: Nextness is Godlier than Cleanliness.

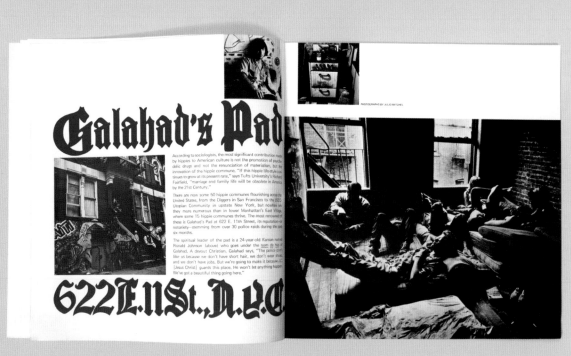

PHOTOGRAPHS BY JULIO MITCHEL

Galahad's Pad

According to sociologists, the most significant contribution made by hippies to American culture is not the promotion of psychedelic drugs and not the renunciation of materialism, but the innovation of the hippie commune. "If this hippie life-style continues to grow at its present rate," says Tufts University's Richard Fairfield, "marriage and family life will be obsolete in America by the 21st Century."

There are now some 50 hippie communes flourishing across the United States, from the Diggers in San Francisco to the USCO Utopian Community in upstate New York, but nowhere are they more numerous than in lower Manhattan's East Village, where some 15 hippie communes thrive. The most renowned of these is Galahad's Pad at 622 E. 11th Street, its reputation—notoriety—stemming from over 30 police raids during the past six months.

The spiritual leader of the pad is a 24-year-old Kansan named Ronald Johnson (above) who goes under the nom de tot of Galahad. A devout Christian, Galahad says, "The police don't like us because we don't have short hair, we don't wear shoes, and we don't have jobs. But we're going to make it because He [Jesus Christ] guards this place. He won't let anything happen. We've got a beautiful thing going here."

622 E. 11 St., N.Y.C.

274

RICHARD LINDNER: THE RUBENS OF THE LOVE GENERATION

"DOUBLE PORTRAIT"
THE HELEN HARDING COLLECTION

THE MARILYN MONROE TRIP:
A PORTFOLIO OF SERIGRAPHIC
PRINTS BY BERT STERN

AVANT
GARDE 2

68. Avant Garde #2

After the sharp kick to the retinas delivered by the cover of *Avant Garde* 1, the cover of 2 is muted and dreamy. It features one of photographer Bert Stern's melancholy images of Marilyn Monroe taken over a three-day period, six weeks before her death. Stern was the last person to photograph Monroe, and pictures from that now famous session had been extensively featured in *Eros*, the precursor of *Avant Garde* (pp.46—48). Stern was a major figure in mid-20th-century American photography. He is perhaps best known for his Monroe pictures, which he published in 1992, in a book called *Marilyn Monroe: The Complete Last Sitting*. His picture of the actress Sue Lyon playing the part of Lolita in the Stanley Kubrick film of the same name is also famous. He stylishly directed the film *Jazz on a Summer's Day*, a 1959 documentary set at the 1958 Newport Jazz Festival. Date: March 1968.

69. Picasso: Portrait of the Artist

Both Ginzburg and Lubalin appear to have had a strong interest in the work of Picasso. A future edition of *Avant Garde* (p.316) was devoted entirely to Picasso's erotic etchings. The photograph of Picasso is by Richard Avedon, one of the giants of American photography. Lubalin characteristically allows the image to fill the entire left-hand page, thus increasing its impact as a psychologically revealing portrait of Picasso.

70—75. The Marilyn Monroe Trip

The psychedelically inclined title of this 12-page feature alludes to Bert Stern's 'phantasmagraphic vision of Marilyn Monroe'. Stern subjects his famous photographs to a series of transformations that render them almost unrecognizable from his sensitive naturalistic originals, about which he said: 'I have never been entirely satisfied with them. Because of photography's technical limitations, they never quite communicated the dazzling image of Marilyn that existed in my mind's eye at the time I photographed her.' After a series of failed experiments, Stern arrived at the idea of an 'amalgam of the dramatic technique of serigraphy and the blazing colors of Day-Glo ink.' The effect is to turn Monroe into an unlikely psychedelic goddess rather than the vulnerable and lovable star of *Some Like it Hot* and her other Hollywood films. Lubalin's opening spread typography, with its eccentric alignments and missing dots over the letter 'i', hints at the derangement introduced by Stern into his otherwise naturalistic pictures.

The Marilyn Monroe Trip by Bert Stern

Hundreds of artists have been hung on Marilyn Monroe ever since she died five years ago (including Dali, De Kooning, Lindner, Rauschenberg, and 38 other greats who participated in an "Homage to Marilyn" show at the Janis Gallery in New York last month). Perhaps none has been more preoccupied with the image of Marilyn, however, than photographer Bert Stern who, through a quirk of fate, became the last man to photograph her. Stern's portraits of Marilyn, shot at the Bel Air Hotel in Hollywood on June 21, 1962, are classic and have been published time and again. "Still, I have never been entirely satisfied with them," says Stern. "Because of photography's technical limitations, they never quite communicated the dazzling image of Marilyn that existed in my mind's eye at the time I photographed her." As a result, over the past five years Stern has been experimenting with various new techniques that would enable him to capture and preserve the image of Marilyn he saw at the time he photographed her. Just this past fall he hit upon the answer: an amalgam of the dramatic technique of serigraphy and the blazing colors of Day-Glo ink. On the next 12 pages the editors of Avant-Garde are pleased to present Bert Stern's phantasmagoric vision of Marilyn Monroe.

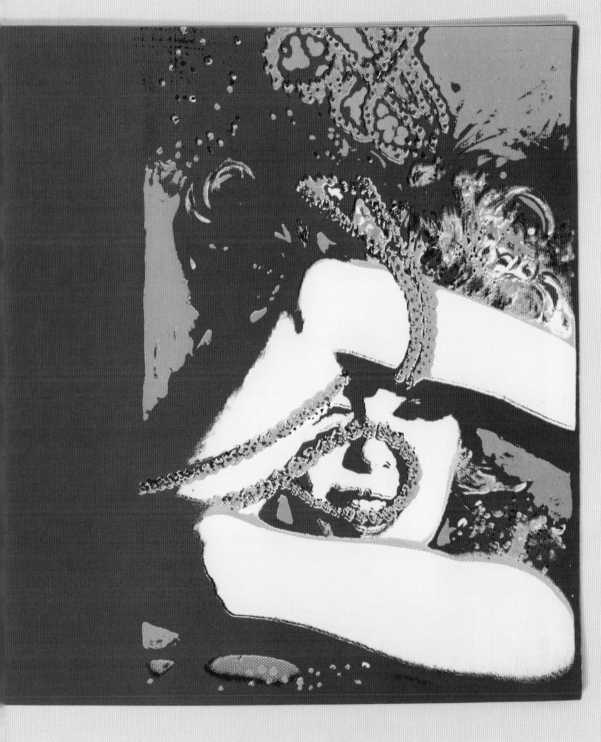

71

Hundred
she died
chenberg
to Marily
Perhaps
Marilyn,
a quirk c
portraits
June 21
again. "S
Stern.
quite co
my mind
the past
techniqu
image o
this pas
techniq
On the
to pres

72

Hund
she c
chen
to M
Perh
Mar
a qu
port
Jun
agai
Ster
quit
my
the
tec
ime
thi
tec
O
to

73

74

Hun
she c
cher
to M
Perh
Mar
a qu
port
Jun
agai
Ster
quit
my
the
tecl
ima
this
tec
Or
to

alter Bowart, Mild-

HYMAN

RAPHS BY JULIO MITCHEL

wart examines a copy of his newspaper,
Village Other.
s made of an American flag.

November evening three years ago, I
ding out in front of the Ninth Circle, a
ich Village café, exchanging idle conver-
with a friend who worked there week-
a bouncer. A couple of young chicks
s, beads, and long straight hair came

by, hawking a newspaper we had never heard of before. They were so enthusiastic and in- sistent that we finally broke down and bought a copy. We were both magazine editors during the week and had a professional curiosity to satisfy. The newspaper, four pages long, was called the *East Village Other* and was folded so that it ripped when it was opened. It was, we quickly agreed, about the most incompre- hensible piece of trash we had ever seen. The articles were so insane, the layout so bizarre, the type so sloppy and riddled with errors, we could only suppose that the thing had been produced by a drunken gang of hebephrenics who had somehow gained access to a printing plant. We were certain that the publication would not possibly survive for a second issue.

Maybe it was the bad light in the street, or the effect of too much weekend booze, or maybe we were just unplugged from what was really happening. In any case, we were wrong. The *East Village Other* has done better than survive. It has prospered.

During the three intervening years it has grown from a fragile four-page seedling into a healthy, giant, 40-page psychedelic flower.

Today, with a fanatic following of 55,000, it is the Voice of Hip, the Headquarters of Flower Power, the heart and soul of the Love Genera- tion.

The offices of the *East Village Other*, or EVO, as the initiated call it, are located in a loft over an old movie house on New York's Lower East Side. As I entered EVO's offices, a few weeks ago, the first thing I noticed was a young girl with a soft smile and long black hair, sitting at a desk. The wall behind her was covered with an unfinished psychedelic mural done, apparently, with Magic Markers. The adjoining wall carried the message, in large red letters, "America has a sexual problem— it can't love." Further inside I entered a large, inner sanctum—EVO's main editorial office. It was brightly illuminated by spots sunk flush to the ceiling. Two windows that faced the street had been converted into mock stained glass, with scenes depicting members of the staff in quasi-holy stances. Between the win- dows hung a monster poster of President John- son's head superimposed on Hitler's uniformed body, which was giving a fascist salute. Graffi- ti abound on the wall surfaces: "Viva Che!," "The season of the witch is now!," "The blos-

$1.00

AVANT GARDE

3

Revaluation of the Dollar: 19 Artists Design a New One-Dollar Bill

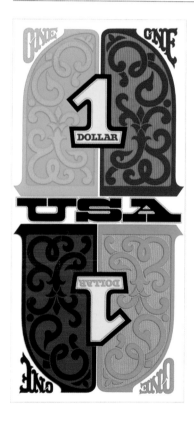

284

76. Avant Garde #3
In the third edition of *Avant Garde*, the magazine invited 19 illustrators to redesign the U.S. currency: 'This wholesale redesign of the dollar bill,' an editorial noted, 'was specially commissioned by *Avant Garde*, on the theory that it's about time someone did. Anyone who has admired French franc-notes, Greek drachmae, even Icelandic kroner, already appreciates the inexpressible ugliness of our sickly-green, turgid-gray, all-powerful American buck.' The three offerings on the cover are, left to right, by; Tom Carnase, Gerry Gersten and Herb Lubalin. Date: May 1968.

77. Revaluation of the Dollar
Opening spread for feature showing work by John Alcorn, Ernie Smith, Etienne Delessert, R.O. Blechman, Edward Gorey and Lionel Kalish.

78—80. Andy's Girls
Herb Lubalin had employed Andy Warhol as an illustrator during his time as an art director at the advertising agency Sudler & Hennessey (p.20). Here, he showcases five women who were part of the Warhol Factory. Photography was by Lee Kraft, a photographer with Warhol assoc-

iations. The women are referred to glibly as five of the 'newest, hottest, female Superstars — the pride and flowering of the breed.' The five Superstars are: Viva (shown with Andy Warhol, fig.78); Katrina and Joy Nicholson (fig.79); National Velvet and Ultra-Violet (fig.80). Ultra-Violet was to return to the pages of *Avant Garde* in issue 9, when she was photographed using infrared photography (p.322). Lubalin's neo-Baroque lettering adds a kitsch note to an otherwise conventional layout. Title lettering (fig.78, left hand page): Tom Carnase.

81, 82. Mr & Mrs Brown go Walking
Powerful photo-essay by Julio Mitchel showing reactions to a mixed-race couple (black man, white woman) walking through the streets of 1960s New York. The essay is presented without commentary. The depiction of mixed-race couples (in admittedly a more intimate setting) in *Eros* (pp.246—249) had already resulted in the prosecution of Ralph Ginzburg for obscenity. Although he was tried and found guilty in 1963, he was not sent to jail until 1972, so this essay was published at the time of his numerous appeals. Lubalin's assured layout tells the story of the couple's stroll with cinematic verve.

83. Was it Good for you?
Light-hearted investigation into sexual research. By embedding the headline in the text, Lubalin is anticipating the phototypesetting of the 1970s, where this sort of integrated layout became quick and easy to do. Back when *Avant Garde* 3 was published, work like this would be done by hand, using razor blades and adhesive. Illustration by Etienne Delessert.

84. The Taming of Denise Gondelman
A boastful and ponderously sexist fictional account of his erotic conquests by novelist Norman Mailer. The tone is set by the opening paragraph: 'On this particular morning, when I awoke, there was a girl propped on one elbow in the bed beside me, no great surprise, because this was the year of all the years in my life when I was scoring three or four times a week, literally combing the pussy out of my hair, which was no great feat if one knew the village and the scientific temperament of the Greenwich Village mind.' Photograph by Alex Greco.

85, 86. The First Church of Love
The short explanatory text introducing the work of an 'anonymous artist' reads: 'The creator [of the work shown] remains anonymous out of distaste for what he calls the "obscene name cult" of modern art.' In fact, the art is recognizable as that of Mati Klarwein. Born in Hamburg in 1932, Klarwein's dazzling psychedelic/surrealist art has appeared on a number of seminal album covers, including *Bitches Brew* by Miles Davis, and *Abraxas* by Santana. The circular painting shown here was subsequently used on a 1970 album by the Chambers Brothers called *New Generation*. Note Lubalin's use of the picture over two spreads; this simple graphic device allows the picture to be reproduced at a size that allows close scrutiny of its vast wealth of detail. Had he printed it smaller so as to fit on a single spread, essential detail would have been lost.

Grain of Sand, oil on canvas, Mati Klarwein 1963—1965
© Klarwein Family
www.matiklarweinart.com

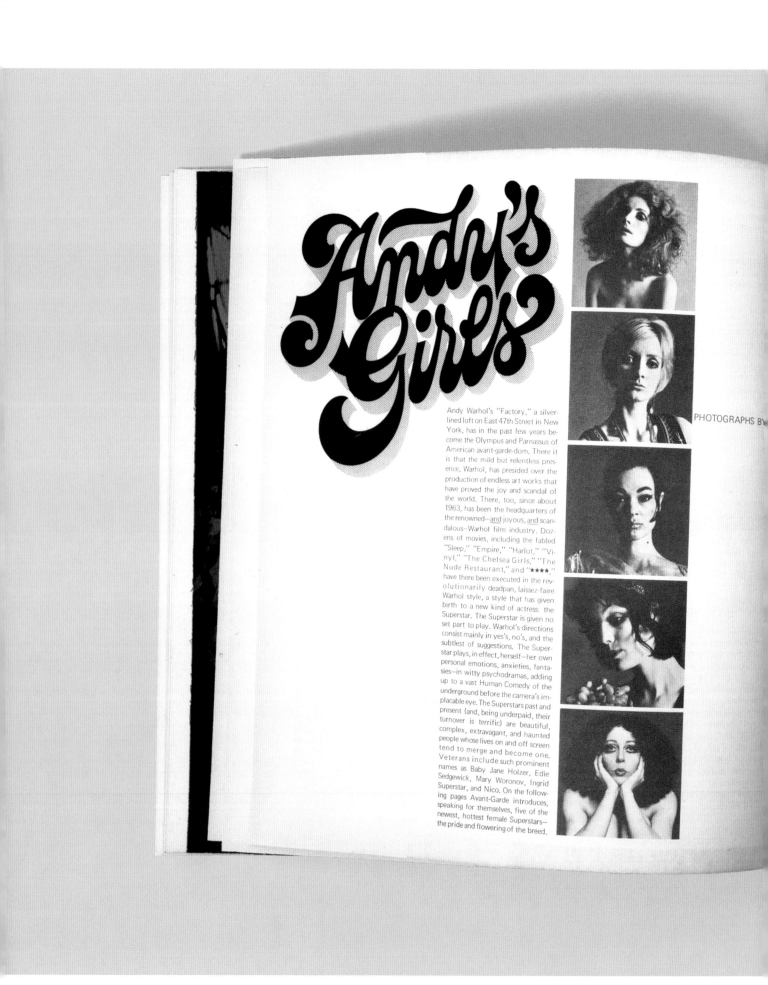

Andy's Girls

Andy Warhol's "Factory," a silver-lined loft on East 47th Street in New York, has in the past few years become the Olympus and Parnassus of American avant-garde-dom. There it is that the mild but relentless presence, Warhol, has presided over the production of endless art works that have proved the joy and scandal of the world. There, too, since about 1963, has been the headquarters of the renowned—and joyous, and scandalous—Warhol film industry. Dozens of movies, including the fabled "Sleep," "Empire," "Harlot," "Vinyl," "The Chelsea Girls," "The Nude Restaurant," and "★★★★," have there been executed in the revolutionarily deadpan, laissez-faire Warhol style, a style that has given birth to a new kind of actress: the Superstar. The Superstar is given no set part to play. Warhol's directions consist mainly in yes's, no's, and the subtlest of suggestions. The Superstar plays, in effect, herself—her own personal emotions, anxieties, fantasies—in witty psychodramas, adding up to a vast Human Comedy of the underground before the camera's implacable eye. The Superstars past and present (and, being underpaid, their turnover is terrific) are beautiful, complex, extravagant, and haunted people whose lives on and off screen tend to merge and become one. Veterans include such prominent names as Baby Jane Holzer, Edie Sedgewick, Mary Woronov, Ingrid Superstar, and Nico. On the following pages Avant-Garde introduces, speaking for themselves, five of the newest, hottest female Superstars—the pride and flowering of the breed.

PHOTOGRAPHS BY

"Andy taught me that everything that I ever thought before was <u>right</u>. My ego has gotten tired from being battered by so many people for so many years; it's a little frayed, like an old camel hair coat. Andy's never battered me, though. He's like a cool running brook....The best drug as an aphrodisiac is peyote; however, it's nauseating. Now I don't take drugs at all. I don't like drugs. I like wine and good conversation around a table. I used to like pot but then found when I used it I was actually coming down. And I don't take acid anymore, because I don't want to warp my chromosomes. Anyway, drugs are for weak people....The last time I took acid I did a dance for the sun on the roof. The man I was with didn't want to make love to me so he told me to go up on the roof--imagine! So I made love to the sun. Since then I haven't made it with many men except an occasional creature who had no place to stay. The sun is the greatest lover in the world. Men can't hold a candle to it....I would like to be Elizabeth Taylor because of all the children she has around her—and the dogs and the cats and the houses—and Richard Burton. A fantastic entourage! I'd like to have a lot of money. I guess I'll have to be a Superstar. Then I could say 'fuck you' to the world....I have a plan to protest the war. As soon as it gets a little warmer I'm going to Washington, and I'm going to ride naked on a black horse with a black saddle and carrying a black flag with the skull and crossbones on it. And my hair won't be long, either. But I guess I'll need some body guards.... In 50 years words will be extinct (and I was saying this before I even heard of Marshall McLuhan!). We'll communicate by ESP--vibrations. Vocal cords will be only for singing with. You might say I'm the last dying gasp of verbosity. I hate talking so much that I do it obsessively!"

VIVA

KATRINA

IVY NICHOLSON

NATIONAL VELVET

ULTRA VIOLET

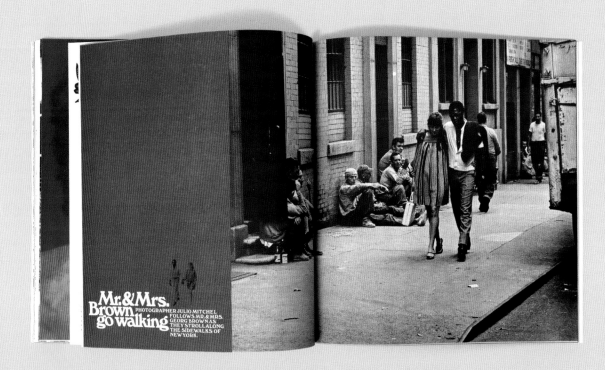

Mr. & Mrs. Brown go walking PHOTOGRAPHER JULIO MITCHEL FOLLOWS MR. & MRS. GEORG BROWN AS THEY STROLL ALONG THE SIDEWALKS OF NEW YORK.

A STORY BY DAN GREENBURG

"Good afternoon," said the interviewer pleasantly to the blond young man on the other side of the desk.

"Good afternoon," said Perlmutter.

There was an uncomfortable pause, which the interviewer savored, studying Perlmutter's discomfort.

"I'm here about the experiment," said Perlmutter, "the one you mentioned in the ad."

"Ah yes, the ad," said the interviewer.

"I ... uh, trust that I'm in the right place?"

"Oh, you're in the right place," said the interviewer smiling blandly. "You want to be in one of our sex experiments, isn't that right?"

"Well, I ... yes," said Perlmutter.

"You're a student here?"

"Yes. Pre-med."

"Ah."

"I, uh, trust that there are still ... openings? In the program, I mean?"

"Tell me," said the interviewer, doodling a possibly erotic doodle on a pad in front of him, "why are you volunteering to participate in a sex experiment?"

"What's the difference?" said Perlmutter.

"I assure you," said the interviewer patronizingly, "we have no wish to pry into your personal affairs, except as they may relate to our business here at the project. Due to the, ah, unusual nature of these particular experiments, we like to have as much information as possible on the people we use, as an aid in determining the potential success or failure of our work."

"I see."

"Now then, what made you volunteer?"

"Well," said Perlmutter, reddening, "outside of the obvious professional interest I have in such activity ..."

"Yes," said the interviewer, "outside of that."

"Well, quite frankly, I consider myself somewhat of a ... actually, *quite a good* ... uh, well, at least a fairly adequate lover, and ..."

"And ...?"

"And also, I thought it might be a good way of meeting girls," he blurted out in some confusion.

"You understand, of course," said the interviewer, "that you will never be permitted to learn the identity of the young lady or ladies whom you will, uh, meet during the course of the experiment?"

"I understand," said Perlmutter.

The buxom middleaged woman in the white lab coat looked up from her papers and motioned Perlmutter into a chair. The hair on her head was dark, frizzy, and pubic. He wondered if the hair in her bush was straight, silky, and blonde. She pointed to the forms he held in his lap. He handed them over.

"Perlmutter?" said Dr. Bronson, adjusting her glasses and glancing quickly and professionally over the forms.

"Right."

"Says here you're volunteering for a straight Hetero-Norm-Coital set-up. That right?"

"Uh, right."

"No interest in any ... in anything more exotic?"

"What do you mean?"

"What I mean to say is that we are concerned in this experiment with the full range of human sexual activity, not just a small segment of it. As I'm sure you realize, not everybody in the world gets his kicks from just coital contact, nor from contact with a partner of a sex opposite to his own, nor from just one partner at a time, nor even from exclusively *human* partners."

"Well, naturally," said Perlmutter.

"So what I am asking is whether, as you've indicated on this form here, you truly wish to restrict your participation in this experiment to a straight coital encounter with just one human partner at a time of the opposite sex?"

"Oh. Well, yes," said Perlmutter, "I believe so."

"All right," said Dr. Bronson.

"At least for the first one," Perlmutter added, not wishing to be thought a total square.

Dr. Bronson pursed her lips and thoughtfully injected a pencil into her mouth.

"You realize, of course," she said at length, "that there are going to be a number of factors present in this experiment of a somewhat distracting nature."

"I realize that," said Perlmutter.

"You realize that you are going to be observed at all times during the experiment by a team of scientists and a battery of delicate and comprehensive measuring equipment?"

"I realize that," said Perlmutter.

"Do you think you will be distracted by being observed while in the act of coitus? That is, do you think it will, ah, impair your function?"

"I doubt it," said Perlmutter. "I have been observed before."

"Oh?"

"I mean, I did live in a fraternity house for almost four years."

On right-thirty of a brisk Saturday evening in fall, Perlmutter arrived at the Extension Offices of the Project on Psychophysiological Research for his 12th and, he hoped, final briefing.

After sitting for about 10 minutes on a folding chair in an otherwise deserted and sparsely-furnished waiting room, the translucent glass door marked STAFF ONLY opened, and a young nurse in a white uniform gave him a pleasant but perfunctory smile.

"We're ready for you now, Mr. Perlmutter," she said.

Perlmutter walked through the door into an examination room with an elevated table, upholstered in brown leather.

"Are you Clothed Foreplay, Semi-Clothed, or Nude?" said the nurse.

"Pardon?"

The nurse consulted her metal clipboard.

"Perlmutter," she said. "Ah yes. You're Semi-Clothed. Would you kindly remove your jacket, tie, shirt, shoes, and trousers, and then follow me into the next room?"

"I've already *had* my physical examination," said Perlmutter, fearing some clerical error. "What examination is this?"

"Oh, this is no examination," said the

"WAS IT GOOD FOR YOU, TOO?"

THE TAMING OF DENISE GONDELMAN

On this particular morning, when I awoke, there was a girl propped on one elbow in the bed beside me, no great surprise, because this was the year of all the years in my life when I was scoring three and four times a week, literally combing the pussy out of my hair, which was no great feat if one knew the Village and the scientific temperament of the Greenwich Village mind. I do not want to give the false impression that I was one of the lustiest to come adventuring down the pike. What it came down to was that I could go an hour with the average girl without destroying more of the vital substance than a good night's sleep could repair, and since that sort of stamina seems to get advertised, and I had my good looks, my blond hair, my height, build, and bullfighting school, I suppose I became one of the Village equivalents of an Eagle Scout badge for the girls. I was one of the credits needed for a diploma in the sexual humanities, I was par for a good course, and more than one of the girls and ladies would try me on an off-evening like comparison-shoppers to shop the value of their boy friend, lover, mate, or husband against the certified professionalism of Sergius O'Shaugnessy.

BY NORMAN MAILER

85

86

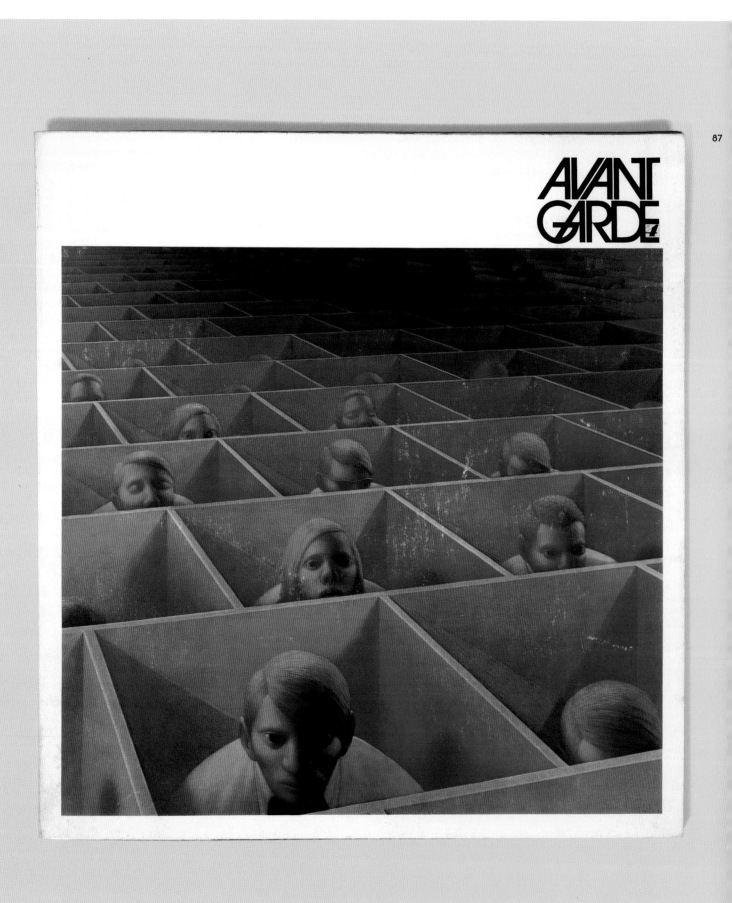

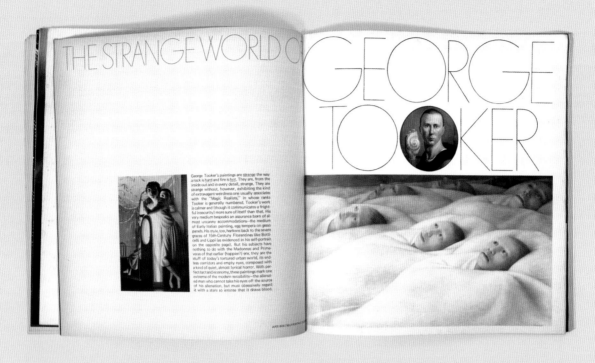

87. Avant Garde #4
The cover features a painting by 'magic realist' artist George Tooker. As his *New York Times* obituary noted: 'He specialized in eerie situations with powerful mythic overtones. Luminous and poetic, his paintings often conveyed a sense of dread, but could just as easily express a lover's rapture or spiritual ecstasy.' He died, aged 90, in 2011. As with *Avant Garde* 1, this cover uses no text other than the masthead. The mysterious painting invites readers to speculate on the magazine's contents. Date: September 1968.

88. The Strange World of ...
More paintings by George Tooker. Lubalin's use of a hairline typeface (L&C Hairline, designed by Lubalin and Tom Carnase), plus his trademark trope of a filled-in 'O' is highly characteristic of his deft use of typography in an editorial setting and his ability to partner images with sympathetic typefaces.©Paintings by George Tooker Courtesy of the Estate of George Tooker and DC Moore Gallery, New York.

89. LeRoi Jones
LeRoi Jones is a poet, writer, political activist and teacher. He was born in 1934 in New Jersey. He was an early associate of the Beat poets. In 1968, he changed his name to Amiri Baraka as part of his Muslim faith. The spread shown is yet another example of Lubalin's skill at selecting typefaces that relayed the editorial tone of the articles. Note his use of interlocking letterforms, particularly the 'L' of 'LEROI' and the F of 'OF'.

90. I Remember Superman
An account of a visit to a live sex show in Havana. Illustration by James Spanfeller.

91. The Battle Hymn of ...
Opening spread for an article about a 'young hawk' who quit college to 'slaughter in Vietnam'. It must be assumed that Lubalin's patriotic typography and colour scheme is ironic — although it is also true that he had affection for patriotic vernacular styles, as he used them repeatedly throughout his career.

92, 93. A Great Year 69
Pages from a privately distributed calendar by New York photographers Steve Horn and Norm Griner. The highly decorative typography, complete with Edwardian embellishments, gives a sense of historical retrospection, neatly complementing the subject matter of the photography. Lettering: Tom Carnase.

LEROI JONES: POET LAUREATE OF THE BLACK REVOLT

PETER SCHJELDAHL

When they say, "It is Roi
who is dead" I wonder
who will they mean?
—LEROI JONES

Photographs of LeRoi Jones show a
~~b~~oth, square, bearded, brown face often
~~pun~~ctuated between the eyes by two apostro-
~~phe~~-shaped wrinkles, bespeaking a kind of con-
~~trol~~led emotional intensity. No less emphatic is
~~the~~ way he holds his body. Bantam, lean, by
~~turn~~s elegant and tough-looking, he stands alert,
~~aggr~~essive, and Napoleonically at ease. I saw
~~him~~ standing that way once, a year or so ago,
~~befo~~re a New York judge's bench. He had been
~~accu~~sed of assault on the complaint of a little-
~~mag~~azine editor who (Jones said) owed him
~~mon~~ey for a play. The editor had quickly cool-
~~ed~~ off and asked that the charges be dropped,
~~but~~ quest the local cops and courts (who had
~~bee~~n coveting a chance to impound Jones for
~~som~~e time) would have laughed at had it not
~~made~~ them so mad. Though any chance of
~~bring~~ing the case to trial, in the absence of
~~plain~~tiff or witnesses, was out of the question,
~~Jone~~s was called before the bench repeatedly
~~in~~ the course of several months for meaning-
~~less~~ hearings. I was present on one of these
~~vario~~us occasions and saw Jones standing in the
~~postu~~re described above, beside his lawyer,
~~direc~~ting at the judge a nonchalant gaze drip-
~~ping~~ with scorn. His Honor didn't like it.

"Counsellor, why is your man looking at
~~me li~~ke that?" he demanded to know.

~~T~~he Counsellor made placatory noises.

~~T~~he judge turned on Jones: "Why are you
~~look~~ing at me like that?!"

~~J~~ones smiled. "Just want to *remember* you,
~~that'~~s all," he said.

~~R~~eading accounts of Jones' equally provo-
~~cativ~~e repartees with Judge Leon Karp at his
~~trial~~ in New Jersey last winter for possession
~~of fi~~rearms during the Newark riot, some other-
~~wise~~ sympathetic whites have wondered why
~~this b~~lack poet can't maintain a civil cool in
~~such~~ situations, thereby disarming the vendetta
~~to w~~hich he has been subjected. It would be
~~mak~~ing a big point about LeRoi Jones to con-

clude that his outbursts are just the result of a
hot temper. Like almost everything else about
him, from the way he looks to the content of
what he says, they are something like two parts
emotion and three parts calculation. They are
part of his new program for black (and his
own) advancement, in opposition to all the
old liberal and integrationist formulae. For Civil
Disobedience, Jones has substituted what
might be called Civil Impudence (with the ultimate goal of Civil War), deliberately spitting
in Whitey's eye—by which he means to be no
less than the hero of an entire generation of
black youth. If this sounds megalomaniacal, it
should be remembered that, as often as not,
it is the megalomaniacs who make history.

That a sensitive, somewhat-dandified poet,
whose works have often been so new as to be
almost incomprehensible, should now be in a
position to "make history" is a sign of the
times. Every black man in America during the
last few years has been brought harshly up
against the question of his blackness, of "Which
side are you on?" This trial has broken the
hearts of some. Martin Luther King, who short
years ago seemed the prophet of an emerging
era, at the end of his life was stranded by the
rising flood of events on an ever-narrowing middle ground. Others, like ex-convict Malcolm X
and precocious Westchester schoolboy Stokely
Carmichael, were caught up by the same flood
and delivered, galvanized and transformed, onto the high ground of black leadership. Each
of these cases is a story in itself, and all will have
to be told one day if we are ever to understand
what has happened to us as a nation. LeRoi
Jones, for his complexity, largeness of talent,
and the drama of his experience, is a good place
to start—though his story will have to be left
only half-complete. Chances are that tomorrow
he will be changed again, and be even more important.

Jones did not always know that historical
prominence was what he wanted. But, on his
own testimony, he always sensed that he was
marked out for something big. Born October 7,
1934, on the genteel-shabby, half-Italian out-
skirts of the Newark ghetto, son of a mailman
and a social worker, he is like most revolution-
aries a product of the middle class. In his own
words, he was "the only 'middle-class' chump
running with the Hillside Place bads. I was
'saved' from them by my parents' determina-

tion and the cool scholarship game which turns
stone killers pure alabaster by graduation
time." These twin identifications—with the
earthy, "bad" ghetto blacks, on the one hand,
and with the celestially white world of intellect
and literature, on the other—coexisted within
him from his adolescence until sometime before his 30th birthday, when he set about to
slaughter his white part. At least this is the version of his life he would have everyone believe.
And, he being no less mysterious than any
other man, it is probably as close to the truth
as we are likely to come.

The stress of Jones' conflicted identity is a
recurring theme in his works, especially in those
looking back on his boyhood and youth. His
play *The Toilet* could not be clearer, and we
have every reason to believe that it is strictly
autobiographical. The incident is alluded to in
other of Jones' writings, and the hero's name
is Ray (Jones' nickname is Roi), described in
the cast notes as "short, intelligent, manic."
Ray is the acknowledged leader of a swaggering
informal gang of Negro students in a boys' high
school. The scene is the school lavatory, where,
after hours, the gang is waiting for a white
student, Karolis, to be dragged in. Karolis has
made homosexual advances to Ray, and Ray is
expected to repay him with a beating. But Ray
is so torn between a sense of what is demanded
of him as leader and a dangerous feeling of
tenderness for Karolis that in the end he almost allows himself to be strangled by the hys-
terical white boy. Then, after the gang members
have interceded and stomped Karolis, Ray re-
enters the washroom, kneels before the broken
body, and, as the curtain falls, stays "weeping
and cradling the head in his arms."

What kind of solicitude a Karolis could expect from Ray/Roi these days is a
moot question. Jones has since ostensibly dis-
owned in himself that order of impulses that
could lead to sympathy for a white man set upon by blacks. The drama of this emotional auto-
surgery hangs like a cloud over his novel, *The
System of Dante's Hell*, a mélange of lyrical
expressionist riffs with snatches of statement
and story. It recounts what Jones calls "the
inferno of my frustration" as he moved, a

I REMEMBER SUPERMAN

AN AMERICAN TOURIST RECALLS THE ASTONISHING COMMAND PERFORMANCE OF A HAVANA BROTHEL SUPERSTAR BY FRANCESCA MILANO

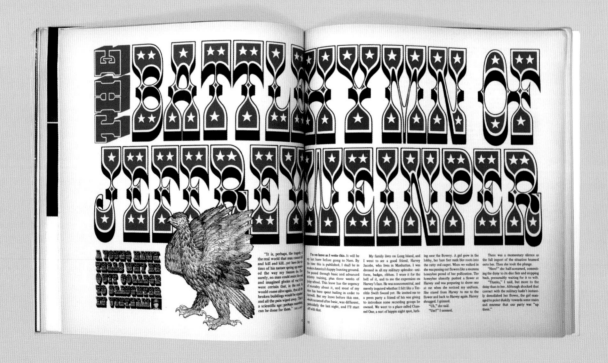

THE BATTLIN OF JEFFREY JUNIPER

A YOUNG MAN'S TWO YEARS WITH THE QUIET COLLEGE TO SLAUGHTER IN VIETNAM

A Great Year...

69

Any Way You Look At It

Yes, '69 promises to be a great year (any way you look at it), and one of the things we're looking forward to is a new page every month from the magnificent calendar that appears on the next 12 pages. It is the creation of two brilliant young New York photographers named Steve Horn and Norm Griner. The Horn/Griner Calendar (sometimes referred to as "The Horny Griner Calendar") has by now become something of an institution in the field of commercial art. For six years Messrs. Horn and Griner have been creating their calendars, basing them upon historical events (and non-events), and distributing them free to some 2,000 privileged characters in art studios, ad agencies, museums, etc., across the land. Despite all sorts of juicy offers, Messrs. Horn and Griner have steadfastly refused to permit distribution of their calendars to the general public, preferring that the calendars remain a special treat for persons within the art world. On the theory that readers of Avant-Garde are really as much a part of that world as anyone, however, Messrs. Horn and Griner have kindly consented to the appearance of their latest calendar upon our pages. For which the editors of Avant-Garde would like to publicly express their gratitude (and yours, too, we hope).

La Belle Otero, the famous courtesan of the nineteenth century, was barred from the casino at Monte Carlo for three days when, after losing over a million francs in a mere 12 hours and the croupier having refused her credit on her gold purse, she jumped up on the roulette table, ripped off her dress and demanded of him, "What's this worth, cochon?"

'69 JANUARY '69

S	M	T	W	T	F	S
			1	2	3	4
5	6	7	8	9	10	11
12	13	14	15	16	17	18
19	20	21	22	23	24	25
26	27	28	29	30	31	

When the emperor Claudius (10 B.C.-54 A.D.) was off in England, Messalina, his empress, challenged the leading harlots of Rome to a non-stop sex bout, the object to see who could sleep with the most men in one night. It is recorded that at dawn, after the twenty-fifth engagement, the last whore conceded her defeat but Messalina carried on until soon.

'69 FEBRUARY '69

S	M	T	W	T	F	S
						1
2	3	4	5	6	7	8
9	10	11	12	13	14	15
16	17	18	19	20	21	22
23	24	25	26	27		

Blanche d'Antigny was so little made to be a courtesan (though quite a successful one) that, according to her friends, she does not know how to get paid when her lover leaves because she sleeps like a log . . . and her admirers host a quick retreat while she slumbered. She finally found a way: ". . . she sews his night shirt to hers before going to sleep."

'69 MARCH '69

S	M	T	W	T	F	S
						1
2	3	4	5	6	7	8
9	10	11	12	13	14	15
16	17	18	19	20	21	22
23	24	25	26	27	28	29
30	31					

94. Avant Garde #5

Highly stylized painting by artist Tom Wesselmann, often associated with Pop Art. Like Lubalin, he was a graduate of Cooper Union. He worked in painting, collage and sculpture, and did not like his inclusion in the American Pop Art school, pointing out that he made aesthetic use of everyday objects and did not intend to criticize them as consumer objects: 'I dislike labels in general and "Pop" in particular,' he said. Wesselmann's languorously erotic art fits seamlessly into the libertine atmosphere of *Avant Garde*. Date: November 1968.© Estate of Tom Wesselmann / DACS, London/VAGA, NY, 2012.

95—97. No More War

Avant Garde attracted 2,000 entries for their 'No More War' poster competition. The winning posters were featured in a six-page layout. Examples shown: Fig.95, left-hand page: untitled work by Lou Myers (USA). Right-hand page: untitled work by Ron and Karen Bowen (USA). Fig.96: left-hand page: 'Love Peace' by James Grashow (USA). Right-hand page: 'Fuck War' by Billy Apple (England) and Robert Coburn (USA). Fig.97: left-hand page: Harvey Stewart and Lawrence Corby (USA). Right-hand page, clockwise top right: 'My Son, The Soldier' by Daniel Schwartz (USA); 'No More Hiroshima' by Hirokatsu Hijikata (Japan); Hans Butter (Holland); 'No More War' by Keiichi Tanaami (Japan).

98—100. Brain Damage

Opening spread (fig.98) and two inner spreads (figs.99 and 100) for feature on work of visionary New York artist/photographer Ira Cohen. Born in New York in 1935, Cohen described himself as an 'Electronic Multimedia Shaman.' In the late 1960s, he developed his 'Mylar Chamber'. This invention used Mylar, a bendable plastic mirrored material that distorts reflections into strange colours and shapes, which enabled Cohen to produce wonderfully twisted and skewed photographic portraits of many of the giants of 1960s radical culture: Jimi Hendrix, Jack Smith, Angus MacLise, Pharaoh Sanders and William S. Burroughs, among others. In 1968, Cohen made his first film, *The Invasion of Thunderbolt Pagoda*, an experimental underground classic. He died in 2011, at the age of 76. Note the distorted typographic headline that mirrors the distorting qualities of the Mylar: Lubalin has run a razor blade through the letters and pulled them into distorted shapes. Yet again, he allows the pictures to dominate his pages — no tasteful acres of white space and postage-stamp images for Herb Lubalin.

"Brain Damage"
SORCERY AS AN ART

QUEEN BONE HAS BEEN TRANSFORMED INTO A ZEBRA BY THE GREAT MIRROR LION!

LORD DOPE FROG AWAITS HIS LADY SOMEWHERE BEYOND TIME.

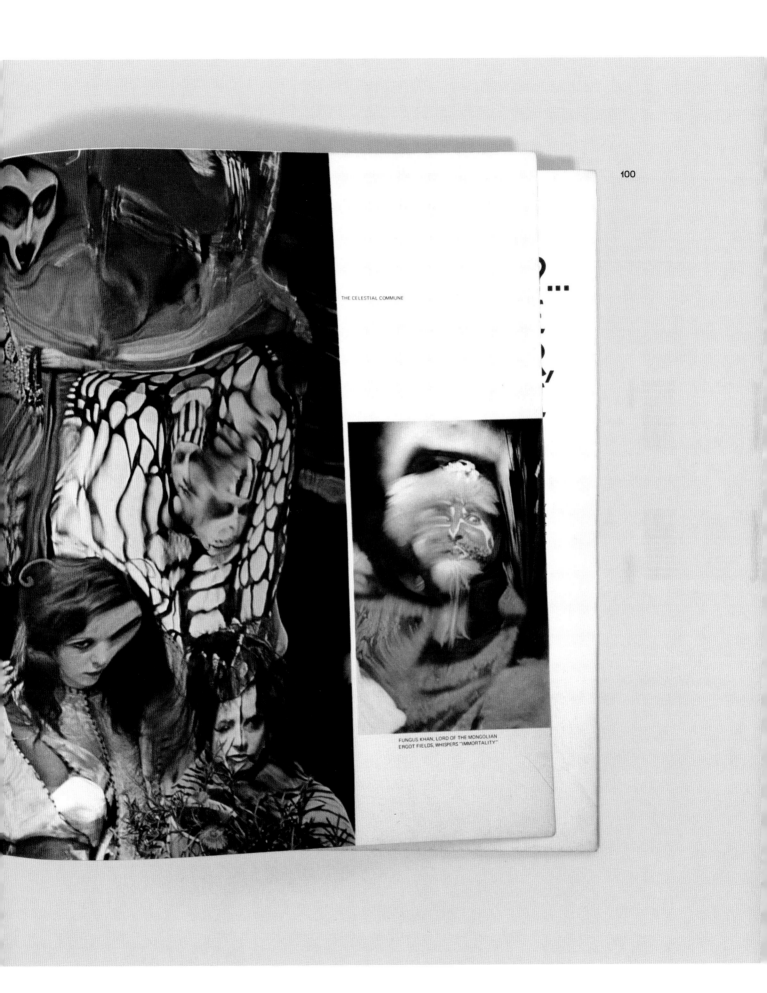

THE CELESTIAL COMMUNE

FUNGUS KHAN, LORD OF THE MONGOLIAN
ERGOT FIELDS, WHISPERS "IMMORTALITY"

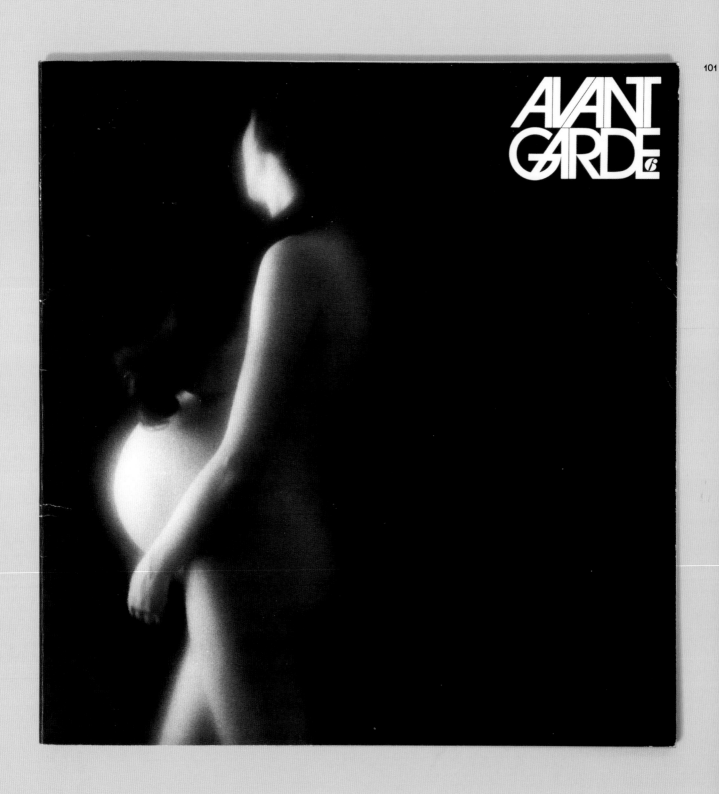

101. Avant Garde #6
Typically taboo-busting front cover showing a photograph of a pregnant woman titled 'In Full Bloom.' There was no such thing as a typical *Avant Garde* cover: apart from the consistent absence of cover lines, each cover was radically different. Even the masthead logotype, which never changed, was allowed to move to a different location on each cover, and its size varied — both attributes that few modern magazines would tolerate. Photograph by Dewayne Dalrymple. Date: January 1969.

102. Melle's Melees
Yet another significant, and recherché, artist showcased in the pages of *Avant Garde*. Melle Oldeboerrigter was born in Holland, and trained as a typesetter. He worked at the *Arbeiderspers* (Workers' Press), but continued to draw and illustrate. Melle has been called a surrealist, but he resisted this categorization and considered himself a visionary artist in the mould of Hieronymus Bosch. The subtle cruciform layout of the text page is pure Lubalin, its drama rendered more powerfully by its position next to a full-bleed image (right-hand page).

103. Breaking Out
Repeatedly, *Avant Garde* turned to the big social and political issues of America in the 1960s. Here, black comedian Dick Gregory offers a politically charged 'Black Manifesto'. Note Lubalin's trademark use of contrasting weights of typeface, and his positioning in the colon under the bar of the 'T' in the word 'OUT'. Photography is by Art Kane, one of the giants of the New York photography scene.

104. Phil Ochs
Opening spread for a 6-page article on Phil Ochs, one of the leading figures of the U.S. folk rock movement of the 1960s. The article begins: 'Phil Ochs wasn't the only shaggy, blue-jeaned young man to trudge into Greenwich Village in 1962 lugging a guitar and fancying that, under a certain light, he looked a little like James Dean.' Lubalin resists the temptation to use a photograph of Ochs, preferring instead to use a highly detailed drawing by frequent collaborator Jim Spanfeller. The typographic headline shows Lubalin's fixation with tightly packed lettering, allowing many internal patterns and relationships to develop. Note the way he allows the 'l' and 'i' of 'Kipling' to intrude into the 'O' of 'Ochs' to create a distinctive graphic motif.

105. The Last Act
Short story by Roald Dahl. As above, the layout is traditional. Illustrations are by Etienne Delessert: by embedding the illustrations in the text, Lubalin makes them almost seem part of the story.

106, 107. The Sexual Revolution
The opening spread has a group of fully clothed men chasing a naked woman (fig. 106). In the second spread, (fig. 107) a lone naked woman is seen chasing a group of clothed men. This is sexual commentary with a uniquely 1960s flavour, and illustrates the confusion that surrounded ideas of sexual liberation with the growing concept of gender equality. Photography is by Ralph M. Hattersley. Lubalin derives maximum effect from these powerful photographs by running them as full-bleed images over two spreads. Anything else would have diminished their potency. They are further evidence, if evidence were needed, that design and layout was as much a part of *Avant Garde* as the editorial content.

PHOTOGRAPH BY ART KANE

BREAKING OUT: A BLACK MANIFESTO BY DICK GREGORY

eorge Wallace was half right when he said, "Gregory's not funny any more." The hole truth is that Dick Gregory is far from <u>merely</u> funny these days. His years of mersion in the caldron of our racial strife have transmuted the master comic into wise, eloquent, and lacerating spokesman for black aspiration, a one-man hot- e from the heart of the ghetto to the conscience of White America. Speaking at llies and on college campuses across the country, running for President, publishing insightful book (<u>Write Me In!</u>), Gregory has spread the word of black liberation th wit and passion. Now that Malcolm X and Martin Luther King are gone, Gregory's ne of the few truth-telling voices left in the land; and, for all its jokes, it leaves no ter truth untold. Turn this page to find out why it makes George Wallace squirm.

Phil Ochs: Kipling of the new left

BY PETER SCHJELDAHL

THE LAST ACT
BY ROALD DAHL

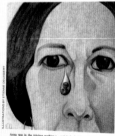

To commemorate America's 100th Birthday in 1876, Cleveland publisher James F. Ryder commissioned A.M. Willard to paint "The Spirit of '76." It depicts the heroes of America's first revolution —the Minutemen who fought for our nation's independence.

To commemorate America's 200th Birthday in 1976, Avant-Garde commissioned Carl Fischer to photograph "The Spirit of 1976." It depicts the heroes of America's present revolution - the avant-gardists who are struggling for sexual freedom, racial equality, and an end to war.

108. Avant Garde #7
By the seventh issue of *Avant Garde*, Ralph Ginzburg and Herb Lubalin had found an editorial and design mix that was both confident and adventurous. Issue 7 contained articles on folk singing, the failure of the black power movement, documentary maker D.A. Pennebaker, Yippie leader Jerry Rubin, and the cat drawings of fashion photographer Guy Bourdin. This frothing mix of subject matter was held together by Lubalin's disciplined handling of the text, and his flair for eye-catching headlines. For the first time the magazine carried a price tag: $1.00. The logotype also acquired a Registered Trade Mark symbol, giving notice that the masthead had been registered with a national trademark office. Cover photograph by longstanding Lubalin associate, Carl Fischer. Date: March 1969.

109. Toward a New Spirit of '76
Spread shows (left) A.M. Willard's 1876 painting *The Spirit of '76*, depicting the heroes of America's first revolution. To commemorate America's 200th birthday in 1976, *Avant Garde* commissioned Carl Fischer to photograph 'the Spirit of 1976'. An editorial note explains that Fischer's photography 'depicts the heroes of America's present revolution — the avant gardists who are struggling for sexual freedom, racial equality, and an end to war.' This quintessentially 1960s declaration neatly sums up the ethos of *Avant Garde*. It also allowed Lubalin to indulge — yet again — his taste for garish vernacular typography. Fischer's photographic tableaux are technically and artistically accomplished.

110. The Demise of Death
Article on scientific advances that might result in the postponement of death. Lubalin's 'deceased' letter 'i' is a trademark gesture, and a fine example of his use of expressive typography.

111—114. Opening spreads
A range of typical opening spreads demonstrating various Lubalin typographic constructions. In the same issue he oscillates between, single-, three-, and four-column grids on the page, and between different text fonts. His accomplished use of dramatic typographic headlines results in fluid, non-repetitive and inviting spreads. Images are by Donna Gortinsky (fig.112); painted plaster sculptures by Herbert George, photography by William E. Watkins (fig.113); illustration (fig.114) by John P. Wagner.

The Demise of Death

THANKS TO NEW SCIENTIFIC DISCOVERIES, THE ONLY THI[NG] WE CAN BE SURE OF N[OW] IS.....TAXES

BY R. MICHAEL DAVIDSON

"Since those first days in Eden, [Man has] been accused of despoiling Nature, of [scorning] her physical wonders, of spurning her [kindest] gifts. I, for one, repudiate these char[ges. In] failing health I can but dwell on Na[ture's] crueler crimes against man. What, if n[ot an] injury, is this natural phenomenon [of] aging? And what, if not the final slu[r, the su]preme insult, is this natural thing we ca[ll death?] Will Man, armed with the guns of [science,] never strike back?"——Dr. Gunnar Bel[ding]

Those guns, unfortunately, did not [arrive] in time to save the irascible Dr. Belding[. But in] the two decades since his death, scie[nce has] begun arming itself—and to the teeth—[for] future assaults. On every scientific fron[t—be] it physics, chemistry, physiology, g[enetics,] electronics, or biology—impressive, an[d some]times bizarre, research is being carrie[d on in] strenuous pursuit of immortality. The [desire] only to live but to live endlessly today [galva]nizes the scientific community that onl[y a few] years ago exhibited nothing but conte[mpt for] the "fictionalists" of life-everlasting.

It is estimated that the National In[stitutes] of Health is now spending nearly $50 [million] annually on hundreds of research projec[ts con]cerned with death and aging. In the [United] States alone there are some 1500 research[ers] whose mission can only be described as [a full] war on death.

Optimism about the prospects for [extending]

ng the world's number-one
-aging—is running high. Dr.
old an assembly at the Royal
ons recently that even those
obably live to be at least 180,
assive research effort now un-
eas of science and medicine.
t massive efforts, however,
mmortality will eventually be
dramatic extensions of youth-
al life span are just around the
xamining the research in pro-
mpasses procedures that could
d now to help man live longer,
understand something about
ing itself.

pects we begin to decline in
tal acuity at the moment of
definition, with each passing
"progressing" steadily toward
real damage begins to set in
twenties. "You don't feel it
e biologist says sardonically,
e you reach 30 your irreplace-
are already dying off at the
every day." Indeed, between
nd 90, provided that one lives
weight drops from an average
ee pounds to a little more than
uscle weight falls off by 30 per
hat fall the heart diminishes in
ping only half the blood that it
The number of nerve fibers in
by a quarter and those that re-
5 per cent more slowly than
bstantially dulling our reaction
that remove waste materials
diminish radically, and even
fall from 250 per papilla in
old age.

mechanism responsible for this
n it be destroyed—or at least

f theories have been advanced
o explain aging and death, but
w seems most viable is the so-
theory. It maintains that senes-
ue to the random failure and
throughout the body. When
the entire individual dies. Par-
ed by this process are those tis-
unable to replace dead cells,
s and nerves. The fact that so
e of heart failure (as opposed,

say, to liver failure) supports this theory. The heart, unlike the liver, is really just a specialized muscle, the cells of which can never be replaced once destroyed. The liver, on the other hand, can regenerate lost cells in old age just as easily as in youth.

But the question remains: *Why* do these cells die? No one is yet absolutely certain. When we know we will be able to decisively control aging and probably eliminate death—if we wish. A number of theories are presently being discounted. The notions that cells simply "run out of gas," become clogged with their own wastes, or are damaged by atmospheric radiation have not fared well under laboratory scrutiny. But a theory proposed by the Finnish chemist John Bjorksten has.

Bjorksten's "cross-linking" theory holds that the long-chain molecules that form the all-important nuclei of the cells become snarled up and thus are unable to function, resulting in cell death. Bjorksten—and now many other scientists—believe that stray protein-like molecules or bits of molecules drift into the cells and accidentally attach themselves at various points to the long-chain molecules. Eventually everything becomes so gummed up that the cell dies. The villains in this case—these stray bits of molecules, the presence of which has been detected chemically and even microscopically—are known as "age pigments."

Bjorksten believes there are bacteria that can dissolve these cross-linkages and thus not only delay aging but perhaps arrest cell death altogether. Scientists do have leads that point to the existence of such bacteria, though they have not yet actually isolated them. But even if such bacteria are never found or controlled, it is likely that modern science will be able to synthesize agents capable of selectively dissolving these pigments.

The cell-death theory, while it may be adequate to explain normal aging processes, cannot, however, account for the phenomenon we call "overnight aging." Some creatures, such as the unfortunate salmon, appear to be naturally "programmed" to die what seems to us to be a premature death. When man turns gray "before his time," however, it would appear to be the result of some defect in a still mysterious cellular mechanism. Eventually, scientists are confident, this life-span mechanism will be understood and subjected to manipulation. The technology for such feats is already being per-

fected by geneticists who are rapidly mastering the new science of "cellular surgery."

While geneticists learn how to make radical and lasting changes in the aging mechanism at the molecular level of life, however, other scientists are exploring different avenues with considerable success. Some of these are not only bizarre but macabre; all are extraordinary. What follows is a sampling of the various approaches:

Fasting for Immortality?—Not at all out of the question, say gerontologists who for years have been pondering the now famous experiments of Dr. C.M. McCay at Cornell University. Dr. McCay took two groups of rats, all the same age, and placed them on different diets. One group was fed on a regimen that, while not excessive, insured a maximum growth rate. The other group was given a skimpy bill-of-fare guaranteed to minimize growth rate. Astoundingly, the "underprivileged" rats lived twice as long as their well-fed brethren. This approach has been followed up by a Chicago research team, which was able to extend the lives of rats 20 per cent simply by forcing them to fast every third day. One of these researchers was so impressed that he began fasting himself. It is certain now that long-range experiments will shortly be conducted with humans.

Dr. Bjorksten theorizes that fasting prolongs life because it diminishes the consumption of "age-pigment" molecules that interfere with cell functions. Others believe that fasting simply delays maturation and extends life in the pre-adult period only. This seems to have been the case, at any rate, with Dr. McCay's rats. Still, it is surely better to add 20 or 30 years to one's life while young rather than while too old to enjoy them.

Peter Pan Is Alive and Well—In a Hormone—It was British physiologist Sir Vincent Wigglesworth who discovered him there. Wigglesworth, experimenting with butterflies and other insects that metamorphose from larval to adult stages of development, found that a specific hormone governs this remarkable phenomenon and keeps the insect young until a preprogrammed time. Excited cosmetics manufacturers immediately dubbed the chemical in question—which Wigglesworth named "ecdysone"—the "Peter Pan hormone" because it seemed to have the power to keep an organism

Sculpture à la Rorschach

In these days when everybody is supposed to be "unshockable," Herbert George's painted plaster sculptures may rattle the sensibilities of even the watchiest connoisseur. Abstract, they are anything but "removed from life"? They are almost too life-like. Derived, so he says, from the morphology of cellular growth, they seem to allude at once to everything organic, fleshly, pulsing or steaming with life. They look almost as if they would cringe if you touched them. And, like Rorschach ink blots, they are what you are dares to be. However, they are not in themselves mere obscene blobs. Their basic model is the head, and George plays on this with nothing wit—inserting, for example, a grinning mouth between the nostril bridges, so deftly suggesting a lewd tongue or beetling brows; making horse and hilarity wink at us in cheerful sobriety.

and aplomb. Herbert George is a tall, emphatically handsome young man, a 28-year-old native of Seattle, Wash., in 1966. He showed a series of bold, elegant wood and canvas constructions at a small New York gallery, here unnamed because, as George tells it, the owner has lately refused to tolerate the "obscenity" of his current work. But these sculptures may seem at first akin to the recent vogue of polymorphously perverse "Funk Art." George denies the influence, pointing instead to modern masters—Arp and Brancusi, Picasso and Lachaise. Most significantly, the concise power of these works which are closely corrective to present trends, proving that sculpture need not be two stories high to capture and hold attention, or a size that can be cradled in the hand, they are about as quiet and docile as a "mushroom."

SCULPTURES PHOTOGRAPHED BY WILLIAM CLAXTON

ILLUSTRATION BY JOHN P. BRUNER

O Precious Balls, Farewell!
JEAN GENET

O prison-home, O sweetness gone, O dream vanished!
Elysium of Beauty: Ocean shored with palm,
Fierce midnights, sated mornings, days of sun-drenched calm:
O shorn locks, O velvet skin close-clutched, deep-ravished.

Come, Love, and dream with me of some tough lover,
Big as the world, hair-shadowed, flecked with dusky grace,
Ready to lodge us tight, and naked, in his dark embrace:
His smoking belly, and his golden thighs, our cover.

A roughneck, hotly glowing, of archangelic make,
His upfling wreathed with scented bloom, the loveliness
Brought by your bright and tremulous hands to bless
A noble flank—now reeling, from the fuck you take.

O sadness in my mouth! O bitter, bitter rue!
O swelling heart! These joys which wrought a fragrant spell
Are leaving me; for lovers go. O precious balls, farewell!
O cock, which chokes my voice with happy insolence, adieu, adieu.

AVANT GARDE #8,
PICASSO'S EROTIC GRAVURES

THIS SPECIAL ISSUE OF AVANT-GARDE IS DEVOTED ENTIRELY TO ONE SUBJECT: A SERIES OF EROTIC GRAVURES, OR ENGRAVINGS, BY PABLO PICASSO, THE PRE-EMINENT ARTIST OF OUR TIME. THEY ARE INTENDED TO STAND, AS PICASSO HIMSELF HAS SAID, "AS AN ABIDING CELEBRATION OF LIFE ITSELF."

115. Avant Garde #8

Special issue of *Avant Garde* devoted entirely to the erotic gravures of Pablo Picasso. The cover text declares Picasso 'the pre-eminent artist of our time'. In the late 1960s, Picasso was indeed almost universally known as the embodiment of contemporary art. Unsurprisingly, his erotic engravings were not well known. The front cover affords Lubalin the opportunity to use his most famous typeface, Avant Garde Gothic, for both the masthead and the issue's title; he also uses Futura Light as an introduction to the magazines content. Note the judicious use of ligatures. Lubalin and Tom Carnase, who jointly devised this famous typeface, were critical of the way their ligatures (made uniquely from capital letters) were used by other typographers. Ed Benguiat, Lubalin's friend and a celebrated type designer, said that the only time the ligatures were properly used was in the masthead of *Avant Garde* magazine. Date: September 1969.

116. Are you Avant Garde?

In an issue otherwise devoted entirely to the erotic work of Picasso, the final two pages are given over to an ad inviting subscriptions. The text offers subscribers a copy of *Nudes of Yesteryear*, a book of Victorian nudes designed by Lubalin and published by Avant-Garde Books (p.48). The rather lugubrious and dated copy refers to the naked models as the 'kookiest, campest, most voluptuous, sportive, and daring women ever to cavort before the winking eye of a camera'.

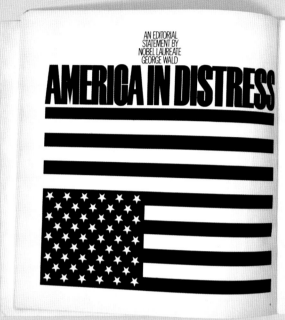

117. Avant Garde #9
Once more, *Avant Garde* features an unconventional artist with marked surrealist and transgressive qualities: on this occasion, the Austrian Ernst Fuchs. Date: November, 1969.

118. America in Distress
Repeatedly throughout his career, Lubalin used the U.S. flag as a basis for his graphic commentary on life, culture and — mostly — politics. Here he incorporates typography into the layout of the flag and reproduces it in black and white. There are numerous instances of his visual riffing on 'Old Glory'.

119. Is the Red Cross Pro-Nazi?
Article by Warren Boroson, accusing the Red Cross ('the richest and most powerful humanitarian organization in the world …') of alerting Nazis in hiding to the likelihood that they were about to be brought to justice. Lubalin's use of red, black and white is redolent of Nazi ensignia, yet unusually for Lubalin, this is a subtle and oddly restrained graphic reference.

120, 121. Ultra-Violet in Infra-Red
Warhol's superstar from issue 3 returns. Ultra-Violet's real name was Isabelle Collin Dufresne. She was born in France in 1935. In the 1970s, she published her autobiography, *Famous for 15 Minutes: My Years with Andy Warhol*. Here she is photographed using infrared film by Eliot Elifson. Like Ginzburg and Lubalin, Elifson was the son of Russian immigrants. He worked for *Life* magazine from 1942 onwards. The photographs of Ultra-Violet were taken on an island off the coast of Maine owned by Elifson. Lubalin's typography is a rather half-hearted attempt at psychedelic lettering: no matter how deranged the subject matter, Lubalin nearly always retained his commitment to formal typographic construction.

122, 123. Deserted Island
Spreads showing Wilton S. Tiffts' elegiac documentary photographs of the now deserted Ellis Island, the former entry point for millions of immigrants to the United States from 1892 until 1954. As the sons of immigrants, Ginzburg and Lubalin would have found these pictures highly expressive, which might explain why the feature has no text. Lubalin's layout allows the images to speak without the need for textual commentary.

IS TH
RE[
CROS
PR(
NAZI

VARREN BOROSON

American Red Cross is also pretty right-wing (it won't help the families of strikers even if they're starving; once, when someone politely suggested that the A.R.C. help the families of strikers in the Kentucky coal fields, the entire governing board of the Harlan County Chapter huffily threatened to resign). Finally, critics have pointed out that the American Red Cross resembles an old folks' home for Junior Leaguers, a place where socialites can dabble at do-gooding. As the late labor leader John L. Lewis once put it, the Red Cross is undemocratic, "surrounded and controlled as it is by a social fringe." "It is too close a corporation," the Great John L. went on. "It is too near the wellsprings of American finance and those who set themselves up as being American aristocracy. There are chapters and units of the Red Cross in various sections of the country that are nothing more nor less than exclusive clubs or social organizations from which the average American is debarred...."

No longer is the Red Cross fair game. Today, criticizing the Red Cross—any branch of it—is akin to praising Ho Chi Minh, and most American newspapers, magazines, and TV stations wouldn't dream of spreading any such heresy—and antagonizing powerful Red Cross leaders. For a case in point, let us look at what happened last year, when the West German Red Cross and several other branches did a terrible thing: They alerted hundreds of Nazi criminals that time was running out for them and justice was closing in.

The protagonist of this tragedy is Simon Wiesenthal, the 60-year-old Nazi-hunter. Mr. Wiesenthal spent four years in over a dozen Nazi concentration camps; 89 of his relatives, including his mother, were murdered by the Nazis. After the war, Wiesenthal determined to dedicate his life to tracking down the most vicious of the Nazis. Today he is in charge of a private organization, the Documentation Center, in Vienna, where he and a few assistants use every scrap of information they can get to locate the whereabouts of wanted Nazi criminals. Once they find out where one is hiding, they pass this information on to the country seeking the Nazi (West Germany, Austria, France, etc.), and the country tries to get the Nazi extradited and prosecuted. It was Simon Wiesenthal who, after 16 years of searching, discovered the hiding place of Adolf Eichmann; it was Simon Wiesenthal who located the Nazi who had arrested Anne Frank.

Since beginning his work, Wiesenthal has amassed a list of 22,500 missing Nazi criminals. How many has he brought to justice? A mere 900. Finding missing Nazi criminals is, after all, backbreaking work. Their names may not even be known: Of the 6000 S.S. men at Auschwitz, for example, only 900 have been identified. Then too, throughout the world there are Nazi sympathizers, people eager to help conceal Nazi criminals and warn them if anybody is asking questions. And many countries just won't extradite Nazi criminals—among them Egypt, of course, but also many South American countries, a few of which (like Paraguay) are indiscriminately pro-German.

Early last year, Wiesenthal compiled a fresh list of 807 Nazi criminals, men and women wanted for crimes in France. The list contained new physical descriptions, new addresses. At the same time that Wiesenthal passed the list on to France, he sent the list to the West German Foreign Office, as is his custom. Somehow, the list came to the attention of Dr. Johannes Gawlik, head of the Foreign Office's Legal Protection Department, which looks out for the interests of Germans living abroad. Dr. Gawlik, by chance, was a lawyer who had defended several S.S. men during the Nuremberg trial.

For a while, Dr. Gawlik thought about what to do with this valuable list of names. Finally he had a brainstorm: He passed the list on to Dr. Kurt Wagner, head of the West German Red Cross Research Center.

Dr. Wagner is the antagonist of this tragedy.

He wasted nary a moment. By letter, by telephone, by telegraph he sent messages to other Red Cross chapters all over the world, informing them where the Nazi criminals were hiding out and urging the Red Cross officials to warn them. The Austrian Red Cross, it has been learned, eagerly cooperated, and 30 Nazi criminals in Austria were told that they were on the list. It is not known which other Red Cross chapters cooperated. With regard to South America, the West German Red Cross decided not to take any chances there, with so many Nazi criminals involved, and several of the Red Cross men flew down to Argentina, Chile, and so forth, to deliver their warnings in person.

As a result of Dr. Wagner's energy and enthusiasm, and as a result of cooperation of Red Cross chapters all over the world, *five-hundred and eighty* of the 807 Nazi criminals were warned. Many, no doubt, chose new places to live and new identities. All will now carefully avoid visiting countries that might extradite them.

Among those who got away:

Alois Brunner, an associate of Eichmann's and a mass murderer. He is the most prominent of the wanted men. Brunner sometimes visits Europe with only his sunglasses to disguise him.

Alois Ennsberger, former S.S. *Hauptsturmführer*, wanted for mass murder.

Heinz Pfanner, former S.S. *Obersturmführer*, tried in absentia in France and condemned to death.

Nice going, Red Cross.

What have you got to say for yourself, Dr. Wagner? Spit it out:

"We are helpers, not judges. We help all human beings in trouble. Nazis are human beings, too. To warn them was in the best Red Cross tradition."

A reporter asked, "Would you help an escaped sex fiend?"

"We help all," Dr. Wagner answered, "even an escaped sex fiend."

A few Red Cross officials in West Germany did admit that the Red Cross had done something improper, and promised to punish those responsible. But Dr. Wagner is still at his post, Simon Wiesenthal informs Avant-Garde. "The Red Cross has punished none of the culprits."

In his Bulletin of Information No. 8, Wiesenthal has eloquently written about the episode. One line, because of Wiesenthal's limited knowledge of English, is strongly reminiscent of the famous letter of Bartolomeo Vanzetti:

"This unusual action to warn mass murderers has been adopted by an honorable organization like the Red Cross, which in other words represents a crime on the ideal of the Red Cross."

When Avant-Garde asked Wiesenthal what effect the Red Cross's warnings would have upon his efforts to bring the missing 580 Nazi criminals to justice, he wrote back dispiritedly:

"At the moment one can hardly measure the setback it caused us."

A suggestion to the reader:

This year, and for a few years to come, don't make any contributions to the Red Cross.

Instead, send the money you intended for the Red Cross to Mr. Simon Wiesenthal, Dokumentationszentrum, 1010 Wien (Vienna) 1, Rudolfsplatz 7/III, Austria.

YEAR, THE
T GERMAN
CROSS WAS
OLVED IN
OCKING
NDAL—A
NDAL THAT
CERTAINLY
N'T READ A
RD ABOUT,
AUSE THE
RICAN MASS
IA DECIDED
USH THE
LE THING UP

Red Cross is the richest and most al humanitarian organization in ld, with chapters in over 100 s and with over 100,000,000 s. Foremost among the chapters American branch, which has 28,- adult members and 18,000,000 members, and which—in fiscal doled out the heady sum of 7,000, all of it obtained from ations.

, you may not remember it, but on a time the Red Cross was sub- criticism. People would point out American chapter is rather racist tance, in World War II it insisted ing all blood that was donated as "black" or "white," so injured en could have a choice). The

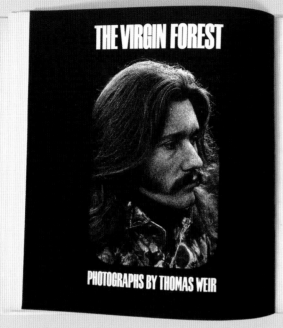

124. Avant Garde #10
The first issue of the 1970s. Cover shows a heliotrope photograph by photographer Thomas Weir. Born in 1935, Weir had associations with the San Francisco psychedelic scene. He photographed the Grateful Dead and their 'extended family' for the back cover of their 1969 album *Aoxomoxoa*. Date: January 1970.

125. The Virgin Forest
Opening spread showing photograph of a hippieish-looking Thomas Weir, and one of his striking nature photographs. Other images (not shown here) feature naked teenage girls. To modern sensibilities, these pictures contravene current mores surrounding the use of pictures of children in art. Weir's intense grainy images are well suited to the matt paper stock that was used for this issue of *Avant Garde*.

126. Israel Captured
Series of pictures that formed a show at the Jewish Museum in New York. The exhibition comprised the work of 50 photographers 'preserving forever the triumphs and tribulations of everyday life in Israel.' Left-hand page, photography by Leonard Freed. Right-hand page, photography by Izis. In this layout, Lubalin uses a full-bleed image to dramatic effect. His love of contrast is evident in this spread: a dark image is placed next to a white page.

127, 128. Israel Captured
Pictures by David Seymour (fig.127); pictures by Leonard Freed (fig.128). Lubalin's mastery of picture editing and his ability to create drama and tension on the printed page are clearly visible in these spreads.

129, 130. The Bigger They Are ...
Feature about the writer Max Hess's obsession with voluptuously bodied women. Lubalin uses the generously proportioned Cooper Black to emphasize the 'full-bodied' nature of the article. His trademark taste for expressive lettering can be seen in the way he treats the word 'Fall'. The line illustrations are by another regular Lubalin collaborator, Rick Schreiter. The left-hand page (fig.129) relates to another article, with an illustration by the Austrian artist Friedrich Hundertwasser, *626 The Way to You*, 1966 ©2012 Hundertwasser Archive, Vienna.

ISRAEL CAPTURED

THE PASSION AND PURPOSE OF ITS PEOPLE ARE PRESERVED FOREVER IN A SET OF MEMORABLE PHOTOGRAPHS

It is likely that the only way that Israel will ever be captured is through the lens of a camera. And a group of the world's most highly creative photographers has done just that: They have shot a series of photographs that preserve forever the triumphs and tribulations of everyday life in Israel. The photographs, numbering 300 and collectively entitled "Israel: The Reality," are currently on exhibition at the Jewish Museum in New York. They commemorate the 22nd anniversary of the U.N. mandate that created the State of Israel. Assembled by the great photojournalist Cornell Capa, the pictures represent the work of 50 photographers, including such titans as Arnold Newman, Leonard Freed, Paul Schutzer, and David Seymour (the last two mortal victims of the Arab-Israeli war). On the next 12 pages, Avant-Garde presents 16 pictures from the show. Each one reflects the enduring inspiration of the people of this small nation, inspiration which has perhaps been most eloquently described by photographer Robert Capa (whose pictures are among the most moving in the show): "Israel is the crudest and hardest place one can live in today. It is also a place where the young sing at night and even the old speak of the future."

TEL AVIV (PHOTOGRAPHER: LEONARD FREED)

SENTINEL

326

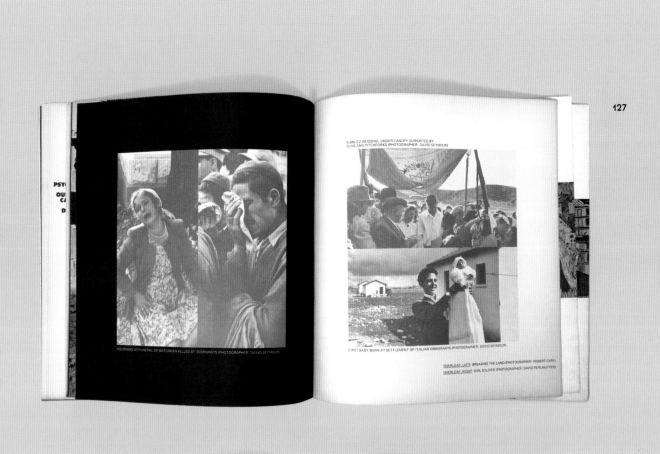

MOURNERS AT FUNERAL OF WATCHMAN KILLED BY TERRORISTS (PHOTOGRAPHER: DAVID SEYMOUR)

KIBBUTZ WEDDING, UNDER CANOPY SUPPORTED BY
GUNS AND PITCHFORKS (PHOTOGRAPHER: DAVID SEYMOUR)

FIRST BABY BORN AT SETTLEMENT OF ITALIAN IMMIGRANTS (PHOTOGRAPHER: DAVID SEYMOUR)

OVERLEAF, LEFT: BREAKING THE LAND (PHOTOGRAPHER: ROBERT CAPA)
OVERLEAF, RIGHT: GIRL SOLDIER (PHOTOGRAPHER: DAVID PERLMUTTER)

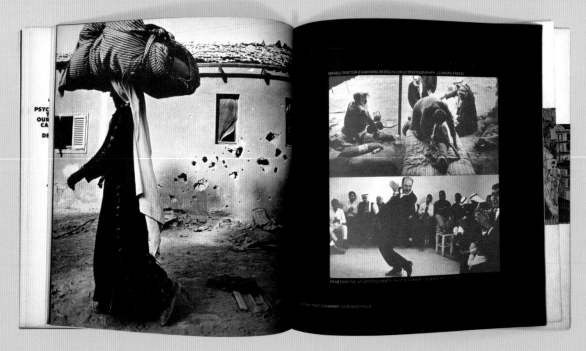

ISRAELI DOCTOR EXAMINING BEDOUIN CHILD (PHOTOGRAPHER: LEONARD FREED)

ARAB DANCING AT WEDDING PARTY (PHOTOGRAPHER: LEONARD FREED)

ON MY WAY TO SEE YOU

The Bigger They Are, The Harder I Fall!

THE MEMOIRS OF A
FAT GIRLS' CASANOVA,
BEING THE FIRST IN
A SERIES ENTITLED
"THE LUST BATTALION:
SEXUAL ADVENTURES
OF THE AVANT-GARDE"
(SEE BACK COVER OF THIS ISSUE)
BY MAX HESS
ILLUSTRATED BY RICK SCHREITER

I have liked and admired
fatgirls; in fact, I have loved and
been loved by fatgirls.
my mind the adjective fat and
the noun girl are words

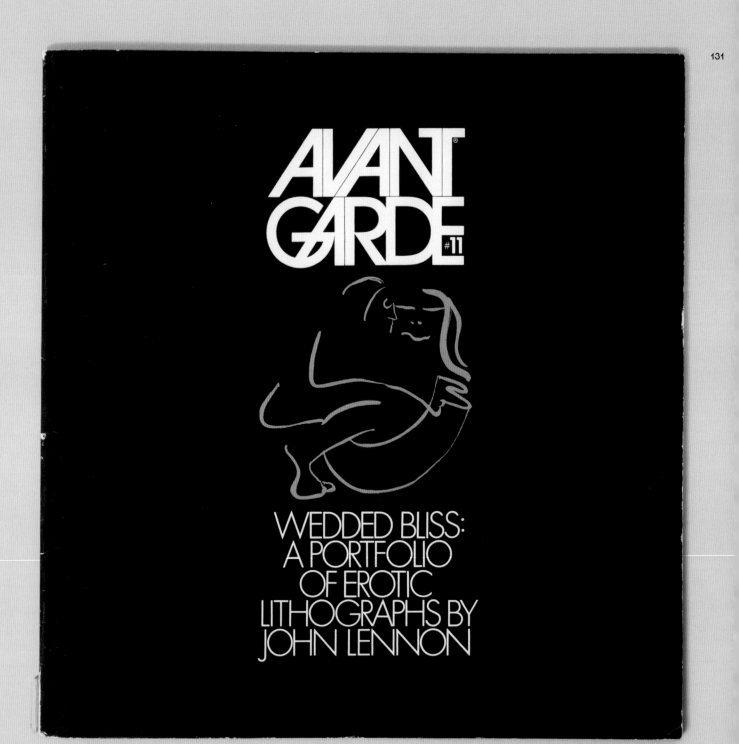

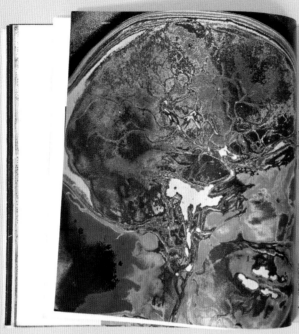

131. Avant Garde #11
This issue features a portfolio of
erotic lithographs by John Lennon.
Date: March 1970.

132. Molecular Mastery of the Brain
Article on developments in molecular
neurology in relation to the human
brain. Image shown is 'produced by
converting into differences in color and
varying intensities of light and dark in an
angiogram through a process developed
by researchers at the Philco-Ford
Corporation, Palo Alto, California.'

133. Oragenitalism
Review of book about 'oral techniques
for genital excitation'. The book is
written by American folklorist Gershon
Legman, and published in 1969. The
Monty Python-esque graphic on the
left-hand page is uncredited. As always,
Lubalin's typographic layout is formal.
At this time, in the late 1960s and early
1970s, it was commonplace for 'underground' magazines to apply printing
and graphic effects to blocks of text.
These were acts of deliberate graphic
obfuscation; the text was no longer
sacred and it was acceptable to make
it hard to read. Not so with Lubalin; he
always respected the sanctity of texts.
His decision to reproduce a column and
a half of text in red (right-hand page)
was as far as he went towards corrupting
body copy.

134. Gustav Klimt: Lost & Found
Article about the Austrian artist Gustav
Klimt. Lubalin mixes paper stocks to
allow the symbolist painter's bejewelled
colour work to be reproduced on coated
art paper. Klimt is described approvingly
in the text as a 'true avant gardist'.

135. A Day for a Lay
Heterosexuality is abundantly
represented in the pages of *Avant Garde*,
but here is a piece of highly explicit
homosexual erotica by one of the 20th
century's major literary poets. Claimed
to be the 'First publication of a long
suppressed masterpiece by W.H. Auden,'
the poem was also known as 'The
Platonic Blow' and was written in the
1940s. The photograph of Auden was
taken in the 1930s by Cecil Beaton.

136, 137. The Silent Majority
Typical of the photo-essays often found
in the pages of *Avant Garde*. The
feature's subtitle — 'Pictures Worth a
Thousand Words' — is almost a manifesto for *Avant Garde*. Here, frequent
contributor Julio Mitchel's vivid pictures
are partnered with Lubalin's patriotic
colour palette, and a heady mix of
vernacular typefaces.

ORAGENITALISM
A BOOK REVIEW

By Anatole Lerer

Oragenitalism: Oral Techniques in Genital Excitation, by G. Legman, The Julian Press, Inc., New York, $15. "Restricted to and Suggested for Mature, Sophisticated Readers (Over 21)."

None of G. Legman's previous books has been tabbed for the Book-of-the-Month Club or the Literary Guild or digested by the *Reader's Digest* or made into a smash movie or a hit musical comedy, and if Mr. Legman has entertained any fond hopes about his latest opus, let me be the first to disabuse him. Why, he'll be lucky if *Oragenitalism* even gets reviewed in the popular press. In fact, when the puzzled editor of the *New York Times Book Review* gets finished looking up "cunnilinctus" and "fellation" in his unabridged dictionary, he'll probably send the book out to be reviewed by J. Edgar Hoover. For the subject of orageni-

talism disgusts and frightens many people, and particularly us Americans: Only in America are the terms for practitioners of this high art used as vicious insults—cocksucker, cuntlapper, and muffdiver.

Cunnilinctus and fellation, in case the reader doesn't know by now, are variants of mouth-to-mouth resuscitation. Mr. Legman quite properly avoids the common spelling "cunnilingus," for although the tongue (*lingua*) does get quite a workout, it doesn't figure in the word's derivation (*linctus* is a Latin past participle meaning "tied"). Legman also introduces this reviewer to a number of useful words and word forms: irrumation, a form of fellation in which the *man* does most of the work; and cunnilingues (as in he c–s her), cunnilinctor, cunnilinquent, clitorides, fellatrix, fella-

tor, and fuckery—the las[t] the practice thereof.

It is an enduring m[ystery?] these varieties of the sex[ual] deprecated in this coun[try] suggests that "The lay an[d] probation of oragenital [acts?] toned by the moral con[demnation?] for the male homosexua[l] with which they are oft[en] might add that this would [be?] a country that prizes ma[nliness?] the United States does, a[nd?] Whatever the cause of or[al?] pute, it is to G. Legman give thanks for the pione[ering?] cunnilinctus he wrote in [?] consists of an updated ve[rsion?] graph, together with new s[?] irrumation, and the 69. [?] mainly devoted to "A Pr[?] the subject, which Legma[n?] by some old French phy[sician?] name, I suspect, was G. Legman write the book in[?] cause, he says in a profound[?] he wanted to undo the [?] suffered upon learning tha[t?] the 69, as he once thoug[ht?] didn't he put a new title o[n?] hiatus between 1940 and [?] roughs beat Legman to the [?] *Naked Lunch*.

Oragenitalism is a valuab[le] book. There is surely no o[ne in the?] world who knows as much [about?] ture and erotic art and sex [?] Pennsylvania's pride and joy[?] Sam Roth, Hugh Hefner, A[?] Rubin, Dr. Wardell Pomero[y?] Ginzburg himself could lear[n by read-?] ing this book. It should pro[ve?] helpful to wives who are ex[pected to?] engage in conventional inte[rcourse?] to men who have passed th[?] well as to women who are [?] men who have not passed [?] Merely as a fund of sexual [?] book should prove fascina[ting unless?] you have a dirty mind. An[d as?] the English lexicographer E[?] said, "is a joy forever." And [if you?] be asked such a question in [?] tion or on a quiz show, on [reading?] *Oragenitalism* you can corr[ectly tell them?] all just what a "flying fuck" [is.?]

On the other hand, som[e?] descriptions of all the orageni[tal?]

...tions are achingly dull. There are no il-
...ons in the book, a terrible lapse, for it
...have saved a lot of space if the author
...evailed upon some couple to demon-
...the tricky positions he is forever des-
...oh, say, Richard Burton and Elizabeth
...or Reverend and Mrs. Norman Vincent
...or David and Julie Nixon Eisenhower.
...of all, Legman's vast, bumptious ego is
...e of continual annoyance. "Some twen-
...s ago, in connection with my invention
...ovulation thermometer...." "The orig-
...brating dildo...was constructed at my
...ion in 1937/8...." "...nor do I give a
...what happens to my tongue after my
...have been asked to will it to the British
...n)...." (Presumably he has been asked,
...the Museum's director, but by a lady
...Indeed, throughout the book one has
...ression that Legman is boasting, "Look
...know, look what I've *done*, you duffer,

...e of the remarkable sexual positions
...gman describes is as follows:

...he man inserts his phallus into the
...'s navel (he having a tiny penis, she an
...us navel, or both), meanwhile with
...forefinger tickling the inside of the
...'s right ear, with his right middle finger
...imb stroking the woman's left nipple
...figure. The man's nose is encased in the
...'s mouth, delicately groping for her
...His hair—and to accomplish this best,
...uld have a crew-cut!—is meanwhile
...the lower-case Greek psi (ψ) inside the
...'s nostrils. His beard—and of course he
...e, you dunce!!—is keeping the woman's
...reast occupied. With his right big toe,
...n is pedicating the woman—or, to coin
...e, pedpedicating her. With his left big
..., of course, he is entering her vulva,
...all the while a figure $\aleph \ \Xi \ \xi \ \hbar \ \varsigma$. The
...herself is ecstatically reciprocating
...ing, in addition to inserting an umbrella
...man's anus and gently opening it, as
...loudly humming The Queen of the
...aria from my favorite Mozart opera,
...*uberflöte*. She cannot whistle it, is
...because of the danger of biting off the
...nose.

...hould the woman be at the same time
...s of cunnilinctus, anilinctus, eyebrow-
...or sacroiliaclinctus, the man should ask
...lly neighbor to assist him—an 11-year-
...ench boy, or girl, will do perfectly.
...hand, of course, he should have per-
...ily introduced the child to the woman
...aring the heat of excitement she peer

down, see a strange face, and shriek bloody
murder. The child should eventually depart,
with a formal bow or curtsy, a *Merci beaucoup,
Madame et Monsieur*, and a good swift kick in
the ass for his trouble.

"In English, this position is colloquially
known as 'Hitting a Grand-Slam Home Run
Off Tom Seaver,' and in French as 'Le Grand
Tour,' or *Cent Soixante et Trois*. Musically,
it is best for the couple to be listening to
Leonard Bernstein leading the New York Phil-
harmonic in 'We Shall Overcome.' Odor-wise,
the pleasure is enhanced tremendously if both
man and woman have generously perfumed
themselves beforehand with a bottle of Pepto-
Bismol. And prior to the assumption of this
position—how could I almost forget to mention this!!!—both partners should have been
painted bright green."

Kidding aside, despite Legman's ego and
his sometimes heavy-handed jokes and his page-
after-page of this-goes-in-here-that-gets-licked-
there, *Oragenitalism* is highly recommended.
If your local bookdealer doesn't have a copy,
you can order one for $15 from the Julian
Press, Inc., 150 Fifth Avenue, New York 10011.
Send a copy to your local library. Send copies
to your friends. Send copies to your enemies.
And send copies to Doris Day, Shirley Temple Black, Ronald Reagan, or whoever you are
sure would benefit from it. Can't you just imagine Governor Reagan's reaction upon getting
the book at his office, puzzling over the title,
taking the book home with him, then late at
night, in bed, opening it up and alighting upon
such passages as...

"...in the 'sixty-nine,' the usual complaint is that
'what is being done to one distracts one from what
one is doing.'"

"...all authentic cases of auto-fellation, or self-
fellation, that have been studied—auto-cunnilinctus is
apparently impossible—have proved to be those of
homosexual men.... (The two usual methods for auto-
fellation are either by simply bending very far forward
in a sitting position, or by lying on the back and
throwing the legs back over the head.)"

"The cunnilinguist's tongue should be kept in good
condition. Excessively bright red color of the tongue,
or heavy grooves or furrows in it, are signs of Vitamin
B deficiencies, which will also destroy the taste buds."

"Clitoral digitation of this kind requires powerful
forearm muscles, and can only come with practice.
The best training for the man...is piano or harp playing,
typewriting, or valve-work on wind instruments. The
playing of the violin or of the ordinary guitar is perhaps the best training of all...."

"In cunnilinctus, the beard—if soft—is likely to
tickle the woman's thighs and vulva in a delicate way
which she will probably enjoy. A bristly beard, on
the other hand, is likely to irritate her thighs and
vulva....In general, the moustache is not likely to irri-

tate the woman, but will probably tickle her fancy or
excite her....A man with a waxed and pointed moustache...should probably refrain from cunnilinctus."

"...it is sometimes practical, if perverse, to cunni-
lingue the woman through her panties or nightgown."

"Probably the most playful practice in connection
with cunnilinctus is the application of liquids such as
wine, champagne (or bubbling soda-pop for the poor!),
orange juice, honey, melted ice-cream, whipped cream,
etc., ad lib., to the vulva....Whipped cream is best, and
the vagina can be quite filled with it....Obviously no
one but an imbecile would attempt to squeeze fruit
juice on a woman's vulva with a lime-squeezer in hand.
It is also not very romantic to pour canned grapefruit
or pineapple juice into a girl out of two holes punched
in a metallic can. If you can't use a blue-glass carafe,
this book is not for you...."

"A similar and very heady flavor is given to the
vulva...by the application of sweet still wines, such as
a good Port, Muscatel, or Malaga."

"Sophisticates often insert into the vagina fruits
such as strawberries or cherries (sweet, pitted cherries),
or sections of an orange (a seedless orange), or slices of
an apple deliciously dipped in honey; thereupon sucking or drawing them out of the vagina again, and eating
them with relish. The classical fruit used in this way
is the banana....I have also heard very often of using
oysters and mussels in cunnilinctus....In any case, the
practice of inserting any solids into the vagina and
sucking them out again should not be attempted by
persons with false teeth or a dental plate...."

"Very often the man can lie between the woman's
legs with his cheek on her pubis, to revel in the feel of
her pubic hair while he eats or drinks (possibly dipping
the leg of a squab into her vagina for sauce, or pour-
ing wine over her vulva and drinking it from there)...."

"The oral inosculation of the penis should...be
done smoothly...the fellator counting the seconds
mentally: 'One big rhinoceros, two big rhinoceroses,'
and so forth....If the man's rhinoceros is not, actually,
so very big, it would be kind of her to use the same
metaphor anyhow, out of a spirit of good fellowship."

"It is rather far...to the elaborate tickling of the
man's fraenum with a violin bow, handled by a voluptuous woman....Actually to be effective, this would
require a good deal of rosin on the bow, and might not
be very pleasant at all."

"Fellation [is] the easiest of all sexual acts—except
for mutual masturbation—to engage in almost without
preamble, or in cramped quarters....For instance, in
adjoining theater-seats in the dark, in a telephone
booth!...When it seems absolutely necessary to have
sexual relations of any kind in a moving vehicle, such
as an automobile, airplane, spaceship, Ferris-wheel, or
hover-craft, it is wise to have someone else do the
driving."

"Let it be remembered to our shame that the
greatest pantomime and comedian of our century
[Charlie Chaplin, of course] was dragged through the
kangaroo-court of American newspaper headlines in
the 1920's, for having resisted an attempted blackmail
divorce suit with the result that he was accused in
court of having 'performed' cunnilinctus on his wife.
'All married people do that,' he replied with dignity.
But it has taken the rest of the Anglo-Saxon world,
and Europe, half a century since then to admit it."

GUSTAV KLIMT: LOST & FOUND

Both as a painter and man, Gustav Klimt was a true avant-gardist. That is, he was well ahead of his time and he paid the price. Although he has since been acknowledged as one of the most inspired painters of the last century, in his own time—turn-of-the-century Austria—he was scorned, degraded, and, eventually, ostracized completely. The sensuality and eroticism of his paintings were too much for his contemporaries to bear. As a result, Klimt's paintings were confiscated, an appointment to the faculty of the University of Vienna was denied him, and his most important commission—to create the allegorical murals "Medicine," "Philosophy," and "Jurisprudence" for a public building in Vienna—was withdrawn after ten years of painstaking labor on his part. Toward the end of his life, Klimt withdrew from the public completely, and he died, in 1918, an all-but-forgotten man. (Even after his death, his works continued to provoke the Philistines. In 1945, retreating SS-men burned several of his most important paintings. For this reason, some of the works on the following pages are not reproduced in full color; no full-color photographs of them were ever taken.) Within the last two years, however, a number of discerning art historians, connoisseurs, and publishers have discovered Klimt's work and have begun to rescue it from oblivion. New York's Guggenheim Museum held a small retrospective. Couturier Oscar de la Renta has based a line of brocades upon the highly ornate fabrics with which Klimt draped his seductive women. Perhaps most important, the publishing firm of Frederick A. Praeger has brought out a ten-pound, 389-plate catalogue raisonné of Klimt's work that is surely one of the most magnificent art books of all time. Klimt would have been pleased by the fact that the Praeger book is priced at $125 and limited to an edition of only 1000 copies. As he once said in a letter to the editor of the Wiener Morgen-Zeitung, "I do not want to waste my time defending my work before the whole population. The important thing for me is not how many people like my paintings, but why likes them." For this reason, we think Klimt would also have been pleased to see his paintings reproduced in Avant-Garde.

A DAY FOR A LAY

FIRST PUBLICATION OF A LONG-SUPPRESSED MASTERPIECE BY W. H. AUDEN

136

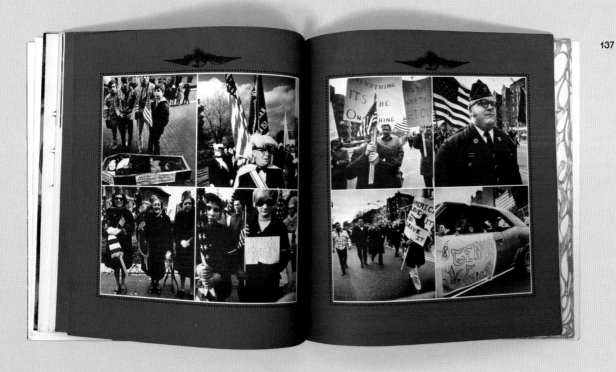

137

335

138. Avant Garde #12
Illustration by Danish artist Jorgen Boberg. Self-taught, he typifies the familiar *Avant Garde* predilection for art with a whiff of myth and magic, hothouse sexuality and consummate draughtsmanship. Date: May 1970.

139. Dial-a-Hawk
In protest at the invasion of Cambodia, *Avant Garde* magazine collected the private home phone numbers of leading figures of the U.S. administration at that time. 'We urge you to call a hawk this evening, or weekend,' an editorial note proclaimed, 'and let them know how you feel about the war.' Telephone numbers provided included those for Vice President Spiro T. Agnew; Senator Barry Goldwater (who had previously sued Ginzburg in connection with an article in *Fact* magazine, p.49); Richard M. Helms, director of the CIA; Henry Kissinger, assistant to the president for National Security; and Richard Nixon, president (last two not shown here). Illustration by Jim Lewis.

140. The Mystery of Jorgen Boberg
Lubalin's bold, unfussy layout allows Boberg's intensely detailed images to stand in splendid isolation.

141, 142. Bell's Belles
Series of moody photographs by Hugh Bell, who was born in St. Lucia in 1927. Raised in Harlem, he became known for his photographs of major jazz stars of the 1950s and 60s, including Billie Holiday, Dizzy Gillespie, Charlie Parker, Louis Armstrong and Duke Ellington. Lubalin's elegant layout gives the pictures a serene quality that might have been lost in a less careful arrangement.

143. The Gang-Bang ...
Survey of the American underground press showing covers from various publications. Although *Avant Garde* was not considered to be part of the 'underground press' (nor did it claim to be), it shared many areas of interest. Lubalin's refined editorial design and his meticulous use of high-quality photography and illustration meant that *Avant Garde* was far more visually sophisticated than the majority of underground journals. On the other hand, many of the articles, with their radical subject matter, would not have been out of place in the underground press.

144. Why Hair has Become ...
A study of long hair throughout history and its role as a continuing badge of rebellion in post-1960s America. Portraits of assorted 'long-hairs' by Benedict J. Fernandez. Thanks to the lack of paid ads, Lubalin was free to indulge his ability to create impressive and engaging layouts.

THE MYSTERY OF JØRGEN BOBERG

Jorgen Boberg, both as an artist and individual, is webbed in mystery. His paintings and etchings are haunted by phantoms from the spirit world and his personal life is a guarded secret. Through an intermediary, who brought us Boberg's thrilling pictures, we learn only that Boberg is completely self-taught and lives in Denmark. From his photograph, we may surmise that he is young, possibly in his twenties. From the titles of his works, we may deduce that he is infatuated with a figure named "Teresa," probably Teresa of Avila, a 16th Century mystic. All else is left to speculation —save one fact: Publication of Jorgen Boberg's work in Avant-Garde marks the emergence of one of the world's great artistic talents. There's no mystery about that.

THE METAMO...

338

DREAM OF CONCEPTION

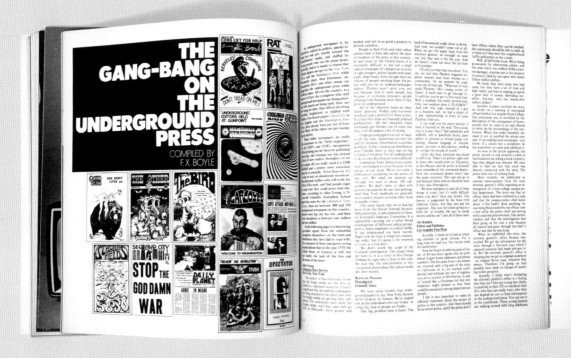

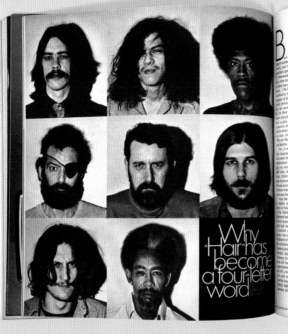

AVANT GARDE 13

PORTRAITS OF THE AMERICAN PEOPLE A MONUMENTAL PORTFOLIO OF PHOTOGRAPHS

145—151. Avant Garde #13
'Portraits of The American People:
A Monumental Portfolio of Photographs',
is one of three issues of *Avant Garde*
devoted to a single subject. The photographs are by Alwyn Scott Turner.
Born in Texas in 1936, Turner grew up
in Detroit. He studied art and later
worked as a photojournalist for *Time-
Life*, *Esquire*, *Look* and other national
magazines. Examples of his work are
in the permanent collection of the
Museum of Modern Art in New York,
New Orleans and elsewhere. The
photographs shown in this issue of
Avant Garde have a poignant black and
white integrity that places Turner in
the grand tradition of classic American
documentary photographers.

The text notes: 'Two months ago, Turner
walked into the offices of *Avant Garde*,
deposited 2,000 of his most recent
pictures, and invited us to devote an
entire issue to publishing the best of
them.' By allocating one image per page
in an uninterrupted flow, something
few magazines then or now could
match, Lubalin affords the photographs
maximum respect. The cover shows
Lubalin's adroit use of Avant Garde
Gothic for both the masthead and the
issue title. As usual, he has kerned the
type with sure-footed aplomb. Ligatures
are kept to a minimum. And once
again, the colour-blind Lubalin uses the
patriotic colour mix of red, white and
blue to good effect. Date: Spring 1971.

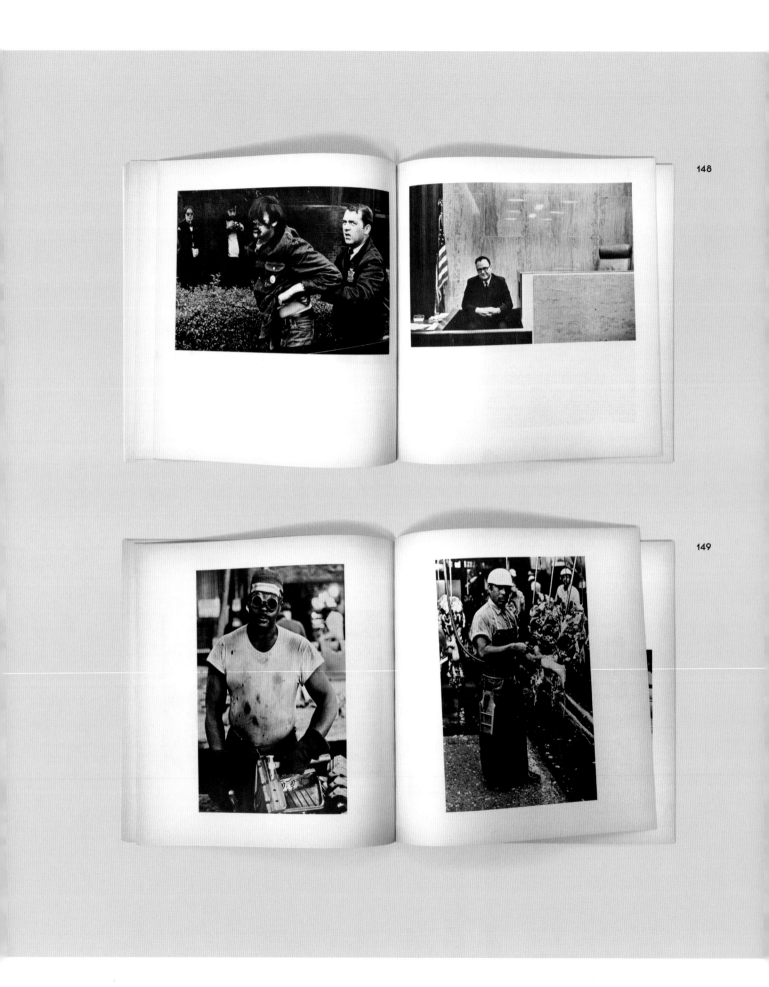

148

149

346

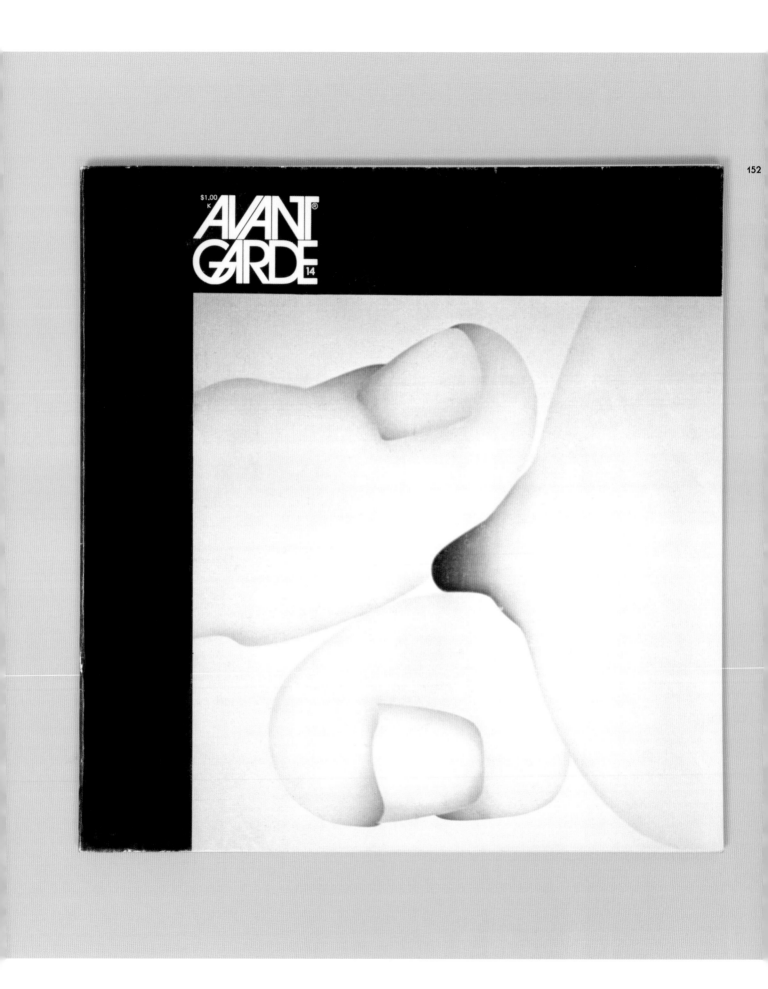

152

348

ON MANHATTAN'S LOWER WEST SIDE, 383 ARTISTS, WRITERS, DANCERS, AND MUSICIANS HAVE CREATED AN AVANT-GARDE COMMUNITY CALLED "WESTBETH"

WAY OUT WESTBETH

A PHOTOGRAPHIC ESSAY BY LEONARD FREED

152. Avant Garde #14
Cover painting by Lambert Wintersberger. This cover is an oddity, since it is unrelated to any of the features inside this issue: all previous cover images had been part of an article within the magazine. This was the final issue of *Avant Garde*. Shortly after its appearance, Ralph Ginzburg was sent to prison to serve the sentence handed down to him by the U.S. authorities for his earlier prosecution for obscenity. (p.45).
Date: Summer 1971.

153. Way Out Westbeth
Article about an artist community created in Manhattan's Lower West Side, now commonly referred to as the West Village. Photography by Leonard Freed. Note the bold, ranged-left use of Avant Garde Gothic.

154—156. High Time
Frank and brutal photographic essay by photographer Mary Ellen Mark on drug addiction. No editorial commentary is supplied. Lubalin's editorial design allows the photographer's striking photographs to assume a quiet dignity that side-steps sensationalism. His arrangement of images has the appearance of a documentary film without a soundtrack, where the images become the sole conveyors of meaning and narrative. Mary Ellen Mark is known for her photojournalism, portraiture and advertising photography. She has said: 'I'm just interested in people on the edges. I feel an affinity for people who haven't had the best breaks in society.' Note Lubalin's use of Kabel Black, and his dovetailing of the lowercase 'i' under the bar of the capital 'T'.

157. Concerning the Maids ...
Short story with illustration by Jerome Snyder. Lubalin's savage reduction of line spacing in the headline anticipates some of his later experiments with phototypesetting.

158. The Machine I Hate the Most
David Frost, Allen Ginsberg, Viva, Claude Levi-Strauss, Norman Rockwell, Roy Liechtenstein and others choose the machines they detest the most. Frost chooses pneumatic drills; Rockwell selects the typewriter; Levi-Strauss nominates the automobile.

159—162. Belles Lettres
Anthon Beeke's 'human alphabet' was first published in 1970 by the Dutch printers de Jong & Co., as part of their experimental publication *Kwadraat Bladen*. Beeke formed his letters out of carefully arranged nude women who he then photographed. The alphabet was a light-hearted response to Wim Crouwel's famous 'new alphabet', published earlier in the same series. Lubalin creates a bold and generous layout where his love of letterforms and *Avant Garde*'s perennial interest in naked women can both be heartily appreciated.

High
Time

PHOTOGRAPHS BY
MARY ELLEN MARK

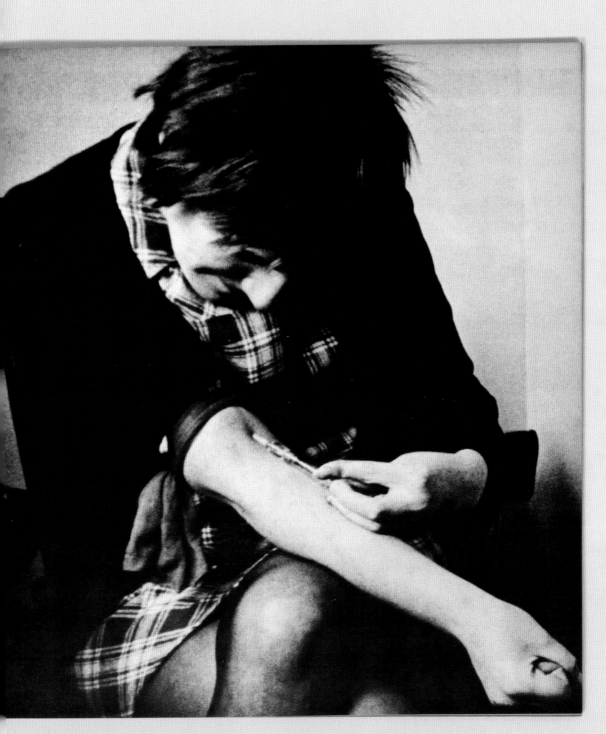

155

156

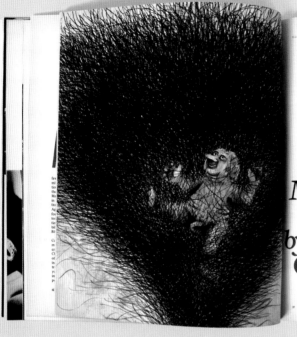

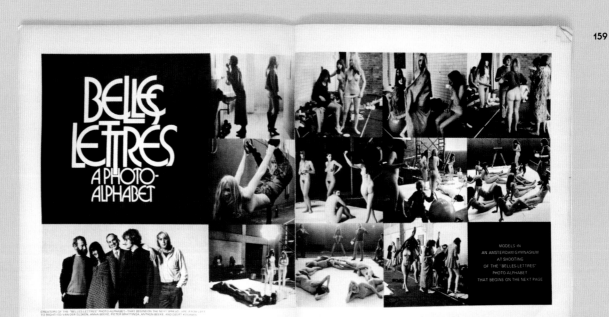

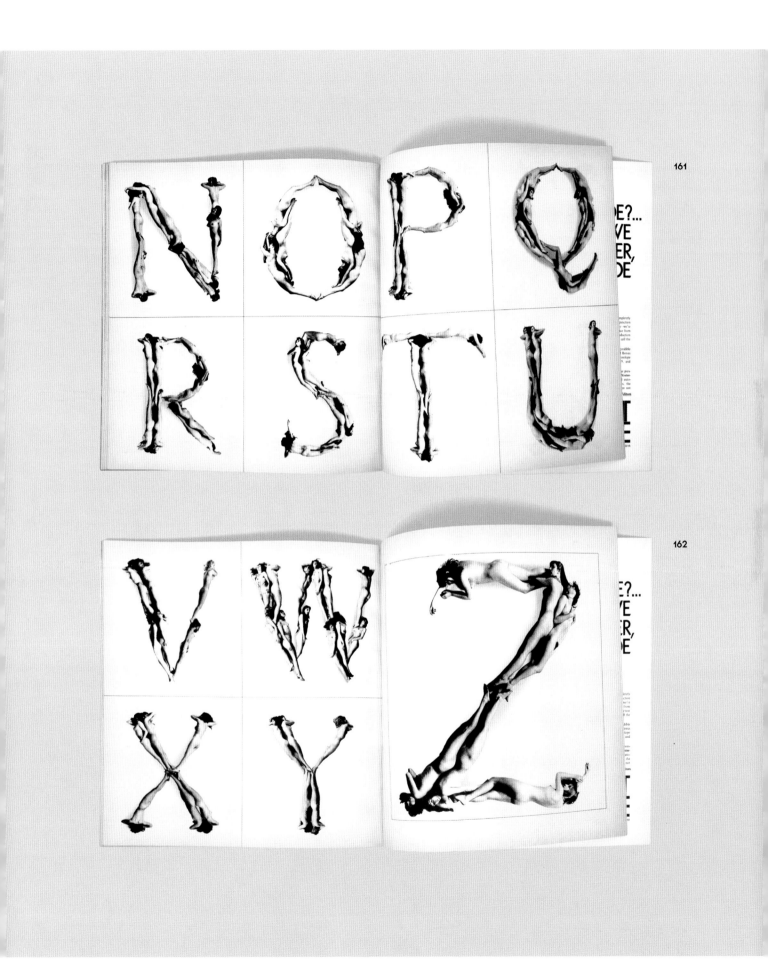

163—167. Avant Garde
After serving his prison sentence,
Ralph Ginzburg and his wife Shoshana
attempted to revive *Avant Garde* as a
tabloid-format newspaper — perhaps
inspired by the success of *Rolling Stone*.
But this bold move took them to the
brink of bankruptcy. The newsprint
version only lasted for one issue (shown
here) and disaster was only averted
by the success of yet another periodical,
the consumer adviser *Moneysworth*,
which attained a circulation of 2.4
million. At the age of 55, Ginzburg retired from publishing and started a new
life as a photojournalist, selling his
very first photograph to *The New York
Post*. He remained a freelance news
photographer until his death in 2006.
Cover Illustration: Roy Carruthers.
Date: 1974.

WILLIAM O. DOUGLAS: A PSYCHO-DIAGNOSIS

REVEALING INSIGHTS INTO THE MIND OF A GREAT AMERICAN ARE MADE POSSIBLE BY HIS CURRENT BEST-SELLING AUTOBIOGRAPHY

BY D. J. BENNETT

Of all the leading personalities America has produced in its 200 years, Justice William O. Douglas stands alone, if for no other reason than the publicly debunks motherhood. Dr. George Draper, the observer who analyzed him in the 1930s, once told him, "The only qualification 90% of women have to be mothers is biological." And Douglas agrees: "I think he was right, and in my view the way we make a fetish of motherhood is sheer nonsense." (For that alone he should have been elected President.)

Instead of trying to conquer his fears through a belligerent machismo, he directed his energies to fighting the fears themselves

WILLIAM O. DOUGLAS AS AN INFANT

Continued on page 22

WHAT IS AVANT-GARDE?

In other words, avant-gardism means simply dedication to earthly pleasures, a sane world and personal freedom, and upon these ideals this paper is founded.

AVANT GARDE

EDITOR-IN-CHIEF: RALPH GINZBURG
ART DIRECTOR: HERB LUBALIN
EXECUTIVE EDITOR: BETTY A. FEIR
ASSOCIATE ART DIRECTOR: HSI LING ONG
GRAPHICS EDITOR: THOMAS BODKIN
CREATIVE EDITOR: SHOSHANA GINZBURG
ARTICLES EDITOR: PAMPER HODGES
ARTICLES EDITOR: PAUL A. RIEDEL
PRODUCTION EDITOR: JANICE VON KAMECKE
MAKEUP EDITOR: OREGON CHIU CHIANG
TYPOGRAPHY EDITOR: MARSHA TREXLER
ASST. GRAPHICS EDITOR: HUGUETTE FRANCO
BUSINESS DIRECTOR: MIRIAM FER
GENERAL MANAGER: PAUL ROMEYKOR
CIRCULATION DIRECTOR: THOMAS ERIKSON
FINANCIAL DIRECTOR: HUYUK CANDEAR
CLASSIFIED AD DIRECTOR: ALICE SLATER

BESTSELLER WELLSPRING

BY R. CLIFFORD WEBSTER

A century ago the space was 20 feet under water. Today, writers like Nancy Milford, author of *Zelda*, radical feminist Susan Brownmiller, critic Hollis Alpert, Ferdinand Lundberg, muckraking member of *The Rich and the Super-Rich*, and Theodore H. White, chronicler of Presidential campaigns, pump out bestsellers from the one-time site of the Croton Reservoir.

"According to Arnold Gingrich, Betty Friedan was the only person nobody could stand. She drove everybody mad with her noise."

Well over 200 books have been written in a decade-and-a-half at 11 desks in just over 500 square feet.

There is theoretically enough space for everyone, but library gossip has it that, at least once, writers have come to blow over who gets which desk when.

Continued from page 3

Before his analysis, Douglas was motivated primarily by the fear of peer ridicule and disapproval

WILLIAM O. DOUGLAS TODAY

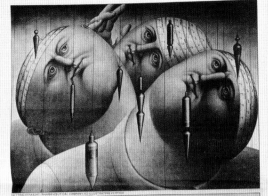

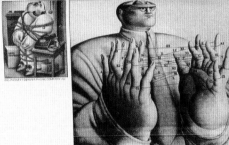

HUGH HEFNER AT THE AGE OF EIGHT

BY PARKER HODGES

THE BOOK HUGH HEFNER IS TRYING TO SUPPRESS

HEFNER

An Unauthorized Biography by FRANK BRADY

"A crucial part of Hefner's success is the image of Hefner as the playboy man—part libertarian, part libertine."

168

U&lc.

Aa Bb Cc Dd Ee Ff Gg Hh Ii Jj Kk Ll Mm Nn Oo Pp   Qq Rr Ss Tt Uu Vv Ww Xx Yy Zz 1234567890 & Æ Œ $ ¢ £ % !? () []

UPPER AND LOWER CASE, THE INTERNATIONAL JOURNAL OF TYPOGRAPHICS   PUBLISHED BY THE INTERNATIONAL TYPEFACE CORPORATION. VOLUME ONE, NUMBER ONE; 1973

In this issue:

PAGE 4

PAGE 6

PAGE 9

PAGE 10

PAGE 12

PAGE 14

PAGE 20

Typography and the New Technologies

When I went to art school, I learned that many of my fellow students had problems when it came to drawing certain parts of the human anatomy. They simply could not draw hands and feet.

I first became conscious of their difficulties when I noticed that the people who appeared in their layouts never had hands or feet. Hands always seemed to be behind peoples' backs or in pockets. Feet were always out of view, either behind a desk, or the people were cropped at the waist or knees.

People, however, do have hands and feet, and very often they must be shown. The advertisements created by these students very often suffered as a result of these simple but important handicaps.

CONTINUED ON PAGE 3

Stop the "Perpetrators"

Danger.
This article has been labeled "Stop the Perpetrators" for good reason.
The alarm is genuine.
No adequate law protects the type designer or photocomposing machine manufacturer from unauthorized duplication of the machine's most vital part: the typeface or font negative. Unauthorized contact duplication of these critical negatives has reached dangerous proportions, and the graphics industry can no longer afford, ostrich-like, to disregard the demoralizing effect it is having on creative talent. It is a blight on the industry's legitimate business practices, and bringing it under control is a worthy endeavor calling for the concerted effort of all. But more about that later; here is the background:
We operate in a free system where ethics and law contribute mightily to the function-

CONTINUED ON PAGE 2

Information, Please

Suppose that you wanted to find out... WHO is the new head of the Johnson Foundation?
WHAT were the basic terms of the General Motors-Curtiss-Wright agreement for the Wankel engine?
WHEN was the Amchitka atomic test conducted?
WHERE will Swindell-Dressler Company build a steel foundry in Russia?
WHY did Secretary Volpe sign a transportation research agreement with the Polish Government?
HOW did Martha Mitchell come to blow the whistle on the Watergate?
Answer:
You'd merely consult the remarkable new Information Bank of The New York Times.
This eminent newspaper has recently taken a giant step into the 21st Century with the introduction of the world's first computerized system for the storage and retrieval of the richly varied contents of newspapers and magazines.

CONTINUED ON PAGE 11

What's so Hot about Robert Indiana?

A lot of friends in advertising–talented designers all–have been talking to themselves lately. "What," they want to know, "is so hot about Robert Indiana?" "What's he got that we haven't?" they want to know. "Look," they say, "we turn out designs like his–only better–every day in the week." "What's so special about Robert Indiana?"
What indeed.
I was mulling this over the other day when I came across an article by New York Times Art Critic, John Canaday. Mr. Canaday was exploring this very idea. He'd just been to a recent new exhibition at the Denise Rene Gallery in New York, which was presenting a one-man show of Indiana's designs, and he hadn't gotten over it yet.
For the uninitiated, Robert Indiana is the creator of LOVE, that cleverly-arranged four

CONTINUED ON PAGE 7

art and typography

let us consider first the function of the artist in society.
the men who handle the antique furniture in my museum have developed a vocabulary of their own when they speak of styles.
they call louis XIV: louis with the twisted legs
louis XV: louis with the bow legs
louis XVI: louis with the straight legs
now the legs of these three kings, i guess, actually did not differ so much from each other.
but it was not the kings who created these styles;
it was the artists, the architects, the painters and sculptors,
the musicians and the authors who tried to render the essence of
the epoch, who made the impact of a certain period visible, audible, perceptible.

the artist creates the face of society; his work enables us to revive the past.
to cite an example, the paintings and posters of toulouse-lautrec
are for us the incarnation of paris around 1900.
how does this come into being?

CONTINUED ON PAGE 15

168. U&lc (No. 1)

Herb Lubalin was the editor, art director and co-publisher of *Upper and Lower Case, The International Journal of Typographics*, from its inception in 1973 until his death in 1981. *U&lc* was a large-format tabloid-sized newsprint publication, issued quarterly until 1999. It was published by ITC, the company owned by Lubalin, Aaron Burns and Ed Rondthaler, and distributed free to any-one who subscribed. Although it was principally a promotional vehicle for ITC typefaces, under Lubalin's editorship it became a highly influential typographic journal. He achieved this by bringing together an eclectic mix of topics and presenting them with verve and panache. The other element that *U&lc* offered its readers was guidance through the maze of technological change that was then sweeping through design and typography. As an early editorial put it: 'The world of graphic arts is alive today with new technological advances, so vast and difficult to comprehend, that they strain the imagination of even the most knowledgeable and creatively gifted among us.' *U&lc* offered a helping hand. *U&lc* masthead lettering: Tom Carnase. Date: 1973.

169. Corporate — Schmorporate!

Spread featuring an article by Ernie Smith, one of Herb Lubalin's former business partners and a longstanding colleague. The inclusion of this article tells us a great deal about Lubalin's affection for Smith, and his generosity to a former business associate. Smith left the Lubalin, Smith, Carnase studio to run a 'resort business in the Adiron-dacks', and it is known that Lubalin severely regretted his departure. Yet he appears to have borne Smith no malice. The article is a light-hearted account of Smith's attempts to establish his new business. Smith was married to Fay Barrows at the time. The pair can be seen standing outside the resort's logo. Barrows was a former assistant of Lubalin's at Sudler & Hennessey, and a major contributor of information and pictures to this book.

170. My Best with Letters

A typical *U&lc* spread revolving around musings on the nature of letterforms. On the right-hand page, four heavy-weights of 20th-century design — Allan R. Fleming, Josef Müller-Brockmann, Paul Rand and George Lois — describe their best typographical work. On the right-hand page, Roger Ferriter (another important Lubalin associate, and a skilled lettering artist) writes about teaching students how to handle letterforms. On display is some student work that Ferriter has collected, and about which he notes: 'They represent an increased awareness on the part of the students as to the function and beauty of typographic forms and their importance in creating a total graphic entity.' This could almost be an encapsulation of Lubalin's philosophy as a graphic designer.

171—174. Something for Everybody ...

The four spreads shown here provide ample evidence of Herb Lubalin's edit-orial and graphic eclecticism: Charles B. Slackman lampoons newspaper mastheads; Lou Dorfsman contributes a thoughtful analysis of the role of design at CBS, the U.S. broadcasting giant; Tom Carnase ('One of the world's finest lettering artists') demonstrates the beauty of Spencerian script; another article discusses the rise of technology in design; and Lubalin himself tells the story of Avant Garde Gothic, albeit in a truncated version (see p.52). As with all *U&lc* layouts, the typefaces used for body copy and headlines are scrupulously identified.

169

MY BEST WITH LETTERS

I suspect that this is the best symbol I have done. Certainly it is omnipresent on the Canadian scene. CN Express trucks drive through every city; CN Trains span the country; most cities have a CN Hotel; and CN Marine has ships on both coastlines. I owe a great debt of gratitude to James Valkus who chose me to do it, and to Donald Gordon (now dead), the former president of CN who agreed to its use. The only regret I have is that my father, who worked all of his short life for CN as a time keeper in the freight yards, did not live to see it appear.

ALLAN R. FLEMING
CANADA

This illustration is o[f] a series of advertis[ing] for Westinghouse r[adios] and record players [that] appeared in the Ph[iladelphia] Symphony Orchest[ra] concert program. [The] problem was to as[sociate] a Westinghouse pr[oduct] with the name of a [great] composer. I wante[d to] avoid the obvious picture of the com[poser] and instead to sug[gest by] typographic mean[s] the spirit of the co[mposer's] music or the instru[ment] with which his work [is] most closely assoc[iated]. This example may not be "my best wit[h letters] but it is perhaps o[ne of] my best demonstra[tions of] descriptive typogr[aphy. It] also demonstrates that a word can so[metimes] say more than a th[ousand] pictures.

PAUL RAND
USA

This poster interprets with pure typographical elements one of the most important principles of film: movement. The overlapping of the word "Film" with "der" produces the impression of motion. The height of the letters of the title "der Film" is equal to 1/5 of that of the poster. The space beneath the title is also 1/5. The space above the title is 3/5. (2/5: 3/5 = the golden section). I like the dual function of the typography in this poster: the cinematic and aesthetic effect within a proportional structure.

JOSEF MÜLLER-BROCKMANN
SWITZERLAND

This is an ad I did in [which] was an unusual lo[ok] (it was a bleed, jus[t to] see it, no package[, just] copy, etc.). It deme[d] to me a fresh use o[f typo] graphy. Letters [have] form (although the[y are] artistic). Letters pu[t into] spell words that sh[ould say] something to com[municate] a selling message. [Ideas] should be interrup[t] tling, fresh, and sh[arp] on a person's life s[o that sell] ing ideas should b[e conten] tious and should tr[eat people] as if they are sharp [enough] to understand a b[ig con] cept. This discussi[on] of a married coupl[e] is a "typographic" [ad] that enhances the [idea] in and of itself, bec[oming] visual.

GEORGE LOIS
USA

THIS FEATURE WAS SET [IN AVANT]
GARDE GOTHIC BOLD.

g Typography

hing students to design with type starts with overcoming
innate fear of "getting involved with technical stuff."
To accomplish this, the first few assignments involve "push-
round" large letterforms and "chunks" of type as though
were pre-formed, abstract pieces of color and design.
No attention is paid to their function as parts of words,
ences or paragraphs. Instead, the student is first asked to
e an analogy between a letterform, or many letterforms,
something other than a letterform, i.e. a letter "O" could
nalogous to an egg, or an eye, or a ball, depending on
orm of the specific alphabet the letter "O" comes from.
The analogy can be one of texture created by the use
any letters or the development of a single form created
een, around, or inside any letter or combination of letters.
The first problem loosens up their "heads" as well as their
so they realize that letters have an intrinsic beauty of their
The next three problems deal with "color" of type (values
light to dark). The students are asked to do a drawing, a
ing, or a pattern with type.
As with the analogy, these three problems are all solved
lage, i.e. pasting up "found" letters from magazines,
spapers, or proofs, from any source. A very useful tool is
ariety of transfer types available in most art supply stores.
Shown here are a few solutions to these starting problems
cted from my classes over the past dozen years. They
esent an increased awareness on the part of the student as
e function and beauty of typographic forms and their
ortance in creating a total graphic entity.

R FERRITER, SCHOOL OF VISUAL ARTS, NEW YORK CITY

TURE WAS SET IN ITC SERIF GOTHIC.

16

THE FLAGS THAT FLY ATOP SOME OF AMERICA'S MOST PRESTIGIOUS NEWSPAPERS AS SEEN THROUGH THE EYES OF SATIRIST CHAS. SLACKMAN.

THE WALL STREET JOURNAL

The DAILY NEWS

THE WASHINGTON POST

DES MOINES REGISTER

The Christian Science Monitor

Salt Lake Tribune

Times

NOTED SEMANTICIST ANATOL RAPOPORT SAID: "TYPOGRAPHY IS TO PRINTING AS ELOCUTION AND DRAMATICS ARE TO THE SPOKEN WORD."

A GREAT ART DIRECTOR IS A MAN WHO KNOWS WHEN SOMEONE ELSE HAS A BETTER IDEA THAN HE HAS

17

Schlemiel

Is a Yiddish word that has become part of the colorful American vernacular. It refers to a man who is in bad luck all the time—a loser, for whom nothing is successful and everything goes wrong. The word actually comes from the Bible, the Book of Numbers, Chapter 2. Shelumiel, the son of Zurishaddai, was the leader of the tribe of Simeon and it is said that, whereas all other leaders were successful in battle, he was the only one who lost all the time. Hence the term schlemiel!

WHEN ROMANCE NEARLY CRASHED ...by Edward Sorel

"O.K."—WHERE DID IT COME FROM?

The most widely held theory about the term O.K., which H.L. Mencken once called "without question the most successful of all Americanisms," is that it came from the Choctaw Indian word okeh, meaning "It is so."

It was also in the spelling okeh that the term appeared as the name of a now-defunct record company beloved by jazz aficionados because under its Okeh label appeared the first important recorded music of such luminaries as Louis Armstrong, the Dorsey Brothers, and Benny Goodman.

The actual origin of O.K., however, is the one that is accepted by virtually all word experts. The first printed example of the term was as part of the name of "The Democratic O.K. Club," an organization of supporters of president Van Buren, who was running for a second term. Van Buren was a native of Old Kinderhook, a village in New York State.

O.K. has become a truly international phrase, and prisoners of war in Japan, Korea, and Vietnam have all reported that every street girl and prison guard have used and understood this term—even though they couldn't speak another word of English.

THE FEATURETTES ON THIS PAGE WERE SET IN AVANT GARDE GOTHIC.

18

Avant Garde Gothic Condensed and Friz Quadrata are new from ITC. Only licensed ITC Subscribers are authorized to reproduce, manufacture and offer for sale, Avant Garde Gothic Condensed, Friz Quadrata and all other ITC typefaces shown in this issue. This mark is your guarantee of authenticity.

AVANT GARDE GOTHIC CONDENSED

In this issue of "U&lc," ITC announces four additions to its highly popular Avant Garde Gothic series. In response to the demand from designers for condensed versions of this versatile face, ITC has added four new members to the Avant Garde Gothic family: Book, Medium, Demi and Bold Condensed.

The Avant Garde Gothic Condensed series retains the same extra-large "x" height of the lower case letterforms, with their shortened ascenders and descenders. This characteristic is one feature that distinguishes Avant Garde Gothic from other sans serif designs.

The large full-bodied lower case letters make for better legibility and offer greater reading ease when large quantities of information require the use of condensed letterforms for compact areas. With very few exceptions, and whenever possible, almost all of the ligatures and variant letterforms of the original Avant Garde Gothic family have been retained in the Condensed series.

Avant Garde Gothic Condensed was specially drawn for ITC by Edward Benguiat and is based on the original Avant Garde Gothic series created by Herb Lubalin and Tom Carnase.

ABCDEFGHIJKLM NOPQRSTUVWXYZ AÄŒŒÆFÆFÅRGHTfIJ lÁLÁLÑTñRÁCÉSSÍT THÚTMNVWVMV (&?!£$%¢°/'±⁻.") 1234567890 abcdefghijklm nopqrstuvwxyzCØ œçœœvWWÝŸB

BOOK CONDENSED

ABCDEFGHIJKLM NOPQRSTUVWXYZ AÄŒŒÆFÆFÅRGHTfIJ lÁLÁLÑTñRÁCÉSSÍT THÚTMNVWVMV (&?!£$%¢°/'±⁻.") 1234567890 abcdefghijklm nopqrstuvwxyzCØ œçœœvWWÝŸB

MEDIUM CONDENSED

ABCDEFGHIJKLM NOPQRSTUVWXYZ AÄŒŒÆFÆFÅRGHTfIJ lÁLÁLÑTñRÁCÉSSÍT THÚTMNVWVMV (&?!£$%¢°/'±⁻.") 1234567890 abcdefghijklm nopqrstuvwxyzCØ œçœœvWWÝŸB

DEMI CONDENSED

ABCDEFGHIJKLM NOPQRSTUVWXYZ AÄŒŒÆFÆFÅRGHTfIJ lÁLÁLÑTñRÁCÉSSÍT THÚTMNVWVMV (&?!£$%¢°/'±⁻.") 1234567890 abcdefghijklm nopqrstuvwxyzCØ œçœœvWWÝŸB

BOLD CONDENSED

19

FRIZ QUADRATA
Award-Winning VGC Typeface Now Available as Photo Text Face from ITC

Letter-consciousness is no longer the private domain of the typographic connoisseur. Just a few years have changed all that. While the man in the street can't tell Caslon from Garamond, he no longer thinks all letters look alike. Not any more.

He's bombarded with posters, brochures, and ads telling him in no uncertain terms that letters can have many forms and very exotic personalities. If he lives in New York and travels by subway he may spend a bumpy hour or two every day pondering the grotesque shapes of transit graffiti. Much as he may dislike both spray can and marker, and much as he may feel that their indiscriminate use on public property is a most unworthy contribution to the art of lettering, nevertheless it has brought millions of John Does like himself to an awareness of letterforms—for good or for bad. Inevitably the more imaginative of these observers have tried to develop a taste for lettering—to learn to distinguish between naive graffiti and the real thing.

A letter-conscious public is precisely what many of us have been hoping for, for many years. And here it is. Thanks to the enormous impact of display lettering—good and bad—the lettering-conscious community has grown from thousands to millions! And in these new millions are those who would like to try their hand at serious letter design.

A few years ago Visual Graphics Corporation recognized this latent potential and pursued it vigorously by launching a typeface-design contest of considerable magnitude. As a result of the contest Visual Graphics issued 2-inch film fonts of 15 Award-Winning faces, all of which have made significant impact on display typography. One wonders to what extent the more conservative of these faces are adaptable to text composition. Text sizes, traditionally, are the first to be developed. Display, as a rule, comes later. Will photo-typography lead to a reversal of this sequence?

ABCDEFGHIJKL MNOPQRSTU VWXYZÆØ abcdefghijklmn opqrstuvwxyz 1234567890 (&!?æøØ$¢%/£°)

ITC QUADRATA REGULAR

ABCDEFGHIJKL MNOPQRSTU VWXYZÆØ abcdefghijklm nopqrstuvwxyz 1234567890 (&!?æøØ$¢%/£°)

ITC QUADRATA BOLD

The question is best answered by action, and to demonstrate the possibilities of the Award-Winning faces, International Typeface Corp., under license from Visual Graphics to develop Friz Quadrata and offer it for sale, is now making two weights of this important design available to all manufacturers of text typesetting equipment.

The original weight of this fine letter was designed by Ernst Friz. Mr. Friz, a native of Switzerland, studied graphics at Zurich with Rudolf Bircher and Walter Koch. He has his own graphic studio and specializes in type, symbol and package design, having won the National Swiss Packaging Award for 1962.

The bold weight adaptation of Friz Quadrata was executed by Victor Caruso, designer with Photo-Lettering Inc.

364

Aa Bb Cc Dd Ee Ff Gg Hh Ii Jj Kk Ll Mm Nn Oo Pp   Qq Rr Ss Tt Uu Vv Ww Xx Yy Zz 1234567890 & Æ Œ $¢ £ % !? ( )[]

UPPER AND LOWER CASE, THE INTERNATIONAL JOURNAL OF TYPOGRAPHICS   PUBLISHED BY INTERNATIONAL TYPEFACE CORPORATION, VOLUME ONE, NUMBER TWO, JAN. 1978

175. Happy Smtwtf&s 1978

The cover shown features a typical interlocking block of type (ITC Garamond Ultra Italic) made out of the word 'Happy' and the initial letters of days of the week. ITC redrew many classic typefaces for the modern era of photographic and computerized typesetting. The controversy this provoked, and the story of ITC and *U&lc* are discussed elsewhere in this book (p.55). Date: January, 1978.

176. 'Ms.' Jacqui Morgan

Despite his status as an alpha male in the New York design scene of the 1970s, Herb Lubalin was an advocate of women in design. 'Ms.' was a regular feature in *U&lc* devoted to the work of female practitioners. Here, the work of Pratt-educated illustrator Jacqui Morgan is featured. As well as his willingness to promote the cause of female designers, he was also a keen admirer of feminine beauty. The designer Diana Wilko, who worked for Lubalin (and is now married to another Lubalin alumnus, photographer Hans Mauli) recalls: 'I first met Herb when he came as a visiting instructor to a design class I was taking at Cooper, and he assigned us a project, to design a poster for the film *The Bible*. Two years later I was working for him. Though he liked my portfolio, he confided much later that when I strode into his office for the job interview in a mini-dress, he knew he had to hire me because I had great legs.'

177. The ABC's of Coloring

Spreads showing an alphabet created by French designer Jean Larcher for a book called *3D Alphabet Colouring Book* (Dover, 1978). It offered the alphabet as multidimensional designs where each letter appears in multiples of itself that interlock, fuse and merge. Readers are then invited to colour in each letterform. It's easy to see why the playful letterforms of Larcher would be appreciated by the equally playful Lubalin.

178—181. Double-page spreads

Various layouts reflecting Lubalin's wide-ranging interest in the world of design, past and present. Note the densely packed layouts conveying his obvious delight in cramming in as much material as possible. Herb Lubalin was no minimalist; he believed in abundance. About his role as editor and proprietor of *U&lc* he said: 'Right now, I have what every designer wants and few have the good fortune to achieve. I'm my own client. Nobody tells me what to do.'

12

The ABC's of coloring. It's hard to believe that anyone can add substantively to the voluminous number of le
that fairly boggle our minds and dazzle our senses. But Jean Larcher has done it again. Just when we think that c
the alphabet have been exhausted, up pops Larcher with still another fascinating variation — this one a spread
forthcoming "Alphabet Coloring Book," which will be on the bookstands in March courtesy of Dover Publicati
prolific multi-talented designer from Paris — who has contributed so handsomely to the editorial excitement
issues with his playful interpretations of both numerals and alphabets — has come up with a bright new co
"audience participation" alphabet, with the readers invited to go for their color markers to fill in the provocative
with their own choice of colors. We suggest that you keep these pages on hand as a reminder to yourselves
typophile friends who might want to go whole hog and buy the book on publication date (on the pretext, natu
it's really "for the children"). Give it a whirl. We think that you, like us, will never cease to be amazed at Larcher'
reach and technical wizardry — brilliantly enhanced, of course, by your own glorious color schemes.

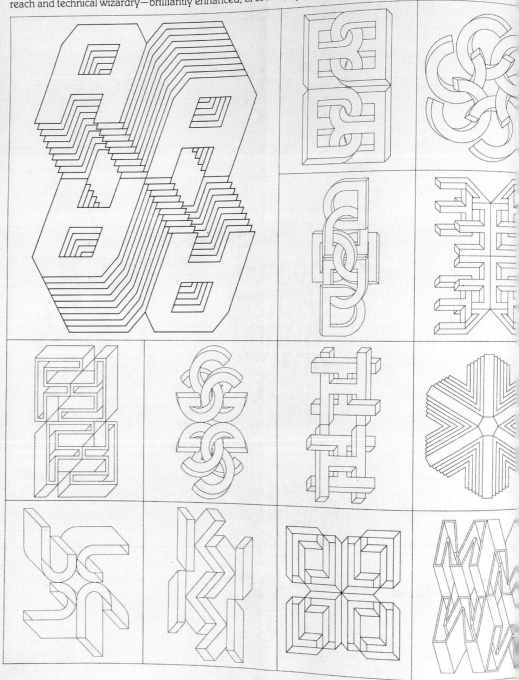

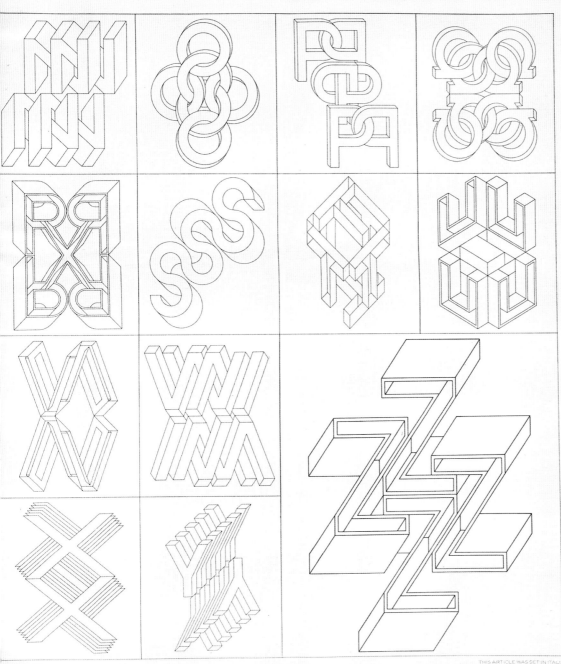

THIS ARTICLE WAS SET IN ITALIA

24

What's New from ITC?

ITC Benguiat Book, Medium and Bold and ITC Benguiat Book Italic, Medium Italic and Bold Italic are new typefaces from ITC. Only licensed ITC Subscribers are authorized to reproduce, manufacture, and offer for sale these and other ITC typefaces shown in this issue. This license mark is your guarantee of authenticity.

These new typefaces will be available to the public on or after January 16, depending on each manufacturer's release schedule.

ITC BENGUIAT

ITC Benguiat Book

It takes no crystal ball to foresee that the future will give ITC Benguiat its firm stamp of approval as the right face at the right time in the right place, for here is a design overflowing with contemporary goodies, drawn with fervor by one whose artistry sees far down the line, and whose pen records in vibrant graphics clear to all.

Benguiat's design confidence reflects in every letter his eagerness to set down the lively shapes with unfaltering boldness; his assurance that in so doing he is taking a firm step forward. These are the traits that give this new typeface such vitality and assure for it a worthy role in tomorrow's typography.

By no means its least important attribute is that, along with other ITC typefaces, it is available under license to manufacturers of scores of different keyboards and manual typesetting machines, transfer sheets, etc. Worldwide. This worldwide coverage brings new ITC faces promptly into the visual mainstream, giving them advance standing in broad dissemination of the printed word. Benguiat is available in three weights, roman and italic, separately designed for text and display.

ABCDEFGHIJKLMNOPQRSTUVWXYZ
abcdefghijklmnopqrstuvwxyz
1234567890

ITC Benguiat Medium

It takes no crystal ball to foresee that the future will give ITC Benguiat its firm stamp of approval as the right face at the right time, for here is a design overflowing with contemporary goodies, drawn with fervor by one whose artistry sees far down the line, and whose pen records in vibrant graphics clear to all.

Benguiat's design confidence reflects in every letter his eagerness to set down the lively shapes with unfaltering boldness; his assurance that in so doing he is taking a firm step forward. These are the traits that give this new typeface such vitality and assure for it a worthy role in tomorrow's typography.

By no means its least important attribute is that, along with other ITC typefaces, it is available under license to manufacturers of scores of different keyboards and manual typesetting machines, transfer sheets, etc. Worldwide. This worldwide coverage brings new ITC faces promptly into the visual mainstream, giving them advance standing in broad dissemination of the printed word. Benguiat is available in three weights, roman and italic, separately designed for text and display.

ABCDEFGHIJKLMNOPQRSTUVWXYZ
abcdefghijklmnopqrstuvwxyz
1234567890

ITC Benguiat Book Italic

It takes no crystal ball to foresee that the future will give ITC Benguiat its firm stamp of approval as the right face at the right time in the right place, for here is a design overflowing with contemporary goodies, drawn with fervor by one whose artistry sees far down the line, and whose pen records in vibrant graphics clear to all.

Benguiat's design confidence re...

25

ITC Benguiat Bold

It takes no crystal ball to foresee that the future will give ITC Benguiat its firm stamp of approval as the right face at the right time in the right place, for here is a design overflowing with contemporary goodies, drawn with fervor by one whose artistry sees far down the line, and whose pen records in vibrant graphics clear to all.

Benguiat's design confidence reflects in every letter his eagerness to set down the lively shapes with unfaltering boldness; his assurance that in so doing he is taking a firm step forward. These are the traits that give this new typeface such vitality and assure for it a worthy role in tomorrow's typography.

By no means its least important attribute is that, along with other ITC typefaces, it is available under license to manufacturers of scores of different keyboards and manual typesetting machines, transfer sheets, etc. Worldwide. This worldwide coverage brings new ITC faces promptly into the visual mainstream, giving them advance standing in broad dissemination of the printed word. Benguiat is available in three weights, roman and italic, separately designed for text and display.

ABCDEFGHIJKLMNOPQRSTUVWXYZ
abcdefghijklmnopqrstuvwxyz
1234567890

ITC Benguiat Medium Italic

It takes no crystal ball to foresee that the future will give ITC Benguiat its firm stamp of approval as the right face at the right time in the right place, for here is a design overflowing with contemporary goodies, drawn with fervor by one whose artistry sees far down the line, and whose pen records in vibrant graphics clear to all.

Benguiat's design confidence reflects in every letter his eagerness to set down the lively shapes with unfaltering boldness; his assurance that in so doing he is taking a firm step forward. These are the traits that give this new typeface such vitality and assure for it a worthy role in tomorrow's typography.

By no means its least important attribute is that, along with other ITC typefaces, it is available under license to manufacturers of scores of different keyboards and manual typesetting machines, transfer sheets, etc. Worldwide. This worldwide coverage brings new...

ABCDEFGHIJKLMNOPQRSTUVWXYZ
abcdefghijklmnopqrstuvwxyz
1234567890

ITC Benguiat Bold Italic

It takes no crystal ball to foresee that the future will give ITC Benguiat its firm stamp of approval as the right face at the right time in the right place, for here is a design overflowing with contemporary goodies, drawn with fervor by one whose artistry sees far down the line, and whose pen records in vibrant graphics clear to all.

Benguiat's design confidence reflects in every letter his eagerness to set down the lively shapes with unfaltering boldness; his assurance that in so doing he is taking a firm step forward. These are the traits that give this new typeface such vitality and assure for it a worthy role in tomorrow's typography.

By no means its least important attribute is that, along with other ITC typefaces, it is available under license to manufacturers of scores of different keyboards and manual typesetting machines, transfer sheets, etc. Worldwide. This worldwide coverage brings new ITC faces promptly into the visual mainstream, giving them advance standing in broad dissemination of the printed word. Benguiat is available in three weights, roman and italic, separately designed for text and display.

ABCDEFGHIJKLMNOPQRSTUVWXYZ
abcdefghijklmnopqrstuvwxyz
1234567890

28

Face to face.

Jean Edouard Robert

Face to face Now exotic "faces" be hidden, waiting for the time when curious eyes will find them in their secret places.

AABCDEFGHIJKLMMNOPQRST
UVWXYZabcdefghijklmnopqrst

29

Pentagram Papers are available from Pentagram Design, 61 North Wharf Road, London W2, 6LB. Five have already been published and two more are in the pipeline. If you would like to receive all seven, please write to Pentagram at the above address. The cost is only $20.00 which we think is the buy of the year.

AaBbCcDdEeFfGgHhIiJjKkLlMmNnOoPp QqRrSsTtUuVvWwXxYyZz1234567890&ÆŒ$¢£%!?()[]

UPPER AND LOWER CASE, THE INTERNATIONAL JOURNAL OF TYPOGRAPHICS   PUBLISHED BY INTERNATIONAL TYPEFACE CORPORATION, VOLUME TWO, NUMBER ONE, MARCH 1978

182. Come Home to Jazz
Here Lubalin makes use of the monumental typeface ITC Machine Bold. The face was designed by Ronne Bonder, a former associate of Tom Carnase. Indeed, Carnase is sometimes credited as the typeface's co-designer. On display is Lubalin's remarkable ability to create seemingly unforced typographic compositions that were both attractive to the eye and highly readable.
Date: March 1978.

183. 'Ms.' Syd Hap
Double-page spread showing the 'marionette artistry' of Syd Hap, a graduate of Pratt and a designer of puppets as well as a puppeteer. On display are puppets of U.S. president Jimmy Carter, Kiss member Gene Simmons, TV soap opera character Mary Hartman, conservative commentator William F. Buckley, Elvis and Rod Stewart. Typeface is ITC Tiffany Heavy.

184. Living Alphabet
Spread showing nature-inspired alphabet by American illustrator Richard Coyne. The letterforms (left-hand page) were inspired by a trip to the jungles of Central East Asia. Also shown (right-hand page) is a trade ad for ITC, the publisher of U&lc.

185–188. Come Home to Jazz
To paraphrase F. Scott Fitzgerald, there are no second acts in graphic design. Or to put it another way, it isn't often that graphic designers get a second chance to improve or redesign their work. To demonstrate the flexibility and versatility of the new phototypesetting technology, Herb Lubalin used the pages of U&lc to recreate a piece of work that he had made in 1960 for Der Druckspiegel, the monthly German graphic arts magazine. The original work was republished by the Composing Room as a 16-page booklet and can be seen on p.416. In the four spreads shown here, Herb Lubalin demonstrates what could be achieved with new typefaces and new techniques of type generation; how type could be wrapped around images, or slotted into odd shapes; and how sizing, letter spacing and line spacing could all be pushed to extremes. Photography: Carl Fischer.

ITC TYPEFACE DIRECTORY 1978

International Typeface Corporation

8   9

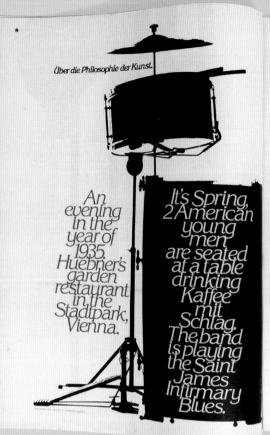

Über die Philosophie der Kunst.

An evening in the year of 1935. Huebner's garden restaurant in the Stadtpark, Vienna.

It's Spring. 2 American young men are seated at a table drinking Kaffee mit Schlag. The band is playing the Saint James Infirmary Blues.

1ST AMER: NOT BAD.
2ND AMER: NOT GOOD, EITHER.
1ST AMER: GIVE THEM A CHANCE; THEY'LL GET IT.
2ND AMER: THE DRUMMER KNOWS THE TRICKS. HE MUST HAVE STUDIED.
1ST AMER: YOU'VE GOT TO STUDY.
2ND AMER: AND YOU'VE GOT TO FORGET YOU STUDIED. JAZZ DRUMMER LIKE BABY DODDS, CHICK WEBB, COZY COLE, HE GIVES YOU THAT MOVE-ALONG FEELING.
1ST AMER: I GUESS THAT'S IT; THAT MOVE-ALONG FEELING.
2ND AMER: THAT'S NOT ALL; YOU'VE GOT TO PASS THE TEST.
1ST AMER: WHAT IS THE TEST?
2ND AMER: THE TEST OF A JAZZ DRUMMER IS: CAN HE MAKE A FAT MAN FALL DOWN A WHOLE FLIGHT OF STAIRS WITHOUT HURTING HIMSELF.

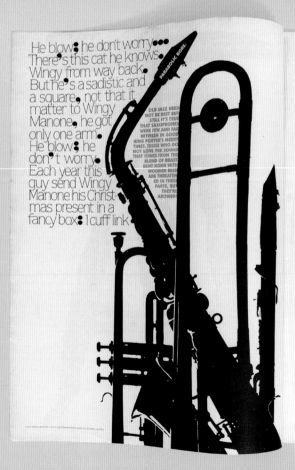

He blows he don't worry●●● There's this cat he knows, Wingy from way back● But he's a sadistic and a square, not that it matter to Wingy Manone● he got only one arm● He blows he don't worry● Each year this guy send Wingy Manone his Christmas present in a fancy box● 1 cuff link

PARABOLIC BONE:

OLD JAZZ NEED NOT BE BEST BUY STILL IT'S TRUE THAT SAXOPHONES WERE FEW AND FAR BETWEEN IN GOOD KING PORTER'S MERRY TIMES. THOSE WHO DO NOT LOVE THE SOUND THAT ISSUES FROM THE BLEND OF BRASS BENT HORN WITH WOODEN REED ARE THREATENED IN THESE PARTS, BUT THEY'RE AROUND

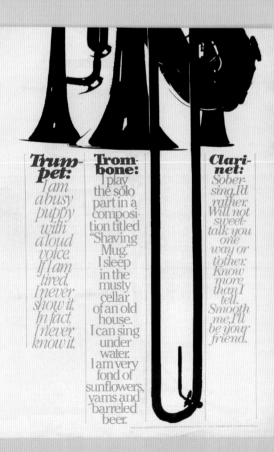

Trumpet: I am a busy puppy with a loud voice. If I am tired, I never show it. In fact, I never know it.

Trombone: I play the solo part in a composition titled "Shaving Mug." I sleep in the musty cellar of an old house. I can sing under water. I am very fond of sunflowers, yams and barreled beer.

Clarinet: Sober-sing, I'd rather. Will not sweet-talk you one way or t'other. Know more than I tell. Smooth me, I'll be your friend.

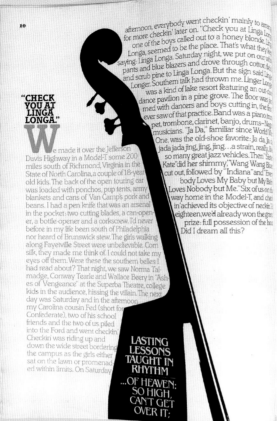
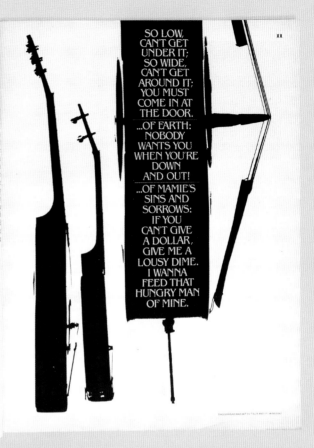

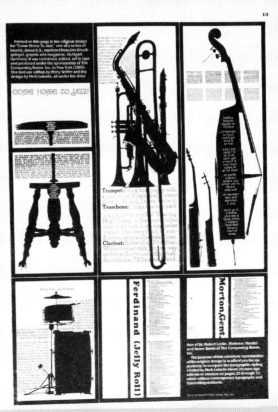

INTERNATIONAL

Aa Bb Cc Dd Ee Ff Gg Hh Ii Jj Kk Ll Mm Nn Oo Pp   Qq Rr Ss Tt Uu Vv Ww Xx Yy Zz 1234567890 & Æ Œ $¢ £%!?()[]

UPPER AND LOWER CASE, THE INTERNATIONAL JOURNAL OF TYPOGRAPHICS   PUBLISHED BY INTERNATIONAL TYPEFACE CORPORATION. VOLUME TWO: NUMBER THREE, SEPT. 1978

189. 'ABCDE ...'
The cover design trails an article inside the magazine titled 'A Brief History of Typography'. The front cover assemblage shows letterforms from 1000 BCE to the computer age. Date: September 1978.

190, 191. Brief History of Typography
Double-page spreads showing adaptation of a calendar issued by the Frederic Ryder Company (advertising typographers based in Chicago). The calendar presented a history of the letterform from ancient times to the present day. Lubalin redesigned the calendar to work within *U&lc*. The written text is by Tom Shortlidge.

192—195. ITC Cheltenham
Spreads demonstrating the versatility of the newly redrawn Cheltenham. The original Cheltenham was designed by Bertram Grosvenor Goodhue, in collaboration with Ingalls Kimball of the Cheltenham Press in New York, during the first few years of the 20th century. Various versions and weights were added by Morris Fuller Benton. Cheltenham became one of the first extensive families of metal types; when, in the 1970s, ITC made 19 new versions, it became one of the largest families available for photographic and electronic typesetting. Here, Lubalin takes a collection of typographic quotations derived from Herman Zapf's 1968 book *Manuale Typographicum*. Each statement has been redesigned using a different weight of the ITC Cheltenham family. This experimental typographic exercise has been specially prepared to show the versatility of the typeface.

easily available. His later contributions to printing, especially small capitals and the first italics, continued this wish to help scholars.

In Venice, at the age of 40, Aldus began to print reference books which brought about a tremendous enlargement of the conception and purpose of all books.

In 1495, he published *De Aetna*, by Pietro Bembo, using a calligraphic Roman of his own design. This is considered to be the first modern book in terms of typographic style.

About 1506, with Francesco Griffo of Bologna, Aldus developed the first italic type. These italics were originally intended to be independent book faces, with no relationship to the Romans. They were used for less important lines on Aldus' title pages, to provide easier reading and to give more emphasis to the capital lines.

The original italics were all lower case and were used with initial Roman capitals, following the practice of calligraphy in the papal chancery. A quarter of a century passed before sloping capitals appeared in type.

1525

Stimulated by printing presses, the wider dissemination of books, and the Renaissance spirit itself, Western Europe showed a great preoccupation with writing and instructional copybooks in the first part of the 16th century.

One of the subjects studied in these books was the classical Roman lapidary capitals. Not only was there an appreciation of these letters, but there were even attempts made to reduce them to a science.

In his *Divina proportione* of 1509, Leonardo Da Vinci demonstrated the construction of the Roman capitals with geometric elements.

And in 1525, Albrecht Dürer wrote an essay entitled "Of the Just Shaping of Letters" as part of a treatise on applied geometry.

In this essay, Dürer constructed each letter by inscribing it in a square of specific size, building the characters from elements of the square and arcs of circles. The constructions were well formed and were not distorted to conform to some predetermined system. Complete instructions and alternate designs for each letter were given in the accompanying text.

Dürer, known for his woodcuts and paintings, had made an important contribution to lettering craftsmanship with a single essay.

1530

Looking back, it could be argued that the greatest contributions to typography were made within a century of its beginning.

The contributions were numerous — the old-style family of types, small capitals, italics, printer's marks, colophons, the movable type itself.

The contributors were people such as Gutenberg, Coster, Fust, Koberger, Ratdolt, Schoeffer, Jenson, Aldus Manutius, Arrighi, Due Pre, DeWorde, Caxton, Pynson, Tory, and Claude Garamond.

Garamond's Romans were introduced in Paris in 1530.

Compared to the Romans of Nicolas Jenson, Garamond's Romans had a greater contrast between thick and thin strokes, more upright round characters, a horizontal cross-stroke on the "e", and serifs that angled sharply out from the stem to form crisp points.

These new letters gained great acceptance in France and were almost single-handedly responsible for displacing the Gothic black letters as the standard printing type.

Curiously, many of the modern typefaces that bear Garamond's name are not really closely related to his types but are based on types that were mistakenly attributed to him.

1720

After Garamond's death in 1561, there was no real substantial change in type design for almost two centuries. Which is not to say that printing went into a decline. Quite the opposite was true.

Printing and printers flourished in the 17th and early 18th centuries. The romantic novel, newspapers, journals, and political pamphlets began to reach the growing ranks of the middle class. At the height of this printing fury, in 1726, William Caslon arrived at his cut known as Old Face.

Caslon Old Face was not a new step in typography. It was just the final definition of the old-style Romans begun by Jenson and Aldus Manutius.

The individual letters were not, in themselves, very distinctive. But they had the ability of combining into exceptionally legible words and pages because no letter flourishes or details would distract the reader.

As others had before, Caslon's type became the standard of an era. It was

eloquently referred to as "the finest vehicle for the printed conveyance of English speech that the art of the punch-cutter has yet devised."

When modern transitional types began to appear 30 years later, Caslon's type fell out of favor. It was "rediscovered," however, in the 19th century because of its great readability.

1757

The transition from old-style to modern-style type design began rather abruptly with the publication of John Baskerville's edition of Vergil in 1757. Baskerville had been dissatisfied with existing types, so for his Vergil, he spent two years designing his own. The result was a relatively heavy face with extreme thins and straight serifs.

These new letters had a near perfection that was very unlike the cruder Caslon type to which England had become accustomed. Part of this perfection had to do with the way the type was printed.

Also dissatisfied with the quality of existing printer's inks, Baskerville made his own extremely black ink, even boiling the oil and burning the lamp-black itself.

The available laid paper did not suit him either, so he manufactured a paper with a smoother surface, the first woven paper ever. He used a harder packing on his press, and when the sheets had been printed he pressed them between hot copper plates to dry and set the ink, thus giving the paper a smooth and polished look.

1788

Although he certainly pushed along the design of modern type, Giambattista Bodoni may have hindered its readability in the process.

The pseudo-classical Bodoni type that was introduced in Italy in 1788 was strongly influenced by the types of Baskerville in England and the Didots in France.

In the Bodoni type, the thick and thin strokes were greatly exaggerated. The round letters were narrow rather than full, and the serifs were thin lines. The fact that the delicate hairlines were reproducible at all is probably a testimonial to the success of copper engraving at the time.

Bodoni's types were used in books that were probably intended to be admired by the affluent rather than read by the masses.

Although the title pages were impressive and the margins were generous, the text in these books was undistinguished, and the editing and proofreading somewhat lax.

Despite its flaws and because of the technical achievements and visual style of his typography, Bodoni gained a great deal of recognition and admirers. One of these admirers was Napoleon, who undoubtedly responded to the classical, almost imperial, look of the Bodoni types.

1816

The letters in the early Greek stone inscriptions were without serifs. But after the Romans added serifs, sans serif letters did not appear again until 1816.

A single size of a sans serif type appeared in the 1816 specimen sheet of William Caslon IV, a descendant of 18th-century type founder William Caslon. Caslon called his single size "sans syrruphs," but it soon became known as "grotesque" because of its strangeness.

By 1832, Stephenson Blake of England was producing a broad range of grotesques. The influence of these "new" letter forms quickly spread beyond Europe to the type foundries of America, where they became part of an explosion of typographic styles in the mid-1800's.

LE TASSE

1820

The year 1820 could be regarded as a kind of boundary line between the purposes of type.

Up to that point, type had been in-

tended primarily [...] fore tasteful "boo[...] dominated.

But around 18[...] America in partic[...] industrially and [...] never known bef[...] merce, advertising [...] ing more express[...] "display faces." At [...] tortion of availab[...] strokes became t[...] even finer.

But soon, the p[...] overflow with fam[...] proportions.

The first shad[...] letters soon appe[...] after a period of c[...] again as the Goth[...] ported to Americ[...]

The most signi[...] were the types ca[...] probably acquired [...] of their "darkness[...] in the archaeolog[...] going on along th[...] and slab serifs of [...] which made them [...] giant advertising [...]

The P.T. Barnu[...] continued throug[...] century, as swolle[...] flowered, shaded, [...] notched, and conv[...] often screamed fo[...] the attention of t[...]

If one type cou[...] the absurdity and [...] period, it would h[...] bet called, approp[...] Monstre."

Although it ha[...] distinct character[...] typewritten lette[...] trically bound to [...] The first recorde[...] typewriter was ta[...] in England in 171[...] 1829, however, th[...] machine — coincid[...] "typographer" — w[...] William Austin B[...] States.

The earliest m[...] embossed writing [...] intended for the [...] model appeared in [...] permitted only ca[...]

The early lette[...] had a purely typo[...] resembled the Bo[...] delicately articula[...]

g thick and thin strokes soon
ed unsuitable for a multiple num-
of copies. The care necessary to
duce something clearly prohibited
apid speed.

order to accommodate both
v and speed, designers began to
don Roman types in favor of letters
nore uniform thickness.

e mechanics of the typewriter
ed the identical space for a narrow
like an "I" as it did for a wide
like a "W." This was unsatisfac-
because the letters then failed to
ve a fluent rhythm, and the legibi-
the typed text was impaired. To
come this obstacle, the lower bars
rrow letters like "I" were empha-
in order to fill out the space they
ied. This new lettering created
ically for the typewriter became
n as "Pica."

though many ornate letters and
ions on Pica were attempted, none
became serious rivals to Pica be-
none could ever achieve its clarity
anufacturing economies.

was only with the invention of the
ic typewriter around 1935 that
designers gained the freedom to
st practical new letter forms for
pewriter.

e regularity with which keys were
k on an electric machine dis-
ed with the necessity for letters
iform thickness.

provements in the electric type-
r allowed the carriage to shift vary-
paces. The new machines would allot
ters of different widths exactly the
they required. With each subse-
t improvement in the typewriter,
desire to create new types for it
stimulated.

1891

y the end of the 19th century,
mercialism and the Industrial Revo-
n had crept into almost all aspects
e in America and Europe. In its path,
of what was craftsmanlike, sensi-
y created, and beautiful had been
hed. Typography was no exception.

revival in typography made by
am Morris was one attempt to stem
reeping blight of industrial ugliness.
nspiration, Morris looked to the first
ted books of the 15th century.
ould have preferred works of an
er, medieval vintage, but of course,
ed books were not available from
period.

ter three years of study into the
of the book, papermaking, binding,
type design, Morris and his Kelm-

scott Press produced *The Story of the Glittering Plain* in 1891. For this book, Morris designed a Roman type modeled after those of Nicolas Jenson. It later became known as Golden type, since it was used for *The Golden Legend*, printed in 1892.

Morris produced a version of Caxton's *Recuyell of the Histories of Troye*, the first book to have been printed in England. For this, he designed a Gothic type known as Troy.

All of the work of the Kelmscott Press is characterized by highly decorated title pages, woodcut illustrations reminiscent of the 16th century, ornamental initials that were inspired by medieval manuscripts, and craftsmanship throughout. Morris' fastidious craftsmanship even extended to the paper of all his books, a linen rag which was woven with a slight irregularity in texture, just like the papers of the earliest printers.

In retrospect, this revival had little bearing on the course of typography, but it did account for the proliferation of private presses at the beginning of the 20th century.

1898

Seldom does a discovery in the field of science have a direct bearing on the course of typography. But when the element neon was discovered by Sir William Ramsay and M.W. Travers in 1898, it would not be long before this discovery gave birth to the most prevalent typographic communication in modern cityscapes.

The first neon sign was created by forcing a small amount of neon gas into a partially evacuated clear glass tube. This gas conducted a current of electricity, naturally producing a bright reddish-orange glow. In order for the sign to glow other than red-orange, the tubing itself needed to be colored.

Once the principle of the neon sign was understood, the complexity of the signs themselves depended on the skill of the glassworkers to bend and form the glass tubes into inventive new shapes.

As the 20th century progressed, neon signs of humble and grandiose varieties were urging people to enter, exit, stop, or start and telling them which way it was to the bathroom. Neon signs identified Salvation Army missions as easily as they did the liquor store right next door.

The flowing, continuous nature of the glass tubing lent itself best to script letter forms, but sans serif styles were

also easily adaptable. In the most elaborate neon typography, strokes were very often doubled, tripled, and quadrupled to produce dramatic pieces of illuminated information in the midst of utter darkness.

1957

Modern sans serif types are basically patterned after a face called Akzidenz Grotesk. This was first cut by the Berthold foundry in Germany in 1898. Much later, when it reached the American market, it became known as Standard.

The legacy of Akzidenz Grotesk can be found in the faces created and popularized by the Swiss school of design — Neue Grotesk (Helvetica), Folio, and Univers.

Although Helvetica has become the most widely used type in modern communication, it can be argued that Univers — because of its extensive range of weights and widths — is a more important typographic landmark.

The Univers family was conceived by Swiss-born designer Adrian Frutiger in 1957. Working in the atelier of the Deberny and Peignot foundry in Paris, Frutiger adopted a rather unconventional approach to type design. Instead of allowing the success of a typeface to dictate its later extension, Frutiger created an entire range of variations at its inception.

Whereas variations in most other typefaces are indicated by words such as 'demi' or 'bold,' the sheer volume of variations in Univers demanded another system. This system became numerical.

Number 55 — Univers 55 — was the norm, and all its variations were based on units of 10. In terms of type "weight," the higher the 10's place in the number, the bolder the type would be; for instance, Univers 75 is bolder than Univers 55.

In terms of type extension or condensation, the higher the unit's place in the number, the more condensed the type would be; for instance, Univers 53 is very extended and Univers 59 is very condensed. Odd numbers such as Univers 57 signified roman, and even numbers such as Univers 58 signified italic.

By carefully altering characteristics within a specific letter, Frutiger ensured an even color and balance for an entire setting of Univers. For instance, the 'free' ends of letters were slightly thickened, and connected ends were somewhat pinched, to lighten the effect of blackness and to prevent smearing during printing. The "c" was narrower

than the "o" because the greater area of white around it made it seem optically as broad as the "o." The "u" was narrower than the "n" because the white area at the top of the "u" was more evident than the white area at the bottom of the "n." There were almost as many similar subtle character changes as there were letters in the alphabet.

The diversity of Univers is most dramatically shown in its original set-up for the composing machine. If you counted the different variations in the 12 different point sizes, altogether there were 17,280 letters and punctuation marks at the disposal of the machine.

1960

For 500 years, the stern limits of metal governed the development of typography. But then, a new tool was added that expanded the capabilities and flexibilities of type — photography.

Experiments in setting type photographically had begun as early as 1876, but it was not until the 1920's that a line-casting machine was successfully converted to a photographic typesetter. At the same time, a revolving disk-type character system on glass and a photographic matrix system were developing.

In 1936, the Uher-type machine, the granddaddy of modern photo typesetters was introduced. And in 1946, the Fotosetter, the first commercially acceptable photographic typesetting machine, was field-tested at the United States Government Printing Office.

The Fotosetter, significant as it was, had all the speed and spacing limitations of hot-metal equipment because it was manually operated and depended on three-dimensional mats to create two-dimensional images.

By the early 1960's, systems had been invented that virtually eliminated vertical and horizontal spacing limitations and that operated at dizzying speeds. Photo lettering suddenly permitted new typefaces to be designed and produced without the crushing cost of casting them in metal.

Photo display lettering could be condensed, expanded, compressed, extended, obliqued, or otherwise made to conform to any desired space.

Photocomposition allowed character fitting in text to be sensitively controlled with the use of plus or minus spacing. Characters could be superimposed, and even solid line spacing could be subtracted from.

With photocomposition, there were no broken letters and no misalignments.

Type was sharper and blacker or more subtle, depending on the typeface. Type could be enlarged as much as 500% without affecting its integrity.

And photocomposition could be more economical because it eliminated steps in the production process.

Phototypography allowed the people who work with type to control their medium, rather than being controlled by it.

1978

Scientists and insurance companies are fond of reminding us that "the future is now." That couldn't be a truer statement when you look at the future of typography. The typesetting equipment for the next generation is already in use.

This Cathode Ray Tube (CRT) system begins by translating the image of a type character into binary (off/on) code. This code in turn controls the image that eventually is projected onto the CRT screen or that is exposed onto a photographic material such as paper or film.

The CRT is made up of lines which form a screen or grid of lines that normally ranges between 1,000 and 2,000 lines per inch. The areas between the lines of the screen create individual squares that can be turned on or off, depending on the binary code.

The binary codes representing a type font are recorded on a storage media such as a 'floppy disk.' When a typeface is needed by the phototypesetter, it is instantly transferred from the storage media to the computer memory. When they are activated, digitized characters are transmitted to the CRT screen.

The characters form on the screen in much the same way that dots form a halftone in a printed picture.

All of this happens with incredible speed. CRT typesetting systems are capable of producing 8,000 characters a second, and 150 to 300 lines of copy every minute.

Any desired unit spacing can be factored into a setting, as well as condensations or extensions of a specific typeface.

A few years ago, a CRT system was a magical, exotic piece of hardware. Today, it's a widely accepted production tool that will perform an important role in typography.

Ultimately, the CRT could be replaced by systems that record directly onto printing plates or even "plateless" printing presses. And maybe that could be the subject of our appointment calendar 25 years from now.

A **LOVE** OF LETTERS IS THE BEGINNING OF TYPOGRAPHICAL WISDOM. THAT IS, THE **LOVE** OF LETTERS AS LITERATURE AND THE **LOVE** OF LETTERS AS PHYSICAL ENTITIES HAVING ABSTRACT BEAUTY OF THEIR OWN, APART FROM THE IDEAS THEY MAY EXPRESS OR THE EMOTIONS THEY MAY EVOKE.

LETTERS ARE THE KEY TO OUR CULTURE. THEY CAN ALSO BE A PICKLOCK TO OUR HEART.

Type gives body & voice to silent thought. The speaking page carries it through the centuries.

Type is one of the most eloquent means of expression in every epoch of style. Next to architecture, it gives the most characteristic portrait of a period and the most severe testimony of a nation's intellectual status.

" ALDOUS HUXLEY JOHANN GOETHE CHARLES DICKENS

GOD BLESS COPPER-PRINTING, AND ALL OTHER REPRODUCTIVE PROCESSES, WHICH ENSURE THAT ANYTHING THAT EXISTS CAN NEVER BE WIPED OUT.

GEORGE B. SHAW VAN WYCK BROOKS THOMAS CARLYLE

We learn to read, in various languages, in various sciences; we learn the alphabet and letters of all manner of Books. But the place where we are to get knowledge, even theoretic knowledge, is the Books themselves! The true University of these days is a Collection of Books. "

TYPOGRAPHY IS A SERVANT—THE SERVANT OF THOUGHT & LANGUAGE TO WHICH IT GIVES VISIBLE EXISTENCE.

This is a major factor in present day photo-typesetting economics and technology and one that presents a demanding design challenge for contemporary typeface designers.

All ITC typeface designs take this factor into consideration and typophiles should bear this in mind when comparing such film-redesigned classics to their original metal-designed counterparts.

It is our hope that the ITC Cheltenham typeface family of nineteen type styles will make as distinguished a contribution to the future of typographic communications as its original forebear has done for more than three quarters of a century.

The original Cheltenham Oldstyle was designed by Bertram Grosvenor Goodhue for and in collaboration with Ingalls Kimball of the Cheltenham Press in New York. Morris Benton handled production of this face at ATF in about 1901; some historians say 1903. Someone, probably Benton, did considerable modification of the original drawings before the design was ready for use. As its success developed, it was natural that variations should be added. Thus in 1904 Morris Benton designed Cheltenham Bold and Italic; in 1905 Cheltenham Bold Condensed; 1906 Bold Condensed Italic, Bold Extended, Bold Extra Condensed. At this time he also created Cheltenham Wide by drawing a new lowercase alphabet to go with the caps of Cheltenham Oldstyle.

More than a dozen other variations came from his drawing board in the following half-dozen years, to make Cheltenham one of the most extensive and successful typefaces of all time. It has become a basic American design, which has gone through perennial revivals without ever really being dead.

Between 1907-1913 Benton added these versions to the Cheltenham family:

7 Bold Outline
1907 Inline
1907 Inline Extended
1907 Inline Extra Condensed
1909 Medium
1909 Medium Italic
1909 Oldstyle Condensed
1911 Extrabold
1912 Bold Shaded
1912 Bold Italic Shaded
1912 Extrabold Shaded
1913 Medium Expanded
1913 Medium Condensed

Other foundries and typesetting machine manufacturers developed their Cheltenham families. Ludlow brought out Cheltenham Cursive caps that were much more elaborate than the foundry italics but usable with the same lowercase letters. Linotype and Monotype Cheltenhams appeared. The Intertype version was known as Cheltonian. In England the face was called Gloucester or Winchester; in Germany, Sorbonne; in Italy, Bodonia. For the first three decades of the century Cheltenham was one of the world's most popular faces.

At the turn of the century Cheltenham became the first extensive family of metal types. Today, with the completion of the 19 ITC versions, it is one of the largest families available for photographic and electronic typesetting.

If some metal type designs required thickening to achieve the same appearance when photoset and offset printed as they once had when cast in metal and printed by letterpress, Cheltenham seems to have anticipated today's technologies; it avoided the very thin strokes of many typefaces of its era yet kept enough difference between light and heavy strokes to avoid monotony.

Tony Stan's ITC Cheltenham features the large x-height and exquisite letterfit demanded today. It avoids the alternate lowercase "r" which was so misused. Designed for use only at the ends of words, it was often found intruding awkwardly between letters. Stan retains the distinctive extended thick stroke of the capital A and the extended bottom right curve of the G.

The extensive ITC Cheltenham family aims to meet the demands of those designers who like to design "in family." To achieve emphasis and set both text and display material within one type family. It is also old enough, and off the stage long enough, to be new and fresh once more. This ITC Cheltenham is a rare blend of fashion and utility, distinction and readability. It is truly a workhorse with style.

On the following pages U&lc presents a collection of typographic quotations taken from Hermann Zapf's classic masterpiece. *Manuale Typographicum*. Each statement has been redesigned by Herb Lubalin using a different weight and style of the ITC Cheltenham family. This experimental typographic exercise has been especially prepared to show the broad versatility of this newly redesigned typeface.

ALPHONSE DE LAMARTINE

LETTERS ARE SYMBOLS WHICH TURN MATTER INTO SPIRIT.

Whence did the wondrous, mystic art arise of painting speech, and speaking to the eyes? That we, by tracing magic lines are taught how to embody, and to colour thought?

Architecture began like all scripts. First there was the alphabet. A stone was laid and that was a letter, and each letter was a hieroglyph, and on each hieroglyph there rested a group of ideas, like the capital on a column. Thus, until Gutenberg architecture is the chief and universal "writing." This granite book, begun in the East, continued by the Greeks and Romans—its last page was written by the Middle Ages. Until the fifteenth century, architecture was the great exponent and recorder of mankind.

In the 15th century everything changed. Human thought discovered a means of perpetuating itself which was not only more lasting and resilient than architecture, but also simpler and more straightforward. Architecture is superseded. The stone letters of Orpheus have been succeeded by the leaden ones of Gutenberg. The book will destroy the edifice. The invention of printing is the greatest event in history. It is the fundamental revolution. Under the printing form, thought becomes more imperishable than ever; it is volatile, elusive and indestructible. It mingles with the very air. Thought derives new life from this concrete form. It passes from a lifespan into immortality. One can destroy something concrete, but who can eradicate what is omnipresent? VICTOR HUGO

After the basic necessities of life there is nothing more precious than books. The art of typography which produces them thus renders countless vital services to society. It serves to instruct, to spread progress in the sciences and arts, to nourish and cultivate the mind and elevate the spirit; the duty of typography is to be the agent and general interpreter of wisdom and truth—in short, it portrays the human spirit. One might therefore call it, above all others, the art of arts and the science of sciences. PIERRE SIMON FOURNIER

I am type!

Of my earliest ancestry neither history nor relics remain. The wedge-shaped symbols impressed in plastic clay by Babylonian builders in the dim past, fore-shadowed me, even foretold me through the hieroglyphs of the ancient Egyptians, descended the beautiful rolls of lettering of the medieval scribes. I was in the making. With the golden vision of the ingenious Gutenberg, who first applied the principle of casting me in metal, the gods and art of printing with movable types was born. Cold, rigid, and implacable I may be yet the first impress of my face brought the Living Word to countless thousands. I bring into the light of day the precious stores of knowledge and wisdom long hidden in the grave of ignorance. I coin for you the enchanting tale, the philosopher's moralizing, and the poet's phantasies. I enable you to exchange the irksome hours that come at times to everyone, for sweet and happy hours with books—golden urns filled with all the manna of the past. To books I present to you a notice of the eternal mind caught in its progress. It is me, the world stamped in its ascent, and preserved forever in type. Through me, Socrates and Plato, Chaucer and the Lords, become your faithful friends who cheer and counsel you. I am type! Of my body the leaden carry that conquers the world.

I am type!

FREDERIC GOUDY

No other art is more justified than typography in looking ahead to future centuries, for the creations of typography benefit coming generations as much as present times. CHARLES ENSCHEDÉ

Have you noticed how picturesque the letter Y is & how innumerable its meanings are? The tree is a Y, the junction of two roads forms a Y, two converging rivers, a donkey's head & that of an ox, the glass with its stem, the lily on its stalk & the beggar lifting his arms are a Y. This observation can be extended to everything that constitutes the elements of the various letters devised by man. Whatever there is in the demotic language has been instilled in to it by the hieratic language. Hieroglyphics are the root of letters. All characters were originally signs & all signs were once images. Human society, the world, man in his entirety is in the alphabet. Masonry, astronomy, philosophy, all the sciences start here, imperceptible but real, & it must be so. The alphabet is a source.

A is the roof with its rafters and traverse-beam, the arch, or it is like two friends who embrace and shake hands. D is the back, and B is also a second D, that is a "double back"—the hump. C is the crescent, is the moon, E is the foundation, the pillar and the roof—all architecture contained in a single letter. F is the gallows, the fork, G is the horn, H is the facade of a building with its two towers, I is the war-machine that throws projectiles, J is the plough, the horn of plenty. K signifies one of the basic laws of geometry: (the angle of reflection is equal to the angle of incidence), L is the leg and the foot. M is the mountain, or the camp within its tents, N is the door, closed with a cross-bar, O is the sun, P is the porter carrying a burden, Q is the croup and the tail. R signifies rest, the porter leaning on his stick, S is the snake, T is the hammer, U is the urn, V is the vase (that is why U and V are often confused), I have already said what Y signifies. X signifies crossed swords, combat; who will be victor? Nobody knows—that is why philosophers used "X" to signify fate, and the mathematicians took it for the unknown. Z is the lightning—is God. So, first comes the house of man, and its construction; church; war, harvest, geometry; the mountain, nomadic life and seclusion; life, astronomy, toil and rest; the horse and the snake; the hammer and the urn which—turned over and struck—makes a bell, trumpets, roads; and finally destiny and God: This is what the alphabet signifies. VICTOR HUGO

U&lc. INTERNATIONAL

Aa Bb Cc Dd Ee Ff Gg Hh Ii Jj Kk Ll Mm Nn Oo Pp · Qq Rr Ss Tt Uu Vv Ww Xx Yy Zz 1234567890 & Æ Œ S $ ¢ £ % !? ( ) [ ]

UPPER AND LOWER CASE THE INTERNATIONAL JOURNAL OF TYPOGRAPHICS · PUBLISHED BY INTERNATIONAL TYPEFACE CORPORATION. VOLUME TWO, NUMBER FOUR, DEC. 1978

MY FAVORITE 6 LETTER WORD

SCARAB

Blissymbols for the Handicapped: A Manner of Speaking

196. My Favorite 6 Letter Word
Herb Lubalin demonstrates the practical and aesthetic effectiveness of ITC Benguiat Condensed, designed by his friend and some-time business associate, Ed Benguiat. Date: December 1978.

197, 198. A Manner of Speaking
Lengthy and detailed analysis of Charles Bliss's 'symbolic language system', designed to help physically disabled adults and children to read.

199. Typomatic
As well as extensive features, *U&lc* carried advertising for the international typesetting industry. This ad announces the arrival of a new typeface: Chwast Buffalo. It features a photograph of Chwast exuding movie-star glamour.

200—203. Double-page spreads
Fig.200 is a continuation of Lubalin's experiments with ITC Benguiat Condensed. Figs.201 and 202 reveal Lubalin's antiquarian streak; here we see some of William Nicholson's 1897 *Almanac of Twelve Sports*. An editorial note (most likely by Lubalin) comments: 'While other artists of the Art Nouveau era were producing veritable colour charts, William Nicholson demonstrated that less can be more.' Fig.203 features a Lubalin-esque verbal and graphic ragbag of typefaces, anecdotes, whimsical information and illustration.

(to) doubt	(to) fly	(to) hold	(to) lift	(to) pray	(to) run	(to) start, begin	(to) wash, bathe	arm	blackboard	business	clock	current events	enclosure	food	glove	house	letter
(to) dream	(to) fold	(to) hope	(to) like	(to) prepare	(to) say, tell	(to) subtract, take away	(to) win	attack	blanket	buttocks	cloth	curtain	energy	foot	glue	ice	life
(to) dress	(to) follow	(to) hug	(to) live	(to) pretend	(to) search	(to) surprise	(to) wish	back	Blissymbol	button	clothing	desk	environment	forest	God	idea	light
(to) drink	(to) force	(to) hurt, feel pain	(to) lose	(to) promise	(to) see	(to) swallow	(to) work	badge	Blissymbol part	cabin	cloud	dessert	example	freedom	gross	insect	lightning
(to) drive (car)	(to) forget	(to) increase	(to) love	(to) protect	(to) seem	(to) swim	(to) write	blood	cake	coat, sweater	dining room	eye	fruit	guilt	island	limits	
(to) dry	(to) get, receive	(to) injure	(to) make	(to) protest	(to) sell	(to) taste	(to) yell	bandage	board	camera	coffee	discussion	eyeglasses	fruit juice	gun	jet plane	line
(to) eat	(to) give	(to) invent	(to) marry	(to) pull	(to) send	(to) teach	thing indicator	bank	boat, ship	car, vehicle	colour	doll	face	frustration	gym	joint	linear thing
(to) end, stop	(to) glue, stick	(to) joke	(to) mean	(to) push	(to) shake	(to) tease	ability	bath, basin	body	cards	container	drawer	fact	fuel	hair	key	lips
(to) enjoy	(to) go, leave	(to) jump	(to) measure	(to) put	(to) share	(to) think	accessory	bathroom	bone	castle	corner	dress	factory	furniture	hamburger	kind, type	
(to) equal	(to) govern	(to) keep, save	(to) meet	(to) rain	(to) shave	(to) touch	action	beach	book	cereal, grain	coat	drink	farm	garage	hand	kitchen	loss
(to) exercise	(to) grow	(to) kick	(to) read	(to) sing	(to) travel	advice	beard	bottle	chair	couch	dump truck	fastener	garbage	handle, switch	knee	machine	
(to) fall	(to) guess	(to) kiss	(to) mix	(to) regret	(to) sit	(to) try	air	bed	bottom	cheese	country, close	ear	feeling	garden	hat	knife	magazine
(to) fasten, join	(to) hang	(to) kneel	(to) move	(to) remember	(to) sleep	(to) turn	airplane	bedroom	bowel movement	chemical product	country(side)	earth	finger	gas	head	knowledge	map
(to) feel	(to) happen	(to) know	(to) multiply	(to) repeat, copy	(to) smell	(to) turn on	alcoholic drink	behaviour	brain	cheryl	crane	east	fire	gasoline	heart	lake	material
(to) fight	(to) hate	(to) laugh	must	(to) request	(to) smile	(to) understand	alphabet	belief	bread	chest of drawers	crayon	edge	fire truck	gathering	hill	lamp, electric light	meal
(to) fill	(to) have	(to) lead, guide	(to) need	(to) resent	(to) smoke	(to) use	ambulance	bell	chin	creation, nature	effort	fish	generalization	hip	language	meaning	
(to) find	(to) hear	(to) learn	(to) open	(to) rest	(to) sneeze	animal	berry	bridge	church, temple	cross	egg	flag	genitals	hobby	leaf	meat	
(to) finish	(to) help	(to) lend	(to) own	(to) return	(to) solve	(to) wait	anniversary	bicycle	broom	circle	elbow	flavouring	gift	hole	leafy vegetable	medicine	
(to) fix, repair	(to) hide	(to) let, allow	(to) play	(to) ride	(to) spin	(to) work, go	answer	bird	brush	city	crutches	electricity	flour	glass	home	leg	metal
(to) floor	(to) hit	(to) lie down	(to) practice	(to) rub	(to) stand	apartment	bath	bus	classroom	cupboard	elevator	flower	glass	hospital	legs and feet	middle	

7

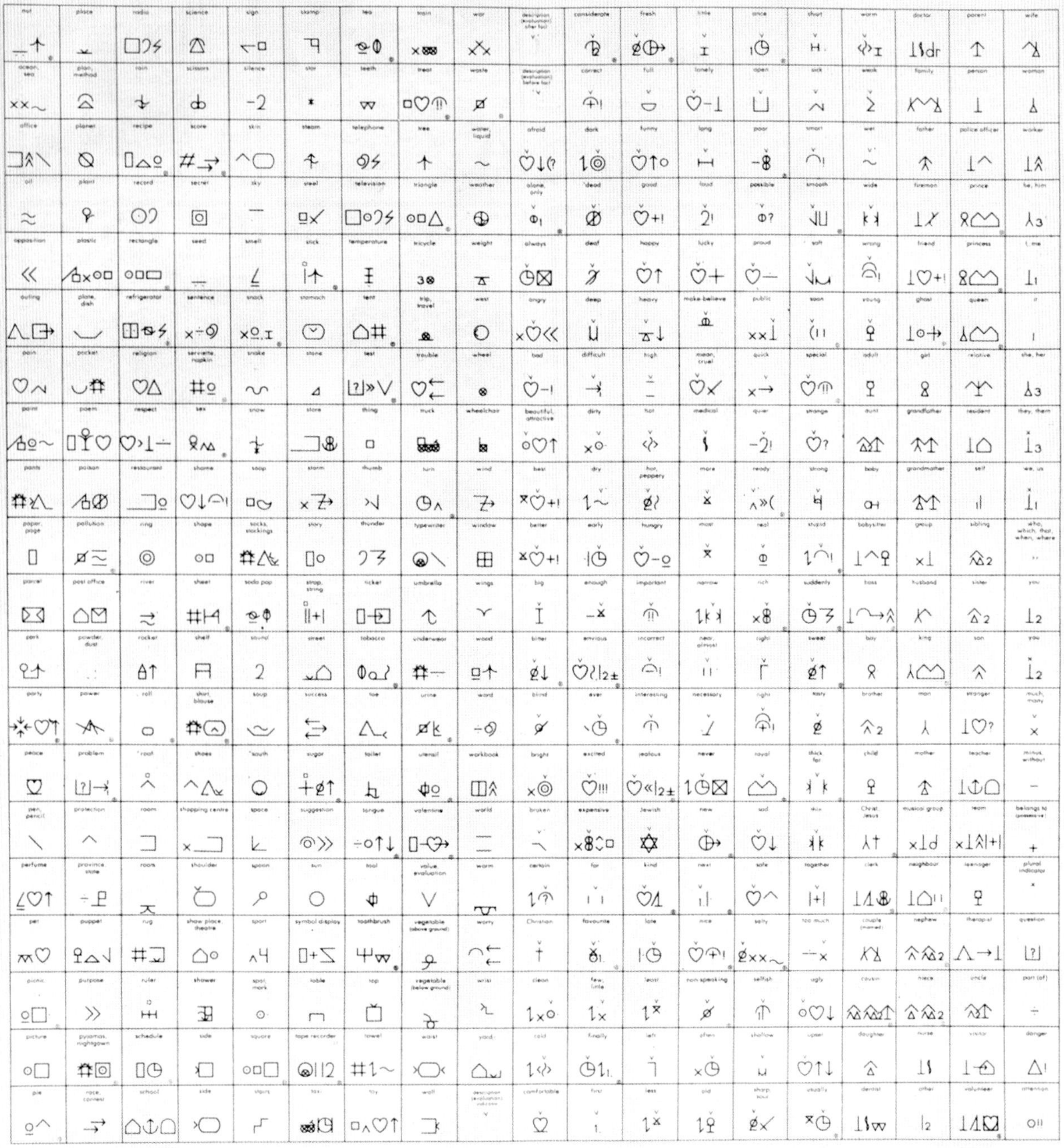
nut
place
radio
science
sign
stamp
tea
train
war
description (evaluation) after fact
considerate
fresh
little
once
short
warm
doctor
parent
wife
ocean, sea
plan, method
rain
scissors
silence
star
teeth
treat
waste
description (evaluation) before fact
correct
full
lonely
open
sick
weak
family
person
woman
office
planet
recipe
score
skin
steam
telephone
tree
water, liquid
afraid
dark
funny
long
poor
smart
wet
father
police officer
worker
oil
plant
record
secret
sky
steel
television
triangle
weather
alone, only
dead
good
loud
possible
smooth
wide
fireman
prince
he, him
opposition
plastic
rectangle
seed
smell
stick
temperature
tricycle
weight
always
deaf
happy
lucky
proud
soft
wrong
friend
princess
I, me
outing
plate, dish
refrigerator
sentence
snack
stomach
tent
trip, travel
west
angry
deep
heavy
make-believe
public
soon
young
ghost
queen
it
pain
pocket
religion
serviette, napkin
snake
stone
test
trouble
wheel
bad
difficult
high
mean, cruel
quick
special
adult
girl
relative
she, her
paint
poem
respect
sex
snow
store
thing
truck
wheelchair
beautiful, attractive
dirty
hot
medical
quiet
strange
aunt
grandfather
resident
they, them
pants
poison
restaurant
shame
soap
storm
thumb
turn
wind
best
dry
hot, peppery
more
ready
strong
baby
grandmother
self
we, us
paper, page
pollution
ring
shape
socks, stockings
story
thunder
typewriter
window
better
early
hungry
most
real
stupid
babysitter
group
sibling
who, which, that, when, where
parcel
post office
river
sheet
soda pop
strap, string
ticket
umbrella
wings
big
enough
important
narrow
rich
suddenly
boss
husband
sister
you
park
powder, dust
rocket
shelf
sound
street
tobacco
underwear
wood
bitter
envious
incorrect
near, almost
right
sweet
boy
king
son
you
party
power
roll
shirt, blouse
soup
success
toe
urine
word
blind
ever
interesting
necessary
right
tasty
brother
man
stranger
much, many
peace
problem
roof
shoes
south
sugar
toilet
utensil
workbook
bright
excited
jealous
never
royal
thick, fat
child
mother
teacher
minus, without
pen, pencil
protection
room
shopping centre
space
suggestion
tongue
valentine
world
broken
expensive
Jewish
new
sad
thin
Christ, Jesus
musical group
team
belongs to (possessive)
perfume
province, state
roots
shoulder
spoon
sun
tool
value, evaluation
worm
certain
far
kind
next
safe
together
clerk
neighbour
teenager
plural indicator
pet
puppet
rug
show place, theatre
sport
symbol display
toothbrush
vegetable (above ground)
worry
Christian
favourite
late
nice
salty
too much
couple (married)
nephew
therapist
question
picnic
purpose
ruler
shower
spot, mark
table
top
vegetable (below ground)
wrist
clean
few, little
least
non speaking
selfish
ugly
cousin
niece
uncle
part (of)
picture
pyjamas, nightgown
schedule
side
square
tape recorder
towel
waist
yard
cold
finally
left
often
shallow
upset
daughter
nurse
visitor
danger
pie
race, contest
school
side
stairs
taxi
toy
wall
comfortable
first
less
old
sharp, sour
usually
dentist
other
volunteer
attention

personality

Typefaces are like human faces; no two are quite alike. Each human face reflects a unique personality; each typeface reflects a unique **typersonality**, shaped by the skill, temperament, and times of the artist who designed it.

Mergenthaler, Linotype, Stempel, Haas now adds to its collection three of the most beautiful, exciting, and timely **typersonalities**, Chwast Buffalo, ITC Benguiat Condensed and Mergenthaler New Baskerville. These new families are additions to the most comprehensive collection of authentic **typersonalities**, the library that sets the standard.

To complete each **typersonality**, we pioneered programmed typography. Our advanced typographic program, ATP 1/54, automatically kerns, tucking one letter closer to or beneath another with any of 432 letter combinations. Automatically sets tight, tighter, or tightest fittings, whichever you prefer. Automatically hangs punctuation for crisp, clean columns.

Mergenthaler Linotype Company
Mergenthaler Drive
Plainview, NY 11803
USA

Mergenthaler, Linotype, Stempel, Haas

Chwast Buffalo Black

The Mergenthaler Linotype Company invited Seymour Chwast to design a face for the library.

Alan Fern, Director for Special Collections, Library of Congress, says of Chwast:

"One of the founders of the Push Pin Studios in New York City, and thus one of the most admired, envied, and imitated graphic designers in the United States, Chwast has both learned to live with the demands of his profession and had a strong influence on it."

"Chwast reacts to letters as he does to other visual objects, in terms of delight in their outlines and sensitivity to their shapes."

Chwast Buffalo Black is the result. A new display series, combines the originality of the designer with the discipline of the Mergenthaler Letter Design Office. This refinements of the ATP 1/54 program provide opportunities for type specifiers to play with kerning and the letterspacing of the Chwast letters to suit their own creative taste.

Chwast Buffalo

CEFGHI
cfhijklmnr

e

Seymour Chwast posing at a 45° angle in order to fit into our format

47

199

389

DOGMA

DOGME GLAUBENSSATZ

U&lc International—
Zusammenfassung
des Textes
in deutsch

AN OLD STYLE HAPPY NEW YEAR!

It's that time of year when we pause to wish our readers the very happiest of holidays. This year we thought we'd present our readers—not one card, but twelve in the form of a calendar. And, the world having gone sports crazy of late, what more fitting subject for our greeting than a sports calendar, each month featuring a different sport?

In the world of words, sports exerts upon our language an influence that is far more flamboyant than that of other fields. It is more of a creator, and its innovations are more picturesque and carry a greater imitation appeal. Few people are fully aware how many of the words and expressions of our common colloquial language stem from sports. To *play ball* comes from baseball, **sudden death** from football, **crestfallen** from cock-fighting, **neck and neck** from horse racing, **straight from the shoulder**, prize fighting; **stymied** comes from golf, **caught napping** from baseball, **behind the eight ball** from billiards, and so on.

An Almanac
of twelve Sports
By William Nicholson

1979.

Hunting.   Coursing.

January.   February.

Racing.   Boating.

March.   April.

Top spread (pages 12–13)

Fishing. Cricket.
May. June.
Archery. Coaching.
July. August.

It is in the world of illustration, however, that a mere glance gives us an entire picture that would take a myriad of words to duplicate—as William Nicholson's "Almanac of Twelve Sports" so graphically points out. The Almanac, drawn in 1897, revolutionized the course of graphic art in the nineties. Originally brought out by William Heinemann, the posters were first drawn with accompanying verses by Rudyard Kipling and, properly, made quite a stir in their day. Printed at the Scolar Press, Ilkley, Yorkshire, they were published in the United States by Alan Wofsy Fine Arts of San Francisco and are reproduced here courtesy of the copyright holder, Elizabeth Banks.

Running the gamut from racing to archery to boxing, Nicholson's backgrounds are composed of earth tones and black with a most purposefully restrained use of color. While other artists of the Art Nouveau era were producing veritable color charts, William Nicholson demonstrated that less can be more.

Enjoy. And have a happy New Year.

Shooting. Golf.
September. October.

Boxing. Skating.
November. December.

Bottom spread (pages 24–25)

Something For Everybody From U&lc

Gesundheitswiederherstellungsmittelzusammenmischungsverhältniskundiger

Wie bitte?

What is the most widely reproduced and distributed painting in the world? The 'Mona Lisa'? No. The 'Last Supper'? Uh-uh. The single most widely reproduced and distributed painting in history is none other than 'The Four Freedoms' by Norman Rockwell.

A spoonerism is an accidental sound transposition. Example: A TV cooking expert started her recipe for vichyssoise with: "First you take a leek..."

THE ELEPHANT IS THE ONLY ANIMAL WITH FOUR KNEES.

No woman ever appeared completely nude on the stage before the 1912 Folies-Bergere in Paris.

The most commonly used word in English conversation is "I".

The word "queue" is the only word in our language that is still pronounced the same way when the last four letters are removed.

What does mean mean?
Well, it means mean:
  mean it.
It means mean:
'I mean you're a mean man.'
It means mean:
'I mean you're a mean man of mean estate.'
And it means mean:
'I mean you're a mean man of mean estate who hews to the golden mean'.

A story of "O".
Giotto was a big ugly Tuscan farmer who dabbled in painting. Pope Boniface VIII wanted to employ the greatest artist in Italy to work on St. Peter's. Nobody in Rome had ever heard of Giotto, but his local neighbors thought he was pretty good and told the papal envoy as much. The latter paid a call on Giotto. "Let's have a sample of your work," he said patronizingly. Giotto laughed, dipped his brush in a bucket of red paint, and drew a circle. The papal messenger thought he was kidding, but Giotto told him that was it. Typical artist. No more samples.

When the Pope looked at the circle, he said: "Get that man; anyone who can draw a perfect circle freehand like that is a genius." That started Giotto on the road to immortality.

A honeybee can carry a burden 300 times its own body weight. To equal this extraordinary feat, a 250-pound man would have to carry a 35-ton truck on his back.

Page	Typeface	Designer
25	Informal Gothic	Tom Holmquaworth USA
26	Weidd	Fredrich Peter, Canada
27	Amou	Walter J. Ospthein, Switzerland
28	Amelia	Stanley Davis, USA
29	Vivo	Raphael Boguslav, USA
30	Domino Antiqua	Karl-Heinz Donning, Germany
31	Wolf Antiqua	Hans-Jürgen Wolf, Germany
32	Arabescu Margaret	Zoltan Nagy, Hungary

204

Aa Bb Cc Dd Ee Ff Gg Hh Ii Jj Kk Ll Mm Nn Oo Pp Qq Rr Ss Tt Uu Vv Ww Xx Yy Zz 1234567890 & ÆŒ $¢ £%!?()[]

UPPER AND LOWER CASE, THE INTERNATIONAL JOURNAL OF TYPOGRAPHICS

PUBLISHED BY INTERNATIONAL TYPEFACE CORPORATION, VOLUME THREE, NUMBER ONE, MARCH 1979

Jim Spanfeller's Fantastic Airplane

What has a fabulous drawing of a fabulous airplane got to do with the state of the typographic arts? The answer is fairly simple. In recent issues of U&lc we have attempted to create exciting formats, reproduced in color, to display as effectively as we know how, our latest featured typefaces. The devices we have employed stray considerably from the purely typographic. In one case we resurrected some old posters to show how they could look—and possibly be improved—with the use of contemporary ITC typefaces. Our issue on ITC Cheltenham included significant commentary on typography by famous literary figures. Our attempt there was to indicate that some very important people, not associated with letterforms, had written astutely on the subject. At the same time we tried to show that good writing and good typography are highly synergistic. Our last issue, featuring the ITC Benguiat Condensed series, sent us scurrying through every page of an unabridged dictionary to select what we thought were the eight most exciting looking words in the English language when set in ITC Benguiat Condensed. All of which brings us back to the answer to the long forgotten question at the beginning of this article.

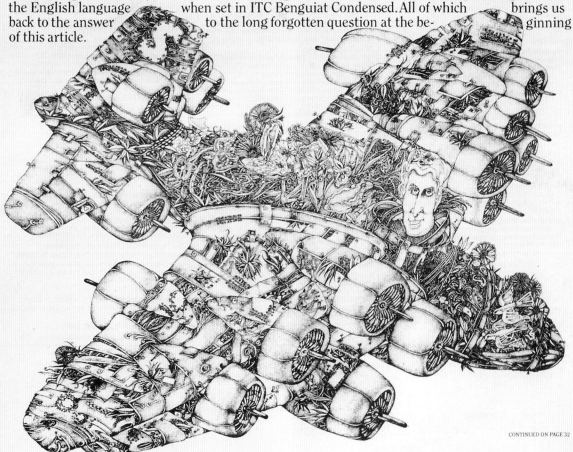

CONTINUED ON PAGE 32

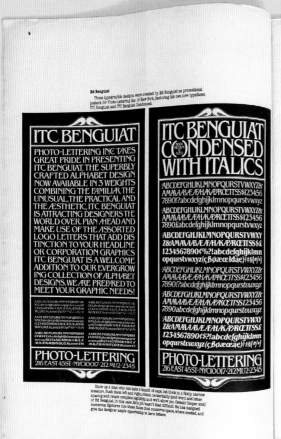

204. Jim Spanfeller's Fantastic ...

This edition of *U&lc* features a tale about a 'universe-wide search for happiness'. Jim Spanfeller, a prolific and regular contributor to Lubalin's various editorial projects, illustrates the story, which is written by Spanfeller's son, Jim Jr. Lubalin sets the tale in ITC Clearface. Largely dormant until revived by ITC, it was originally designed in 1907 by Morris Fuller Benton for the American Type Founders Company. Victor Caruso redrew it with small, almost slab, serifs, and the customary ITC large x-height and minimal stroke contrast. Date: March 1979.

205, 206. Spreads

Lubalin the editor at his most back-slapping and generous. He devotes four pages to eulogizing the work of five colleagues (and his own work). Fig.205 (left-hand page) finds him giving space to his friend Ed Benguiat, while on the opposite page he sings the praises of partners Ernie Smith and Alan Peckolick. Fig.206 (left-hand page) is reserved for some of his own work, which sits opposite a page devoted to the typography of Tony Di Spigna and Bob Farber ('a principal in Lubalin Burns & Co. Inc.')

207—210. Spreads

Fig.207 features two alphabets (left-hand page) submitted to *U&lc* by readers; (top) alphabet by Carla Sigurdson, an illustrator; (beneath) alphabets by Morris Zaslavsky, graphic designer and teacher. The right-hand page is devoted to a feature on ITC Clearface with italics. Fig.208 (left-hand page) shows the end of the story by illustrator Jim Spanfeller and his son, and the beginning (right-hand page) of a feature on Alpha Series by Robert Sellner. Lubalin writes: 'Sellner, who is chairman of the fine arts at Dwight Morrow High School, Englewood, NJ, has achieved something that, in our opinion, neither Robert Indiana nor Jasper Johns has been able to do. He's made art out of graphic symbols without the need of a gilt-edged frame.' Fig.210 shows a selection of work from the Society of Scribes' 1979 Engagement Calendar. Lubalin had a lifelong interest in calligraphy.

6

Herb Lubalin

Like Ed Benguiat, Herb Lubalin uses Oswald Cooper's early 20th century designs as a source of inspiration for squaring up type. Lou Dorfsman of CBS once said, "Give Herb any piece of copy, short or long, large or small, and he'll square it up effectively without batting an eyelash." The Art Kane announcement does just this by taking advantage of the myriad of possibilities for design exploration offered in ITC Avant Garde Gothic Extra Light.

Herb Lubalin's special design technique, which he calls expressive typography, turns typographics into story-telling illustrations as evident in "The Turned-On Crisis," a short animated film for PBS, the Public Broadcasting Service, using ITC Avant Garde Gothic Medium to tell the tale of drug addiction in the U.S.A. "The Missing Link" (a rejected film title—thus the client shall remain nameless), set in ITC Machine Bold, tells the story through the device of omitting a couple of "I"s.

Fanny Hill, set in an exaggerated ITC Benguiat, was designed for the Erotic Art Book

Society and published by Ralph Ginzburg. The fancy swashes were Lubalin's way of establishing a 19th century quality with a 20th century typeface. And the spread from the Art Directors Club Annual was set in ITC American Typewriter. This versatile typeface can be set in extremely wide measures (in this case, 48 picas) and still retain a high degree of legibility.

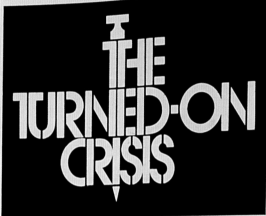

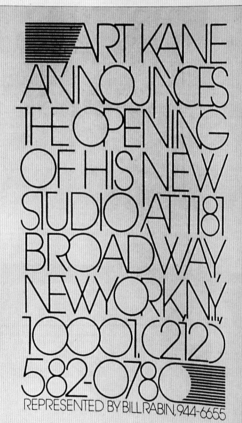

Tony DiSpigna

Tony DiSpigna fits right into the mold of Herb Lubalin Associates. As you can see, his is a dedication to fine typography more as a decorative medium than an illustrative one.

Below left, his design for ABC Television is an imaginative adaptation of ITC Korinna Heavy in 3 dimensions. Mark Johnson was the art director. The Lenali poster was designed for Tony's cousin in Naples, Italy, who owns a beauty boutique. It effectively combines ITC Bernase with ITC Serif Gothic. Note particularly the excellent spacing, kerning and use of ligatures in the ITC Serif Gothic. The Citroën logo, in ITC Machine Bold, displays the clever use of their trademark in the "T." This design was done for Lubalin, Delpire, in Paris.

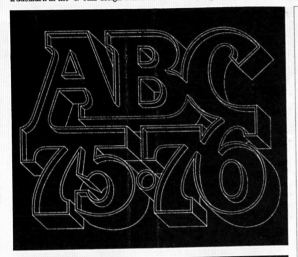

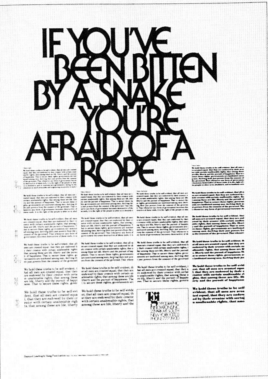

Bob Farber

Bob Farber, a principal in Lubalin, Burns & Co. Inc., and ITC, designed the posters above as promotions for TGI, Typographic Innovations, Inc., New York. The comments about Alan Peckolick's use of ITC Serif Gothic apply as well to Bob Farber, only more so. Bob has used ITC Serif Gothic to create a maximum of impact sacrificing only a minimum of legibility.

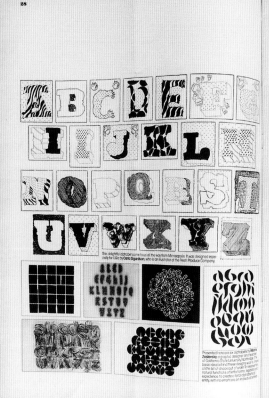

What's New From ITC

ITC Clearface Regular, Bold, Heavy and Black with Italics, and ITC Clearface Outline, Outline Shadow and Contour are new typefaces from ITC. Only licensed ITC Subscribers are authorized to reproduce, manufacture, and offer for sale these and all other ITC typefaces shown in this issue. This license mark is your guarantee of authenticity.

These new typefaces will be available to the public on or after April 15, 1979 depending on each manufacturer's release schedule.

ITC CLEARFACE WITH ITALICS

REGULAR
BOLD
HEAVY
BLACK
OUTLINE
CONTOUR
& OUTLINE
SHADOW

Clearface, as its name implies, is a highly utilitarian type, yet the full potential of its utility has long remained dormant. When originally designed by Morris Fuller Benton for the American Type Founders Company in 1907, it was fashioned primarily for handset display, and the subtle refinements needed to adapt it to text mass have been long neglected. From time to time efforts to redesign Clearface have been made, but to date no complete family had emerged with the enrichment of the original flavor. **In 1978, under license from American Type Founders Company** to adapt the original designs for use in contemporary typography, ITC undertook to devote the care and in-depth study that the letterforms of this beautiful typeface truly deserve. To achieve this, ITC commissioned Victor Caruso, Alphabet Designer with Photo-Lettering Inc., to develop a full family of four weights with rigorous italics. The italics have a merit of their own and reflect the same meticulous development as the uprights. **Here, in ITC Clearface,** is a truly definitive interpretation of Clearface, made to stand the test of time.

ITC CLEARFACE REGULAR

abcdefghijklmnopqrstuvwxyz
ABCDEFGHIJKLMNOPQRSTUVWXYZ
1234567890$$¢£%ÀÇĐĚŁØÆ̃ĈĚß
açdęłøäëœefi(:;,.!¡?:·-""/#*)[†§«»1234567890]

ITC CLEARFACE REGULAR ITALIC

abcdefghijklmnopqrstuvwxyz
ABCDEFGHIJKLMNOPQRSTUVWXYZ
1234567890&$$¢£%ÀÇĐĚŁØÆ̃ĈĚß
açdęłøäëœefi(:;,.!¡?:·-""/#)[†§«»1234567890]*

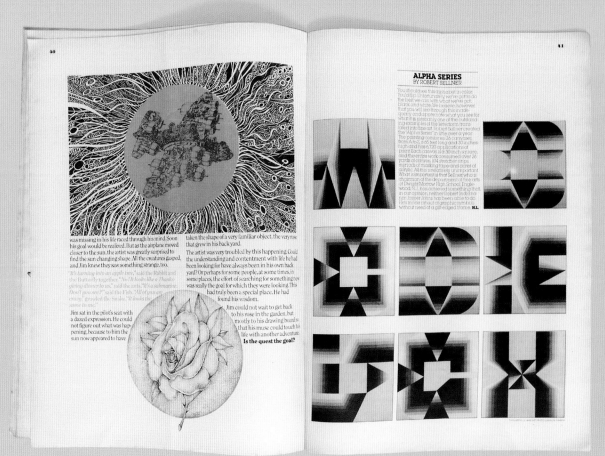

ALPHA SERIES
BY ROBERT SELLNER

U&lc.

INTERNATIONAL

Aa Bb Cc Dd Ee Ff Gg Hh Ii Jj Kk Ll Mm Nn Oo Pp   Qq Rr Ss Tt Uu Vv Ww Xx Yy Zz 1234567890&ÆŒ$¢£%!?()[]

UPPER AND LOWER CASE. THE INTERNATIONAL JOURNAL OF TYPOGRAPHICS   PUBLISHED BY INTERNATIONAL TYPEFACE CORPORATION, VOLUME THREE, NUMBER TWO, JUNE 1979

PETER BEARD'S DIARY

BY CAROL DIGRAPPA

I first saw the remains of Peter Beard's diaries in November 1977 at the International Center of Photography. Earlier that year, over twenty years of diaries had been destroyed in a fire that razed Beard's Montauk windmill residence. Only two books survived. The 1976 **Bicentennial Diary,** which was at Meriden Gravure on the night of the fire, hung on the walls in lithographs—a colorful and portentous frieze in a bright white room. **The Elephant Diary,** filled with photographs dating from 1971 to 1976, had been with Beard the night of the fire and now lay open in a black box in the center of the room. The casket also held the soggy pile of burned books—ashes, mold and all.

Marvin Israel designed the show of diaries and dying elephants (from Beard's book **The End of the Game**) as a conceptual installation. To give the viewer the feeling of African imbalance, photographs of starved elephants, disintegrating carcasses, and ravaged land were theatrically lighted in the dark. Elephant dung, animal skulls, stress boxes jammed with progress reports from Kenya Colony, and jungle sounds carried out the themes of over-population, stress and destruction of habitat.

The elephants stood out as a metaphor for men. In contrast to the rest of the museum, the diary room seemed modern and light—an embellishment of the theme. The pages overlapped on the wall in a detailed bas-relief which, like death itself, seduced and repelled simultaneously.

After seeing pictures of so many rotting carcasses, the diaries conjured up a dream of the primeval forest—of a dense chaos. On each page, a wild landscape of "piddling trivia and absurdities" grew like a fungus. Each image was woven into another, blending and layering arcane truths and media nonsense until open space seemed as rare as in the forest, as meaningful as silence. Almost as if the diaries had designed themselves, they reflected a strange order in a complex growth of visions.

CONTINUED ON PAGE 3

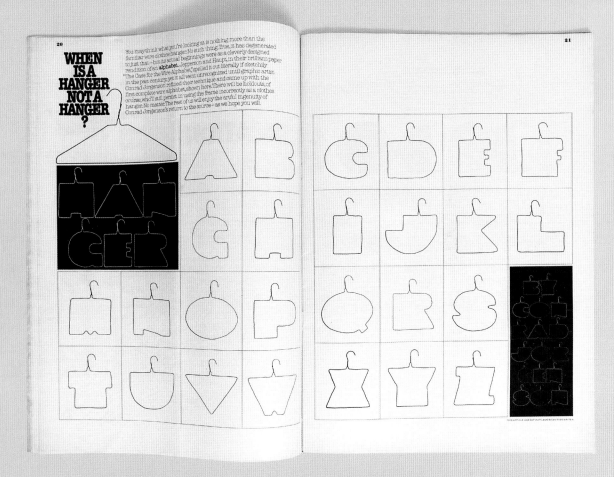

211. Peter Beard's Diary
Peter Beard is a celebrated photographer, best known for his portraits of Africa. Born in New York in 1938, he went to Yale, studying under Vincent Scully, Joseph Albers and Richard Lindner. During his travels in Africa he photographed and documented the demise of elephants and rhinos. Carol Digrappa writes about his extraordinary diaries: 'The crinkled edges are coated in blood which splashes across one page with a handprint. As the pages turn, the diary begins to resemble, a modern book of the dead.' Date: June 1979.

212. When is a Hanger not a Hanger
Lubalin's ongoing programme of publishing weird alphabets submitted by readers. This one, by Jepperson and Haupt, is made out of wire hangers. The text face is ITC American Typewriter.

213. A Collection of Characters
Brilliant literary caricatures by William D. Bramhall Jr., taken from the Literary Engagement Calendar, 1979. Lubalin uses ITC Clearface for the text.

214—217. Spreads
Fig.214 is an eclectic selection of graphic work submitted by readers. Figs.215 and 216 are from an eight-page 'attempt to show suggested uses for ITC Zapf Chancery in both display and text to help solve various graphic problems. Problems such as one finds in a wedding announcement; a diploma; a legal document; a restaurant menu; a bible page; a book jacket; a greeting card; cosmetic and other packages; and a corporate letterhead, etc., etc.' Fig.217. shows a photographic blow-up of the 'vanishing' (due to 1970s inflation) U.S. dollar bill.

212

A Collection of Characters from The Literary Engagement Calendar by William D. Bramhall, Jr.

The interaction of art and language and literature is a question that has long agitated academicians, causing them to divide into three more or less well-defined camps. Should art be viewed primarily as a visual activity; should language be viewed as strictly a speaking activity, and the written literary language be considered only ancillary to speech? Or should all three be equally important in the academician's consideration?

Take caricature, surely an art form in itself. And, properly illustrated, a form that is heard and read as well as seen. A year ago, we came across some extraordinary work by a young caricaturist named William Bramhall, Jr., and we've been anxious to show at least some of his efforts on the pages of U&lc. In the fall of '78, Bramhall's work first appeared publicly in an edition of The Literary Engagement Calendar, quickly selling out 15,000 copies for its publisher, The Brandywine Press, which distributes through E.P. Dutton.

A quick look at the illustrations on these pages will indicate why. From Bernard Shaw to Kafka to Oscar Wilde to Charles Dickens, Bramhall has subtly captured a particular

ALEXANDER POPE

HERMAN MELVILLE

T.S. ELIOT

GUSTAVE

VIRGINIA WOOLF

OSCAR WILDE

BRENDAN BEHAN

RALPH WALDO EMERSON

JOHN MILTON

EZRA POUND

ANDRÉ MALRAUX

G.B. SHAW

FRANZ KAFKA

CHARLES DICKENS

MARY SHELLEY

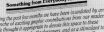

Something from Everybody for U&lc

During the past few months we have been inundated by an avalanche of exciting graphic contributions from our readers. We thought it appropriate to devote this space to these works as a showcase for the designers, and as a stimulant to all those who hesitate to send their stuff in. We will resume our illustrated letters in the next issue.

Lonnie Sue Johnson didn't supply us with a title for these illustrations, but we think they're an intriguing interpretation of the phases of the moon.

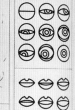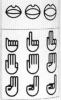

Robert Berguson, an Associate Professor at Louisiana Tech University, submitted these examples of his calligraphic painting which have been on exhibition at the Lauren Rogers Library and Museum of Art in Laurel, Mississippi. Berguson calls this calligraphy, which is highly reminiscent of Arabic, Bergo marks. His work has been described as an emotional, mental and physical arrangement of lines to create visual esthetics. They most certainly do.

These "Signs of Life" by Wolfgang Schmidt were sent to us by Pieter Brattinga of the Pratt Gallery in Amsterdam, Netherlands. They are a program of geometric letters and pictographs that describe human qualities and capacities.

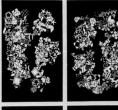 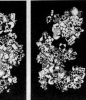

EDUCATION
TOURISME
PORTRAITS
CULTURE
FOU
CÉLÈBRES
BRUIT
CLANDSTIN
CLUB
BRICOLAGE
CUISINE
ENFANTS
BEAUTÉ

Félix Beltrán is undoubtedly one of Cuba's most gifted designers. He has studied extensively in the United States where he was granted scholarships at the New School and Pratt Institute. He also studied at the Art Students League. In appreciation for our sending him U&lc he has kindly reciprocated by sending us these fascinating graphic abstractions created from many of his previously designed symbols. Olé, Félix Beltrán.

Jean Larcher, a constant contributor to U&lc, has again sent us a sampling of his expressive typography. This work, created in French, certainly needs no translation.

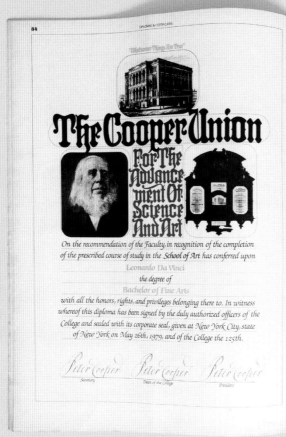

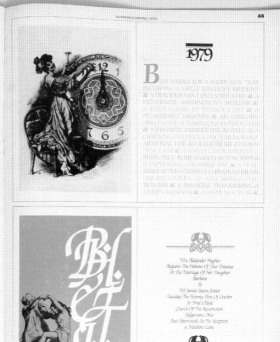

U&lc.

Aa Bb Cc Dd Ee Ff Gg Hh Ii Jj Kk Ll Mm Nn Oo Pp   Qq Rr Ss Tt Uu Vv Ww Xx Yy Zz 1234567890 & Æ Œ E $ ¢ £ % ! ? ( ) [ ]

UPPER AND LOWER CASE. THE INTERNATIONAL JOURNAL OF TYPOGRAPHICS   PUBLISHED BY INTERNATIONAL TYPEFACE CORPORATION, VOLUME SEVEN, NUMBER FOUR, DEC. 1980

5741 (1981)

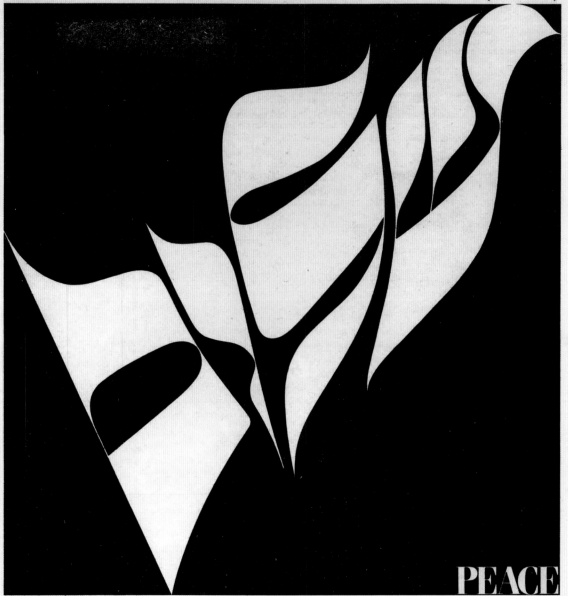

PEACE

218. Peace
One of the last editions of *U&lc* under
the editorship of Herb Lubalin. The front
cover shows another of Lubalin's recurring interests (and a formative influence
on his development of 'expressive
typography'): Hebrew letterforms. The
cover uses lettering by Stan Brod, a
typographer who had been 'designing
New Year and Hanukkah cards since
5715. That was the year, according to
the Hebrew calendar, that he and Ruth
were married and decided to send out
their own hand-crafted greeting cards.'
The date 5741 translates into 1981,
and the fluid Hebrew letterforms spell
out 'Peace'. Date: December 1980.

219. Oswaldo Miranda
Herb Lubalin spotted the Lubalin-esque
work of Brazilian designer Oswaldo
Miranda at an awards presentation of
the Society of Publication Designers,
and again at a Type Directors' Annual
Show. He notes: 'Out of a wealth of
excellent graphics, his work struck me
as extraordinary. I copied his address
from the back of one of his entries and
promptly wrote to him in Brazil, request-
ing some samples of his work for a
feature article in *U&lc*.' In another note,
he notes that Miranda's 'gifts are his
inventive mind, his willingness to take
risks and his masterful graphic skills.
But it is especially rare to find someone
who can dazzle you with design without
obfuscating meaning. The way he
manipulates his use of space, his sense
of scale, his black-and-white patterning
— all contrive to stop you dead in
your tracks.' It's clear that Lubalin
recognized a fellow traveller: he might
well have used these words to describe
his own work.

220. Have a Happy 5741 (1981)
A range of New Year greetings cards
by Stan Brod using Hebrew letterforms.
As the editorial introduction notes:
'Since graven images are taboo (see
Commandment #1), Hebrew greeting
cards present a special challenge
to designers. But they also have the
singular advantage of working with
letterforms that have an innate unity and
rhythm. There is potential for dynamic
contrasts ... for creating a squared-off,
bold modern look, or a voluptuous,
undulating exotic flavor. Mr. Brod has
enjoyed experimenting with different
proportions of line, weight and mood,
as is obvious from the work reproduced
on this double-spread.' This could be
a description of the typographic work
of Herb Lubalin. The links between
Lubalin's practice of typography and
Hebrew letterforms is discussed elsewhere (p.13). Stan Brod taught experimental typography at the Art Academy
of Cincinnati and Graphic Design at
the University of Cincinnati. He worked
for the firm of Lipson Assoc., Inc.

221—224. International Calligraphy ...
Spreads from an eight-page feature
showing art culled from a juried
exhibition of calligraphy sponsored
by the ITC Center. Lubalin's love of
calligraphy is evident in an introductory
comment: 'In the face of electronic and
mechanical "marvels," calligraphers
thrive!' Spreads include work by
Raphael Boguslav, one of the most
inventive contemporary calligraphers.
A graduate of the Cooper Union,
Boguslav worked for Lippincott &
Margulies for many years designing
logos for companies such as New
York Life, PPG and Chrysler.

225. Portraits of Italian Masters
When confronted with a series of portraits of the Italian Renaissance masters
by Stephen Alcorn, son of John Alcorn,
Herb Lubalin decided to devote eight
pages to them. 'We recently became
intrigued,' he notes, 'with a portfolio
of prints — 31 portraits of famous artists.
There was something about these prints
— not just the archaic look of them —
but the sentimental idea of them, like
somebody's collection of rock stars
or sports heroes, that completely dis-
armed us.' Stephen Alcorn had spent
time in Florence before returning to
New York to study fine art. Lubalin
partnered Alcorn's imposing portraits
with densely packed blocks of type
set in ITC Isbell; 'our new Roman
typeface designed by Dick Isbell and
Jerry Campbell.'

Stan Brod has been designing New Year and Hanukkah cards since 5715. That was the year, according to the Hebrew calendar, that he and Ruth were married and decided to send out their own hand-crafted greeting cards. With only thirty to fifty people on their list, it was not too taxing to block print and decorate their cards by hand. But as their list grew to over a hundred names, they had to go semi-commercial. They now print mechanically, and add the decorative touches—doilies, tissue streamers and legal seals by hand. Ruth is the conceptualist; Stan does the graphics. The whole family licks the stamps.

Since graven images are taboo (see Commandment#1), Hebrew greeting cards present a special challenge to designers. But they also have the singular advantage of working with letter forms that have an innate unity and rhythm. There is potential for dynamic contrasts… for creating a squared-off, bold modern look, or a voluptuous, undulating exotic flavor. Mr. Brod has enjoyed experimenting with different proportions of line, weight and mood, as is obvious from the work

reproduced on this double-spread.

Between holiday seasons, Stan has tackled graphic problems in academic and commercial circles. He has taught Experimental Typography at the Art Academy of Cincinnati, Graphic Design at the University of Cincinnati, and is currently with the firm of Lipson Assoc., Inc.

HAVE A HAPPY 5741 (1981)

Then it was that a miracle was wrought. The oil in the cruse burned eight days. / Babylonian Talmud, Shabbat 21 b.　　　Greetings from the Stan Brods

New Year Greetings from the Stan Brods

A Sweet Year

Ruth Stan Deb Dan and Mike Brod

Peace　Ruth, Stan, Debbie, Daniel and Michael Brod

Grant Peace　　　Ruth, Stan, Deb, Dan and Mike Brod

New Year Greetings

Stan, Ruth, Deb, Dan and Mike Brod

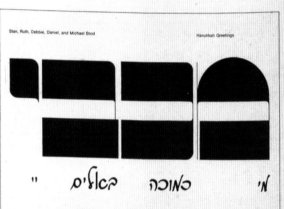

Stan, Ruth, Debbie, Daniel, and Michael Brod

Hanukkah Greetings

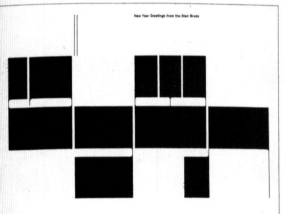

New Year Greetings from the Stan Brods

A Good Year

Stan, Ruth, Deb, Dan and Mike Brod

Greetings from Stan, Ruth, Debbie, Daniel and Michael Brod

THIS ARTICLE WAS SET IN ITC FENICE

28   29

PUT YOUR BEST FACE FORWARD

For the past few years, the city of Baltimore has been working on a major project: Operation Image-Lift. Aside from the actual physical rehabilitation of its waterfront and other historic areas, certain civic-minded organizations have been counting up and celebrating Baltimore's cultural contributions.

In that connection, the University of Maryland recently sponsored an Edgar Allan Poe Festival, to rediscover his work

and to honor Baltimore where his writing talent was first recognized and nurtured. Poe also died in Baltimore, and is buried on what-is-now University grounds.

The Eucalyptus Tree Studio sent us a copy of the brochure they contributed to the Festival. Each of the studio artists created and rendered his own graphic interpretation of Poe. They put their faces together with our faces* and turned out a jewel of a book. It is neat, compact—a scant 5"x 5"—but

what it lacks in physical dimensions, it makes up for in imagination and style.

Designed by Jerry Dadds; illustrated by Jerry Dadds, Gary Yealdhall, Richard Waldrep, Nancy Urbanski and Cameron Gerlach. Typesetting by The Composing Room, Inc.; Printing by Collins Lithographing and Printing Company, all of Baltimore, Md.

*The ITC typefaces chosen for the brochure are ITC Garamond Condensed and ITC Benguiat.

---

30   31

NUTS AND BOLTS

Aristotle dreamed of mechanical machines in the 4th century B.C. Only a hundred years later Archimedes thought that steam could be used to power them. And in the first century B.C., Hero of Alexandria wrote about the basics of machinery. But theory and technology didn't get together until the Middle Ages.

During the next 500 years automatons were the same on the outside, but new and improved on the inside. As our knowledge of technology grew, so did they. And they became more lifelike.

Then in 1921, they became better than human. At least they did in Karel Capek's play **R.U.R.** As a literary masterpiece it was a minor piece. But if all else was forgotten about the play one word wasn't. Robot. Capek took the name he gave his mechanical men from the Czech word 'robota.' Or drudgery. The robots were to do all the menial tasks humans dislike. Unfortunately, the robots didn't like doing them anymore than we did. And, since they could do them better, they decided they'd be better off without us.

From then on robots became our foes as well as friends. Only five years later, in 1926, Fritz Lang's movie 'Metropolis' created another evil robot, Maria. Star Wars fans might remember her as C-3PO's evil grandmother. In this case, bad blood (or bolts) didn't run in the family.

Today we're surrounded by robots. But we don't always see the forest for the transistors. Because today's robots don't look like us anymore. Yet they help build our cars. And they've been to Mars. They're as much a part of our lives as our pocket calculator. (Which, by today's definition, **is** a robot.)

The word 'robot' may have meant drudgery. But we think you'll find our puzzle no great chore. So turn on your memory bank and program yourself for fun.

Man vs. robot. It was the early 1930's. And Jack Dempsey was sure of the outcome. "I wouldn't be afraid of any robot or mechanical man. I could tear it to pieces, bolt by bolt, and scatter its brain wheels and cogs all over the canvas." But alas, as fate would have it, the fight never came a bout.

ACROSS   **DOWN**

ANSWERS ON PAGE 89

This is Number 13 in a series of Very Graphic Crossword Puzzles by Al McGinley and Lee Gardner.

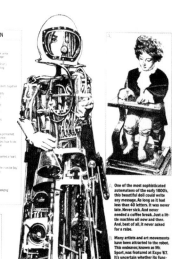

One of the most sophisticated automatons of the early 1800's, this beautiful doll could write any message. As long as it had less than 40 letters. It was never late. Never sick. And never needed a coffee break. Just a little machine oil now and then. And, best of all, it never asked for a raise.

Many artists and art movements have been attracted to the robot. This endeavor, known as Mr. Sport, was featured at Expo '67. It's uncertain whether its function was to cheer the home team or frighten the opponents. But it probably didn't matter too much, the game was called because of rain.

One of the first automatons (as they were called then) was designed in 1350. It was a magnificent bird that crowned the top of the Strasbourg Cathedral. And every day at noon he spread his wings, thrust out his tongue and squawked the hour. A bit of technology that was really something to crow about.

1541-1614

BY NOW EVERYONE KNOWS THAT DOMENIKOS THEOTOKOPOULOS WAS BORN GREEK (IN CRETE TO BE EXACT), WORKED MOSTLY IN SPAIN AND WENT THROUGH LIFE WITH THE ITALIAN NICKNAME EL GRECO. BUT WHY, AFTER STUDYING WITH SEVERAL GREAT ITALIAN MASTERS (HE LEARNED TO WIELD A BRUSH FROM TITIAN AND HOW TO PAINT CROWD SCENES FROM TINTORETTO) DID HE ABANDON ITALY AND EMIGRATE TO SPAIN? THE TRUTH IS HE RUINED HIMSELF PROFESSIONALLY IN ITALY BY MAKING DISPARAGING REMARKS ABOUT MICHELANGELO'S PAINTINGS. BUT HE ALSO OBJECTED TO CERTAIN FASHIONS IN ITALIAN RENAISSANCE PAINTING—THE MINGLING OF CHRISTIAN AND CLASSIC IMAGES, AND THE "NATURALISM" THAT WAS CREEPING INTO SUPERNATURAL THEMES. AFTER ALL, WHAT KIND OF MYSTICAL FEELINGS COULD ONE HAVE FOR A HOLY VIRGIN SITTING IN A LOCAL VENETIAN PALAZZO? OR FOR A STARK NAKED CHRIST ON THE CROSS? IN SPAIN, HE DEVELOPED A STYLE OF HIS OWN, WHICH WAS HIGHLY SPIRITUAL AND CLOSER TO THE BYZANTINE AND MEDIEVAL FORMS. IN SPITE OF HIS OWN VOCIFEROUS OBJECTION TO NATURALISM IN SPIRITUAL THEMES, HE CONSISTENTLY USED HIS WIFE'S FACE FOR THE VIRGIN MARY, AND POSED HIS BROTHER AND SON AS SAINTS AND HOLY MEN. HE, HIMSELF, CAME IN FOR TONGUE-LASHINGS FOR OTHER LIBERTIES THAT HE TOOK. IN A WORK FOR THE TOLEDO CATHEDRAL, HE PAINTED A CHRIST IN A "TOO-RED" TUNIC, AND SURROUNDED HIM WITH HOLY WOMEN WHO LOOKED "PROFANE" TO THE CRITICS. THEY CALLED HIS ELONGATED FIGURES "INACCURATE" AND WROTE HIM OFF AS A KOOK WITH DEFECTIVE VISION. FORTUNATELY, A SMALL ELITE GROUP OF CONNOISSEURS ASSURED HIS SUCCESS THEN. AND TODAY WE KNOW, OF COURSE, HOW MUCH HIS DISTORTIONS AND LIGHT-AND-SPACE PYROTECHNICS INFLUENCED THE MODERNS—ESPECIALLY THE EXPRESSIONIST MOVEMENT.

EL GRECO

1577-1640

In the 17th century, painters were not generally counted among the cultured elite. But with Peter Paul Rubens, they had to change the rules. Rubens was a cultivated man in every sense of the word. He had grace, intellect, was a linguist, an archeologist of sorts, respected for his knowledge of the classics and antiquities, a giant of a painter, an very rich. His house was the showplace of Antwerp, and still is. Dukes, duchesses, queens and marquises encouraged his friendship, just to get an invitation to his magnificent estate, and they weren't shortchanged. The baroque portico, the classic statuary, the formal gardens, the gold-embossed tooled leather walls, his studio, his paintings and his collection of antique art objects were eye-poppers, even to royalty. The grand house was also the scene of his greatest pleasures and sorrows. His first son was born there, and his first wife died there. But after a few disconsolate years, at the age of 53, he took a beautiful 16-year-old girl for a bride. It naturally turned his life around. He painted with renewed vigor, using his child-bride in almost every picture. She was his model in religious paintings and in Dionysian scenes of goddesses and nymphs. He posed her in costume, and painted her in the natural setting of their garden, too, sometimes alone, sometimes with their children. He simply couldn't get enough of her. Although Rubens was a bit fuddy-duddy in his personal habits—he ate very little meat because the cooking smells upset his painting appetite, and he rationed his painting hours so as not to "tire his spirit"—he was voracious in his appetite for painting women. And how he painted them. Voluptuous...exuberant...Titian-inspired figures. To this day, women who fit the description are called Rubenesque.

RVBENS

606-1669

LIKE SOME OTHER GREAT ARTISTS
O LEFT NOTES, JOURNALS AND LET-
RS BEHIND, REMBRANDT LEFT VERY
W MESSAGES ABOUT HIMSELF...ONLY
WORK. BUT IF YOU HOPE TO CON-
RUCT A REASONABLE PSYCHOLOGI-
PORTRAIT OF THE MAN BASED ON
PAINTINGS AND ETCHINGS, YOU'LL
N COME TO A SCREECHING HALT.
RE ARE TOO MANY CONFLICTING
TS. ❧ HIS MOTHER, THREE INFANT
LDREN AND HIS BELOVED WIFE
KIA ALL DIED WITHIN A FEW YEARS
EACH OTHER. HE WAS IN A FINAN-
L MESS. HE HAD PURCHASED A HUGE
USE, ON WHICH HE NEGLECTED TO
EP UP THE PAYMENTS. HE HAD WILLY-
LY SPENT LARGE SUMS OF MONEY
HIS PRIVATE ART COLLECTION. AT
E TIME OF DEEP PERSONAL TRAGEDY,
WAS ALSO FINANCIALLY BANKRUPT.
THESE CIRCUMSTANCES INHIBIT
M? FOLLOWING HIS FAMILY'S TRAGIC
MISE, HE PAINTED HIS MOST GRAN-
OSE PICTURES. (THE FAMOUS NIGHT
TCH WAS COMPLETED THE YEAR
KIA DIED.) A PRODIGIOUS NUMBER
RELIGIOUS WORKS FLOWED FROM
STUDIO, TOO. IF YOU IMAGINE THE
RITUAL THEMES POURED FORTH
OM SOMEONE AFFLICTED BY GRIEF,
U MUST ACCOUNT FOR THE FACT
AT HE WAS ALSO TURNING OUT HUGE
ANTITIES OF ETCHINGS AND PAINT-
GS WITH CLASSICAL AND PAGAN
AGES, AS WELL AS LANDSCAPES,
RTRAITS, NUDES AND STUDIES OF
O MEN AND WILD BEASTS. IF YOU
NK HE WAS A DEVOUT CHRISTIAN,
D INTERPRET HIS ETCHINGS OF THE
RIST LEGEND AS SPIRITUALLY IN-
RED, YOU SHOULD KNOW THAT THE
SPIRATION FOR THE COMPOSITION
ME STRAIGHT OUT OF RAPHAEL, THE
LY FIGURES FROM HIS OBSERVA-
ONS OF POOR OLD JEWS OF AMSTER-
M, AND THAT RELIGIOUS PICTURES
RE VERY BIG SELLERS IN THE MAR-
TPLACE. ❧ FINALLY, WHAT KIND OF
N BUSIES HIMSELF ETCHING A POR-
AIT OF THE AUCTIONEER, WHILE HIS
ME AND HIS TREASURED ART COL-
CTION ARE BEING SOLD OUT FROM
DER HIM? ONLY A MAN WHO IS AN
TIST TO HIS BONES.

REMBRANDT

GOYA

1746-1828

In any popularity contest among painters of his day, Francisco de Goya y Lucientes would have won the title "Mr. Spain." He was in constant demand for religious paintings, tapestry designs and portraits by the dozen. His portraits, especially of royalty, were painted with a brutal eye, and were less than flattering. But there was never a murmur of dissent. Either his royal patrons were too dense to perceive the truth, or too intimidated by his stature to protest. Aside from a hectic career as a painter, Goya found time for traveling, hunting, bullfighting and a little hanky-panky with the Duchess of Alba. ❧ But in his mid-forties, his expansive life style ended. He fell gravely ill from a "mysterious" disease. (It might have been lead poisoning brought on by his habit of working in haste and using his fingers to push the paint

around.) Whatever the cause, he was left almost totally deaf, and his work took on a decidedly morbid note. He painted in somnolent gray tones, with only a few strokes of clear feverish color. Within that period, a savage war between France and Spain intensified his personal trauma. He created a series of tragic etchings depicting the horrors of war and the sufferings of mankind. In his own home, he covered the walls with frescoes of nightmarish fantasies, as black in mood as they were in color. Eventually, he exiled himself to France in protest against the oppressive regime of Ferdinand II. ❧ In his 82 years, he produced a phenomenal quantity of work. There was hardly a subject or technique he didn't explore, and all his admirers claim to be his direct descendants. Romantics claim him for his expressiveness; social realists for his revelations; surrealists for his phantasmagorical outpourings. Could it be he was also the inspiration for Picasso's and Casals' self-exile from Spain?

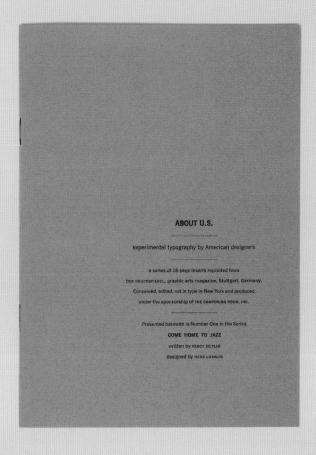

ABOUT U.S.

experimental typography by American designers

a series of 16-page inserts reprinted from
DER DRUCKSPIEGEL, graphic arts magazine, Stuttgart, Germany.
Conceived, edited, set in type in New York and produced
under the sponsorship of THE COMPOSING ROOM, INC.

Presented herewith is Number One in the Series
COME HOME TO JAZZ
written by PERCY SEITLIN
designed by HERB LUBALIN

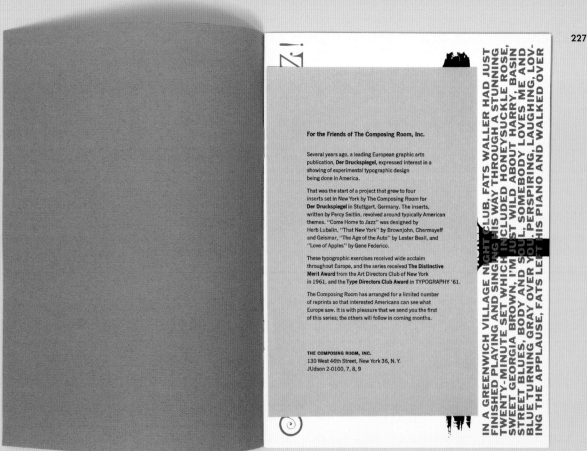

For the Friends of The Composing Room, Inc.

Several years ago, a leading European graphic arts
publication, **Der Druckspiegel,** expressed interest in a
showing of experimental typographic design
being done in America.

That was the start of a project that grew to four
inserts set in New York by The Composing Room for
Der Druckspiegel in Stuttgart, Germany. The inserts,
written by Percy Seitlin, revolved around typically American
themes. "Come Home to Jazz" was designed by
Herb Lubalin, "That New York" by Brownjohn, Chermayeff
and Geismar, "The Age of the Auto" by Lester Beall, and
"Love of Apples" by Gene Federico.

These typographic exercises received wide acclaim
throughout Europe, and the series received **The Distinctive
Merit Award** from the Art Directors Club of New York
in 1961, and the **Type Directors Club Award** in TYPOGRAPHY '61.

The Composing Room has arranged for a limited number
of reprints so that interested Americans can see what
Europe saw. It is with pleasure that we send you the first
of this series; others will follow in coming months.

THE COMPOSING ROOM, INC.
130 West 46th Street, New York 36, N. Y.
JUdson 2-0100, 7, 8, 9

IN A GREENWICH VILLAGE NIGHT CLUB, FATS WALLER HAD JUST
FINISHED PLAYING AND SINGING HIS WAY THROUGH A STUNNING
TWENTY-MINUTE SET WHICH INCLUDED HONEYSUCKLE ROSE,
SWEET GEORGIA BROWN, I'M JUST WILD ABOUT HARRY, BASIN
STREET BLUES, BODY AND SOUL, SOMEBODY LOVES ME AND
BLUE TURNING GRAY OVER YOU. PERSPIRING, LAUGHING, LOV-
ING THE APPLAUSE, FATS LEFT HIS PIANO AND WALKED OVER

COME HOME to JAZZ!

THAT'S WHAT HE SAID, WHEN ASKED

IN A GREENWICH VILLAGE NIGHT CLUB, FATS WALLER HAD JUST FINISHED PLAYING AND SINGING HIS WAY THROUGH A STUNNING TWENTY-MINUTE SET WHICH INCLUDED HONEYSUCKLE ROSE, SWEET GEORGIA BROWN, I'M JUST WILD ABOUT HARRY, BASIN STREET BLUES, BODY AND SOUL, SOMEBODY LOVES ME AND BLUE TURNING GRAY OVER YOU. PERSPIRING, LAUGHING, LOVING THE APPLAUSE, FATS LEFT HIS PIANO AND WALKED OVER

TO THE BAR WHERE HE ENCOUNTERED A FASHIONABLY-DRESSED WOMAN. "OH," SHE SAID, "JUST THE MAN I WANT TO SEE. I'M SURE YOU CAN ANSWER MY QUESTION. TELL ME, MR. WALLER, WHAT IS SWING?" FATS REACHED FOR HIS DRINK WITH ONE HAND, MOPPED HIS FACE WITH THE OTHER, LOOKED AT THE WOMAN SQUARELY AND REPLIED, "LADY, IF YOU GOTTA ASK, YOU AINT GOT IT!" RELAXING BETWEEN SETS, ART TATUM SAT AT A TABLE IN A FIFTY-SECOND STREET BISTRO DRINKING BEER FROM A BOTTLE. "BUT FAITH IS YOUR SALVATION," SAID THE BROWNSKIN GIRL. AND ART TOOK A SWIG OF HIS BEER. "WITHOUT IT YOU ARE LOST," SAID THE BROWNSKIN GIRL, AS BLIND ART TATUM SADLY SIPPED HIS BEER. "ALL GOD'S CHILDREN ARE LOST," SAID ART, "BUT ON YA FEW CAN PLAY THE PIANO."

ART TATUM, 1910-1957 (LOST MAN PLAYED FINE PIANO)

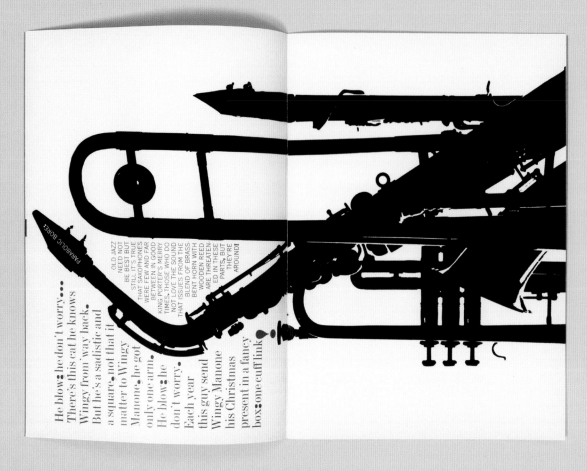

He blow; he don't worry... There's this cat he knows Wingy from way back. But he's a sadistic and a square...not that it matter to Wingy Manone...he got only one arm... He blow; he don't worry. Each year this guy send Wingy Manone his Christmas present in a fancy box:one cuff link

PARABOLIC BORE+

OLD JAZZ NEED NOT BE BEST BUT STILL IT'S TRUE THAT SAXOPHONES WERE FEW AND FAR BETWEEN IN GOOD KING PORTER'S MERRY TIMES. THOSE WHO DO NOT LOVE THE SOUND THAT ISSUES FROM THE BLEND OF BRASS, BENT HORN WITH WOODEN REED ARE THREATENED IN THESE PARTS, BUT THEY'RE AROUND!

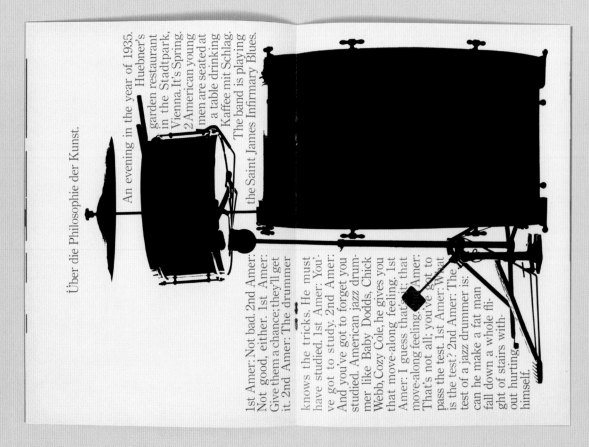

Über die Philosophie der Kunst.

An evening in the year of 1935. Huebner's garden restaurant in the Stadtpark, Vienna. It's Spring. 2 American young men are seated at a table drinking Kaffee mit Schlag. The band is playing the Saint James Infirmary Blues.

1st Amer: Not bad. 2nd Amer: Not good, either. 1st Amer: Give them a chance; they'll get it. 2nd Amer: The drummer knows the tricks. He must have studied. 1st Amer: You've got to study. 2nd Amer: And you've got to forget you studied. American jazz drummer, like Baby Dodds, Chick Webb, Cozy Cole, he gives you that move-along feeling. 1st Amer: I guess that's it; that move-along feeling. 2nd Amer: That's not all; you've got to pass the test. 1st Amer: What is the test? 2nd Amer: The test of a jazz drummer is: can he make a fat man fall down a whole flight of stairs without hurting himself.

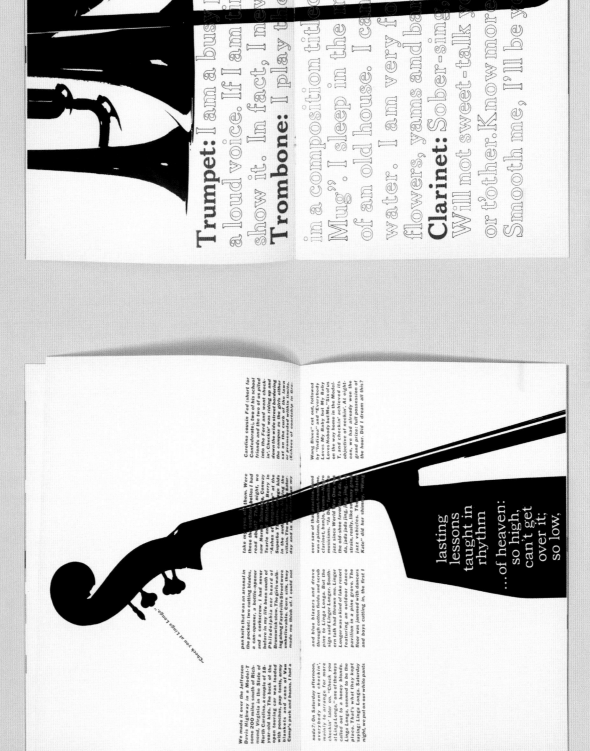

Trumpet: I am a busy puppy with a loud voice. If I am tired, I never show it. In fact, I never know it. **Trombone:** I play the solo part in a composition titled "Shaving Mug". I sleep in the musty cellar of an old house. I can sing under water. I am very fond of sun-flowers, yams and barreled beer. **Clarinet:** Sober-sing, I'd rather. Will not sweet-talk you one way or t'other. Know more than I tell. Smooth me, I'll be your friend.

lasting lessons taught in rhythm ...of heaven: so high, can't get over it; so low,

"Check you at Linga Longa."

We made it over the Jefferson Davis Highway in a Model-T some 200 miles south of Richmond, Virginia in the State of North Carolina, a couple of 18-year-old kids. The back of the open touring car was loaded with ponchos, pup tents, army blankets and cans of Vienna Camp's pork and beans. I had a penknife that was an arsenal in the pocket: two cutting blades, a can-opener, a bottle-opener and a corkscrew. I had never before in my life been south of Philadelphia nor heard of Brunswick stew. The girls walking along Fayetteville Street were umbrella-nude. Cars still they made me think of. I could not

Carolina cousin Fed (short for Confederate), two of his school friends and the two of us piled into the Ford and went checkin'. Checkin' was riding up and down the wide street bordering the campus as the girls either sat on the curb or they-ca promenaded within invita-... (Echoes of courtship in Gra-...)

take in, in them. Were these ladies I had night, we saw Moresi Talmadge, Conway Twarle and Wallace Barry in Superba T at the in the aud selling the villain. They and in day and in my

ever saw of the practice band was a piano, trumpet, trombone, clarinet, banjo, drums—too musicians. "La Da Dee Dee da jazz since World War One. In the old-shoe favorites da da, jada jing jing, the strain, really, like some great jazz vehicles. The "Sister Kate" did her shimmy, Wang

Wang Blues" cut out, followed by "Indiana" and "Everybody Loves My Baby but My Baby Loves Nobody but Me." Six of us on the way home in the Model-T, and checkin' achieved its objective of neckin'. At eighteen, we had already won the grand prize: full possession of the hour. Did I dream all this?

nada?) On Saturday afternoon, everybody went checkin', mainly to arrange for more checkin' later on. "Check you at Linga Longa," one of the boys called out to a honey blonde. Linga Longa seemed to be the place. That's what they kept saying: Linga Longa. Saturday night, we put on our white pants and blue blazers and drove through cotton fields and scrub pine to Linga Longa. But the sign said Linger Longer. Southern folk had thrown me. Linger Longer was a kind of lake resort featuring an outdoor dance pavilion in a pine grove. The floor was jammed with dancers and boys cutting in, the first I

◆ He was a waif,
cared for by his Creole godmother,
called Eulalia Echo, voo-doo woman.
("She had plenty money.").
It was absurd of him to say
he invented jazz.
It's a good thing
for the record, though,
that he made the claim,
because, in doing so,
he gave us positively
a fine specimen of his egotism.
▶ Mister Jelly was not merely counted
among those present.
With candy-striped shirt,
tan, pointed shoe
and diamond-studded tooth,
he was a telegram to the world
announcing: I am here!
He came here to write:
The Queen of Spades,
The Crave,
Granpa's Spells,
I Hate a Man Like You,
The Big Fat Ham, and
Hello, Central, Give Me Doctor Jazz.
As a piano-playing professor
in the resorts of Storyville.
he set the Naked Dance to music.
But his ambition
was as high as heaven:
he wanted to be
the champion pool-player
of the world.
◆ In the tenderloin of the old city
at the mouth of the Mississippi,
the police "guaranteed safety
to all concerned"
but there were shootings
and stabbings aplenty
and Mister Jelly saw his share.

◆ Most of the trouble was about money.
Sportin' men and their je-bets,
angry with themselves
for buying dear and selling cheap,
were always spoiling for a fight.
Jazz was what they were selling,
but we'll never know
whether jazz named the commodity
or it named jazz.
▶ But this New Orleans music
was much more than the background
for a saloon brawl.
Jazz, said Jelly,
was to be played sweet and soft
with plenty rhythm.
A glass that's full of water, he said,
you can't put any more in it;
but if it's only half full,
you've got to hand it to the Europeans.
you can still put in more.
When they took up jazz,
they went right to the source.
Jelly was discovered by
the French critics around the time
he was broke up north
and had to pawn his diamond garters.
Here he would be,
frail aristocrat of early jazz,
"a historical figure" now,
gigging at a left-wing affair
in Webster Hall.
With him on the bandstand,
Harlem entertainers,
turning jazz into a loud vaudeville
of commercial rhythm music.
And, saddest of all,
the audience,
cheering indiscriminately
the counterfeit and the genuine.

Ferdinand (Jelly Roll)

226—234. U.S: experimental ...
Front cover and spreads from a series
of booklets reprinted and distributed
as souvenirs by The Composing Room.
The pages had originally appeared in
Der Druckspiegel, the monthly German
graphic arts magazine. There were
four in the series: *Come Home to Jazz*
by Herb Lubalin; *That's New York* by
Robert Brownjohn and Chermayeff
and Geismar; *The Age of the Auto* by
Lester Beall; and *Love of Apples* by Gene
Federico. Herb Lubalin was known to
be a jazz fan, and attended concerts in
the 1930s with his friend Lou Dorfsman,
although his son Peter has no recollection of jazz being played in the Lubalin
family home. Much later, Lubalin was
to recreate these pages using the new
phototypesetting technology (p.372).
Writer: Percy Seitlin. Photography: Carl
Fischer. Client: The Composing Room.
Date: 1960.

Folio 11

has been written and designed by Herb Lubalin primarily as a public service to all those students of the Graphic Arts who have an uncontrollable desire to make it big in a hurry.

Its impact on this aspiring group has yet to be recorded.

Its secondary purpose was to give Sanders Printing Corporation a hard time,
to test their metal,
as the saying goes.
In this effort we have unquestionably succeeded.

However,
we are happy to report,
that despite overwhelming odds,
Sanders has come through,
once again,
with flowing colors.
Mostly metallic.

How to become successful,
though an art director,
and achieve immortality.

For a while.

235. Folio 11
Cover and spreads from promotional booklet for printer, designed to demonstrate the range of print processes on offer. Lubalin wrote the witty copy, which gives the reader an insight into his lack of commercial piety. Photography: Anthony Hyde, Jr. Artists: John Alcorn, Charles B. Slackman. Client: Sanders Printing Corporation. Date: 1967.

And with these kudos—fame.
Headlines,
travel,
speeches,
friends,
worshippers,
idolatry.
You are a hero.

HOW TO BECOME SUCCESSFUL THOUGH AN ART DIRECTOR

An "O" can mean money.
Money talks.
A successful career is often built on a sound foundation of it.
Set your sights on this valuable commodity.

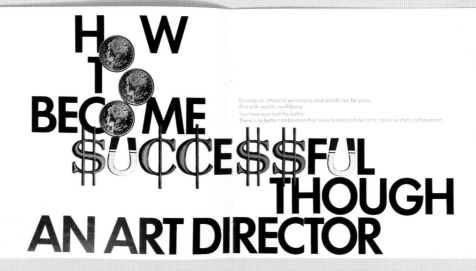

HOW TO BECOME SUCCESSFUL THOUGH AN ART DIRECTOR

Develop an attractive personality and wealth can be yours.
And with wealth, confidence.
You have won half the battle.
There is no better combination than security and confidence to inspire aesthetic achievement.

So,
achieve.
And,
with a little luck,
glory can be yours.
Certificates.
Certificates of Merit.
Certificates of Distinction.
Certificates of Distinctive Merit.
Awards.
Awards of Merit.
Awards of Distinction.
Awards of Distinctive Merit.
Medals.
Silver medals.
Bronze medals.
Gold medals.
Gold Cleos.
Gold Andys.
Golden T-Squares.
Etc.

HOW TO BECOME SUCCESSFUL THOUGH AN ART DIRECTOR

236. The Sound of Music
Front and back cover for souvenir
brochure to accompany the film *The
Sound of Music*. Rather than accept
payment by royalty, Lubalin insisted on
a large fee. By so doing, he missed
an opportunity to make a great deal of
money; *The Sound of Music*, released
in 1965, went on to be one of the most
successful movies of all time. Publisher:
National Publishers. Lettering: Tom
Carnase. Date: 1965.

237. McGraphic
Newsprint publication designed to
support the 1972 presidential
campaign of U.S. Democrat Senator
George McGovern (see p.67). The liberal
McGovern failed to beat Republican
incumbent Richard Nixon in one of the
biggest landslide victories in American
history. Page size is approximately
15" × 23". It was designed and edited
by Seymour Chwast, Herb Lubalin,
Bill Maloney and Ellen Shapiro.
Contributing illustrators include
Marshall Arisman, Jules Feiffer,
Paul Giovanopoulos, Norman Green,
Robert Grossman, David Levine,
James McMullan, Burt Silverman and
Ed Sorel. Publisher: Graphic Artists
and Writers for McGovern Shriver.
Lettering: Tom Carnase. Date: 1972.

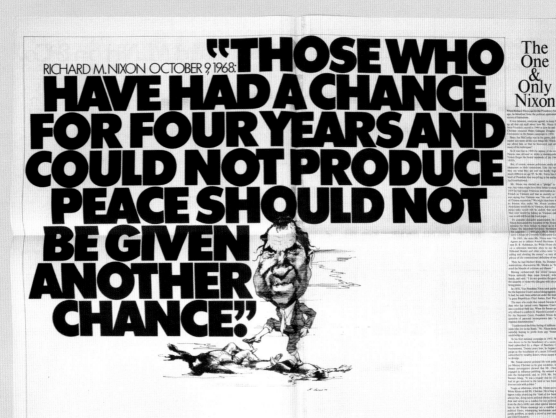

RICHARD M. NIXON OCTOBER 9, 1968: "THOSE WHO HAVE HAD A CHANCE FOR FOUR YEARS AND COULD NOT PRODUCE PEACE SHOULD NOT BE GIVEN ANOTHER CHANCE."

The One & Only Nixon

McGovern on the Issues.

"I want America to come home from the alien world of power politics, militarism, deception, racism and special privilege.
Then our children will love America, not simply because it is theirs but because of the great and good land all of us together have made it."

light-line gothics and grotesks, and the newly re-discovered swash initials.

These actions, reactions and gyrations in taste continue, but a more significant development occurred when magazines began to recognize design as an editorial force and art directors as contributors to editorial ideas and decisions.

In the mid-1960's, American magazines are again turning to European sources for new trends in design: the continuing excellence of *Du* in Switzerland, the bold layouts of *Paris Match* and *Elle* in France, and *Epoca* in Italy, the sparkling new ideas in page design and typography in Germany's *Twen* and England's *Queen* and *Town* and in London's new newspaper supplements.

Thirty-five years ago in 1930, Dr. Agha wrote an article for *Advertising Arts* in which he discussed the modern magazine and some of the questions already being raised about it. He referred to the challenge of the "*Artistes Decorateurs Français*" to the German *Werkbund*, "that there are other things in life and art besides the cold and organized conceptions of the technician and manufacturer."

EROS

1962: First cover for *Eros* by Herb Lubalin

Dr. Agha ended his discourse with the question, "Does this [challenge] mean that the modern typographers will have to store away their little dots and black rules and put frames on their pictures? Or will the modern magazines follow their own educational campaign, and by trial and error finally achieve harmony between material and its presentation?"
Today, after thirty-five years of trial and error, our design destiny is still dependent on that "harmony between material and its presentation."

Allen Hurlburt

1962: *Eros* spread designed by Herb Lubalin, photographs by Hattersley

1962: *Show* spread by Henry Wolf, photograph by Gordon Parks

THE GREAT CRAFTSMEN

1963: *Snow* spread designed and photographed by Henry Wolf

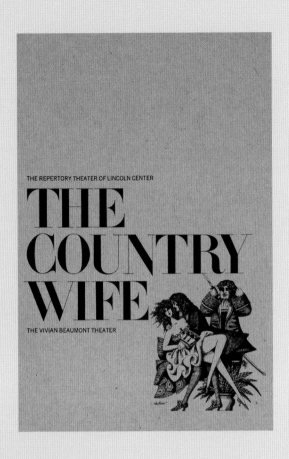

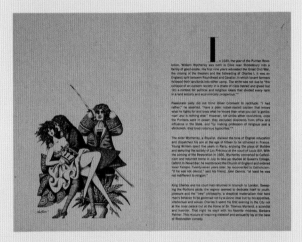

238. Magazine USA, AIGA
Front cover and spreads for booklet
surveying magazine design of the
period. Hand-lettering on the cover:
Tom Carnase. Client: The American
Institute of Graphic Arts. Date: 1965.

239. The Country Wife
Brochure cover for theatrical performance of Restoration comedy written
in 1675 by William Wycherley. It is likely
that the bawdy nature of this play would
have appealed to the broad-minded
Lubalin, especially the intentional pun
in the title. Illustrations: John Alcorn.
Client: Repertory Theater of Lincoln
Center, Inc. Date: 1966.

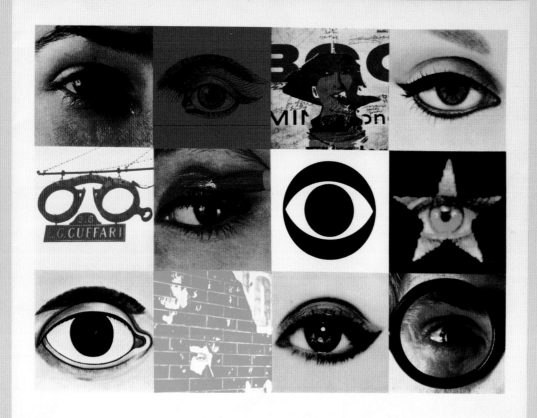

ИСКУССТВО, ПОРАЖАЮЩЕЕ ГЛАЗ

Помещенные выше изображе-
ния глаз взяты из работ Ир-
винга Блуменфелда, Уильяма
Голдэна, Арта Кейна, Джона
Мансела, Ирвинга Пенна,
Карла Фишера, Фернанда
Фонссагривса, Хиро и фирмы
«Американ тайп фаундерс».

Искусство, поражающее глаз, искусство, ласка-
ющее глаз! За последнее время в Соединенных
Штатах прикладная графика достигла небыва-
лого расцвета, и ее произведения разнообразят и
украшают повседневную жизнь. Всех — от типо-
графа до упаковщика консервов — восхищают эти красочные произведения
искусства. Передовая роль в развитии прикладной графики принадлежит
Гербу Лубалину, известному мастеру художественного оформления. Его та-
лант и новаторские идеи немало способствовали изменению внешнего вида
американских журналов. На этих страницах Лубалин наглядно показывает
нам, что происходит в области прикладной графики Соединенных Штатов.

240, 241. Amerika Illustrated
Pages from a glossy magazine published
by the U.S. Information Agency for
distribution in the USSR during the Cold
War. This special edition of the magazine
(no.83) had a cover designed by Saul
Bass (printed on silver foil), and a 16-
page section designed by Herb Lubalin,
titled 'Art that Strikes the Eye...,' focusing
on the graphic arts and featuring work
by Lubalin and other leading figures of
the American graphic arts scene. Client:
United States Information Agency.
Date: 1960. Magazine kindly supplied
by Robin Benson, Past Print Blog -
www.westread.blogspot.com

Notes on attribution, credits and image sources: the nature of graphic design is that it is nearly always a collaborative venture. Individual designers often claim authorship of work, but more often than not, the work is the result of collaboration: the genuinely solo graphic designer is a rare thing indeed.

With this in mind, the editors of this book have approached the question of 'who did what?' with caution. It is not possible to identify everyone involved in the execution of every piece of work included in these pages. But what is clear, however, is that all the work from 1964 onwards emanated from the studios that Herb Lubalin ran from that date until his death in 1981.

Although he was a highly individualistic designer with a signature style, Lubalin's work was invariably dependent on others. Accordingly, he surrounded himself with graphic specialists of all kinds. Intriguingly for a designer of his undoubted status, Herb Lubalin acknowledged the contribution made by his collaborators, partners and employees. Repeatedly, in interviews and studio press releases, he emphasized that the credit for the work he was known for, should, in fact, be shared. This is rare in such circles.

It is also worth noting, however, that despite Herb Lubalin's acknowledged dependence on other professionals, there is such a thing as a universally acknowledged 'Lubalin style'. Mention

of this can be found in countless books and articles. Like a great film director, Herb Lubalin surrounded himself with creative partners, yet nevertheless produced a style that was palpably his own.

It is against this backdrop that the editors have approached the question of attribution and creative credits. Our method can be summarized as an overarching assumption that all work shown in these pages produced from 1964 onwards can be legitimately and fairly referred to as the work of Herb Lubalin, but with the implicit understanding that he was not necessarily the sole author of the work.

Where individual credits are available to us in reputable published sources

such as design awards annuals, magazines and studio publications, we have included them. The editors would be happy to rectify omissions in future editions.

Note on image sources: all the images in this book are reproduced from photographs of material held in the archive of The Herb Lubalin Study Center of Design and Typography at The Cooper Union, unless otherwise stated.

The Editors.

END MATTER

THE HERB LUBALIN STUDY CENTER OF DESIGN AND TYPO-GRAPHY

ESTABLISHED IN 1984 IT WILL BE THE WORLD'S FIRST STUDY CENTER FOR THE GRAPHIC ARTS. IT WILL BE AN INTERNATIONAL EDUCATIONAL RE-SOURCE, UNPRECEDENTED IN IT'S MAGNITUDE. INITIALLY, THE LUBALIN CENTER WILL HOUSE HERB'S VAST ARCHIVE OF WORK. WORKS OF THE MOST PROMINENT NAMES IN OUR INDUSTRY WILL BE ADDED TO FORM A PERMANENT COLLECTION. THE LUBALIN STUDY CENTER WILL PROVIDE THE MEANS WHEREBY THE ENTIRE DESIGN COMMUNITY CAN STUDY INNOVATIVE WORK & IDEAS PRODUCED BY LEADING COMMU-NICATORS. IT IS A MONUMENTAL WAY TO HONOR HERB LUBALIN

Number.... of an edition of 1001

Poster announcing the opening
of the Lubalin Study Centre at the
Cooper Union.

Herb Lubalin Study Center

The Herb Lubalin Study Center of Design and Typography opened its doors in September 1985. It was established by a group of about 100 benefactors who felt compelled, after Herb Lubalin's death in 1981, to preserve his vast collection of work. The founders' goals were to provide the design community with a place to study Lubalin's innovative work, and for the center to function as his living memorial. The Lubalin Center testifies to his pre-eminent influence, both in the design community and the public eye.

The original founders of the Herb Lubalin Center of Design and Typography are: Aaron Burns, Louis Dorfsman, Carl Fischer, Marilyn Hoffner, George Lois, Rhoda Lubalin, Peter Lubalin, Robert Lubalin, Irwin Lubalin and Alan Peckolick. Past curators and directors include Philippe Apeloig, Georgette Ballance, William Bevington, Mike Essl, Ellen Lupton, Lawrence Mirsky and George Sadek.

The core of the Center's collection consists of an extensive archive of Herb Lubalin's work, including promotional and editorial design, typeface designs, posters, journals, magazines, letterheads, logos, identity programmes and packaging, dating from c. 1950 to 1981. Included in the collection are numerous original tissues that were the core of Lubalin's work process. Most of what is seen in this book is available in the Center.

The founders intended the Center to expand to include other important work documenting 20th- and 21st-century American and European graphic design. The collection currently includes work by eminent graphic designers and design studios, including Paul Rand, Lou Dorfsman, Push Pin Studios, George Lois, Alvin Lustig, Will Burtin, Lester Beall, Lou Silverstein, Bradbury Thompson, Otl Aicher, Karl Gerstner, Anthon Beeke, Tibor Kalman and M&Co, Massimo Vignelli, Chip Kidd, and countless others. The collection also includes a library of books and magazines relating to graphic design and typography, an extensive collection of posters, and myriad type specimen books and pamphlets, some dating back to the 19th century.

Our main objective for the Lubalin Center is to make the entire archive accessible to the public. We hope to engage researchers with historic ephemera in an informal, hands-on manner that is only possible by physically interacting with examples of graphic design and typography. There is nothing more gratifying than to be able to interact with an original piece of ephemera, to experience it in the way it was supposed to be experienced rather than as a reproduction. Additionally, the Center sponsors a public programme that includes exhibitions, lectures and publications that focus on graphic design and typography (and its role and impact on culture), which provide an opportunity to place the archive's work within a historical context. The exhibition programming was initiated by the Center's first director George Sadek, and Ellen Lupton, the Center's first curator. Together they fostered a standard of innovative exhibitions and publications. Their first exhibition, 'Global Signage: Semiotics and the Language of International Pictures' (1986) explored the history and theory of modern pictographic sign systems.

Other seminal exhibitions sponsored by the Lubalin Center include 'Period Styles: A History of Punctuation' (1988); 'Numbers' (1989); 'Anthon Beeke's Stage: Holland's illusionist poster designer' (1990); and 'The Bauhaus and Design Theory, from Preschool to Post-Modernism' (1991). Catalogues acted as extensions of the exhibitions, providing new ways of looking at and thinking about design. Lupton is currently the curator of contemporary design at Cooper-Hewitt, National Design Museum in New York City and director of the Graphic Design MFA program at Maryland Institute College of Art (MICA) in Baltimore.

Exhibitions curated by the Center have investigated a wide range of subjects, as evidenced by these two exhibitions: 'Blackletter: Type and National Identity' (guest curated by Peter Bain and Paul Shaw) and 'Lift and Separate: Graphic Design and the Quote/Unquote Vernacular' (guest curated by Barbara Glauber). Other exhibitions have showcased the work of important individuals such as Paul Rand, Jean Widmer, Willem Sandberg, Massin, Otl Aicher and Chip Kidd. Additional exhibitions have surveyed work ranging from contemporary Chinese Graphic Design, Swiss Design from 1955 to 2000, and the work of Chermayeff and Geismar, as well as graduate student projects from the MIT Media Lab's Aesthetics and Computation Group.

In 2009, the Lubalin Center moved from the Cooper Union Foundation Building, designated a National Historic Landmark in 1961, to '41 Cooper Square', designed by Thom Mayne, and recently endowed with the prestigious LEED Platinum award by the U.S. Green Building Council (USGBC). With more space, better access and greater visibility, the new Lubalin Center is better equipped to receive visitors.

We have reorganized the collection to showcase some of Lubalin's work that was previously less accessible, as well as pieces that were in storage. Since the move there has been a tremendous increase in researchers, particularly from international institutions. We've gleaned from our visiting researchers that the amount of ephemera that we house is simply overwhelming.

In its new environs, the Center has staged three exhibitions in the adjacent '41 Cooper Gallery'. The first exhibition in the new space, 'Lubalin Now', was curated by Mike Essl and Alexander Tochilovsky (2009). It made use of contemporary graphic design that reflected the formal and conceptual approach of Herb Lubalin's work and legacy, with posters, publications and motion graphics spotlighting an emerging trend towards expressive lettering and typography. Original work by Herb Lubalin and his studio, culled from the collection, illuminated Lubalin's influence on this growing design movement. This exhibition, 60 years after Lubalin's graduation from Cooper Union, reaffirmed the relevance of his ideas to contemporary design. Designers included in the exhibition ranged from Marian Bantjes to HunterGatherer; from Non-Format to Post Typography.

'Appetite: a reciprocal relationship between food and design' (2010), and 'Pharma' (2011), were both curated by Alexander Tochilovsky. The former investigated how design influences the way people perceive food and highlighted the process of design as well as the details that shape our experience of food. The latter examined the evolution of graphic design in the service of the pharmaceutical industry. It examined the birth of the industry and its accompanying relationship to the marketing industry, and showcased rarely seen graphic design ephemera created during the golden age of pharmaceutical marketing.

Over the years, the Lubalin Center has sponsored many lectures, often in conjunction with exhibitions. Speakers have included Paul Rand, John Maeda, April Greiman, Wolfgang Weingart, Alexander Gelman, Leonardo Sonnoli, Bruno Monguzzi, Massin, David Tartakover, Wendy Siuyi Wong, Luba Lukova, Fang Chen, Malcolm Garrett, Mervyn Kurlansky and Uwe Loesch among many others. During 2010 Lubalin Center began sponsoring the public lecture series of 'Type@Cooper', the recently launched post-graduate certificate program in typeface design at the Cooper Union. The lecture series was renamed the Herb Lubalin Lecture Series and all the lectures were made free of charge, greatly increasing attendance. The Center is also involved in the selection of the speakers, who have included Stephen O. Saxe, Mike Daines, Christian Schwartz, Roger Black, Matteo Bologna, Paul Shaw, Sebastien Morlighem, John Downer, Matthew Carter, Doug Clouse, Ken Barber and Ed Benguiat, Jonathan Hoefler and Sumner Stone. Additionally, the Lubalin Center provides the basis for research to many of the Type@Cooper participants, making it an important part of the students' work.

In support of the educational mission of the institution, the founders conceived of the Lubalin Study Center as a vehicle for integrating visual practice and humanist scholarship. The Center has a steady stream of local, national and international visitors, which include both professional designers and students. Visitors come to the Center from countries ranging from England, France, Argentina, Israel, Australia, South Korea and Iceland. Their research is then disseminated into projects in the global graphic design community. Class groups from New York metropolitan institutions and across the country frequently visit for guided, and often custom-tailored, tours of the collection. The Center also collaborates with the design

faculty to provide access and assistance to students studying graphic design at Cooper Union, as well as other institutions. Many of the instructors integrate assignments into their curriculum that utilize the archive and expose students to design history via the collection.

The Center is constantly changing to keep abreast of the evolving communication tools, to allow a better connection to the wider public audience. The ultimate goal would be to allow viewers to be able to access the contents of the collection remotely in order to be inspired to come and view the materials in person.

In closing, we would like to acknowledge and thank the original founders and past directors and curators whose hard work and dedication has preserved and cultivated an amazing repository of graphic design and maintained the Center as an evolving laboratory for graphic design. It is a testament to them that the Center, as well as all programs, continues to be open to the academic community and the general public free of cost. The Lubalin Center is serious in its ambitions and scope, but is also friendly and accessible; exactly the way we prefer it to be.

We would also like to thank the publishers and authors of this book for conceiving it and for the tremendous work they have accomplished. We are certain that it will allow a wider audience to see and appreciate the amazing breadth and quality of Herb Lubalin's and his collaborators' work, and we hope that the readers will share in the pleasure that we derive out of seeing this work every day in the archive.

Alexander Tochilovsky, Curator
Emily Roz, Archive Co-ordinator

Inside the Lubalin Study Center at the
Cooper Union.

A Lubalin Biblio-graphy

Barry, John D., 2005
U&lc: Influencing Design & Typography
Mark Batty Publishers

Blake, Peter, 1993
No Place Like Utopia
Norton

Challis, Clive, 2005
Helmut Krone: The Book.
Graphic Design and Art Direction
(concept, form and meaning) after
Advertising's Creative Revolution
Cambridge Enchorial Press

Conradi, Jan, 2010
Unimark International
Lars Muller Publishers

Cracknell, Andrew, 2011
The Real Mad Men: The Remarkable True
Story of Madison Avenue's Golden Age
Quercus

Friedman, Mildred, 1989
Graphic Design in America:
A Visual Language History
Harry N. Abrams

Graphic Designers aux Etats-Unis 1, 1971
Office du Livre

Heller, Steven, & Pettit, Elinor, 1998
Design Dialogues
Allworth Press

Heller, Steven, 2002
The Graphic Design Reader
Allworth Press

Heller, Steven, 1999
Paul Rand
Phaidon Press

Herb Lubalin, 2002
GGG Books

Hess, Dick Hess & Muller, Marion, 1987
Dorfsman & CBS
American Showcase

Hollis, Richard, 1994
Graphic Design. A Concise History
Thames & Hudson

Lou Dorfsman, 1996
GGG Books

Loxley, Simon, 2004
Type: The Secret History of Letters
I.B. Tauris

Lubalin, Herb, 1966
Herb Lubalin's Iconochrestomathy:
A Graphic Interpretation of a Carefully
Selected Collection of Literary Passages
Harlin Quist

Lupton, Ellen & Miller, J. Abbott, 1996
Design; Writing; Research Kiosk

Lupton, Ellen, 1996
Mixing Messages
Thames and Hudson

Meggs, Philip B., & Purvis,
Alston W., 2006
Meggs' History of Graphic Design,
John Wiley & Sons

Meggs, Philip B., 1992
Type and Image: The Language of
Graphic Design
John Wiley & Sons

Monem, Nadine Käthe, 2008
Font, the Sourcebook
Black Dog Publishing

Remington, R. Roger, 2003
American Modernism Graphic Design
1920 to 1960
Laurence King Publishing

Snyder, Gertrude & Peckolick,
Alan, 1985
Herb Lubalin: Art Director,
Graphic Designer and Typographer
American Showcase

Surhone, Tennoe, Henssonow, eds.
Herb Lubalin
Betascript Publishing

Thomson, Ellen Mazur, 1997
The Origins of Graphic Design in America,
1870—1920
Yale University Press

Weill, Alan, 2004
Graphics
Thames & Hudson

Wlassikoff, Michel, 2005
The Story of Graphic Design in France
Ginko Press

Zapf, Hermann, 1987
Hermann Zapf and his Design Philosophy
Society of Typographic Arts

Articles:

'A Talk With Herb Lubalin.'
Graphics Today
(July/August, 1976)

Bird, David. 'Obituary:
Herb Lubalin, Graphic Designer
for Publications and Advertising.'
New York Times
(26 May, 1981)

'Bouquets: Herb Lubalin.'
Magazine of the
New York Art Directors Club
(December, 1964)

Burns, Neil.
'Herb Lubalin: Grand Master.'
How (Feb, 1993)

Durniak, John. 'Herb Who?'
Idea, Herb Lubalin Special Issue (1969)

'Herb Lubalin,
A Towering Figure.'
Adweek (8 June, 1981)

Hoffner, Marilyn.
'Herb Lubalin, Designer and Art
Director.'
Graphis (September, 1964)

'How Herb Lubalin
Creates a Campaign at
Sudler & Hennessey.'
Print (January/February, 1958)

Kinser, Bill & Lanny Sommese.
'Herb Lubalin and the Journal of
Typographics U&lc.'
Novum Gebrauchsgraphik (1981)

Kolatch, Myron. 'Introduction.'
The New Leader
(January/April, 2006)

Leu, Olaf.
'Herb Lubalin: American Design
Influence Abroad.'
Print (January, 1968)

Lubalin, Herb.
'Individual Squelchers.'
Idea 77 (July, 1966)

Lubalin, Herb.
'The Graphic Revolution in America:
40 Years of Innovative Typography,
1940 to 1980.'
Print (May/June, 1979)

Nishio, Tadahisa.
'Dialogue with Herb Lubalin.'
Idea, Herb Lubalin
Special Issue (1969)

Nishio, Tadahisa.
'On Herb Lubalin.'
Idea 77 (July, 1966)

Snyder, Gertrude.
'Herb Lubalin. Art Director, Graphic
Designer, and Typographer.'
Graphis (January/February, 1985)

'Tony Di Spigna.'
The Typographer (May/June, 1984)

Wickens, Mark.
'Reappraisal: Herb Lubalin.'
Campaign (31 August, 1990)

Author's thanks

I owe profound and heartfelt thanks to the numerous friends and colleagues of Herb Lubalin who so generously shared their memories of him; without them, and others, this book would never have been written.

Rhoda Lubalin told me many facts about her late husband that helped me to understand him better.

Peter Lubalin granted me a long interview and provided many glimpses into his early life growing up with his father, and what it was like to enter a profession (advertising) where Herb Lubalin was already a dominant figure. Both Rhoda and Peter showed me enormous kindness and unstinting support from the outset.

Emily Roz and Sasha Tochilovsky of the The Herb Lubalin Study Center of Design and Typography at the Cooper Union contributed enthusiasm, patience, and of course, permission to invade the archive they look after so diligently. Emily's contact book, combined with Sasha's encyclopedic knowledge of the archive, made for a happy and productive association.

Fay Barrows supplied me with much unpublished information about Herb Lubalin's early working life in advertising, and also provided many marvellous photographs.

George Lois and Alan Peckolick invited me into their Manhattan apartments and talked about Herb Lubalin at length and with affection and insight. Alan Peckolick and his wife Jessica Weber generously read the text and made important comments and suggestions.

Tony Di Spigna supplied me with an email interview despite the interruption of Hurricane Irene.

Marilyn Hoffner and her husband Al Greenberg devoted an afternoon at the Cooper Union to sharing their memories.

Carl Fischer supplied pictures from his private collection, and many recollections about life with Herb Lubalin.

Louise Fili contributed many memories and one of the best photographs in this book (p.77).

Bernie Zlotnick supplied numerous interesting facts and volunteered some outstanding photographs of Herb Lubalin and his circle of friends and colleagues from the New York design and advertising scene of the 1960s and 70s.

Mike Aron, Jason Calfo, Lynda Decker and Kevin Gatta all worked closely with Herb Lubalin towards the end of his life, and all generously allowed me to quiz them about working with him.

Fran Elfenbein, Diana Wilko and her husband Hans Mauli worked for Herb Lubalin at a critical time in his career. All three provided help and insight.

David Pocknell and Mike Daines contributed a British perspective to the Lubalin story. John Bateson kindly supplied copies of U&lc for photography.

Steven Heller, as the reigning heavyweight champ of American graphic design history, kindly read the manuscript and suggested a number of important changes and additions. I also relied on his writings for many facts and insights, especially in relation to Lubalin's work with Ralph Ginzburg, and the story of Avant Garde (magazine and typeface.)

Claudia Klat photographed almost the entire Lubalin archive during an intense week of activity at the Lubalin Study Center in the summer of 2011. She also worked tirelessly on the design of the book.

The Spin studio, including production manager Sam Stevenson and designers Elena Carl, Dan Cottrell and Callin Mackintosh, who worked on the design, and undertook the huge task of retouching hundreds of images. Also Sarah Schrauwen for proofreading and Daniel Flynn for film and audio work.

Trish Finegan supervised the contractual and production development of this book.

Lastly, Tony Brook, my co-editor and publishing partner, whose idea it was to produce a book on Lubalin. Without his prompting and clear-eyed delight in the work of Herb Lubalin, I would never have written this volume.

Index

Colophon

First published in the
United Kingdom in 2018
by Unit Editions Ltd

This edition published in
the United Kingdom in
2024 by Thames & Hudson
Ltd, 181A High Holborn,
London WC1V 7QX

First published in
the United States of
America in 2024 by
Thames & Hudson Inc.,
500 Fifth Avenue, New
York, New York 10110

*Herb Lubalin: American
Graphic Designer* © 2018
Unit Editions Ltd

*Herb Lubalin: American
Graphic Designer* © 2024
Thames & Hudson Ltd,
London

Illustrations © 2018 Herb
Lubalin, courtesy of the
Herb Lubalin Study Center
of Design and Typography

Special thanks to Peter
and Rhoda Lubalin

British Library Cataloguing-
in-Publication Data
A catalogue record for this
book is available from the
British Library

Library of Congress Control
Number 2023948784

ISBN 978-0-500-02809-4

Printed and bound in
China by Everbest Printing
Investment Ltd.